D0622877

MODERN CAPITALIST PLANNING: THE FRENCH MODEL

MODERN CAPITALIST PLANNING: THE FRENCH MODEL

STEPHEN S. COHEN

Updated Edition

UNIVERSITY OF CALIFORNIA PRESS
Berkeley, Los Angeles, London

FOR MY PARENTS

University of California Press
Berkeley and Los Angeles, California

University of California Press, Ltd.
London, England

California Edition 1977
ISBN: 0–520–02793–0 (clothbound)
0–520–02892–9 (paperbound)
Library of Congress Catalog Card Number: 74–79762

Printed in the United States of America

CONTENTS

ACKNOWLEDGEMENTS vii

INTRODUCTION ix

PREFACE TO THE PAPERBACK EDITION xi

PART I A PRELIMINARY MODEL OF THE PLANNING PROCESS 1

1 *Educative Planning* 3
2 *Coercive Implementation* 21
3 *The Plan in the Bureaucracy: A First View of the Power Structure of Planning* 28

PART II THE PLANNING PROCESS: A NARRATIVE 31

4 *Stages One and Two: The Plan and the Ministry of Finance* 33
5 *Stage Three: Parliament and the Plan* 58
6 *Stage Four: Big Business and the Plan* 60
7 *The Fifth Stage: Coherence* 78

PART III THE MONNET PLAN: A HISTORY 81

8 *Priorities* 83
9 *Inflation and Priorities* 91
10 *Priorities Three: Housing* 104
11 *Priorities Four: Other Criteria* 109

PART IV THE SECOND PLAN: A RESPONSE TO CHANGE 117

12 *Changed Conditions* 119
13 *The New Planning Process: A Two Component Model* 129
14 *The Targets of the Second Plan* 136
15 *The Second Plan: Results and Explanations* 149

PART V PLANNING MODELS: THEIR POLITICAL MEANING 155

16 *Planning as a Political Process* 157
17 *The Second Plan and Actual Economic Policy* 164
18 *The Common Market and the Planning Process* 176

PART VI PLANNING AND DEMOCRACY 189

19 *Democracy as Direct Participation* 191
20 *Trade Union Participation and the Institutional Structures of the Plan* 220
21 *The Plan and Parliament* 228

CONTENTS

POSTSCRIPT

1 *The 'Events' of May 1968* 238

2 *The Recent Evolution of French Planning* 258

APPENDIX I THE FOURTH PLAN 280

APPENDIX II THE THIRD PLAN 282

APPPENDIX III AVERAGE ANNUAL RATE OF GROWTH OF THE GNP 290

BIBLIOGRAPHY 291

SUPPLEMENTARY SELECTED BIBLIOGRAPHY 325

INDEX 327

ACKNOWLEDGEMENTS

This book could not have been written without the generous cooperation of over one hundred planners, civil servants, politicians, businessmen, trade unionists, journalists and 'experts' who found the time, energy and tolerance for extensive conversations with the author. Many of those discussions continued, at growing levels of sophistication, through several meetings over a three year period. I should like to thank all of those people; their sheer number precludes listing them by name.

The author benefited from the personal support of the late Governor and Mrs Herbert H. Lehman in both a financial and a moral sense. I should like to express my respect, appreciation and obligation. This project also received financial assistance from the University of London Central Research Fund, from Brandeis University and from the Economic Development Administration of the US Department of Commerce.

Major portions of this study were presented as a doctoral dissertation at the London School of Economics. They benefited from the guidance and criticism of Professor A. C. L. Day, Mr William Pickles and Mr Andrew Shonfield.

My good friend, Mr George W. Ross has been the most important influence in developing the author's level of social awareness and his methods of social analysis. Finally, I should like to thank Miss Laura M. Slatkin for her continuing assistance.

INTRODUCTION

French style economic planning has become an export product, and it has captured the market once dominated by American lectures on the virtues of a free-enterprise economy and Soviet sermons on the necessity for central planning. Claims for the 'French model' reduce to two contentions. It is effective, and it is inoffensive.

The first contention – its efficacy – is supported by correlation and imitation. France has now had her economic plan for more than twenty years, and during that time the French economy has maintained an average rate of growth of gross national product of 4-5%. This rate is substantially superior to those of Great Britain and the United States during the fifties, and quite comparable to that of the Soviet Union during the sixties.[1] The British study and imitate the French Plan. American city and regional planners draw models of it. Eastern European economists continually visit the Planning Commission's offices in Paris. The Common Market talks about a French Plan for Europe, and the European Left thinks it significant enough to view it as a paradigm model of post-war European capitalism.

The second contention – the inoffensiveness of French planning – is based on claims that French planning is characterised by a minimum of coercion and bureaucracy and a maximum of private decentralised decision-making and flexibility. In brief, it proclaims the total compatability of French style planning and modern capitalism. Proponents of the plan argue that some variant of the French model—the middle way between coercive central planning and unchecked private enterprise – has become a necessary element in a Western, democratic régime.

The following study is presented as an essay in Political-Economy. It examines the role of the plan in the political-economy it has come to symbolise. It analyses the machinery of French planning – the economic and administrative techniques

[1] See Appendix III for data.

and the institutional framework in which they are applied. But an analysis of French planning confined to an abstract model of the planning machinery alone would be, at best, incomplete. Thus, this study goes beyond such a model to place the plan in its social and historical context and to focus on the interplay of a changing environment and a changing planning process. The principal framework of this study is the power structure of the modern capitalist political economy in which the plan operates. These power relations are the principal determinants of the plan's role and its modes of operation. In short, any attempt to answer the basic question of what French planning does and how it does it – the purpose of this study – must situate planning within the broader configurations of the social, economic and political forces of French society.

PREFACE TO THE PAPERBACK EDITION

Publication of this new paperback edition comes at an opportune moment: the United States is just beginning what promises to be a long and serious debate about setting up a national economic plan. Timeliness is an irresistible but straightforward temptation for a publisher. For an author, it can be more subtle, for it often carries the illusion of modest, but real, usefulness.

The basis of that illusion is right at hand. The theme of the book is how to talk about planning in the context of an economy like ours, and the opening rounds of the current American debate on planning demonstrate that we do not seem to do that very well.

A few prominent Americans have already set out their initial views on the subject; many more will soon follow. Even by the norms of talk about economic policy—where the rules of rigor and common sense are generally relaxed—homily, metaphor and homespun wisdom dominate these pronouncements to a remarkable degree. Vocabulary is rudimentary. Definitions are private; they convey personal images. There seems to be no agreed-upon way to distinguish among different kinds of planning and to make those distinctions stick. In the absence of common definitions and referents, discussion does not advance. John Dunlop, Secretary of Labor and a sophisticated economist, remarked about this kind of discussion that in America 'it is hard to discuss planning because almost no one knows what it means.'[1]

What is important about such discussions is not their substantive content but the political fact of their existence; they become interesting only when understood as an early part of a long and complex political process. Their principal function is

[1] Cited in *New York Times*, 13 May 1975.

to put the question of national economic planning on the political agenda.

Towards that end, an initial political scaffolding was quickly erected. The first pieces were a series of individual public pronouncements in favor of planning by prominent public figures as seemingly disparate as Hubert Humphrey, Henry Ford II, Leonard Woodcock, R. V. Roosa and Wassily Leontief, which were featured in key media such as the *Wall Street Journal* and the *New York Times*.[2] The *Times* itself, in a lead editorial, solemnly suggested that the time had come to set up a national economic plan.[3] Business and political leaders suddenly found themselves asked to state their views on planning; quite a few did, prompting still others to try. Various journals picked up the theme and amplified the discussion. *Challenge* ran articles on the subject issue after issue; *Barron's* swiftly denounced planning as a danger to both liberty and efficiency and noted that the *New York Times*' suggestion was 'the opening gun of a well-orchestrated campaign' which had quickly become 'almost a movement.' *Social Policy* announced its intention to 'open discussion of planning to the widest variety of viewpoints possible' including radical views.[4] An Initiative Committee for National Economic Planning was formed, co-chaired by Professor Wassily Leontief and Leonard Woodcock, President of the United Auto Workers.[5] The work of the Initiative Committee was nicely synchronized with the introduction of the Humphrey-Javits Bill (The Balanced Growth and Economic Planning Act of 1975) which provides the initial focus for debate. Within small, but influential, circles planning is becoming an acceptable—even a necessary—subject of discussion, and those circles are rapidly widening.

Behind these efforts lie serious fears generated by a worsening economic situation and exacerbated by a deepening disenchant-

[2] *New York Times*, 10 December 1974; 12 December 1974; 1 December 1974; 16 February 1975; 16 March 1975 and 13 May 1975. *Wall Street Journal*, 12 August 1975.

[3] 23 February 1975.

[4] See *Challenge*, esp. issues of July–August 1974 and March–April 1975; first quotation is from *Barron's* 24 March 1975; *Social Policy* editorial from April 1975 issue.

[5] For composition of the Initiative Committee and its initial statement see *Challenge*, March–April 1975.

ment with 'mainstream economics.' A conviction reluctantly grows that manipulating demand, however adroitly, is simply not enough; something more is needed, and that next step seems to take the evocative name of 'planning.'

THE CREATION OF A POLITICAL ISSUE

Thus far we seem to be hurriedly following the early stages of a classic case of 'the creation of a political issue.' The elements are in their appointed places. Underneath it all there is a substantive problem area of broad dimensions: what to do about the economy, especially now that it is doing so badly and the old remedies seem not to be working. A small, but influential group of 'responsible people' collected from Wall Street, the universities, the unions, big business and the political-administrative realm responds to that situation in a particular way. It translates the situation into a problem, then tries to make that definition of the problem into a public issue. Its initial formulation of the problem is quickly amplified by diverse media. A bill, preferably bi-partisan, is introduced in the Congress, creating a central focus and forum. Committee hearings follow, as do more articles, more speeches and more bills. Momentum accumulates. It would be interesting to compare this effort to make planning a public issue with our recent experience of how hunger, or pension reform or, especially, poverty became public issues of particular formulation. The process has its own very powerful political logic—and its own dangers. The search for coalition—and not just any coalition—is its hallmark. Divisive distinctions must be avoided, and the initial step, the definition of the problem, is crucial. R. V. Roosa, formerly a ranking Treasury official and currently a Wall Street statesman, demonstrated this logic nicely when he expressed both the urgency of planning and the purpose of this first stage of the debate: 'The time has come to develop a truly home-grown American form of national economic planning. . . . Our concern is to find a planning approach that will be American in character and democratic in form.'[6]

[6] Cited in F. Reisman's editorial in *Social Policy*, March–April 1975. For a similar view see *New York Times* editorial entitled "The Need to Plan," 23 February 1975.

Such responsible initiative by an established elite—leading a movement for corrective reform—insulates discussion from sharp and fundamental distinctions. But as American political debate generally follows this form something more is needed to account for the particularly insubstantial quality of these preliminary discussions about planning.

WHAT KIND OF PLANNING?

First, we have not as a nation accumulated much experience with national economic planning, and like everyone else, we do not seem able to learn very much from the experience of others. Second, the academic and intellectual communities, especially the economics and political science branches, have not provided us with a set of analytic tools appropriate for discussing planning. As a result, we have no structured way to address the question: What kind of planning? Because these structures are so blatantly absent, the discussion does not develop—it just grows bigger, with everyone talking about something else. For some planning is just research, an exercise in pure information gathering and organizing that could help to spot future bottlenecks by improving available information. For others it means replacing a market system with massive federal bureaucracies that will destroy both personal liberty and economic efficiency. For still others it is a device to rescue a paralyzed economic system where a profusion of organizations, both public and private, control different pieces of the economy: it is essentially an effort to nationalize a feudal system. Others have more concrete visions of the purpose of planning: for some it is an employment program, for others, a national investment bank. Some see it as a tool of big business, while others see it as a weapon against big business. Each of these private visions may be perfectly reasonable—or not. The point is that together they do not add up to a discussion. Aaron Wildavsky entitled a provocative essay on economic planning 'If Planning is Everything, Maybe it's Nothing.'[7] If we are to get anywhere in the politically, as well as intellectually, important task of talking publicly and seriously about planning, his

[7] In *Policy Sciences*, No. 4, 1973.

epigram must be changed: If Planning is Everything, Maybe It's Time to Make Some Distinctions.

Several bedrock distinctions must be made at the outset. First, a discussion of 'Whether or not to plan?' is just nonsense in the context of an economy such as ours. The only serious question, both intellectually and politically, is: What kind of planning? For what ends? Through what means? By whom? Whether or not we ever had a self-regulating market economy, we do not now. The structures of our economy simply preclude leaving it all to the market, and it would take a real revolution to change them. A retreat from discussion about the reality of planning in its various forms and locations to talk about restoring an automatic system through deregulation and dismantling is, at best, romantic. And romantic reactions, whether they call for free markets and invisible hands, self-sufficient rural communes or *gemütlich* old neighborhoods, lead to political disasters.

Second, apolitical planning is a fiction. Planning is either political or it is decorative. Planning can never be purely technical or politically neutral. Planning means changing the political process; it means changes in who decides what about the evolution of the economy and how the choices are made. The kind of change in the political process defines the kind of planning. The 'One Best Way' approach that dominated American city planning for decades behind the slogan 'Keep Planning Out of Politics' was political planning; it kept planning out of one kind of politics and confined it to another. It is the same with economic planning at the national level. There is no meaningful content—but there is a good deal of political obfuscation—in any reified notion of 'Planning' that has no specific substance and context. There are only particular kinds of planning—particular changes in particular political-economic contexts.

Third, planning is not necessarily Left Wing—as a quick look at the French planning experience will demonstrate. Nor is planning necessarily about economic efficiency. Indeed, it most often is not—as a glance at the agricultural sector of any Western nation will reveal. And finally, although the craft-union type of demarcation between politics and economics may serve some useful purpose, it makes no sense at all in discussing planning, because planning is where economics and politics fuse. A political economy approach is necessary.

FRENCH PLANNING AS A RELEVANT MODEL

The best way to begin talking about planning is to examine concretely how a changing planning process interacts with an evolving political-economy. This book attempts to do just that —to develop a structured approach to studying planning by analyzing the thirty-year history of French planning. It treats French planning as a prototype model of modern capitalistic planning: 'modern' to indicate the broad structural transformations that distinguish the actual French political-economy, or the German or the American, from the textbook world of perfect competition; 'capitalism,' so as not to ignore fundamental continuities; and 'prototype' because the French experience is particularly rich in near-classic formulations of the logic and the workings of different kinds of planning within a context analogous to our own.

French planning has become the premier example of modern capitalist planning, the most frequently cited example in the US planning debate. The *Wall Street Journal* ran a front-page analysis of the strengths and weaknesses of French planning under the headline 'French Five Year Plan, Possible Model for the U.S.'[8] Herbert Stein, Chairman of Nixon's Council of Economic Advisers, told the economists' convention that the 'U.S. might create a planning agency like the French.'[9] And just last year, French planning was officially declared to be a kind of economic system: Samuelson devoted almost a full page of the 9th edition—about the same as for 'China' or for 'Socialism'—to what he calls 'French indicative planning.'

The problem is that these frequent references to the French experience are used to illustrate divergent points. For some, like Stein, it is an example of how a strong planning bureaucracy can use a lot of clout with great effect. For others, like Samuelson, it is a model of how a lightweight study bureau, which produces only 'indicative' information, can have remarkable success, while still others, like the *Wall Street Journal*, question its effectiveness. Though there is solid agreement that French planning constitutes a relevant model for the United States, there is nothing but confusion about what it is and what it does, let alone about how well it does it.

[8] 12 August 1975.
[9] Cited in *New York Times*, 30 December 1973, p. 1.

The French planning process is not a streamlined design of smoothly fitting parts. Its formal structure tells little about its functional structure. Its explicit targets do not define its operational role. The plan is a collection of activities that have never been integrated into a single, coherent process. That is one reason there has been so much confusion about the way it operates; it operates in several ways at once. There is, however, a deeper reason for the confusion manifest in these efforts to evaluate the performance of the French planning and to assess its applicability to the US context. They all begin from the premise that planning is fundamentally technical, that it is basically an economist's device. But despite the presence of sophisticated techniques, planning is not fundamentally a technology. It is a change in the form of political discourse, one that implies change in the way political decisions are made.

This book discusses French planning as an evolving political-economic process, not as an economist's tool. The questions it focuses on revolve around the theme of how can we distinguish among different kinds of planning in terms of the political choices each presents and how can planning be made to serve democracy?

For this paperback edition, I have added a long second postscript which analyzes the development of French planning since May 1968. It shows how the French, after thirty years of experience with planning, now find themselves, once again, forced to search for answers to the same question the US debate is trying to address: What kind of planning do we now want?

Fall, 1975 S.S.C.

PART I

A PRELIMINARY MODEL OF THE PLANNING PROCESS

1 EDUCATIVE PLANNING

The methods of French planning can be classified under two general headings: 'educative' and 'coercive'. Educative methods concentrate on clarifying the fundamental harmony of interest shared by the plan and expansion-minded business, and on disseminating information about production techniques, managerial methods and, crucially, about market conditions. Coercive methods are based on power.

Educative planning consists of two simultaneous and interrelated processes. The first is analogous to an adult-education programme designed to introduce top-level businessmen and ranking civil servants to modern managerial methods and attitudes: planning becomes a series of forums for the study of production techniques, industrial organisation, government policies, foreign competition and similar concerns of progressive management. The second type of educative process, 'indicative planning', transforms planning into a giant, cooperative market-research project: representatives of the major economic groups participate in the preparation of an input-output table for the principal sectors of the economy.

Both forms of educative planning depend upon one precondition: enlightened self-interest.

PLANNING AS ADULT EDUCATION

(*A*) *ENLIGHTENING SELF-INTEREST*

Unless we ourselves take a hand now, they'll foist a republic on us. If we want things to stay as they are, things will have to change. D'you understand?

Giuseppe di Lampedusa, *The Leopard*

In order for educative planning to work, the business community must accept the idea of participating in the planning process and profiting from it. Before the French business community could come around to such a position, they had to recover from the fear that the word 'planning', following so closely on a series of nationalisations, had aroused in them.

At the beginning, business reluctantly co-operated with the plan, largely because M. Jean Monnet, a respectable member of the business community in his own right, 'had convinced them that the only alternative to planification was nationalisation.'[1]

Reluctant co-operation from business would not, however, suffice for long-term success in educative planning. Nor could the threat of nationalisation and the general insecurity of the business leadership be expected to last very far into the post-war period, as it was becoming increasingly apparent to everyone that no further large-scale nationalisations were likely.[2]

Fortunately for the Monnet planners, the short period of 'forced co-operation' was sufficient for businessmen to begin to see the plan not as a threat to their own independence, but rather as an instrument with a great potential for serving their own ends – at least the ends of the more progressive firms.

Once businessmen had had some direct contact with the form of planning practised by Monnet, they could begin to think of the realities of current French planning practice instead of the vague and, for businessmen, nightmarish images the word evoked. The business community realized that the plan sought no further nationalisations; that it was not 'socialist', but rather had a great respect for profits and the profit motive; and that it did not seek to impose a bureaucratic control on all stages of production and distribution. Businessmen realized that the Monnet Plan was an instrument to strengthen (or if you prefer, to save) private enterprise. They discovered that the French planning process was designed to accommodate itself to the existing environment of private, decentralized decision-making and to the existing power-structure within the State bureaucracy. The plan aimed at transforming the stagnant, non-competitive industries that the planners associated with the sclerosis and decadence of the inter-war period into expansion-oriented,

[1] Quotation is from W. P. Blass, 'Economic Planning European Style,' *Harvard Business Review*, Sept.-Oct. 1963, p. 110. François Perroux writes 'The first plan served as a brake on a majority opinion favouring nationalisation . . . the liberal plan was a substitute for plans that the French left would most willingly have made more authoritarian.' *Le Plan Français* (Paris, 1962), p. 11.

[2] See *L'Express*, 6 juin 1953, p. 10; John Sheahan, *Promotion and Control of Industry in Postwar France*, Harvard University Press, 1963, p. 32.

internationally competitive industries. Above all, the plan sought to 'modernise' French industry. Its activities were largely limited to promoting industrial development and modernisation by encouraging investment and restructuring in certain 'key' sectors. The plan, business felt, was not very much concerned about what would come after this change, which French journalists are fond of labelling 'the transition to neo-capitalism.' After a few years of contact with the plan, businessmen came to feel that it was unlikely that planning would lead to more fundamental changes in the economic system.

(*B*) *THE ROUND TABLE*

Monnet's planners were proselytisers, out to make conversions among French businessmen. They sought to change the directing attitudes, methods and styles of French business, as well as its outmoded productive plant and obsolete industrial structures: 'Modernisation to them was not so much a condition of things as a state of mind which they wished to propagate widely.'[1]

Their method was classic. It had an unlimited number of precedents. It was King Arthur's method, and it was directed towards similar ends.

King Arthur's Round Table was created to promote Chivalry: to educate the cruder Knights of the Kingdom in the beliefs, the techniques and the modes of comportment of chivalry, the proper code of behaviour for a 'modern' knight. Arthur selected representatives of the old-fashioned knights who were causing his kingdom such distress by their uselessness, bickering and generally anti-social attitudes and sat them around a table next to such shining examples of knightly chivalry as Lancelot, Tristram, Galahad and himself. There Arthur expounded the doctrines of Chivalry: public-service knight errantry instead of wasteful aimlessness and carousing, interrupted only by the serious business of keeping the fief in the family. He and his colleagues explained the advantages that would be derived from the change: the kingdom would be more peaceful and more prosperous, the knights themselves more useful, more prosperous, more respected, more likely to live longer and, more fashionable – more modern. The presence of certain of their colleagues who were acknowledged models of

[1] Henry W. Ehrmann, *Organized Business in France* (Princeton, 1957), p. 285.

neo-knighthood (Lancelot, *et al.*) was a critical factor in the educative process. As much educating went on while jousting, questing and quaffing as went on at the round table. It worked well. England prospered and knighthood flowered.[1]

Monnet tried to do the same thing. He invited selected old-fashioned French businessmen to participate in the round-table forum of the plan and sat them next to living examples of the kind of modern businessman he was hoping to see dominate the economy: Pierre Massé (Electricité de France), Paul Huvelin (Loire et Centre, then Kléber-Colombes), Louis Armand (SNCF), Joseph Roos (aviation), Raoul de Vitry (chemicals).[2] While Monnet and the planners explained to them the advantages and techniques of expansion-minded management, daily contact with their more progressive colleagues helped bring them over to the complex set of attitudes and methods that Monnet and the planners were trying to spread. A national modernisation and development plan is an institution particularly well suited to such an educative task. The plan provides the framework for discussion and decision. The plan's framework of investment, output and sectoral growth analysis differed enormously from the outlook of strictly financial concerns, and from the strict financial orthodoxy which was long characteristic of French economic administration. The plan's framework forced participating businessmen to see things – especially their own role – from a new perspective. It was the principal educative tool.[3]

The educative round-table approach to planning is no mere trapping of the French system. It is an integral and important part of that system. The great transformation of business attitudes which began during the period of the Monnet Plan has been among the most important changes in the post-war French economy. Without that change, the long-term development and modernisation of the economy could never have been achieved, despite the heavy investment programme. Professor Kindleberger argues:

[1]This interpretation of the Arthurian legend owes more to T. H. White *The Once and Future King*, than to Malory.

[2] See *First Plan*, pp. 189–193 for a preliminary list of participants in the modernisation commissions; and *Année Politique*, 1949, pp. 420–436 for a more complete listing.

[3] We will have a great deal to say about what constitutes the plan's framework and about its effects on attitude and behaviour in the following chapters.

> The economic recovery of France after the war is due to the restaffing of the economy with new men and new attitudes . . . the new men were found in private as well as nationalized industry, in family firms as well as corporate enterprises, in administrative positions as well as technical ones. Some of them had 'a passion for innovation,' some for expansion, all for efficiency of one sort or another . . . Dissatisfaction with the past led them to substitute change for stability as the operating guide. To conclude that the basic change in the French economy is one of people and attitudes is frustrating to the economist . . . marginal analysis, compound interest, growth as a function of fixed resources, evolving technology and growing capital are more compatible with the economic modes of reasoning. It is true that capital has grown, and technical progress has been made, but these are accompaniments of a more far-reaching process, rather than exogeneous variables. . . .[1]

The plan was by no means uniquely responsible for this revolution in personnel and attitudes. But it was, as we shall see, an important centre and force in encouraging the rapid post-war change in the personnel, attitudes and methods that directed the French economy.

INDICATIVE PLANNING OR PLANNING AS MARKET RESEARCH

> French planning . . . is essentially the extension to the national level of the kind of planning effort made by any private business with thought for the future.[2]
>
> Any large firm, operated on modern lines, draws for itself medium and long term programmes, in which market forecasts, equipment programmes, and all aspects of the firm's policy are made mutually consistent, and ends and means are checked against each other. We really do nothing else, at the level of the whole economy.[3]

Indicative planning is the most talked-about feature of the French planning process. Often, it is taken to be the defining characteristic of French planning.[4] It has been called, by serious

[1] Charles P. Kindleberger, 'The Postwar Resurgence of the French Economy,' in Stanley Hoffman *et al.*, *In Search of France* (Cambridge, Mass., 1963), pp. 156–157.

[2] Pierre Massé, speech to U.S. Council on Foreign Relations, autumn 1962, Commissariat du Plan, mimeo, p. 1.

[3] Pierre Massé, speech to Detroit Edison Co., Nov. 1962, Commissariat du Plan, mimeo, p. 3.

[4] As in *Ibid.*, or Jean Fourastié, *La Planification Economique en France* (Paris, P.U.F.), 1963; or Bernard Cazes, *La Planification en France et le IV Plan* (Paris, Editions de l'Epargne), 1962.

men, 'planning without planners', and has been portrayed as the way to promote rapid and orderly economic growth without coercion or bureaucracy, the way to reconcile economic planning with decentralised decision-making, private property, democracy and efficiency.[1]

Indicative planning is a way to influence economic behaviour without recourse to power; it works on a purely informational basis. The technical process of preparing an indicative plan is complicated, but the logic of indicative planning is simple.

A brief abstract of the most commonly received interpretations of 'the logic of indicative planning' follows.[2]

(*A*) *THE AIMS OF INDICATIVE PLANNING*

The immediate aim of the indicative, or market research, approach to planning is to improve the information available for making decisions.

If the management of any firm could be provided with accurate estimates of future demand for its products, it would govern its investment and output programmes 'rationally', i.e., by the obvious dictates of demand. The price system does not provide management with adequate information about future market conditions; the indicative plan tries to fill this gap. It does not replace the market and the price system. It supplements the information supplied by the price system. It improves the market mechanism by reducing uncertainties.[3]

The firm benefits from the information provided by indicative planning. Decisions are based on more complete information. Security is increased; so are efficiency, profits and growth.

[1] Quotation is from P. Massée, Detroit Edison Co., p. 4; see also his *Le Plan ou L'anti-hasard*, Paris, NRF, 1965, p. 144. Andrew Shonfield describes the way French planning has been urged on Western nations by 'the technique of the soft sell,' and the way its proponents 'seemed to go out of their way to cast a veil over the experience of the public authorities in France in persuading business to abide by the aims of the Plan in their day-to-day decisions. It was like describing a battle without ever taking account of the fact that anyone had been killed—or at least had been threatened with slaughter.' *Modern Capitalism*, New York, OUP, 1965, p. 146.

[2] These works include the numerous articles and speeches by Commissioner Pierre Massé and his staff at the Planning Commission listed in the bibliography as well as Fourastié, *Planification*, Cazes, *le IV Plan*, and Pierre Bauchet, *Economic Planning, the French Experience*, London (Heineman), 1964.

[3] See J. Bénard, 'Le Marché Commun et l'Avenir de la Planification Française,' *Revue Economique*, no. 5, Sept. 1964, p. 762; Pierre Bauchet, 'La Regulation par le Plan,' *Revue de l'Economie Politique*, juin 1964, pp. 692–697; Bernard Cazes, *le IV Plan*, pp. 8–11.

The economy too benefits from indicative planning:

(1) Production bottlenecks are reduced, making possible higher rates of growth. If each industry could plainly see what demand for its products would be, each industry would expand its capacity to meet that demand. In this manner, the overall growth rate will not be held back by one (or several), key industries which, because of over cautious estimates of future demand, did not expand capacity enough to meet the needs of the growing economy. One such bottleneck, e.g., inadequate productive capacity in the construction or machine tool industries, can hold back growth in an entire chain of activities. It can also strain foreign exchange reserves and lower the economy's inflation threshold. Both these effects further retard the rate of overall expansion. The informational effects of the indicative plan eliminate one very important cause of such bottlenecks – inaccurate and conservative estimates of future demand by management. Similarly, they reduce wasteful investment in excess capacity resulting from over optimistic estimates of demand, and in this manner contribute to a more efficient use of resources.[1]

(2) The informational effects of indicative planning also increase the over-all rate of expansion in a more general way. Uncertainties about future demand tend to reduce the rates of investment and expansion in the private sector. Indicative planning reduces such uncertainties, thus providing a climate conducive to higher investment and more rapid expansion.[2]

(3) Fluctuations of investment between over-and-under capacity is one of the principal causes of booms and busts and of less catastrophic swings in the business cycle. According to Keynes and thousands of 'play-it-by-ear' businessmen, most investment decisions are taken on the basis of inadequate information about future demand.[3] The uncertainty surround-

[1] See P. Massé, *French Affairs*, pp. 10–11; Bernard Cazes, *le IV Plan*, pp. 8–11.

[2] See B. Cazes, *le IV Plan*, pp. 8–11; Davis and Whinston, 'The Economics of Urban Renewal,' *Law and Contemporary Problems*, vol. 26, 1961, pp. 105–118; J. R. Hicks, *Value and Capital* (London, 1946), chapter X; F. K. Knight, *Risk, Uncertainty and Profit*, no. 16 in the London School of Economics series of reprints of scarce tracts in economics and political science, New York (Houghton Mifflin), 1921, chapter VII.

[3] See B. Cazes, *le IV Plan*, pp. 8–22; J. M. Keynes, *General Theory* (London, 1947 edition), pp. 149–150; J. McDonald, 'How Executives Make Decisions,' in *The Executive Life* by the editors of *Fortune Magazine* (Dolphin Paperback), 1956.

ing those decisions is a prime cause of unstabilising investment fluctuations. By providing better information about future demand the indicative plan reduces investment fluctuations and helps to smooth out the growth path.

(4) The information provided by the indicative plan aids decision-making for government as well as for business. The plan provides a clear picture of the effects on the entire economy of any change in government policies. By making apparent the implications of any contemplated change in government policies the indicative plan leads to more rational decisions and more coherent policies.

These advantages are obtained on the cheap with indicative planning: it costs almost nothing in terms of the values and freedoms of a liberal economy. There is no appreciable increase in bureaucracy or red-tape; no threat to decentralised decision-making; no diminution of the rights of private property. Indicative planning functions on a purely informational basis. Information is collected, organised and made available to all. It 'works' because it becomes a universal guide for decisions. It guides decisions because, its proponents maintain, the information so processed is more complete and more accurate than that which any firm – even the biggest – could obtain through its own market research.[1] The information is better not only because it is more comprehensive, but, crucially, because it is consistent. Demand projections for all sectors are prepared on the basis of a uniform set of assumptions and checked against one another for consistency. That consistency is what guarantees each industry a cleared market. The motor of indicative planning is a benign circle: the more industry follows the plan, the more accurate the plan's information will be; the more accurate the plan's information, the more reason industry will have to follow the plan.

(*B*) *HOW THE INDICATIVE PLAN IS PREPARED: THE TECHNIQUE OF INDICATIVE PLANNING*

Representatives of the major industries, the Treasury, the tutelary ministries, the banks, the trade unions, the state statistical agencies, and outside 'experts' work together, under

[1] See, Massé, *French Affairs*, pp. 10–11.

the direction of the planners, in the preparation of a co-ordinated set of detailed demand projections for the major sectors of the economy.[1]

The demand projections take the form of an input-output table which shows the sectoral interdependencies in the economy: the table relates the effects of an action in any industry on all other industries. For example, agricultural production is strongly influenced by government support policies. A change in government policies will result in a change in output from the agricultural sector, a change in inputs purchased by that sector and, a change in final demand generated by farm incomes. Tractor sales are therefore strongly influenced by government farm policies, and rubber production is in turn affected by the demand for tractor tyres.

The first step in preparing an indicative plan is to assemble a set of detailed inter-industry accounts for the latest year for which information is available. The accounts may be organised in the form of a table in which each industry appears twice, as a producer of outputs and as a purchaser of inputs. The elements in each row (see table I on following page), show the uses made of the output of each industry. For example, of the total output of industry 1, which we shall call X_1, x_{16} is used by the railroad industry, x_{1n} is used by industry n, x_{11} is used by industry 1 (the steel industry) itself, and Y_1 goes directly to final uses, government, private consumption, exports and investment (G_1, C_1, E_1, and I_1). The role of the steel industry as a purchaser of inputs is shown in column one. Total produced inputs purchased from all industries by the steel industry is U_1. It is the sum of x_{11}, x_{21}, x_{31}. . . the amounts of steel, automotive machinery, coal, etc., used by the steel industry during the given accounting period. P_1 represents the primary or unproduced inputs used by industry 1, in this case, labour, capital and foreign exchange. $U_1 + P_1 = X_1$, total production of industry 1.

Such a table provides a clear picture of economic activity for the latest completed accounting period, (usually the year before preparation of the plan begins). Emphasis is on inter-

[1] A twenty-eight sector model was used in the initial preparation of the fourth plan; see P. Massé, *Histoire Méthode et Doctrine de la Planification Française*, La Documentation Française, 1962, p. 7.

TABLE I

				PURCHASERS OR USERS												
				Intermediate Use							Final Use					
Suppliers or Producers	Producing Industries	Steel	1	x_{11}	x_{12}	x_{13}	x_{14}	x_{15}	x_{1n}	Z_1	Y1	G1	C1	E1	I1	X1
		Autos	2	x_{21}	x_{22}	x_{23}	x_{24}	x_{25}	x_{2n}	Z_2	Y2	G2	C2	E2	I2	X2
		Coal	3	x_{31}	x_{32}	x_{33}	x_{34}	x_{35}	x_{3n}	Z_3	Y3	G3	C3	E3	I3	X3
		Electricity	4	x_{41}	x_{42}	x_{43}	x_{44}	x_{45}	x_{4n}	Z_4	Y4	G4	C4	E4	I4	X4
		Agriculture	5	x_{51}	x_{52}	x_{53}	x_{54}	x_{55}	x_{5n}	Z_5	Y5	G5	C5	E5	I5	X5
		Railroads	6	x_{61}	x_{62}	x_{63}	x_{64}	x_{65}	x_{6n}	Z_6	Y6	G6	C6	E6	I6	X6
		Industry	N	x_{n1}	x_{n2}	x_{n3}	x_{n4}	x_{n5}	x_{nn}	Z_n	Yn	Gn	Cn	En	In	Xn
			U	U_1	U_2	U_3	U_4	U_5	U_n							
	Primary Inputs	Labour	L	L1 L2	L3	L4	L5	L6	Ln	ZL	YL	GL	CL	EL	IL	XL
		Finance	F	F1 F2	F3	F4	F5	F6	FN	ZF	YF	GF	CF	EF	IF	XF
		Foreign Exchange	$	$1 $2	$3	$4	$5	$6	$N	Z$	Y$	G$	C$	E$	I$	X$
		Total Primary Inputs	P	P1 P2	P3	P4	P5	P6	PN	ZP	YP	GP	CP	EP	IP	XP
		Total Production	V	V1 V2	V3	V4	V5	V6	VN							

dependence; the flow of goods is traced from final demand, through inter-industry uses to primary inputs.

An important characteristic of such a descriptive table is that it can be a useful tool for prediction – the essential element of planning. In order to go from a descriptive table of last year's market to a predictive table of future market conditions, two further categories of information must be obtained. They are: coefficients of inter-industry demand (or input coefficients) and estimates of final demand for the target date of the plan.

Input coefficient (a_{ij}) represents the amount of the product of industry *i* needed to produce one unit of the product of industry *j*, or the demand of each industry for each commodity as a function of its own output. Input coefficient $a_{ij} = X_{ij}/X_j$, where X_{ij} represents the demand of industry j for product *i*, and X_j represents total output of industry j.

The input coefficient is assumed to represent an essentially technical relationship. It is therefore established on the basis of past practice. Each inter-industry purchase is divided by the total output of that industry. The data are taken from the interindustry accounts recorded in table I. Two important assumptions lie behind the establishment of these coefficients. First, the technical relations that obtained in the year for which the accounting matrix was drawn up represent fixed-coefficient production relationships so that each industry will continue to produce its product with exactly the same inputs regardless of relative price changes in inputs.[1] Second, the coefficients are independent of the level of production, so that the total intermediate demands of an industry are determined only by the total level of production of that industry.[2]

In practice of French planning, the difficulties associated with these basic assumptions of input-output theory are handled in a simple, but imperfect way. If innovations have

[1] See H. B. Chenery and Paul G. Clark, *Interindustry Economics* (N.Y. 1959), chapters 2 and 6, or any good text on basic input-output theory. More sophisticated examination of the no substitution assumption can be found in C. F. Christ, 'A Review of Input-Output Analysis,' in National Bureau of Economic Research, *Input-Output Analysis: An Appraisal* (Princeton, 1955), and R. Dorfman, 'The Nature and Significance of Input-Output,' *Review of Economics and Statistics*, XXXVI, no. 2, May 1954. For a discussion of the 'no substitution' assumption with special reference to French planning practice see F. LeGuay, 'Les projections à long terme en France,' paper presented to the International Conference on input-output techniques, Geneva, September 1961.

[2] See, Chenery and Clark, *Interindustry Economics*, chapters 2 and 6.

hours or higher output, higher wages or higher rates of investment, price stability or more rapid expansion. These choices are all conflict situations; they are trade-offs: more schools than there would have been without a plan means less of something else than there would have been without a plan. Indicative planning cannot make such choices. It assumes away all questions of conflict. It treats them as having been previously resolved elsewhere. The function of the indicative plan is to publicise the terms of the settlements. Only because there are no conflicts can indicative planning operate on a purely informational basis. There is nothing in the indicative planning mechanism that prevents it from being undertaken by a substantial private institution instead of a state agency. If the government and the major industries were willing to make their own programmes known to the planning institution, it could organise that information, check it for consistency, make the results known to all the independent participants (including the state), ask those participants to revise their programmes in light of the more complete information they now possess. Then they would return the revised programmes to the planning institution which would repeat the process, again and again, until the desired level of accuracy is achieved. Because the absence of conflict is what characterises indicative planning and defines its boundaries, those boundaries are narrow. Indicative planning can help accelerate and regularise (smooth-out) growth by reducing bottlenecks that result from ignorance of final demand. It can help to increase efficiency in the use of resources and the rate of investment by reducing uncertainty. It can even exert an important indirect influence on the *direction* of development by revealing to the decision-makers the implications of their actions, and in this way, perhaps, lead them to somewhat different actions. These are important functions, but they constitute a far narrower role than that which the French plan publicly defines as its own.

A spokesman for the planning Commission states that:

> The aim of the Plan is first to regularise the current of economic life and then to orient it in a direction other than that which would have been taken spontaneously.[1]

Parliament defined the plan as 'an instrument for the orientation

[1] Ministère de la Co-opération, *Le Plan Française*, 1963, p. 29.

of economic expansion and social progress'[1] The planners have always described the plan as an instrument to steer expansion. The goals of the plans are couched in terms of accelerating and directing growth – with coherence, and smoothness given secondary consideration. Thus Commissioner Massé describes the first plan in these terms:

> The first plan had to opt either for a modest development of all sectors, or a strong progression in certain sectors. . . . A hardy choice was made in favour of the second option.[2]

A foreign observer describes the principal objective of the third plan in terms of the conflicts necessary to influence the direction of development:

> [the 3rd plan] stressed the importance of allowing essential investment projects to go ahead even at the expense of a slower growth in consumption.[3]

The indicative planning mechanism is not an adequate tool to accomplish the objectives of the third plan. A planning process suitable to the goals of the third plan would have to be something different from the purely indicative model. For higher investment and lower consumption than there would have been without the plan is a target that implies conflict. And the mere publication of a chart predicting fewer consumer goods will not affect behaviour. The indicative planning tables must be supported by a universally held conviction that the projected pattern of resource allocation will, in fact, be realised. This implies that the conflict has been resolved and that action which will result in higher effective demand for investment goods and lower demand for consumption goods has been taken – or, at least, is sure to be taken in the future. Without such a certitude there is no reason for the consumer goods industries to guide their production by the indicative plan. The conflict between higher investment and higher consumption breaks down the self-implementing machinery of indicative planning. The only way such an objective can be realised is by coercion: the resource allocation priorities must be forced on the economy in some way or another.

[1] *Journal Officiel, Lois et Décrets,* Août 1962, p. 7810.

[2] Massé, *Documentation Française*, p. 5.

[3] Malcolm MacLennan, 'French Planning: Some Lessons for Britain,' *Planning* (P.E.P., London) Vol. XXIX, No. 475, 9 September 1963, p. 335.

The resolution of a resource allocation problem may take many forms – but they are all power solutions; they all imply conflicts. First there is the familiar classical, or laissez-faire, model: the market mechanism allocates the resources. There is no *conscious* effort made to steer development by orienting large amounts of economic activity: an infinity of small decisions allocate the resources and shape the future. This model is the complete denial of planning.

At the other extreme is the model of authoritarian central planning. The planning institution decides how resources are to be allocated. Its decisions are direct commands to the principal economic agents. The control system is essentially hierarchical: information is conveyed directly, by fiat. The power instrument for implementing all decisions is direct command. The market allocates little. Development is consciously controlled, not just guided.

An intermediate approach, the 'modified market' model is more relevant to the French economy than either extreme. As in the laissez-faire model there is no need for a formal plan, although, as we shall see, the modified market model implies some planning. In order to see how the model works, let us assume that under conditions of rapid growth and full employment, the government decides to shift resources in a particular direction, for example, into a new programme of highway construction. This decision means, of course, that other sectors will not be able to expand as quickly as they would have in the absence of the highway programme. The government can use any of a multitude of means to bring about the desired shift in resources. It can act directly on final demand by increasing taxes, by raising hire-purchase terms, or by changing the pattern of government expenditures. It can act on the supply side by raising interest rates, by limiting the inflow of foreign goods, or by increasing business taxes. Or it can do nothing and print money to pay for the highway programme thus letting inflation reallocate resources through the market mechanism. The range of possible actions is enormous. But once the initial action (e.g., an increase in interest rates) is taken, the market mechanism will handle all subsequent adjustments by itself. It will allocate the remaining resources among competing uses. These adjustments to the initital action are made automatically, without systematic efforts at guiding them, but they are not unforeseeable. The choice of the initial action implies a choice as to the subsequent adjustments. For example, an increase in interest rates will affect the construction industry more than, say, the soap industry; an increase in hire-purchase rates will cut demand for consumer durables more than it will affect demand for medical services. In the modified market model there is a conscious effort to direct expansion. There is planning, even though no formal planning institution exists. The planning consists in the wilful direction of economic activity; its sophistication depends upon the way the implications of the initial resource shift are considered. The more consciously, the more systematically the adjustments to the initial action are anticipated (one could just as easily say 'planned'), the more sophisticated the planning process.

Here is where the indicative planning mechanism can be added to the modified market model. An indicative plan is an excellent instrument for studying the implications of a contemplated shift in resources. It provides a clear picture of the adjustments that will follow from that action. Suppose that in the example we have been using, the government decides to increase interest rates in order to fit its highway programme under the economy's inflation ceiling. Some planning, however rudimentary, is present once the government attempts to anticipate the effects of higher interest rates. But a casual analysis of those effects might not go beyond noting the initial impact of higher interest rates on residential construction. It might not consider the effects of a slow down in housing starts on the paint, plaster, furniture and porcelain industries, let alone third round repercussions on forestry, railroad traffic and chemicals.

The indicative plan, as we have seen, provides a systematic analysis of the effects throughout the economy of any major shift in resources. It provides that information not only to the government which will make the initial decisions, but also to all the economic agents who will have to adjust their behaviour because of that decision. Herein lies its function in planning. The analytical machinery of indicative planning can be used to increase the sophistication with which decisions are made, by better informing the decision-making centre of the adjustments that will follow from their decisions: it can also be used to increase the sophistication with which those adjustments are made, by supplementing the information the market provides about the effects of the initial action on the environment of each major economic agent.

If the French plan is to influence the direction of development it must be able to deal with conflicts: it must make decisions. If it is to do this with any sophistication it must incorporate the kind of systematic analysis provided by the indicative plan. And if it is to operate in an environment of decentralised decision-making and dispersed power, where it cannot convey and enforce its decisions by direct command, it must work through the market mechanism.

The commonly received indicative planning model for French planning must, therefore, be put aside in favour of a model that is relevant to the three functions French planning attributes to itself: orienting, regularising and accelerating development. That model must show the interrelations between the systematic analysis, decision-making and decision-implementing processes that constitute planning.

In addition, therefore, to 'educative' methods of planning there is a substantial body of 'coercive' devices employed in French planning for dealing with conflict situations.

2 COERCIVE IMPLEMENTATION

1 SELECTIVE INCENTIVES: IMPLEMENTATION IN THE PRIVATE SECTOR

The coercive methods of French planning are designed to promote growth and modernisation in selected industries: they are not aimed at controlling business activity. The plan compels industrial development and rationalization through the discriminatory use of a complicated assortment of state economic favours. The way these powers are generally used is easy to understand: the plan buys the co-operation of private firms.

The French state disposes of a wide assortment of economic favours, commonly called *incitations*, or incentives, which can be used to make a project desired by the state profitable to the firm. The most important of these incentives fall into four broad categories: cheap investment capital, accelerated depreciation allowances, special tax reductions and outright grants. These incentives are used selectively: they are granted to certain firms, or to certain categories of firms, and not to others.

Until 1949 an elaborate system of direct controls regulated building, borrowing, importing and the allocation of scarce materials. Implementation of the planned investment programme would have demanded little more than a co-ordinated policy of issuing such permits. The Monnet planners, however, never relied heavily on this form of direct, bureaucratic planning. In the first place, everyone, including the planners, knew that these controls were only temporary: it would be self-defeating to establish what was hoped to become a permanent institution upon so unpopular and transitory a base. Furthermore, the planners felt that they could achieve their limited objectives in the private sector through the use of selective incentives, without having to depend upon direct physical controls. Acute shortages of investment goods, foreign exchange and investment financing in the first years of the Monnet Plan greatly increased the planners' reasons for confidence in their incentives: they transformed incentives into controls.

In the immediate post-war period it was practically impossible to finance any major investment programme without government support.[1] Self-financing (financing out of retained earnings and depreciation allowances), the traditional form of financing investment in private industry, amounted to less than one-third of total investment in the sectors covered by the plan's analysis during the years 1947-1950.

SELF-FINANCING AS A PERCENTAGE OF TOTAL INVESTMENT FINANCE[2]

1947	1948	1949	1950
22.7%	23.7%	30.1%	34.7%

Almost two-thirds of total investment was financed out of public, or publicly controlled funds.[3]

Investment projects undertaken within the framework of the plan received priority access to these funds. Approved projects could secure long-term loans at low interest rates through state controlled credit institutions. Rates and terms varied according to the sector and the project, but they were far below the 'going' interest rate and below the opportunity cost of capital.[4] Borrowing from the state was borrowing cheaply; borrowing in the private market was impossible at anything approaching 'normal'

[1] See John Sheahan, *Promotion and Control of Industry in Postwar France*, Cambridge, Mass. 1963, p. 173.

[2] Source: Comm. du Plan, *Rapport Annuel*, 1951 (*Cinq Ans d'Exécution de Plan*), Paris, 1952, table 131, p. 322.

[3] Issues of stocks and bonds accounted for the residual of total investment

1948	1949	1950	1951
8.5%	6.4%	6.4%	6.1%

financing (including nationalized industries).But these security issues had to have the approval of the Plan. See, *Ibid.*, p. 323.

[4] Interest rates on loans from publically controlled funds ranged around 4½% for nationalized and private firms in the basic industries: EDF, SNCF, steel, aluminium, ship-building. EDF borrowed from the state at 4½% for the construction of its hydroelectric power stations. Many economists insisted that the rate was artificially low; Pierre Massé then a director at EDF, used an 8% interest rate in his linear programming analysis of the projects – and even this 8% rate was considered artificially low. See, Massé and Gibrat, 'Applications of Linear Programming to Investment in the Electrical Power Industry,' *Management Science*, January 1957, pp. 149–166. On 'going' interest rates, and rates for state loans, see BRAE (Bureau de Recherche et d'Action Economique), *La Politique d'Incitation*, Paris, 1960, pp. 58, 64.

rates and terms. Non-approved projects had great difficulty obtaining access to publicly controlled funds.

As long as business was dependent on the state for upwards of two-thirds of investment finance, and approval of a proposed investment project by the Planning Commission was an important determinant of the allocation of public investment credits, business would be compelled to co-operate with the plan.

By 1952, however, the sources of investment finance were beginning to change. About forty-five per cent of investment in the sectors covered by the plan was now financed out of retained earnings and depreciation allowances (self-financing):

SELF-FINANCING AS A PERCENTAGE OF TOTAL INVESTMENT[1]

1952	1953	1954	1955	1956	1957	1958	1959
47.6%	43%	44%	45%	46.9%	42.6%	44%	43.6%

Business was no longer so dependent upon the state for financing: a state loan was an important aid to business, but it was no longer an absolute necessity.

Throughout the 'fifties over half of investment continued to be financed out of borrowings, and

> more than eighty per cent of capital borrowed by firms was at artificial interest rates decided or reduced by the public authorities.[2]

The plan retained an important influence over the allocation of these funds. Supplying cheap investment credits remained an important means by which the planners were able to *promote* selected investment projects. But the withholding of cheap credits was no longer a means to forbid investments that the plan did not wish to see realized. The granting of cheap investment credits was thus transformed by business' increased capacity to self-finance into an incentive: it had formerly been a control.

Other incentives supplement access to cheap investment credits. These incentives are awarded by the ministries to approved investment projects under several titles that correspond with the aims of the plan. Those titles included aid the

[1] Source: for 1952–1955, Comm. du Plan, *Rapport Annuel* 1956, table 13, p. 21; for 1956–1959, *Rapport Annuel* 1960, table III p. 12.

[2] François Bloch-Lainé, *Encyclopédie Française* Vol. XX, p. 22–12. Andrew Shonfield, *Modern Capitalism*, p. 86 also uses an 80% estimate for the early sixties; his source is Chazel and Poyet, *l'Economie Mixte*, p. 102.

encouragement of exports; regional development; scientific and technical research; industrial conversion, restructuring, concentration and specialisation; investment and savings; productivity, modernisation and international competitiveness.[1] A single investment project can receive a package of incentives, which could include, for example:

a loan of investment funds at 4–5% (instead of 8%).

tax reductions on that portion of capital raised in the market: a sum equal to 5% of an approved increase in capital can be subtracted from profits tax for a period of up to seven years. On an issue of one million francs, the advantage comes to 175,000 francs.[2]

state guarantees of loans in private market.

reduction of building taxes from 13.20% to 1.40% for construction needed for industrial regroupings, conversion or regional development.[3]

accelerated depreciation rates of up to 50% in the first year for investment in scientific and technical research.[4]

accelerated depreciation rates (up to 50% in the first year) for workers' housing to accompany new industrial developments.[5]

accelerated depreciation allowances for firms which are awarded a *Carte d'Exportateur* (over 20% of business goes to exports).[6]

subsidies for equipment of up to 10–20% of costs for plants located in specially designed regions.[7]

This list is merely suggestive. The number of incentives is enormous and constantly changing, as are their specific provisions. Two important characteristics of the plan's incentives ought to be noted now; we will discuss them at some length below. They all operate on the supply side and they all serve to promote expansion; none aims at constraining expansion. As we shall see, the plan relies on positive incentives. These incentives can generally be counted upon to induce a firm to undertake a project by making that project profitable. But they cannot prevent a firm from expanding beyond the targets of the

[1] See M. Delcourt, *Les Moyens d'Exécution du Plan*, Comm. du Plan (mimeo); also G. de la Perrière, L'*Exécution du Plan*, Comm. du Plan (mimeo) and BRAE, *Politique d'Incitation*, chapter 11.

[2] See decree of 29 August 1957; for arithmetic of 'net advantage,' see BRAE, *Politique d'Incitation*, p. 66.

[3] La Perrière, *Exécution du Plan*, p. 16.

[4] Ordinance of 25 September 1958.

[5] Law of 25 July 1953.

[6] Decree of 10 August 1957.

[7] Decree of 10 April 1960.

plan or in some unplanned direction. The task of orienting growth implies more than just promoting the development of certain sectors; it often implies constraining expansion in other sectors. The plan's incentives cannot be relied upon to accomplish that task. Action on the demand side would, of course, be an excellent means to hold back expansion in certain sectors. But government action on demand has not been systematically co-ordinated with the objectives of the plan. Price policy – even when direct price controls were widespread – was not used in close conjunction with the plan, nor was short-term monetary and fiscal policy. This lack of tight co-ordination between short-term action on the demand side and the medium term goals of the plan, has been, as we shall see, the greatest source of the plan's weakness.[1]

2 IMPLEMENTATION IN THE PUBLIC SECTOR

In the nationalised industries and the public sector in general, the plan aspires to be more coercive (or imperative) than in the private sectors. This is because the publicly-owned industries are the basic industrial sectors, and consequently the focal point of the planned investment programmes, and also because of the theory which unflinchingly holds that:

> the adoption of the Plan by the government is the same thing as an order for its execution by the nationalized enterprises.[2]
>
> 1946
>
> execution in those sectors [the nationalized industries] poses no serious problems since it is the state that decides.[3]
>
> 1962

Direct investment by the state represents about 35% of total gross investment in France.[4] By controlling the public sector the planner can direct more than thirty-five per cent of total investment; they could use the great leverage of the public sector's market power to influence the large volume of private investment that is closely tied to the public sector. The purchasing policies of the public sector and the nationalised industries

[1] Part IV below, examines the relation of government action on demand to the programmes of the plans.
[2] *Rapport Annuel*, 1946–47, pp. 102–103.
[3] Delcourt, *Moyens d'Exécution*, p. 1.
[4] See chart on following page.

TABLE II

DIRECT State Investment: Year 1959

		millions of francs
Direct State Investments (Budget Titles)		1,390
Investments by Local Governments		3,920
Investments by Nationalised Sector*		
Power		6,885
Coal (C.D.F.)	1,340	
Electricity (E.D.F.)	3,393	
Co. Nat. du Rhone	187	
Gas (Gaz de France)	648	
Gas (Gaz de Lacq)	361	
Atomic Energy	785	
Mining Research	21	
Petroleum	250 e.	
Transportation		3,579
French Railways (SNCF)	2,352	
Paris Transport Authority (RATP)	68	
Inland Waterways	25	
Maritimes trans.	150	
Air transportation	278	
Paris airport	144	
Ports	20	
Post Office (PTT)	542	
Navigation	57	
Regional development	117	
TOTAL DIRECT STATE INVESTMENTS		15,900
Total Investments		45,860
Direct State Investments as percentage of Total Investment		35%

* Does not include investment of national enterprises in competitive sectors, e.g., Régie Renault, nationalized banks, or public financing of housing, and 46% of housing expenditures were financed from public funds.

Source: FDES, *Rapport du Conseil du Directeur du FDES* (1959), pp. 10–11, 13 and 36 et Comm. du Plan, *Rapport Sur l'Exécution du Plan* 1961 *et* 1962, p. 254. On housing see Angus Campbell, *Economic Growth in the West* (Twentieth Century Fund) 1964, table IV-4.

could be used to control the private industries for which they are the principal clients.[1] For example, Electricité de France purchases about eighty per cent of the output of the heavy electrical equipment industry.[2] Its influence on the electrical

[1] See, Comm. du Plan, *Rapport Général sur le Premier Plan de Modernisation et d'Equipement*, Nov. 1946–Jan. 1947 (hereafter referred to as *The First Plan* or the *Monnet Plan*), chapter VI, para. 6.

[2] G. de la Perrière, *Exécution du Plan*, p. 13.

equipment industry is almost as complete as if the electrical equipment manufacturers were vertically integrated with EDF. Similarly, the pricing policies of the public sector could be used to control other industries.

As we shall see, the planners have encountered great difficulties in trying to get the investment budget of the public sector to conform to the plan; and they have had even less success in using the economic power of the public sector as a tool to influence private firms.

The major source of difficulty is that the public sector is not a simple hierarchy that responds to the commands of the plan. Rather, it is a giant cluster of ministries, agencies and firms, each of which has its own constituency to satisfy, a traditional area of competence to protect from encroachment by the Planning Commission or by any other agency, a different order of investment priorities, and a different conception of its own role. If any one institution can be said to hold the system together and control it, that institution is the Ministry of Finance, and not the Planning Commission.

Coercive planning operates through two distinct control processes: direct command (*Herrschaft* or imperative control)[1] for the public sector, and incentives (direct field control)[2] in certain branches of the private sector. Both depend upon the ministries, especially the Ministry of Finance. For it is the Ministry of Finance that controls direct public investment. The Ministry of Finance – not the plan – issues orders to the public sector. And it is the Ministry of Finance which has authority and final responsibility over the financial incentives used to implement the plan. The Planning commission does not control the incentives; the Ministry of Finance does. The *critical* link in the coercive process is the relation of the plan to the Ministry of Finance.

[1] See Max Weber, *The Theory of Social and Economic Organization*, New York, 1947, p. 152, and Dahl and Lindbloom, *Politics, Economics and Society*, New York, chapter I.

[2] *Ibid.*, chapter I.

3 THE PLAN IN THE BUREAUCRACY: A first view of the power structure of planning

The most prominent characteristics of the Planning Commission as a bureaucratic entity are its size and power. The Planning Commission is small. Its payroll is probably one of the shortest in the entire French bureaucracy: full-time staff numbers under 130 people, including the usual contingent of chauffeurs, typists, secretaries, *huissiers* and concierges; full-time 'planners' number about forty.[1] The size of the Planning Commission's staff has not changed during its twenty year existence. More than just a curious exception to Parkinson's Law, this fact of size has important consequences. It means that the Planning Commission is totally dependent upon the ministries in the conduct of its day-to-day business.

> the management of a modern public office . . . is based on 'the files,' along with a body of officials and the respective apparatus of material implements.[2]

The Ministry of Finance also has the files, the material implements and the officials. Most of the statistical information fed into the plan comes from the economic information service of the Ministry of Finance, the SEEF, as do most of the econometricians, statisticians and experts who work with that information in the preparation of the plan. Thus, for the traditional agencies of the state bureaucracy – especially the Ministry of Finance – the smallness of the Planning Commission is an *initial* guarantee against the threat (once posed by the Ministry of the National Economy) of the

[1] Massé, *French Affairs*, pp. 4–5. Bernard Gourney and Pierre Viot, provide an excellent description of the personnel of the Planning Commission in 'Les Planificateurs et les Décisions du Plan,' paper presented at the Colloque sur la Planification at Grenoble, 2–4 May 1963, mimeo, Comm. du Plan, 26 April 1963, Part II, section A, pp. 19–22.

[2] Max Weber, 'On Bureaucracy,' *From Max Weber*, Mills and Gerth translation, London, 1961, p. 196.

planning agency growing into a super-ministry of the economy.[1]

> No department, no ministry can reasonably fear that the Commissariat will encroach upon its functions. . . . In this way, the risks of the administrative calamity that is a conflict of competence are straight-off reduced.[2]

The unusually small size of the Planning Commission is no accident. The lesson of the Ministry of the National Economy was fresh in mind when Monnet designed the French planning process. He could try to establish the plan as a super-ministry of the economy – with the considerable risk of total defeat – or he could try to fit the plan into the existing structure of bureaucratic competence and power. Monnet chose the latter course.[3]

The size of the Planning Commission is an important element in a definition of the relation of the plan to the ministries. Its permanent staff of forty planners necessitates the participation of the ministries in every phase of planning: its lightweight and open structure assures them that their traditional areas of competence will be respected and,

> the fact that some of the Planning Commission's experts are merely on loan from their original departments provides additional security to the ministries.[4]

The power at the disposal of the Planning Commission provides a second, and greater, assurance to the ministries. The Planning Commission by itself exercises no direct powers over the economy. None of the targets and programmes of the plan is enforceable by law. Business (including the nationalised industries) is under no legal obligation to follow any of the plan's programmes. Nor does the planning Commission have any direct authority within the state bureaucracy over the administration of the whole range of state economic activities.[5] The coercive implementation methods of planning are all under

[1] See below, pp. 64ff for a brief history of the Ministry of the National Economy.

[2] Massé, *French Affairs*, p. 4.

[3] See Comm. du Plan, *Les Motifs d'Exécution du Plan*, mimeo (1963 ?), Part II, Section 4a, p. 32; David Granick emphasizes this point. 'The effective functioning of the Planning Commissariat . . . is explained by the fact that none of its big-brother ministries has considered it a threat worth clobbering.' *The European Executive* (Anchor Paperback), New York, 1964, p. 150.

[4] Massé, *French Affairs*, p. 4.

[5] Recent reforms, and recent proposals for reform aimed at linking the state budget and the instruments of monetary and fiscal policy to the plan are discussed in Part V, below.

the control of the various ministries (mostly the Ministry of Finance).

Within the government and administrative apparatus, *the Planning Commission's role is solely one of conception, counsel and appraisal. It takes part in the procedure and the preparation of decisions, but it has no power of its own and administers no funds for economic action.*[1]

This distribution of power shapes the planning process and determines the role of the Planning Commission. The Planning Commission must act as a broker among several power groups, of which big business and the Ministry of Finance are by far the most important. But the Planning Commission is not a 'neutral' broker, disinterested in the outcome of the power clash; it sees itself as more than a mere mediator or go-between. It has a clear objective – to get a plan drawn-up and implemented that best reflects its own ordering of priorities.

One way it can translate its list of priorities and programmes into a force in the economy is to secure voluntary commitments from business and from the ministries to implement the plan. Failing voluntary agreements, the Planning Commission must use force. But like a highly skilled judo expert it harnesses the other fellow's force to its own ends. The ministries have the power to compel business to carry out the plan's programmes, and big business can pressure the ministries into taking certain actions sought by the plan. Planning operates on combinations of these forces and voluntary commitments; the Planning Commission organizes and mobilises these combinations.

The countervailing powers of the ministries on business and business on the ministries are not equal, nor are they of equal importance to the success of planning. The ministries' powers over business are stronger, and they are more central to the functioning of the planning process. The planners' influence on the exercise of these powers is the key variable in the entire process of planning.

The power structure in which French planning operates determines the nature of the planning process. It is a bargaining process in which the contents of the plan are worked-out among the three principal parties: the Ministry of Finance, Big Business and the Planning Commission.

[1] Massé, p. 5; his italics; see also F. Ridley and J. Blondel, *Public Administration in France*, London, 1964, pp. 202–205.

PART II

THE PLANNING PROCESS: A NARRATIVE

4 *STAGES ONE AND TWO:*
The Plan and the Ministry of Finance

According to official accounts, the planning process is a simple progression of clearly defined actions taken by clearly defined institutions. The Planning Commission prepares several preliminary growth models around alternative sets of hypotheses. The hypotheses concern such variables as aggregate growth rates (4%, 4½%, 5%, 5½%), length of work-week (40, 42, 44, 46 hours), major shifts in investment and foreign trade projections. The growth models project the implications of each set of hypotheses for the entire economy. The government and Parliament study these models and choose a general outline for planned development. The outline plan then goes to the modernisation commissions – the round tables of planners, government officials, businessmen, trade unionists and experts where detailed investment and output programmes are filled in for each industry. A set of similarly composed 'horizontal' commissions then check the industry programmes against one another for consistency. Such, *en principe*, is the general outline of the planning process.[1] The reality is something else.

An operational model of the planning process, as distinct from a purely formal organigramme, also begins with a set of preliminary growth models which serve as basic study documents for subsequent discussions and decisions. Only the Planning Commission does not prepare those models on its own: it works in close conjunction with the SEEF and the other state statistical services.[2] It has to. The Planning Com-

[1] As, for example, in Jean Fourastié, *La Planification Economique en France*, Paris (P.U.F.), 1963, pp. 98–102; or Etienne Hirsch, 'French Planning and its European Applications,' *Journal of Common Market Studies*, Vol. 1, #2, 1962, pp. 118–121.

[2] The SEEF, Service des Études Économiques et Financières, is part of the Ministry of Finance. The *SEEF* prepares the budget and the national accounts. It is the most important information and statistical agency of the state. It is also the one most directly attached to the Ministry of Finance. It was created

mission lacks the staff necessary for such an enterprise and, as argued above, that lack is no accident. The *SEEF* supplies the data, the statisticians and the econometricians. It also brings to the first phase of planning the presence of the Ministry of Finance.

In theory, the projecting of alternative preliminary growth models is a technical, or an apolitical, phase of planning, in

---

during the period of the Monnet Plan when there was 'an acute consciousness among senior civil servants . . . of the backwardness of French statistical apparatus and analysis.' (Hackett, p. 105). The problems posed by planning added urgency to these widely felt needs for reform. The planned allocation of resources, during the post-war period of scarcity and direct controls, was passing from the Ministry of Finance to the Director of Economic Programmes and the Plan, as a result, in part, of the different methods of economic accounting and analysis used by the two agencies. The Director of Economic Programmes was charged with the direct allocation of scarce resources. Its calculations were, therefore, in terms of physical quantities and specific industries. The accounts and accounting methods of the Ministry of Finance were in traditional financial terms. There was thus, a certain feeling in the Ministry of Finance that their traditional area of competence was being encroached upon; that their only participation in the planned allocation of resources was to translate the programmes of the Plan from tons of steel, aluminium and cement into francs and write them into the budget. The *SEEF* was created to rework the accounting methods of the Ministry of Finance and introduce more up-to-date econometric techniques capable of dealing with the questions and type of analysis raised by planning. By 1952, the *SEEF* had taken over the functions of the Director of Economic Programmes, and was supplying econometricians to the Plan instead of borrowing such experts from the Plan. Most of the information in this note was obtained through interviews. The following works tell something of the history of the *SEEF*: Alain Chevalier, 'Le Ministère des Finances,' *Revue Economique*, Nov. 1962, p. 935; A. de Lattre, *Politique Economique de La France*, Paris, 1961 (Polycopié les Cours de Droit), pp. 48–49; J. & A. Hackett, *Economic Planning in France*, London, 1963, pp. 104–108 provides a more detailed but less analytical description.

INSEE, Institut National de la Statistique et des Etudes Economiques, was originally part of the Ministry of the National Economy. *INSEE* is now attached to the Ministry of Finance. It prepares the general statistical studies (e.g. *l'Annuaire Statistique*) and specialises in large scale surveys and censuses. It is also the centre for teaching modern statistical methods. Its director, M. C. Gruson, has had a great influence on the recent improvements in French statistics.

CREDOC, Centre de Recherches et de Documentation sur la Consommation, was originally attached to the Commissariat of Productivity. CREDOC is now a semi-independent agency, but the Ministry of Finance appoints its directors. It specialises in research about the consumption functions.

INED, Institut National d'Etudes Démographiques, is attached to the Ministry of Health and Population. It supplies demographic information and undertakes population censuses.

CREMAP and *CREPEL* are two small study groups, established in 1961. They are concerned with research into the application of mathematical and computer techniques to planning.

which several alternative models are prepared by a technical agency for presentation to an elected decision-making body. In practice, it is inseparable from the second phase of planning where the single outline plan is chosen – not by Parliament but by the Ministry of Finance and the Planning Commission.[1] There is no clear shift from one institution to another – as implied in the official model – between the preparation of alternative preliminary models and the choice of one outline plan. The crucial decisions that shape the plan are made during the second stage of the planning process.

The second stage consists of protracted consultations between the Planning Commission and the Ministry of Finance, with the Government sometimes acting as arbiter, and sometimes playing a purely passive role.[2] Its end product is a skeletal, or outline plan.

The Planning Commission must secure the active participation of the Ministry of Finance in the preparation of the plan in order to secure its active participation in the implementation of the plan. The problem is to overcome 'the natural difference in views between services, each charged with its own particular responsibilities'.[3]

As Professor Bauchet observed:

The extreme distrust of the various Ministries, jealous of their prerogatives, and the priviliges of certain nationalised firms, did more to prevent the Planning Commission from playing a decisive role, did more to menace its existence, than all the political forces hostile to the idea of planning . . . to avoid alienating the administration, the Planning Commissioners have followed a policy of conciliation and not of authority and co-ordination. One is right to think that only this policy has preserved the Plan from being completely destroyed.[4]

[1] See pp. 58–9 below, for an outline history of Parliamentary participation in planning. Part VII of this study examines the question of parliamentary participation in greater detail, and discusses recent suggestions for reform as well as the reforms intended to increase Parliamentary participation introduced with the fourth and fifth plans. Only for the 5th Plan (1966–1970) were alternative growth hypotheses (4, 5, 5½% per yr.) made explicit, and only one hypothesis was developed into an outline plan; see *J. O. Lois et Décrets*, 23 Dec. 1964, and *J. O. Conseil Economique*, 14 Oct. 1965, and below pp. 229–30.

[2] Part III provides an historical examination of the changing role of the various Governments in the planning process.

[3] Massé, *La Documentation Française*, p. 4.

[4] Pierre Bauchet, *La Planification Française, Quinze Ans d'Expérience*, Paris, 1962, pp. 59–60.

This diplomatic aspect of French planning seems to have captured the imagination of foreign observers. In its never-ending quest for romance, mystery and a touch of intrigue across the Channel, the *Economist* sees the planners as a small group of enlightened modernisers and expansionists, confronting a status-quo minded, cumbersome and mildly silly bureaucracy, and besting it by sheer wit: the planners convince the Treasury (the Ministry of Finance) of the soundness of their programmes by convincing treasury officials that the plan's programmes are quite the same as their own ideas.

Some French Treasury officials say privately that the influence of the Commissariat – of that office of economic technocrats – has been exaggerated. 'The Commissariat people discuss their latest four-year plan with us for three years in advance,' they will say, 'and the target figures for annual production that they eventually wrote into it was exactly the figure that we thought right on financial grounds. Probably the greatest triumph of the Commissariat is that the French Treasury genuinely believes this.'[1]

The Ministry of Finance, however, is rarely persuaded to do anything it does not want to do. If there is any persuasion in French planning – and there is – it is best located not in the persuasive skills of the planners, however great they may be, but rather in the receptivity of the Treasury officials to new ideas.

The profound changes in attitudes, methods and men that have transformed the French business community since the war have hit the higher civil service with an even greater force. This change in official thinking is the most important element in the successful co-operation between the plan and the Ministry of Finance. It is responsible for the survival of the planning institution and for whatever success the French plans have had.

M. Etienne Hirsch, Monnet's successor as Planning Commissioner explains the relations between the plan and the Ministry of Finance in the following manner:

Let us take, for example, the question of the Ministry of Finance, the object of so much reproach. I think this attitude is unrealistic because the power is where the money is, and no matter what you do you cannot escape the fact. What is necessary, therefore, is to

[1] *The Economist*, 28 October 1962, p. 314; for a similar view, see Charles Frankel, 'Bureaucracy and Democracy in the New Europe,' *Daedalus*, Winter, 1964.

convert the Ministry of Finance and show it that the Plan is a good thing. . . . I must say that to a very great extent, the plan's success has been due to the conversion of the Ministry of Finance, an extremely profound conversion, similar to the one that radically transformed the attitudes of the business leadership.[1]

ATTACKING THE OLD MINISTRY OF FINANCE

During the 'thirties the *Rue de Rivoli*[2] was characterised by strict financial orthodoxy and political conservatism. The *grand corps*, especially the Inspectorate of Finance was popularly considered to be the agent of the devil and the banks. The Treasury was associated in the popular imagination, and in the works of many serious thinkers, with the business community, and the business community in the late 'thirties was associated with stagnation: it was failing the nation. This situation led the Popular Front to create the Ministry of the National Economy, a new super ministry of economics, as a direct attack on the political conservatism and financial orthodoxy of the Ministry of Finance. The new super ministry was a failure from the beginning. The Ministry of Finance kept control of the important levers of economic power until a Conservative government returned to power, attached the Ministry of the National Economy to the Treasury and put an end to the experiment. But the creation of an effective super ministry of economics that would seize power from the Ministry of Finance and use that power to initiate, modernize and plan remained a key Leftist objective.[3]

Immediately after the war, the Left resurrected the idea of a

[1] Etienne Hirsch, in 'Colloque pour une Planification Démocratique,' *Les Cahiers de la République*, no. 45, juin 1962, p. 465; Pierre Massé, M. Hirsch's successor as Planning Commissioner, makes a similar statement in *Hommes et Techniques*, No. 218, jan. 1963, p. 10.

[2] Address of the Ministry of Finance: used like Whitehall, Quai d'Orsay, Capitol Hill, Downing Street, etc.

[3] See Giles Gozard, 'le Ministere de l'Economie Nationale,' *Productions Françaises*, July 1947 and August-Sept. 1947; L. Bertrand, 'Economie Nationale et Finances,' *Revue Banque et Bourse*, April 1954; R. Nathan, *Politique Economique de la France*, Cours de l'I.E.P. 1957–58, Paris, Le Cours de Droit, 1958, pp. 27–28; B. Chenot, *Organisation Economique de l'Etat*, Paris, Dalloz, 1951. paras. 114–128 and, esp. 143; C-J Gignoux, *l'Economie Française Entre les Deux Guerres*, p. 322; Shepard B. Clough, *France, A History of National Economics*, New York, 1939, p. 346; Paul Delouvrier, *Politique Economique de la France*' Cours de l'I.E.P., 1957–58, Paris, Les Cours de Droit, 1958, pp. 53–57, and following two footnotes.

Ministry of the National Economy that would finally remove the obstructions the Ministry of Finance seemed to put in the way of all economic reform, reorganisation and dynamism. In the autumn of 1944, the Provisional Government resuscitated the Ministry of the National Economy, placed it under the direction of Pierre Mendès France and charged it with 'the overall direction of economic policy, with the preparation of the plan and its execution.' In order to accomplish this it was supposed to 'guide and control the actions of Ministries charged with industrial production, food supply, reconstruction and to co-ordinate the actions of those and all other departments and ministries in the economic domain.[1]

This second attempt to overcome the Treasury with a super ministry of the economy also failed. The Treasury kept control of the critical levers of economic power and launched a counter-attack that effectively crippled the fledgling ministry which found itself unable to obtain the basic economic and statistical information it needed in order to operate (the Treasury had it), and unable to obtain a competent staff (career civil-servants – especially in the *grands corps* – got the hint and would not go near it). It was not even able to obtain a proper building for itself; its offices were scattered in eighteen different buildings throughout Paris. Finally, a new Conservative government came to power, dismantled the ailing Ministry and attached most of the pieces to the Treasury.[2]

[1] Decree of 23 November 1944, article 4; see also, decree of 4 Sept. 1944.

[2] There is almost no literature on the role of the Ministry of the National Economy as a precursor of the Monnet Plan and as a rival to the Ministry of Finance. None of the standard works on French planning discusses it. General political and economic histories of the immediate post-war period focus on the currency reform which led to the resignation of Mendès France and the appointment of René Pleven as both Minister of Finance and Minister of the National Economy. The story-with-a-moral presented here did not grow out of that literature (cited below). Rather it came out of the interviews with M. Louis Franck and M. Andre Philip. In only one other place in this study (pp. 101–3) is material gathered in interviews used to support a specific, substantive argument.

The following works touch upon the history of the Ministry of the National Economy. The argument presented here, would not, I think, come immediately to mind on reading these sources. But once the argument has been suggested it can be checked against the different aspects of the Ministry's brief career that are discussed in these works and the principal thrust of the argument as well as the specific assertions and facts will be corroborated—all except one: 'its offices were scattered in eighteen different buildings.' This estimate ought to be read in a metaphorical sense even though it may be, in addition, numerically correct.

See R. Nathan, *Politique Economique de la France*, pp. 27–28 and Chenot, *Organisation Economique de l'Etat*, para. 143, whose purposes in discussing the

THE NEW MINISTRY OF FINANCE

Since the early 'fifties there has been no widespread enthusiasm for doing away with the Ministry of Finance. There are still demands for administrative reforms and occasional proposals calling for a super-Ministry of the economy, but the original impetus behind the Ministry of the National Economy – to overcome the dead weight of the Treasury – no longer exists. The reason is that the Treasury has changed, and there is no longer the same urgent need to destroy it.

The Treasury has become an initiating force: it has assumed a role of actively promoting expansion. The dominant attitude among ranking Treasury officials is complete commitment to economic rationalisation, full employment, high investment, and rapid growth. The change from the pre-war preoccupation with budget balancing is striking. The state is now the partner of big business and it is an active, initiating partner. Whereas in the pre-war period interventionism meant protectionism, today it means the promotion of rationalisation and the stimulation of expansion. Interventionism is not clandestine. It is not exceptional. The job of the managers of the state is to intervene in order to realize their objectives, and their objectives are simple: growth and efficiency. 'They are managers, not revolutionaries.' The rate of increase in the GNP is their most important measure of growth, and international competitiveness is their most important measure of efficiency. As we shall see, this new attitude and its accompanying style in the upper ranks of the civil service are what have permitted the plan to function. It is, without any question, the most important factor in the success of French planning.[1]

---

question are nearest to our own; Philip Williams, *Politics in Post-war France*, Longmans, 1954, pp. 391–392; Alain Chevalier, 'le Ministère des Finances,' *Revue Economique*, Nov. 1962, pp. 933–35; Henry Harbold, *Le Plan Monnet*, Ph.D. Thesis, Harvard, 1953, unpub., p. 18; Harold Lubell, *The French Investment Plan*, Ph.D. Harvard, 1951 (also mimeographed by the OEEC), pp. 52–53; G. Pallez, *Finances Publiques*, Cours de l'IEP, 1961–62, Paris, Les Cours de Droit, 1962, pp. 33–34; *Année Politique*, 1949, p. 249; Delouvrier, *Politique Economique de la France*, pp. 55–57, 78–79, 161–9; Gozard, 'Economie Nationale', Bertrand, 'Economie Nationale et Finances', and below, pp. 95–6 where the resignation of Mendès France is discussed in reference to the currency reform.

[1] The assertions of this paragraph are central to the argument. They are developed and supported in the following pages and throughly re-examined from the critical perspective of the Left in Part VI. My primary sources of information are the interviews described in the introduction. The published works of many

The changing attitudes and roles of the managers of the state have been closely associated with the influence of the *Ecole National d'Administration* (the National School of Public Administration), usually called the *ENA*. A drastic reform in the recruitment and training of higher civil servants followed the Liberation. The reform had three general aims. The first was to broaden the social base of recruitment. The second was to unify the upper ranks of the civil service and end the rigid compartmentalisation of action and thought. The third was to change the outlook and modes of thought of the administrative élite.[1]

---

high ranking Treasury officials are also an excellent means for understanding their thinking. See, especially, the works of François Bloch-Lainé listed in the bibliography. Mr Bloch-Lainé is one of the most powerful and prominent *hauts fonctionnaires*; he is also the man most esteemed by the younger generation of ranking officials. C. Gruson, and P. Delouvrier, and Louis Armand, to name but a few, provide good examples of this mode of thought. So do the journals *Promotions* and *Patrie et Progrès*, and, especially, the numerous publications of the Club Jean Moulin. The following works support the general argument of the paragraph; they are used to support the more detailed development of thsee assertions in the following pages: Jean-François Kesler, 'Les Anciens Elèves de l'Ecole National d'Administration,' *Revue Française de Science Politique*, Vol. XLV, no. 2, April 1964, esp. pp. 244–247 (the quotation in the paragraph is from Kesler); Philippe Bauchard, *La Mystique du Plan*, Paris, 1963, esp. pp. 51–97. 199–246; Jean Meynaud, 'Administration et Politique en France,' *Il Politico*, no. 1, 1959, pp. 5–32; Alain Chevalier, 'Le Ministère des Finances,' *Revue Economique*, Nov. 1962, pp. 930–937; Etienne Hirsch in *Cahiers de la République*, Charles Kindelberger, 'Post-war Resurgence . . .', Charles Brindillac, 'Les Hauts Fonctionnaires,' *Esprit*, June 1953; J. Billy, *Les Techniciens et le Pouvoir*, Paris, 1960; Pierre LaLumière, *l'Inspection des Finances*, Thèse pour le doctorat en droit, U. de Paris, P.U.F., 1959; Andrew Shonfield argues that this change in attitude and in role in the managers of the state is the difference that made a difference in economic performance: see, *Modern Capitalism*, especially pp. 61–7, 87, 121–175; Bernard Gourney, 'Un groupe dirigeant de la société française: les grands fonctionnaires,' *Revue Française de Science Politique*, XLV, no. 2, April 1964. Louis Armand and Michel Drancourt, *Plaidoyer pour l'Avenir*, Paris, 1961; J. Touchard and J. Solé, 'Planification et Technocratie,' in *La Planification Comme Processus de Decision*, Cahiers de la Fondation Nationale des Sciences Politique, #140, 1965, and Jean Meynaud, *La Technocratie*, Paris, Payot, 1964.

[1] Literature on this reform effort is plentiful and quite good. See, T. Feyzioglu, 'The Reforms of the French Higher Civil Service Since 1945,' *Public Administration*, XXXIII, Spring and Summer 1955; Herman N. Finer, 'The French Higher Civil Service,' *Public Personnel Review*, IX, 1945; J. Chapsal, *France Depuis* 1945, pp. 485–487; W. J. Siffin, ed. *Toward the Comparative Study of Public Administration*, Bloomington, 1959; P. Campbell, 'The French Civil Service,' *Public Administration* (New Zealand), XVII, Sept. 1955; P. Bauchard, *La Mystique du Plan*, J. F. Kesler, 'L'Anciens Elèves . . .'; F. Bloch-Lainé, l'Administration Economique,' *Revue Economique*, Nov. 1962; Club Jean Moulin, *L'Etat et le Citoyen*, pp. 136–142. A. Chevalier, 'Le Ministère des Finances'. See also *J.O.*

Prior to 1945, appointments to the higher ranks of the civil service and to the *grands corps* were made on the basis of competitive examinations prepared and administered separately by the individual *corps* or department.[1] Training was geared to the examinations and specialized for each agency. It was rigorous – especially for the *grands corps* – but its rigour consisted in mastering vast quantities of highly specialized knowledge. The result was a system of isolated closed circles. There was little mobility between departments and almost none between *corps*. Allegiance was to the *corps*, not to anything comparable to a civil service caste as in Britain – the model in the minds of the post-war reformers. Communication between departments was limited. The higher civil service was compartmentalised, not only by function, but by training.[2] The social origins and attitudes of the pre-Liberation higher civil service was the major reason for the reformers' zeal.[3] The *grand corps*, and the higher civil service in general, was recruited from the Parisian *haute bourgeoisie* 'which was not energetically democratic.'[4] They were extremely conservative and in their world conservatism often included outright anti-Republicanism.[5] The *Ecole Libre des Sciences Politiques* was the training ground for the higher civil servants. It has long been the object of much well-documented, well-reasoned and virulent criticism – as well as a great deal of polemic. The school was private, expensive and 'snobbish.'[6] Its students and professors had little interest,

---

Assemblée Nationale Débats, 22 Juin 1945, The Decrees, Ordinances and Laws of Oct. 10 1945, and works cited on following pages.

[1] There were about 75 separate examinations for entrance into the upper and middle ranks. See, La Documentation Française, *l'Organisation Gouvermentale, Administrative et Judicaire de la France*, 1952, pp. 72–73.

[2] See Finer, 'French Higher Civil Service', *passim*; T. Feyzioglu, 'Reforms of Civil Service', pp. 69–78; Chapsal *et al.*, *France Depuis* 1945, pp. 485–486; Campbell, 'The French Civil Service', pp. 37–38; F. Bloch-Lainé, *R. Economique*, pp. 862–863; *J.O.*, *Débats*, 6/22/45, pp. 1168–1172; and *La Réforme de la Fonction Publique*, Paris, Imprimérie Nationale, 1945, a 96-page official report of Michel Debré's commission which prepared the reforms of Oct. 1945.

[3] See, *J.O. Débats*, 6/22/45, pp. 1168–1171; Petrinax (A. Geraud) *The Gravediggers of France*, 1944, *Passim*; T. Feyzioglu, 'Reforms of the . . . Civil Service,' pp. 74–78; André Ferrat, *La République à Refaire*, Paris, 1945, *passim*.

[4] Quotation is from H. Finer, 'French Higher Civil Service', p. 168.

[5] See also, in addition to *ibid*, Campbell, '*French Civil Service*', pp. 42–43; Pertinax, *Gravediggers*, pp. 360ff.; La Lumière, *l'Inspection des Finances*, pp. 7, 219 and A. Diamant, 'French Administrative System', p. 186.

[6] 'Snobbish' is from Ridley and Blondel, *Public Administration in France*, p. 37; see references in preceding two footnotes.

and less sympathy, for the problems of the masses. The tone of the institution was fiercely anti-democratic.[1]

The education at the *Ecole Libre* 'was of a high grade, the highest in the world in point of the severity with which the student was compelled to attend to his studies.'[2]

But it was strangely removed from any reality other than that which prevailed in the closed circles of the *grands corps*. The trainees studied manuals on administrative procedure and treatises on financial administration. They were taught how to do what *hauts fonctionnaires* did by *hauts fonctionnaires*. Nobody seemed to question the purpose of that activity; nobody seemed eager to do different things, or to do the same things differently. Procedures were taught and they were taught from a bureaucratic catechism.

> The formulae were all cut and dried. They were answers, but not thought-provoking problems. They did not whirr as reality whirrs. The studies had a thin, remote, antiquated flavour about them. The truth was that France had slipped dangerously from any proper level of excellence in economic and political science studies.[3]

Keynes was not read; economics was not studied. Instead, financial administration was taught.[4] The intellectual deficiencies of the educational system were reflected in the intellectual inadequacies of the *hauts fonctionnaires*. They were extremely intelligent and rigorously educated, but they were not extremely effective. Their education was not relevant to the problems confronting the nation, but rather it was relevant to the jobs they chose to do. The *hauts fonctionnaires*, it was believed, managed the state, and the state had failed the nation.[5]

As a result of the administrative reforms of October 1945,

[1] All the above references in this section deal with this question. The attacks on the *Ecole Libre* by André Phillippe and Pierre Cot, and Andre Sigfried's defense of the school in *J.O. Débats*, 6/22/45 are worth reading; A. Diamant, *French Administrative System*, p. 186 offers a more tempered judgement. Campbell, '*French Civil Service*', p. 43 refers to the staff of the school as 'acknowledged enemies of the Republic'; Finer, pp. 168–170 and esp. Feyzioglu, part I, are thorough in this subject.

[2] H. Finer, 'French Higher Civil Service', p. 167.

[3] *Ibid.*, p. 167.

[4] *Ibid.*, p. 167; Kesler, 'Anciens Elèves . . .', pp. 262–263; *J.O. Débats*, 6/22/45, pp. 1168–1171; La Lumière, *l'Inspection des Finances*, pp. 179–182.

[5] See La Lumière, *l'Inspection des Finances*, pp. 179–190; *France Observateur*, 24 jan. 1963, p. 6; Pertinax, *Gravediggers; La Reforme de la Fonction Publique*; Kesler, *Anciens Elèves*, pp. 245–257; *J.O. Débats*, 6/22/45, pp. 1168–1171; T. Feyzioglu, 'Reforms of . . . Civil Service', part I.

the system of separate examinations was abolished and replaced by one common examination. The *Ecole Libre des Sciences Politiques* was nationalised, renamed the *Institut d'Etudes Politiques*, and incorporated into the University of Paris. And a new graduate school of public administration, the *Ecole National d'Administration*, was established.[1]

The reforms have helped to unify the higher civil service.[2] There is now far more horizontal mobility and far more communication within the upper echelons of the civil service. The *grands corps* still draw off the best students and still command a certain allegiance, but the fierce loyalty to the *corps* has been replaced by a wider identification with the *ENA* and by a sense of caste.[3]

'The social aspects of the reform had only limited success.'[4] Equality of opportunity cannot be reconciled to efficiency and excellence unless the entire education system is democratised; reforms confined to the apex of the pyramid are necessarily superficial. The 'democratisation' of recruitment aided the middle classes, especially the managerial and professional strata.[5] It did not bring the higher civil service closer to 'the people.' Only 2.5% of the students admitted to the *ENA* from 1952–61 were sons of workers. At the *ENA* the workers' sons strive to be like the others, and usually over-succeed.[6]

It was in changing the attitudes, concerns and modes of thought of the administrative élite that the reformers had their

[1] See the Laws, decrees and ordinances of 10 Oct. 1945; Ridley and Blondel, *Public Administration in France*, p. 37.

[2] *Ibid.*, p. 37.

[3] On 31 March 1963 over 75% of the *ENA* graduates in the *Inspection des Finances* were on assignments outside the *corps*; the rate was 40% for the *Conseil d'Etat* and the *Cour des Comptes*, Kesler, 'Anciens Elèves', p. 255; Kesler is very good on this subject; see also, P. Bauchard, *La Mystique du Plan*, pp. 64ff; B. Gourney, 'Un groupe dirigeant . . .', pp. 222–224; Ridley and Blondel, *Public Administration* . . . , p. 37; F. Bloch-Lainé, *R. Economique*, p. 863; La Lumière, pp. 180–190; Chapsal, *France Depuis* 1945, pp. 485–486.

[4] Quotation is from Ridley and Blondel, *Public Administration in France*, p. 37; see Feyzioglu, Reforms of . . . Civil Service', part II for a similar judgement.

[5] See, Ecole National d'Administration, *Recruitment and Training for the Higher Civil Service in France*, Paris, 1956; Kesler, 'Anciens Elèves . . .', pp. 250–251; P. Bauchard, *La Mystique du Plan*, chapter 3; *France-Observateur*, 24 Jan. 1963; p. 6; Feyzioglu, 'Reforms of . . . Civil Service', part II, and Gourney, 'Un groupe dirigeant . . .', p. 225.

[6] See Kesler, 'Anciens Elèves . . .', p. 251 for observations on the comportment of working class students at the *ENA*; Feyzioglu, 'Reforms of Civil Service', part II provides a thorough and documented analysis of the social origins of the students at the *ENA*; see also Meynaud, *La Technocratie*, pp. 50–54.

greatest success, for this change revolutionised the French higher civil service. The manuals and treatises which were the mainstays of the curriculum at the *Ecole Libre* have been replaced by a heavy emphasis on the 'practical' at the *ENA*. In addition to attending lectures and reading the established texts, the student participates in seminars and prepares numerous written case studies of current problems. Crucially, he gets practical, on-the-job training. The first year is devoted to an apprenticeship, normally in a provincial administration where the student handles actual problems. The practical value of the apprenticeship period compares favourably with the old system of probationary appointments upon completion of schooling 'which had become a dead letter in practice.'[1] The second year is devoted largely to formal classroom training. At the end of the year the students take an examination which determines who will enter which *grands corps* – and who will merely join a ministerial department. The examination is crucial to a young man's career. Membership in a *grand corps* means higher pay, greater prestige, more power, more interesting work – and, a top position in private industry when, as often happens, the civil servant decides to enter a more lucrative situation in one of the giant corporations or banks.[2] The third year often includes an apprenticeship in a private (or nationalised) firm as well as specialised training for the particular administration the student will be joining upon completion of his course.[3] The curriculum of the *ENA* with its practical orientation, is highly regarded by students of political administration.[4]

More important, perhaps, than the 'practical' orientation of

[1] Quotation is from Finer, 'French Higher Civil Service', p. 172. Special value is placed by the School on the stages of practical training. It is, above all, desired to remedy the defect of all previous methods of recruitment, namely, to overcome the entirely theoretical knowledge by practice before the candidates enter on their own executive experiences.' *Ibid.*, p. 174. See also, Ridley and Blondel, *Public Administration in France*, pp. 39–40; *France Observateur*, 24 Jan. 1963, p. 6; Kesler, 'Anciens Elèves . . .', p. 246.

[2] See, Ridley and Blondel, *Public Administration in France*, p. 39; Chapsal, pp. 486–487; On switching to the private sector—or pantouflage, as it is commonly called – see below, p. 66.

Ridley and Blondel, *Public Administration in France*, p. 39; Finer, 'French Higher Civil Service', 174 often the 3rd year is reduced to six months.

[4] For example, Ridley and Blondel write: 'The Ecole National d'Administration . . . constitutes a great experiment in the recruitment and training of higher civil servants, and is likely to be watched carefully by other countries throughout the world. Rarely, if ever, have young administrators been given the opportunity of acquiring such a wide range of practical knowledge, particularly in provincial

the curriculum is the general atmosphere of the school. Most great schools have a characteristic tone which affects the student's outlook and style quite as strongly as does the content of his courses. Oxford in the 'twenties and the City College of New York in the 'thirties are well known examples. It would be misleading to describe the impact of CCNY on the generation of the nineteen-thirties after examining only the curriculum.

The atmosphere of the school is a set of collective attitudes. The attitudes shared by the *ENA* students and graduates are difficult to define, but perilous to ignore. Although they have yet to be defined satisfactorily, they have certainly not been ignored.[1] They have been the object of considerable concern, vast quantities of discussion and even a good deal of serious, if none-too-scientific, analysis.

The same labels appear over and over again in numerous analyses – both serious and casual – of the post-war change in the higher civil service. The new *hauts fonctionnaires* are not called bureaucrats; 'technocrats' has become the favourite designation. The search for a new label reflects a widespread feeling that something has changed in the administration. The choice of 'technocrat' indicates something of the way the popular imagination sees that change. Modernisers, managers, experts, expansionists, planners and rationalisers are other terms freely used in attempts to understand and describe the new administrative stance.[2] They are all vague epithets, myths as well as metaphors, but they differ markedly from the equally

---

administration. The period of practical training serves as a fruitful basis for thought and discussion during their second year at the school. Their approach to administration is consequently broader and more practical when they start their life in the service in earnest.' *Public Administration in France*, p. 40.

[1] Prof. Jean Meynaud remarks that: 'there has never been a serious study of the ideology of the higher civil servants, and one is still obliged to rely on impressions.' *La Technocratie*, p. 20.

[2] See, Kesler, 'Anciens Elèves. . . .' His article draws on the research M. Kesler is doing for a thesis for the Doctorat ès lettres at the University of Paris entitled, *l'Ecole National d'Administration et son Influence sur les origines, le recrutement, les idées, l'ésprit et les méthodes des hauts fonctionnaires.* In addition to this article – which is quite good – I have drawn upon the rudimentary draft and copious notes that M. Kesler has been good enough to let me study. I also rely heavily on my own interviews and personal impressions. Concerning this and the following paragraphs see also *France-Observateur*, 24 Jan. 1963, p. 6; P. Bauchard, *La Mystique du Plan*, chap. 3; La Lumière, *l'Inspection des Finances*, pp. 219ff; A Chalendon, 'une Troisième Voie, 'Economie Concertée', *Jeune Patron*, dec. 1960; D. Granick, *The European Executive*, N.Y., 1964 (paperback) chap. 5; J. B. King *Executive Organization and Administrative*

vague terms used to describe the pre-war administration: bureaucrats, and mandarins. These tags do not define the new administration, but they summon up an image, and they serve as an abbreviation for a long list of characteristics. The characteristics evoked by the popular descriptions 'technocrats' and 'modernisers' – distinguish the newly dominant group of French administrators. These characteristics include a disdain for ideology; a pragmatic, or technical mentality; a commitment to modernisation; a compulsion to get things done; and a strong sense of caste and duty.

The ENA graduates, now dominant in the higher civil service, are a vigorously non-ideological group. They treat ideological argument with condescending indifference, sometimes with impatience and scorn. For the new technocrats, ideological discussion means endless and sterile debate while the opportunity for action passes.

> In general, they abhor political commitment [*engagement*]. . . . They are scornful of ideologies. They have no taste for doctrinal debates. They disdain words ending in *ism*. In this they reflect the current 'end of ideology.' But they preceded it. A decade before the others, the ENA alumni renounced political metaphysics, and its jousts and joys.[1]

The technocrats have replaced ideological references and commitments with their own brand of radical pragmatism. At the centre of their system of beliefs is the conviction that social problems are susceptible to technical solutions.[2] They see social situations as sets of specific, solvable problems. In this,

---

Practice in the Fourth Republic (unpub. Ph.D. thesis) Stanford University, 1958; B. Gourney, 'Technocrats et Politiques', *Economie et Humanisme*, no. 136, Nov.-Dec. 1961, p. 13; A. Shonfield, *Modern Capitalism*, chaps. 5, 7 and 8; A. Louvel, 'Grands Corps et Grands Commis,' *Revue des Deux Mondes*, 1 Jan. 1959; J. Sabatier, 'l'Avenir de l'ENA,' *Promotions*, Jan. 1952; F. Pietri, 'l'Inspection . . . au Pouvoir'; G. Vedel, 'Les Problèmes de la Technocratie dans le Monde Moderne et le Rôle des Experts; Rapport sur la France,' paper presented to the Fifth World Congress, International Political Science Association, Paris, Sept. 1961, and Meynaud, *La Technocratie*, part II.

[1] Kesler, 'Anciens Elèves . . .', pp. 345–246; for similar observations see Bauchard, *La Mystique du Plan*, pp. 72–76; B. Gourney, 'Un Groupe Dirigeant . . .', pp. 230–236; François Bloch-Lainé, 'Economie Concertée et Planification Démocratique,' *Cahiers de la République*, juillet 1962, p. 574, Touchard and Solé, 'Planification et Technocratie', pp. 29–34.

[2] See Kesler, 'Anciens Elèves . . .', pp. 245–247; André Philip, 'France's New Elite', p. 14; Bauchard, *La Mystique du Plan*, pp. 72ff; Gourney, 'Un Groupe Dirigeant', pp. 229–236. Meynaud, *La Technocratie*, pp. 99–238.

their outlook is reminiscent of the 'social engineering' mentality which had such a vogue in the USA during the nineteen-thirties. Principles do not matter; only results count. Their economic policies often combine classical liberalism and extreme *dirigisme*. For example, direct price controls coupled with the abolition of tariffs is one of their favourite means for controlling prices in a given line of goods. The policy package is coherent in terms of the specific end, not in terms of any body of traditional economic theory. And it was not conceived in terms of any body of theory, but only in terms of the specific objective.[1] Each question is isolated and given a specific solution. It is the case-by-case approach of pure pragmatism, and it is in perfect harmony with the training at the *ENA* where the 'case method' is the mainstay of the curriculum.[2]

The case-by-case approach takes the place of a traditional ideology. Economic rationalism becomes their goal, efficiency their standard of judgement. Their ideas tend to take the form of projects because projects are specific, concrete realisations, and because the yardstick of efficiency can be applied to them. The *hauts fonctionnaires* were willing to gamble on the Super-Caravelle. It was a specific project. It had a calculable, if risky, pay-off. They understood the problem – because it could be understood as a specific problem. But they had great difficulty understanding the coal miners' strike of March 1963 with its animus of conflict, and their insensitivity showed up in the difficulties they had 'solving' that problem.[3] The problem solving mentality, with its fixation on concrete, specific solutions and its denial of ideological considerations, asserts itself in the Constantine Plan for Algeria. The *ENA* alumni set out to do something about the Algerian problem. Many of them had taken their apprenticeship in Algeria. They had great resources at their disposal, and 'they could exercise the power of proconsuls.'[4] They divided the Algerian situation into two cate-

[1] Kesler, 'Anciens Elèves . . .', esp. pp. 246 and 263. The restructuring of the steel industry in the early fifties is an excellent example of this approach. See Sheahan, *Promotion and Control* . . ., pp. 174–175.

[2] See Kesler, 'Anciens Elèves . . .', p. 247; Meynaud, *La Technocratie*, pp. 205–224.

See George W. Ross, 'The French Miners' Strike,' *New Politics*, May 1963 and P. Bauchard, *La Mystique du Plan*, pp. 77–78. Meynaud, *La Technocratie*, pp. 193ff describes the kinds of projects that the new *hauts fonctionnaires* find most attractive.

[4] Kesler, 'Anciens Elèves . . .', p. 264.

gories: solvable problems, and all the rest, and set about devising solutions to the solvable problems. They studied the quantifiable, 'rational' variables and produced a glamorous, coherent and bold programme designed to foster economic and social progress underneath the viscissitudes and irresponsibilities of the ideological, political and military struggle. The Constantine plan concentrated on building up the physical infra-structure of Algeria. The *ENA* graduates built bridges, roads and schools. But they ignored the ideological heart of the Algerian situation. They treated it somehow as irrelevant to their serious and constructive work for that Nation (or Department? – they could never be sure what it was they were building). But they kept on building infra-structure. Rather like the British Colonel in Pierre Boule's *Bridge on the River Kwai* for whom the construction of an excellent bridge became an end in itself, the *ENA* graduates simply would not look beyond the concrete realisations of the Constantine plan.[1]

A technical, or pragmatic mentality by itself cannot fill the ideological void in which the ENA graduates function. Some set of values and goals must inform their behaviour; something must give them direction. For the new *hauts fonctionnaires* myth has replaced ideology. Myths – vague associations of motivating images – provide their direction. Myths – rather than traditional ideologies – inform their behaviour. And the most powerful of these myths is the myth of modernisation.

There is an *ENA* style. The *ENA* style is bourgeois, but it is a modernising and enlightened bourgeoisie, a bourgeoisie which looks towards the future rather than the past, and which takes its models from the USA rather than from the Belle Epoque, a bourgeoisie which has deliberately chosen expansion and progress.[2]

The *ENA* alumni are committed to modernising France. As we shall see in the final chapter, their myth of modernisation is not a complete substitute for a consistent ideology. But it

[1] See the periodical *Patrie et Progrés*; see also, Bauchard, *La Mystique du Plan*, pp. 89–91. Kesler, 'Anciens Elèves . . .', p. 246, offers a slightly different interpretation of 'l'ésprit de l'ENA' in Algeria.

[2] Quotation is from Kesler, 'Anciens Elèves . . .', p. 244; see the works by Bloch-Lainé, Gourney, Bauchard and Brindillac, already cited, for similar observations on the new, modernising stance of the higher civil service. On behaviour-informing myths see, of course, Sorel. Herskovits, *the Myth of the Negro Past*; L. Coser, 'The Myth of the Peasant Revolt,' *Dissent*, May-June 1966, and P. Rahv, *The Myth and the Powerhouse*, New York, 1964, also deal with the role of myths.

does fill some of the functions of an ideology. It does inform their daily actions. It gives them direction. In daily life their committment to modernisation becomes a committment to economic expansion and economic rationalisation. For production is the aspect of French life where modernisation has its least ambiguous meaning.

Here is where the *ENA* graduates are most confident; they know what constitutes a modern productive plant. They agree on the paramount importance of increasing productivity as the prerequisite to any future good society. No temporary change in political structures, foreign policy, or income distribution turns their attention from the crucial, long term task of economic rationalisation. Even constitutional changes are studied opportunistically that they might be better used to serve the serious and enduring end of productivity. Furthermore, the *ENA* graduates believe that many of the traditional divisions and problems of French society can be dissolved in rising levels of economic well-being. They feel that economic rationalisation has its own dynamic which has made or soon will make obsolete many of the traditional questions and divisions of French political life.[1]

They concentrate their efforts on economic modernisation. They restructure industries consisting of many small scale, multi-product, 'old-fashioned' firms into a small number of specialised, large scale, expansionist firms that produce the most advanced products with the most advanced techniques. The ideological pedigree of the means they use to 'rationalise' the industry is irrelevant. They will work through a trade association that operates as a tight *entente*, if it can be made into a rationalising *entente*; they will intervene directly with subsidies and threats in order to promote mergers and modernisation; they will even resort to nationalisation, not for ideological reasons but for the 'technical' reason that no other means has been able to make that industry perform satisfactorily.[2]

[1] Gourney, 'Un Groupe Dirigeant . . .', pp. 228–231; Bauchard, *La Mystique du Plan*, p. 77.

[2] See François Bloch-Lainé, *Pour Une Réforme de l'Entreprise*, Paris, Editions du Seuil, 1963, pp. 129–137 and his article in *Cahiers de la République*, Jan-Feb. 1962, pp. 66–67; Hackett and Hackett, *Economic Planning in France*, pp. 348–349; Club Jean Moulin, 'La Planification Démocratique, II,' *Les Cahiers de la République* Jan.-Feb. 1962, pp. 66–67; André Delion, *l'Etat et les Entreprises Publiques*, 1958, pp. 168–169; *Le Monde*, 17–18 June, 1960.

They are far more concerned with raising the level of production than with equalising its distribution.[1] They favour high profits because they consider profits the motor of capitalist expansion, but they frown on profits from non-productive activities such as real estate speculation.[2] They ardently favour an incomes policy.[3] They believe that the fundamental interests of labour and management do not necessarily conflict; the 'true interest' of each party is in expansion and productivity. The *ENA* graduates are constantly, and rather desperately, searching for a 'good' trade unionist, the man who sees and discusses social and economic problems in the same terms as the civil servants, the man capable of bringing the trade unions into the partnership of modern business, and the modern state – which is the goal of the new civil servants.[4]

The higher civil servants see themselves as representing the general interest. The general interest has nothing in common with any summation of particular interests, nor with the expressed wishes of the citizens:[5] the notion is straight out of Rousseau. It is something intrinsically different and higher; and they are its agents. The new *hauts fonctionnaires* hold to this view with even greater vigour and integrity than their predecessors.[6] The State is the embodiment of the general interest; its purpose is to serve that general interest. And the ranking civil servants see themselves, and not Parliament, as

[1] Gourney, 'Un Groupe Dirigeant . . .', p. 236; Kesler, 'Anciens Elèves . . .', p. 248.

[2] *Ibid.*, p. 248.

[3] F. Bloch-Lainé, *Cahiers de la République*, pp. 585–586; La Documentation Française, 'Rapport sur la politique des revenus . . . Oct. 1963–Jan. 1964' *Recueils et Monographies*, no. 47, 1964.

[4] On their search for a dialogue with the trade unions see André Philip, 'France's New Elite', p. 14; Bauchard, *La Mystique du Plan*, pp. 75, 79, 81; and B. Gourney and P. Viot, 'Les Planificateurs et les Décisions du Plan,' paper presented at the Colloque sur la Planification at Grenoble, 2–4 May 1963, mimeo, Comm. du Plan, April 1963, esp. pp. 8–9, and 23–24.

[5] Gourney is good on this question. See 'Un Groupe Dirigeant . . .' pp. 228–242, and so is La Lumière, *l'Inspection des Finances*, p. 181. See also, Massé, *French Affairs*, closing paragraph, where he quotes Paul Valéry on the crucial difference between the peoples' true wishes and their expressed wishes, and A. Gourdon, 'Les Grands Commis et le Mythe de l'Intérêt Général,' *Promotion*, #38, 1956.

[6] Gourney, 'Un Groupe Dirigeant . . .', pp. 228ff; La Lumière, *l'Inspection des Finances*, p. 181. Réalités, Dec. 1958, pp. 114–127 where the loyalty of the *hauts fonctionnaires* to the State and the General Interest is examined and applauded in a popular style.

the embodiment of the State.[1] The *hauts fonctionnaires* act for the State and the State acts for the general interest. If their conception of what the general interest demand happens to clash with the views of some other groups, their job is to act, if need be over the objections of that group. Inequality is the essence of the relations between the State and the citizens.[2] Pending the realisation by the social and economic groups of their true interest – and the *hauts fonctionnaires* as we shall see, recognise an obligation to lead these short-sighted groups to an understanding of their true interest – the State must act. The *hauts fonctionnaires* must sort out and solve the problems and quarrels of the governed. They must not only maintain order, but also steer the nation towards a better order; in brief, they must rule, and they must rule by their own concept of the general interest.

These twin conceptions – the primacy of the general interest and the ruling role of the *hauts fonctionnaires* – are traditional in French administration.[3] They come together nicely with the newer attitudes of the higher civil servants – a disdain for ideology, a pragmatic mentality, a commitment to modernisation and a compulsion to get things done – in the final expression of their social thinking, the *Economie Concertée*, with its premier institution and chief symbol, the plan.

The *economie concertée* is a notion popularised by François Bloch-Lainé, the most prominent of the *hauts fonctionnaires*. We will have a lot to say about it in the concluding chapter of this study. For our present purposes a brief sketch will do. The *économie concertée* is a partnership of big business, the state, and, in theory though not in practice, the trade unions. The managers of big business and the managers of the state run the modern core of the nation's economy – mostly the oligopoly sectors. Positive co-operation – not conflict, as in a market ideology – is its motor. The state is not a silent partner; it is an initiating, active partner. It intervenes in every aspect of economic affairs, encouraging, teaching, sometimes, even threatening. Its purpose is to promote economic modernisation:

[1] Gourney, 'Un Groupe Dirigeant . . .', pp. 228–231 is clear on this traditional theme.

[2] *Ibid.*, p. 228.

[3] See A. Diamant, 'The French Administrative System', pp. 186–187; Gourney, 'Un Groupe Dirigeant . . .', pp. 227–231, and A. Shonfield, *Modern Capitalism*, chapter V.

greater efficiency, greater productivity, greater expansion. The partnership works for the general interest; and it works outside the traditional political arena. Parliament and the constellation of institutions that surrounds Parliament are not necessary for the smooth functioning of the system; indeed, as we shall see, an active Parliament can be an embarrassment to the *économie concertée*. The *économie concertée* is the new higher civil servants' favourite model of economic and social organization. It is fundamentally an attitude of co-operation between the stewards of the state and the managers of big business. The Plan is the most visible, and most glamorous institutionalization of the *économie concertée*; consequently it is also its principal symbol.[1] For the plan is the embodiment of all the social attitudes we have been attributing to the new *hauts fonctionnaires*; and they have become its strongest supporters. The new *hauts fonctionnaires* are planners. They have been completely won over to the way of thinking that the plan represents.[2] One observer called the plan 'their supreme reference.'[3] Its appeal lies in its basic core of order and control, its aura of intellectual elegance and sophistication, its modern, scientific mystique, and its apparent freedom from ideological commitment. The plan represents an attempt to take charge of events, an effort to shape the nation's future. In the political and ideological vacuum in which the new generation of ranking civil servants lives, it is the ideal instrument for an enlightened, non-ideological élite to lead the nation; it is also an ideal retreat from the vagaries and vulgarities of Parliamentary politics and ideological commitment.[4]

When planning first began, the *hauts fonctionnaires* were its

[1] Very often the plan is used as a symbolic reference for the *économie concertée*. Confusing the plan as an institution with the plan as a symbol for the general partnership between big business and the interventionist state tends to make the planning institution seem far more influential than it now is. Shonfield, *Modern Capitalism*, does this in his generally excellent chapter on French planning. Gourney notes the symbolic role of the Plan for the ranking civil servants, 'Un Groupe Dirigeant . . .', pp. 237–238, as does Bauchard, *La Mystique du Plan*, *passim*, and Meynaud, *La Technocratie*, pp. 193–206.

[2] See statement by Planning Commissioner Hirsch cited above, p. 63.

[3] Kesler, 'Anciens Elèves . . .', p. 247; see also, Bauchard, *La Mystique du Plan*, p. 73, and Meynaud, *La Technocratie*, pp. 193–206, for similar observations.

[4] See François Bloch-Lainé, 'Economie Concertée Planification Démocratique,' *Cahiers de la République*, juillet 1962, esp. pp. 573–589; note how he explicitly places the *économie concertée* in an ideological void, p. 574. See also, Gourney, 'Un Groupe Dirigeant . . .', p. 228ff, and below, part VI.

most potent enemy; now they are its most enthusiastic supporters. This 'conversion,' as Planning Commissioner Hirsch called it, is responsible for the survival and success of French planning, but it is also responsible for the character and content of the plans. For, as we shall see, the *hauts fonctionnaires* and the values and ideas they personify have come to dominate the plan. It has become their instrument.

Important areas of disagreement continue to exist between the Planning Commission and the Treasury. But because of this 'profound conversion,' disagreement is no longer the result of fundamentally opposed ways of thinking. Suspicion, fear and hostility have subsided. Conflicting aims and methods no longer colour the relations between the plan and the Treasury. Instead, disagreements now result from the different responsibilities of the two institutions: conflicts are now structural rather than attitudinal *and* structural. The two most important differences in the responsibilities of the plan and the Treasury concern their scope and duration (or time span).

Scope: The Ministry of Finance is responsible for all economic policy; the plan is actively concerned with a more limited range of economic activities. Consequently, the Treasury tends towards a greater awareness of limitations imposed upon the plan's investment programmes by the demands of overall economic balance, the demands of sectors not included in the plan, and the demands of powerful pressure groups. The danger of inflation is a constant preoccupation of the Ministry of Finance. The Treasury is directly responsible for holding back wages and prices, for safeguarding France's foreign exchange position, and for keeping resources available for high priority projects outside the plan, such as military and para-military projects.[1] The Planning Commission on the other hand, has often sacrificed considerations of overall equilibrium, especially

[1] The concluding paragraphs of this chapter contain many references to historical patterns of behaviour much like those in the above paragraph. These statements are drawn from the findings presented in Part II which examines, in great detail, the influence of the plan on the behaviour of the principal economic agents–especially the Ministry of Finance. The only published piece that deals directly with these questions is Planning Commission mimeo, *Les Motifs d'Exécution du Plan*. It is excellent. See pp. 12–15, which discuss the conflicts between the plan and the Treasury.

as regards inflationary pressures, to the need for rapid growth and modernisation.[1]

The Ministry of Finance is also responsible to organized interest groups that the plan is able to ignore. Small business groups, agricultural interests, war veterans organisations, pensioners' lobbies, public works lobbies, local interests, the Foreign Office and the military establishment are all powerful and active forces in the Treasury's environment; for reasons which will become apparent later, the plan is relatively insulated from their direct influence. And, it is the Ministry of Finance, not the Planning Commission, that is ultimately responsible for dealing with Trade Union demands. Certain industrial sectors participating in the plan also have strong influence within the Ministry of Finance. (This category includes many of the nationalised industries as well as privately owned oligopolies such as Chemicals, Steel, or Aluminium). The Ministry of Finance, consequently, looks after their interests in the planning process as well as elsewhere.[2] Furthermore, the Ministry of Finance, as the senior Ministry, has to protect the competence of the lesser agencies of economic administration such as the Ministry of Public Works and the Ministry of Industry, which all wish to maintain the highest possible level of expenditures and preserve their own traditional control over those funds.[3] The Ministry of Finance has to consider the demands of these pressure groups when drawing up and implementing the plan. The Planning Commission does not.

Thus the Treasury is apt to find itself disagreeing with the Planning Commission on a considerable number of issues. As the Treasury has the power, this limits the range of the Planning Commission's influence so that, for example,

the influence of the Planning Commission . . . has been minimal

[1] See, below, Part III, chap. 1, for a detailed examination of the Monnet planners' decision to add to the inflationary pressures in order to accelerate the rate of industrial modernization.

[2] *Les Motifs d'Exécution du Plan* is quite explicit on these points, see, esp. pp. 12–15. These questions are developed below, in part III.

[3] On the general tendency of a higher bureaucratic office to protect the competence of its subordinate agencies see Max Weber, 'On Bureaucracy,' *From Max Weber*, C. W. Mills, ed. (London), pp. 197–199. On the French practice see Laurence Wylie's essay in *In Search of France*, by Stanley Hoffman *et al.*, pp. 220–224. Planning Commission mimeo entitled *Les Motifs d'Exécution du Plan*, part I, provides the most sensible discussion of this and other bureaucratic phenomena and their relation to French planning.

in the sensitive areas of agriculture, public works and overseas projects.[1]

The plan has no real influence on the decisions to devalue the franc, nor on the decision to join the Common Market.[2] Its influence on military affairs has been nonexistent.

As we shall see, from the point of view of the Treasury, the plan is only one consideration among many – albeit a most important one.

In addition to the differences between the Planning Commission and the Treasury concerning the choice of targets for the plan – differences which result from the greater scope of the Treasury's responsibilities – their greatest problems in working together arise after the plan has been drawn up, at the critical stage of implementation.

Time: The Ministry of Finance is responsible for short-run economic policy as well as for longer-range programmes; the Planning Commission is not. During the four year life of a plan, changes in the economic situation necessitate constant initiatives of a short-term nature. These daily actions concern increases or decreases in wages, military spending, foreign aid, family allowances, imports, exports, and prices. Sometimes the urgency of immediate pressures forces the Treasury to undertake a set of short-term actions such as an austerity programme in response to mounting inflationary pressures and a deteriorating foreign exchange position. These short-term actions are usually taken without reference to the plan's middle term programmes. They often jeopardise the planned investment programmes and destroy the coherence of the plan's overall growth pattern.[3]

Lack of co-ordination between short-term policy and the middle term programmes of the plan is the most serious source of difficulty in relations between the Treasury and the

[1] Sheahan, *Promotion and Control*, p. 172.

[2] *Les Motifs d'Exécution du Plan*, pp. 4–5, 10–14. On p. 13 the planners state: 'On peut néanmoins s'étonner que, par example, ni sur le plan des principes ni sur celui de la négociation quotidienne, le Commissariat au Plan ne soit pratiquement pas associé à la définition et la mise en oeuvre de la position de la France à l'égard de la construction économique européene.' See part IV below where these themes are developed.

[3] Part IV of this study examines the problem of co-ordinating short-term economic policy with the middle-term programme of the plan.

plan; it has been, without question, the most serious obstacle to successful implementation of the successive plans.

The personality at the head of the Treasury, that of the Minister of Finance, is often an additional obstacle to smooth co-operation between the Plan and the Treasury. The Minister's influence is felt less at the initial stages of the plan's preparation than at the critical stage of its implementation when action by the Treasury is necessary. Often the Minister comes from the traditional political arena, and not the administrative elite of the *grandes écoles*. M. Antoine Pinay is a recurrent case in point. He does not share the attitudes, ways of thinking, or vocabulary that are so closely connected with planning. Furthermore, he does not think too highly or too much about planning in general. In addition to the question of the Finance Minister's attitude towards the plan there is also the question of his limited range for manoeuvre. Often, especially under the Fourth Republic, he knew that he would not be in office for the full life of the four year plan. Consequently, he preferred to focus his efforts, and popular attention, on a shorter programme, that would be closely identified with his own name. The Faure plan (during the second plan), and the Giscard d'Estaing Stabilisation plan (during the fourth plan) are excellent examples of the important lack of co-ordination.

FIRST AND SECOND STAGES: SUMMARY

During the second stage of the planning process, the Planning Commission and the Treasury make the big decisions. Alternative growth models are prepared, then choices are made as to the rate and direction of planned development.

The Treasury's close co-operation is necessitated by the power structure in which French planning operates: the Treasury has the power needed to implement the plan. It has been made possible by the post-war change in attitude of the ranking Treasury officials. The Treasury is no longer the principal road block to the ideas represented by the plan, nor is it any longer a threat to the existence of the planning institution. Instead, it has espoused those ideas as its very own, and has become the most powerful advocate of economic planning. The enthusiasm of the new generation of higher Treasury officials for planning has been the most important factor in the success of French planning. But the Treasury's wholehearted commitment to planning does not preclude disagreements between the Planning Commission and the Treasury. The different responsibilities of the two institutions is the primary source of such disagreements. The larger scope of the Treasury's concerns is the major source of difficulty in the preparation of the plan. The fact that the plan and the Treasury frequently operate with different time horizons in view is the major source of difficulties in implementing the plan once it is drawn up.

The second stage of the planning process begins with the preparation of economic alternatives – or planning models – by the Planning Commission and the Treasury. It results in a single outline plan that delineates the planned rate and pattern of development. The major decisions of French planning are taken, during this second stage, by the Planning Commission and the Treasury: they are merely modified during the subsequent stages of planning.

5 *STAGE THREE:*
Parliament and the plan

In theory, the third stage of the planning process consists of active participation by Parliament in the choice of national economic goals and of means to attain those goals.[1] In practice Parliament has had almost no influence on the contents of the plans; its participation in the planning process has been so slight as to be totally ineffective, yet real enough to be derisive. The third stage has been effectively by-passed. The big decisions on the broad outlines of the plans, the decisions Parliament is supposed to make, are made in the second stage – by the Ministry of Finance and the Planning Commission.

The first plan was promulgated by executive decree without any Parliamentary debate or approval.[2] Parliamentary power has historically been associated with its control of the purse. One observer conscious of this fact remarked that 'Parliamentary control begins with the granting of credits necessary for the Plan.'[3] Credits for the projects of the first plan were voted by Parliament in 1947, along with the annual budget presented by the Ministry of Finance. The plan's programmes, however, were not distinguished from the rest of the budget. Finding this situation intolerable, Parliament insisted that in the future the plan's programmes be presented separately. They were, in 1950. And in 1950, without debate, Parliament cursorily voted the credits necessary to complete the investment projects.

> The plan was already more than half realised and its execution continuing smoothly. This gave Parliament the feeling of the uselessness of a difficult debate without any object.[4]

[1] See, for example, Jean Fourastié, *La Planification Economique en France* (Paris, P.U.F.), 1963, pp. 98–102.

[2] See Decree of 16 January 1947, signed by Léon Blum.

[3] Pierre Bauchet, *La Planification Française, Quinze Ans d'Expérience*, Paris, 1962, p. 102.

[4] P. Bauchet, *Planification*, p. 127.

Parliament voted its approval for the second plan (for the years 1953–57) on 27 March 1956.[1]

The third plan was not submitted to Parliamentary discussion or approval. It was promulgated by Executive decree.[2]

The interim plan (1959–60) was also put into effect without Parliamentary debate or approval.[3]

The fourth plan underwent a different procedure. It was submitted to Parliament *before* it went into effect. And Parliament did make some minor changes in the plan: a prefatory statement concerning the importance of 'Social Policy'[4] and minor changes in the body of the text, mostly small increases in credits for agricultural education, highways and telephone service.[5]

These changes are significant only if one chooses to see them as the beginning of a new and active role for Parliament in planning. By themselves, they constitute no departure from the previous practice of a plan prepared without Parliamentary influence. Many authors of studies on French planning as well as official spokesmen for the Planning Commission maintain that the Parliamentary debate on the fourth plan was the beginning of active parliamentary participation in planning – and that the fifth plan represents a second step forward toward that end.[6] A detailed examination of the role of Parliament in the plan will be found in Part VI below which concerns the democratisation of planning. For the purposes of our initial simplified model of the planning process, Parliamentary participation will be taken to be non-existent.

[1] See *J.O.*, *Lois et Décrets*, loi de 27 mars 1956.

[2] Décret no. 59–443 of 19 mars 1959, *J.O.*, *Lois et Décrets*, 11 avril 1959.

[3] See *Plan Intérimaire*, Paris, Imprimerie Nationale 1960.

[4] Article one, law no. 62–900, *J.O.*, *Lois et Décrets*, 1962, p. 7810.

[5] *J.O.*, *Assemblée Nationale*, *Débats*, 21 juin 1962, p. 1912.

[6] Hackett, *Economic Planning in France*, pp. 194–204 is a good example of this approach. Bernard Gourney and Pierre Viot (both of the Planning Commission) present a different, and I think more realistic, view. They argue that Parliament has had no effective influence on any of the first *four* plans. See, 'Les Planificateurs et les Décisions du Plan,' paper presented at the Colloque sur la Planification, at Grenoble 2–4 May 1963, mimeo, Comm. du Plan, 26 April 1963, part II, section 3, pp. 30ff.

6 *STAGE FOUR:*
Big business and the plan

In the fourth stage of the planning process, the outline prepared by the Planning Commission and the Treasury is coloured in with detailed programmes for industrial investment, output and modernisation. The work takes place in the most often discussed institution of French planning, the modernisation (or vertical) commissions. The modernisation commissions are composed of selected representatives of management, the trade unions, agricultural interests, consumer groups, the financial community, Government officials, the planners and 'experts.' For the fourth plan there were twenty-three vertical commissions in which 991 persons sat. The membership of the various subcommissions, working groups, and special commissions brought the total number of participants to 3,138.[1]

The members of the commissions are named by the Government upon recommendation of the Planning Commission. They serve without pay and, in theory, in an individual capacity.[2] There is no fixed proportion of seats allotted to various groups. There are no minutes kept, no votes taken. Commissioner Massé explains that

> No rigorous dosage is demanded in the composition of the commissions. The spirit counts more than the letter. The commissions seek a general accord and not a majority vote. *The goal of their work is not to separate the winners from the losers, but to come up with a common view.*[3]

[1] La Documentation Française, *Notes et Etudes Documentaires*, no. 2,846, 30 décembre 1961, p. 9. See below, part VI, Chap. 19 for a social and occupational breakdown of membership of modernisation commissions.

[2] Official works on the plan explain that the participants are invited as individuals and not as representatives of interest groups. See, for example, J. Fourastié, *La Planification Economique en France* (Paris, P.U.F.) 1963, pp. 26–27; or P. Bauchet, *Planification*, p. 47.

[3] Massé, *French Affairs*, p. 5 (italics added); Bauchet, *Planification*, p. 47 makes a similar statement.

Not everyone concurs with this official view:

> The largest union (the CGT) withdrew from participation in the 2nd and 3rd plans, (though it returned at the start of preparations for the 4th plan). According to officials of the Planning Commission, the trouble was that these groups conceived of participation in . . . the unacceptable terms . . . of group interest and fought to dominate the Plan for their own purposes. According to labour union officials, they were not the only ones trying to influence the planning in their interests. They were simply the losers.[1]

There exists a large body of literature that describes the formal structure, the composition and the theoretical functioning of the modernisation commissions. What actually goes on in these commissions, however, is another story.

> Books about French planning attach much interest to the institutional procedures involved in establishing the plan, but provide very little analysis of the reality of this procedure, contenting themselves, despite slight correctives, with noting that hardly anyone opposes the Plan in France nowadays . . . Hacket and Bauchet are two of the best known of these books.[2]

This chapter sketches out a highly simplified model of the activities of the modernisation commissions. What is excluded from a model of a power structure is as significant as what is included. Parliament, the trade unions, unorganised small business, consumer groups and agricultural interests are excluded from this chapter's model. Discussion is confined to the managers of big business, the planners, ranking civil servants and 'experts.' This simplifying assumption eliminates complicating detail in order to permit a clearer look at the decision-making process. Subsequent chapters restore the detail. They discuss the roles of the groups excluded from this chapter's model. By excluding these groups in the first place, little accuracy is sacrificed. Their representatives constitute only about 10–15 per cent of the commissions.[3] Their participation in the discussion and business of each commission is limited;

[1] John Sheahan, *Promotion and Control of Industry in Postwar France*, Cambridge, Mass., 1963, p. 180.

[2] J. Lautmann, *Recherche sur les Nouvelles Rélations Entre les Pouvoirs Publics en le Secteur Privé* (unpub. mimeo, 1964), p. 2.

[3] See tables I and II of Part VI below.

their influence on the decision-making process is negligible.

Business enters the planning process at the modernisation commission stage. 'Indicative planning' and the 'educative round tables' (described above) constitute the official agenda for the modernisation commissions. While these educative activities are under way the power relations of French planning reassert themselves in the form of tri-partite bargaining among the planners, the managers of big business and the ranking civil servants.

The planners come to the modernisation commission phase with specific objectives for each sector concerning output, investment, foreign trade and often several special projects such as changing the structure or geographic location of the industry. They also bring with them, from the second stage of the planning process, the support of the Treasury, so that behind the planners' programmes lies the incentive system of French planning.

The businessmen expect to negotiate with the planners; they do not expect to take orders. They do not have to acquiesce to the planners' commands; they have the power to bargain.

The giant firms and the powerful trade associations maintain their own direct access to the ministries and the Government. They can often count on obtaining state co-operation without the active support of the Planning Commission. If absolutely necessary, they can pressure the ministries to make the Planning Commission change its programmes in order to accommodate their own wishes. Furthermore the businessmen can ordinarily count on the support of the tutelary ministries. The tutelary ministries generally support their industries in any dealings with outside forces.[1] But neither the Planning Commission nor the business community wants a direct confrontation. And such confrontations are rare. The planners know that if the Treasury or the Government should have to arbitrate a direct conflict of will between the plan and a powerful business lobby, the outcome would by no means be certain.[2] This independent access to the state provides business with an element of control over

[1] See Shonfield, *Modern Capitalism*, p. 139; Ehrmann, *Organized Business in France*, pp. 262–263.

[2] Shonfield tells how the steel industry disagreed with the Planners' programme for steel and was able to rally enough support in the Treasury and the Government to force the Planners to change that programme. See. *Modern Capitalism*, p. 139.

the planners. It limits the demands that the planners can make, and when skilfully used, it creates a situation where the implementation of essential parts of the plan depends upon the influence of the business interest with the Ministries and the Government. For example, shortly before the outbreak of the Korean War, when the Pinay Government sought to curtail investment funds for the plan's projects, 'the industries that were particularly benefiting from the plan, such as steel, electrical equipment, shipbuilding and petroleum, proved to be invaluable allies of the Planning Commission, in its successful efforts to have those credits restored.'[1]

Giant firms can also simply ignore the Planners' information and incentives, and undertake a major investment project without the plan's approval or support.[2] As explained above, though incentives are an aid to a large firm, they generally are not a necessity. But most important, as far as bargaining strength is concerned, are the output and modernisation programmes which business firms prepare on their own and bring with them to the plan. Often these programmes overlap with those of the Planning Commission, so that the industry's own expansion and modernisation programme is quite similar to that sought by the planners.

As a top-executive of one of the largest industrial enterprises in France explained:

No, the Plan is not at all authoritarian. It does not force us into anything we do not want to do . . . the investment projects that the Plan urges us to undertake are usually the same as we ourselves want, with or without the Plan. . . . I don't know enough about other

[1] Ehrmann, *Organized Business in France*, pp. 289–290; see also Shonfield, *Modern Capitalism*, pp. 139–140; Granick, *European Executive*, pp. 143–144.

[2] Shonfield tells the story of Renault's open conflict with the Plan about adding new capacity and about the location of that new capacity. Renault – a nationalised firm – did without the Plan's incentive and financed its non-approved expansion, in a non-approved location out of its own funds. See, *Modern Capitalism*, pp. 139–140 and *Le Monde* 17 July 1963, p. 16, 23 July 1963, p. 12. See also the Plan's conflict with the steel industry reported in Shonfield, pp. 139–140 and *The Economist*, 8 February 1964; J. Marchal, 'Investment Decisions in French Public Undertakings,' *Annals of Public and Co-operative Economy*, Oct.-Dec. 1964, Vol. XXV, no. 4, pp. 266–267 touches on this same theme. Planning Commission mimeo, *Les Motifs d'Exécution du Plan* is the best published source on what actually goes on in the modernisation commissions – and on the relation of the Plan to the other agencies of the State administration. See, esp. pp. 7–9 and 12.

industries, but we are a very modern firm in a growing industry and we have no trouble with the Plan.[1]

When, as often happens, the planners' projects overlap with the firm's own expansion programme, it is decidedly in the interest of the firm to be forced by the plan's incentives (read: subsidies) to undertake the project.

> To what degree is an incentive a determinant for the accomplishment of an investment project? If it is not a determinant – that is, if the investment project was likely to be undertaken even in its absence, one can only consider it to be an outright gift.[2]

François Bloch-Lainé, one of the most important supporters of the plan, raises the same question:

> It is very probable that a certain number of extensions which benefitted from such aid would have been made without it, and it is quite certain that in such a case the subsidy was more of a reward than an incentive.[3]

There seems to be no way of knowing what percentage of investment projects that benefited from the plan's incentives would have been undertaken without them. The question is particularly pertinent to the very big firms such as St. Gobain, Pécheney, or Michelin which are constantly undertaking major investment projects. It is a relatively simple matter for such a firm to alter certain elements of an investment programme (often very minor elements) so as to fit the entire project under one of the titles for which incentives are granted.[4] For example, when part of the output of a new plant is explicitly reserved for exports (sometimes representing a change no greater than an

[1] Private interview. The interpretation of the workings of the modernisation commissions, especially the descriptions of the bargaining between big business and the planners, is drawn largely from the interviews described in the introduction.

[2] Prof. Hubert Brochier, 'Les Effects de la Planification Française,' exposé fait au Colloque sur la Planification à Grenoble, 2–4 mai 1963. Reprinted in *Cahiers Reconstruction*, 63–1 mai 1963, p. VI–18.

[3] François Bloch-Lainé, 'Sept Années d'Incitation à l'Expansion Régionale: Bilan et Leçons,' *Revue Juridique et Economique du Sud-Ouest*, no. 4, 1962, p. 941. See also, *Les Motifs d'Exécution du Plan*, p. 17.

[4] The titles under which incentives are granted (aid to encourage exports, regional development, productivity, modernisation, specialisation, research, etc.) are listed above, p. 24. François Bloch-Lainé discusses just this problem in reference to the effectiveness of incentives for encouraging regional development in 'Sept Années d'Incitation . . .', pp. 940ff. See also, *Les Motifs d'Exécution du Plan*, pp. 17–18.

official declaration of intention), then the whole project receives a state subsidy; a plant is built in one of the many areas singled out for industrial development, and the project benefits from considerable state aid under the blanket assumption that the project is necessarily situated in such a region at a financial disadvantage, and would 'normally' have been located elsewhere. Whatever the title under which incentives are granted and whatever form the incentives take, a big company will always have some project on hand that will qualify for subsidisation. For example, the Plan's approval is an important aid for obtaining permission to issue new securities. But,

> The fact of the matter is that only the biggest companies raise additional capital by public issues . . . and they can always list some of their activities under the Plan's 'approved' categories. It is easy for them to choose from among the numerous operations they undertake each year those which will most interest the Planners and finance the others out of their own resources.[1]

Even François Bloch-Lainé concludes that the

> Incentive power of the Plan's subsidies is generally strong only in the Plan's dealings with small and middle size firms where the subsidy is often financially indispensable.[2]

But for the giant firms which are always undertaking some projects that fall under the plan's subsidisation categories the 'incentives have a tendency to become automatic.'[3] They lose their value as stimulants to change and become rewards for good behaviour.

Bargaining in the modernisation commissions between the managers of the giant corporations and the planners is not a series of direct conflicts, with undertones of hostility, as traditional labour vs. management image of bargaining suggests. Rather, it takes place in a context of fundamental agreement. The planners, the ranking civil servants and the managers of big business share the same attitudes, the same modes of thought and expression, the same outlook. They come from the same social background; they attended the same schools. They know

[1] BRAE (Bureau de Recherche et d'Action Economique) Rue Royale, *La litique d'Incitation*, Paris, 1960, p. 63.

[2] F. Bloch-Lainé, 'Sept Années d'Incitation . . .', p. 491.

[3] *Les Motifs d'Exécution du Plan*, p. 7.

one another.[1] Indeed, to an alarming extent, they are the same people. Over twenty-five per cent of the Inspectors of Finance shift over into executive positions in the largest industrial firms and banks.[2] This is not to make a charge of corruption. There is no 'graft' involved, although a certain reluctance to antagonise a potential employer is to be expected. The important thing about common background shared by managers of the state and managers of big business is that it creates an atmosphere of understanding and trust, a feeling of working together toward a common end. Trade unionists and representatives of small business groups complain that the managers of big business and the managers of the State have such an automatic understanding of one another, such an extreme sensitivity to each other's interests that when a trade union representative arrives in a modernisation commission he feels like an uninvited guest at a family reunion.[3] David Granick remarks that

> the key fact in French planning is that the same type of men are sitting in the management and civil service posts in this cartel: men of the *grands écoles*, present or former civil servants, who consider themselves technocrats.[4]

Recognition of this fundamental sympathy and agreement is crucial to an understanding of French planning. The plan is a small affair. It is a series of discreet arrangements among people who know one another, who trust one another and who generally see eye-to-eye on things.

One can conclude, therefore, that planning is done by big

[1] See Granick, *The European Executive*, chapters 5 and 11; *Le Monde* 7 Oct. 1953, article by G. Mathieu; Pierre La Lumière, *l'Inspection des Finances*, esp. pp. 179–190; Club Jean Moulin, *l'Etat et le Citoyen*, Paris, 1961, pp. 136–145. André Philip in the *New Leader*, 22 June 1959, p. 15, and below, chapter I, part VI.

[2] 'Pantouflage' as the French call the switch from the civil service into a well-paid managerial position in big business has been the subject of a good deal of serious study. Pierre La Lumière, *l'Inspection des Finances*, is very good. See esp. pp. 69–90. The firms to which civil servants most often transfer include: Air Liquide, Pechiney, De Wendel, Simca, and, of course, the Banques d'Affaires, Dreyfus, Indochine, C.I.C., Lazard, Worms, etc. (*Ibid.*, p. 87). See also, Club Jean Moulin, *l'Etat et le Citoyen*, pp. 141–142; *Le Monde*, 7 Oct. 1953, Granick, *European Executive*, chapters 5 and 11; Kesler, 'Anciens Elèves . . .', p. 261, Ehrmann, *Organized Business in France*, p. 267–271.

[3] See below, Part VI, chapters I, III, where the modernisation commissions are studies from the critical perspective of the Left. See also, Granick, pp. 213–214; R. Jacques, 'Pour une Approche Syndicale au Plan,' *Esprit*, juillet 1961.

[4] Granick, *European Executive*, p. 147.

business for big business.[1] While this is quite true, it can direct attention away from the real, if non-revolutionary influence of the plan. For the planners are not simply the dupes of big business. They are not revolutionaries, but they do have their own goals and they do try to change things. They try to promote efficiency and expansion. They have a healthy respect for profits, and will raise no objection whatever to business benefitting from state subsidies – as long as business performs in a manner consistent with their own objectives. That is, as long as business is forever becoming more productive.

To view the workings of the modernisation commissions as a puppet show in which big business pulls all the strings is just as misleading as to view it as a battle. The modernisation commissions are part of a partnership, part of a co-operative venture between the managers of big business and the managers of the State. Open conflict is unusual. The plan does not wish to run the firm. It wishes to guide the firm to its true interest – and it believes that that interest defined as expansion and international competitiveness is the National Interest. Sometimes the plan wants 'favours' from the firm such as a special regional location for a new plant. The plan is willing to pay for those favours. This is where the incentives function. The plan may also want business to undertake projects that for one reason or another, business has been reluctant to undertake. This is the most important use of the incentives – to bribe business to do something the planners are confident business will find to its own advantage. Rarely, if ever, are incentives used to subsidize what the planners expect to be a wholly unprofitable venture. Nonetheless, a cost-effectiveness analysis of the plan's incentives might prove embarrassing if such a study could be made. Many of the subsidies are not incentives; they are rewards.

PLANNING WITHIN THE INDUSTRY

'Concerted Economy' and 'Flexible Planning' are expressions

[1] As most Leftist critiques of the plan have concluded: see, for example, Jean Anciant, 'Economie Concertée: Mythe ou Réalité,' *La Revue Socialiste*, no. 166, Oct. 1963, pp. 274–276, or CGT: *Le Plan, Mythes et Réalitiés, Supplément du Journal Le Peuple*, no. 643 *passim*. Many staunch middle-of-the-roaders have reached this same conclusion. See, for example, David Granick, *European Executive*, chapter 11.

that could well be replaced by Concerted Cartelisation and Flexible Cartelisation.[1]

According to official descriptions of the planning process, planning is done by branches (or sectors), and not by individual firms:

> The plan is . . . established by branch of activity. It does not dictate a course of action to private enterprise. It simply states the general objectives fixed for economic development and the particular goal for each branch. But, within the framework thus outlined, each firm is free to choose its own target. It can maintain its position within its branch, it can enlarge it, it can diminish it: that is its own affair.[2]

Such a procedure might seem to pose the problem of potential discrepancies between the sum of investment projects for each firm and the total planned for the sector. However, in practice

> There is, in general, no noticeable discrepancy between the target of the branch and the sum of the targets of the individual companies, because of the concerted planning procedure which I am now going to describe.[3]

Two kinds of decision are made in the private sector modernisation commissions: (1) the choice of growth and modernisation objectives for the industry as a whole, and (2) the division of that development among the firms. The methods most commonly used to deal with both questions vary with the characteristics of the industry and the commission.[4] The most important of these characteristics is the structure of the industry. Is it a highly concentrated industry? Is it a low-concentration industry with a competitive structure? Or is it a low concentration industry structured into some sort of *entente*? A highly concentrated sector, dominated by a few giant, modern firms is best for the planners; and an *entente* is often workable. The competitive structure, however, is awkward because, among other reasons, the operations of the modernisation commissions are all geared to industrial situations in which collusion, in some form or another, and not competition, is the principal mode of action.

[1] Jean Anciant, 'Economie Concertée: Mythe ou Réalité,' p. 276.
[2] Pierre Massé (in English) to U.S. Council on Foreign Relations, Washington, D.C., Mimeo, Comm. du Plan, p. 2.
[3] *Ibid.*, p. 2.
[4] See Gourney and Viot, (Grenoble paper), pp. 3–5.

In the modernisation commissions for highly concentrated industries, the planners generally work closely and informally with one key man, usually the director of a leading firm in that industry who acts as the bargaining agent for management. He is in close contact with the plan not only when the commission is in session, but throughout the year. The Planning Commission generally assigns one permanent staff member to keep in constant contact with the industry, so that a steady dialogue is maintained between the leader of management and a spokesman for the plan.[1] The key businessman floor-manages the planners' programmes. He presents the plan's projects (and offers of subsidisation) to the firms and negotiates the terms of business co-operation. His position as a respected member of management enhances his value as negotiator.

Furthermore, negotiations with (and through) one dependable businessman, permit maximum discretion, and discretion (or secrecy) is indispensable to French planning.[2] Bargaining is central to French planning: the bargaining between the planners and businessmen about developmental objectives and about the contents of the flexible packages of incentives; the bargaining within the state administration about initial targets and about where to cut when retrenchment becomes necessary; and the bargaining among the firms in an industry about the division of planned expansion. To say that such bargaining could not take place in public is merely to assert the basic premise of neo-realist international relations, or of any form of bargaining analysis: open covenants, openly arrived at, tend to be meaningless; serious negotiation can only be done in private.

> Critics of 'secret diplomacy' have demanded public sessions on the assumption that full publicity is 'democratic' and promotes honesty, understanding and agreement. In reality, the reverse is more nearly true. . . . Whatever the other evils of private sessions may be, they unquestionably facilitate compromise among divergent views – which is the *sine qua non* of success in every conference.[3]

This 'key man' method of negotiation is the planners'

[1] Shonfield describes the relation of a planner to 'his' industry in *Modern Capitalism*, p. 137. Gourney and Viot mention the latitude given to the 'leader' in the modernisation commissions, (Grenoble paper), pp. 3–4.

[2] Andrew Shonfield makes this point. See, 'Who Controls the Planners?' *The Listener*, 13 Dec. 1962, pp. 992–993.

[3] Frederick L. Schuman, *International Relations* (New York, 1958), p. 192; see also, pp. 166–170, 191.

favourite. It seems to be the most commonly used means for making important decisions that concern business participation in the plan. A variant of this method consists in a similar 'private agreement' between the planners (backed by the Treasury) and two or three such key businessmen. The two firms, after of course a long period of bargaining, agree to undertake the planners' project. Often the planners' programme for an industry includes specific projects aimed at specific firms as well as general performance objectives for the entire industry.[1] These specific projects are negotiated directly between the planners and the firm concerned: it is planning for the firm, not the branch. When the plan's programme demands the co-operation of the rest of the firms in an industry, it is largely through the personal efforts of the two or three business leaders that the planners negotiate with the entire industry.

In many industries, especially the less-concentrated ones such as textiles, hotels and tourism and many of the manufacturing industries, the planners work primarily through the trade association.[2] The trade association plays an important role in planning for certain highly concentrated sectors as well – particularly steel – where, for various reasons, it is especially strong and active.[3] In such cases the trade association replaces the key businessman as the industry's bargaining agent. Investment, output modernisation and in particular, restructuring programmes are prepared in consultation with the trade association, which also assumes responsibility for overseeing the breaking down of the industry's plan into programmes for individual firms. An excellent example of the active role of a trade association in planning is offered by the cotton-textile trade association (along with steel among the strongest in France), which in 1953, in co-operation with the Planning Commission, prepared and implemented a far-reaching five-year plan for the modernisation and restructuring of the industry.[4]

Important decisions contained in the over-all plan for an

[1] Some typical examples include the location of a Citroen motorcar complex in Brittany, or the deal worked out between the plan and *Aciers et Forges de la Loire* in which the steel company renounced its intentions to close down its plant at Boucau, in exchange for financial aid to its other plants.

[2] See Houssiaux, *Pouvoir de Monopole*, for concentration statistics.

[3] See, J. Sheahan, *Promotion and Control*, p. 135.

[4] Syndicat Général de l'Industrie Contonnière Française, *Programme d'Ensemble de l'Industrie Cotonnière Française*, Paris, 1953; Sheahan, *Promotion and Control*, p. 135.

industry are not taken in plenary sessions of the modernisation commissions: they are made elsewhere, informally, in private, among a few key individuals. They are discussed in the commissions. Secondary considerations are decided in full meetings, and the resulting programme is eventually written into the commission's report. But all this is after the fact, and everyone participating knows it. The modernisation commissions as formal meeting places are not where the important decisions are made. To listen to a Parliamentary debate on the plan is to learn nothing positive about the way French planning works. To attend a meeting of the Social and Economic Council and to assume that the discussion (often animated and intelligent) will lead to important decisions is sheer naïveté. To sit in on a meeting of a modernisation commission, and imagine that the questions being discussed have not already been decided is to mistake the essence of French planning:

> The essence of French planning . . . is the planning of each industry by its own members, acting as a great cartel, with the civil service sitting in on the game and sweetening the pot.[1]

And the outside investigator cannot sit in where the key decisions are made, in consultations between the Planning Commission and the Treasury (stage two of the planning process), where basic choices of the plan are made, and the broad outline of the plan drawn-up. Nor can he attend the bargaining sessions between the planners and the key businessmen, where the outline plan is coloured-in with detailed programmes for each industry, and the terms of business co-operation are bargained out. Nor can he attend the informal meetings where the industry's leaders and one or two planners, acting as a cartel, translate the industry's plan into programmes for individual firms.

For once an industry's over-all plan is established it must somehow be broken down into investment and output programmes for individual firms. The way this is done in French planning is by some form of 'collusion' within the industry.

> The French system of detailed target planning involves . . . the

[1] David Granick, *European Executive*, p. 155.

toleration of agreements between firms to fix the share each will take of the planned expansion.[1]

Collusion is an accurate term; there is no need to search for a euphemism, for French law, unlike US law, traditionally distinguishes between 'good' and 'bad' collusion.

The form of collusion usually follows the pattern of the initial negotiations in the modernisation commissions; i.e., where the trade association bargained for the industry with the planner, it generally directs the operations of the 'planning cartel.'

It is absurd to assume that a group of the leading businessmen in an industry who are assembled together to prepare a set of investment, output and modernisation programmes for the industry will not continue to act co-operatively when the time comes to break down that plan into programmes for each firm – especially if the industry has a long tradition of co-operative rather than competitive behaviour, and if there is no active opposition to such practice.

Most French industries have such a tradition. French businessmen have never placed much faith in nor even rendered lip service to the doctrines of open competition as the best method of industrial organisation. An *entente* of some kind to 'regularise' activity has always seemed more reasonable, and has almost always developed.[2]

Before the war, it has been argued, competition was more widespread in France than in Germany or the United States.[3] John Sheahan points out that the only basis on which this assertion could have been defended is purely structural: the degree of concentration was unusually low. But low concentra-

[1] Quotation is from, Malcolm MacLennen, 'French Planning: Some Lessons for Britain,' *Planning*, Vol. XXIX, no. 475 (PEP, London), 8 Sept. 1963, p. 347. See also, Shonfield, *Modern Capitalism*, p. 138; Gourney and Viot, (Grenoble Paper), p. 3; J. Anciant, 'Economie Concertée', *passim*; J. C. R. Dow, 'Problems of Economic Planning,' *Westminster Bank Review*, Nov. 1961, p. 19; A. Soulat in *Cahiers de la République*, #45, p. 475. W. Baum, *The French Economy and the State*, Princeton, 1958, pp. 280–281, and below, part IV, pp. 139 ff.

[2] John Sheahan, *Promotion and Control*, chapter 14 is very good. See also, David S. Landes, 'French Business and the Businessman . . .' in E. M. Earle, ed., *Modern France*, Princeton, 1951; R. Goetz-Girey, 'Monopoly and Competition in France,' in E. H. Chamberlain, ed., *Monopoly and Competition and their Regulation*, London, Macmillan, 1954; Ehrmann, *Organized Business in France*, pp. 368–391; and Conseil Economique, *Etudes et Travaux*, no. 13, *Contrôle des ententes professionnelles*, Paris, 1950.

[3] Goetz-Girey, p. 21.

tion is, by itself, no guarantee of competition; there is an important difference between positive competitive pressure and the absence of monopolistic control. In the French case, low concentration took the form of *ententes* in which all producers were kept alive, with the more efficient 'accepting above-average returns, but foregoing possible growth.'[1]

In France, *ententes*, cartels and monopolies are traditional, omnipresent and encouraged.[2]

French law, pre-war and post-war, accepts *ententes*, cartels and other forms of restrictions on competition, but on the basis of a distinction as to their aims. The law-case *Comptoir Longwy* (1902) is perhaps the best-known judicial assertion of the distinction between good and bad cartels, and provides a legal definition of a good one. The court ruled that a steel cartel which controlled more than half of French steel production, fixed prices and output quotas, and imposed specific penalties for breaking the cartel's rules was not in violation of the law because its principal objective was 'to regulate the operations of its members . . . in the general interests of production in a great industry.'[3]

In August 1953 the Laniel Government issued a decree 'concerning the maintenance or re-establishment of free competition in industry and commerce,'[4] which *Le Monde* called 'the Sherman Act of the IVth Republic.'[5]

Section four of the decree categorically prohibits all cartels, *ententes* or other forms of co-operation in restraint of trade. But article 59*ter* of that section resurrects the traditional distinction between good and bad cartels.

[1] Sheahan, p. 251.

[2] Houssiaux, *Le Pouvoir du Monopole*, provides the best concentration studies; Sheahan, *Promotion and Control*, chapter 14 is good on the general tone of restrictive practices; so is, Conseil Economique, *Etudes et Travaux*, no. 13. See also J. H. Jeannéney, *Forces et Faiblesses de l'Economie Française*, Paris, 1955, pp. 258ff. The legal position of restrictive practices and the attitudes of the public authorities towards them are discussed in the following pages, and below in part IV, esp. pp. 138ff. Corwin D. Edwards, *Trade Regulations Overseas*,. N.Y., 1966, pp. 3–75 provides the clearest survey in English, of French laws about restrictive practices.

[3] La Documentation Française, *Notes et Etudes Documentaires*, no. 1736, 'Ententes et Monopoles dans le Monde,' (Paris, 1953), p. 41.

[4] Décret No. 53–704 du 9 août 1953, *Journal Officiel, Lois et Décrets*, 10 août 1953, p. 7045.

[5] *Le Monde*, 20 August 1953, p. 10. See also Corwin D. Edwards, *Controls of Cartels and Monopolies, An International Comparison*, N.Y., 1967, pp. 128–129, 347–350.

excluded [from the prohibition of the decree] are concerted actions, convention or ententes . . . that serve to improve . . . the market or to assure the development of economic progress by rationalization and specialization.

Neither the letter nor the spirit of the law is opposed to *ententes per se*. The law distinguishes broadly between good and bad ones. The planners and the economic administration of the State go further; they are positively in favour of good (rationalising, modernising, and specialising) *ententes*, and actively promote such arrangements. And they do not seem, in practice, to make great efforts to distinguish bad *ententes* from good. *Ententes* are encouraged almost, indiscriminately, under the theory that an *entente*, under the supervision of the plan is a better form of industrial organisation than a low-concentration, competitive structure, and an industry structured into a few giant firms operating as a cartel with the planners participating is the best form of industrial organisation.

Successive plans posit the goals of increasing the size of French firms and improving co-operation within the industry through the promotion of mergers and intra-industry agreements.[1]

The Report of the Commission on manufacturing industries for the Third plan includes a long section which lists the impediments to the promotion of 'mergers and agreements.'[2] The first impediment the report mentions is psychological: 'many businessmen still see their colleagues as competitors rather than as possible associates'.[3] The second is legal: 'The realisation of mergers and agreements seems to be slowed down by the laws concerning *ententes* . . . the laws should be modified.'[4]

The report goes on to describe the 'embarrassment' of the Secretary of State for Economic Affairs who had to reply to a Parliamentary question concerning the contradiction between anti-*entente* legislation and the Plan's policy, backed by the State, of actively promoting mergers and industrial restructuring

[1] See below, pp. 72–5, 138 ff.

[2] Commissariat Général de Plan, *Troisième Plan de Modernisation et d'Equipement, Rapport Général de la Commission des Industries de Transformation* (Paris, 1958), p. 126.

[3] *Ibid.*, p. 126.

[4] *Ibid.*, p. 127.

around forms of organisation other than competition.[1]

The report concludes by asking the public authorities to make it clear to business that

> their efforts to accomplish in common the rationalisation of their production, far from falling under the sanctions of the law, will benefit from real encouragements from the public authorities.[2]

The French attitude towards concentration and *ententes* differs from that of American economists. The American generally studies industrial concentration with the assumption that high concentration prevents competition, permits monopoly profits and reduces general efficiency. The French economist generally looks at industrial structures to see whether concentration is high enough to allow for big, efficient firms. The French planners categorically and indiscriminately encourage mergers. In no published statement has the Planning Commission opposed a merger – not even when two such giants as St. Gobain and Pèchiney combined their chemical operations.[3] They reject competition as the basis of industrial organisation; *ententes* are not to be eliminated, they are to be converted by the planners' participation into the means for rationalising industrial structure and spurring co-operative growth and modernisation. Rationalisation invariably takes the form of increasing the size of the firms by promoting mergers and specialisation. Size, in the planners' thinking and in their statements, is equated with efficiency, innovation and, crucially, modernisation. One government report concluded:

> The large firm appears today to be the most efficient unit of production . . . its role as a motor of growth should be underlined . . . it favours improvements of techniques and the quality of products . . .[4]

[1] *Ibid.*, p. 127.

[2] *Ibid.*, p. 128.

[3] See *Le Monde* 22–23 novembre 1959, p. 9 for the story of this merger. The Celtex mergers is another good example. See *Le Monde* of 30 March 1952 and 24 June 1961. See also *Le Monde* of 23 Sept. 1964, p. 20 where the administration's attitude is made quite clear; also *Le Monde*, 17 juin 1964, p. 18; the *New York Times* (Int'l edition), 28 July 1964 story entitled 'European Big Businesses get Bigger,' and *Le Monde* 21–22 Nov. 1965, p. 11.

[4] INSEE, 'l'Industrie Française de 1951 à 1956,' *Etudes Statistiques*, jan-mars., 1960, p. 53. See also G. Pompidou's speech reported in *Le Monde* of 17 juin 1964 under the title 'La taille des entreprises françaises doit grandir.' The Gaullists seem to have added national *Grandeur* to the Planners' already lengthy list of the virtues of corporate bigness.

The planners give no evidence of any study of this correlation between size and efficiency. They never seem to take notice of, let alone take issue with, studies such as Joe Bain's classic of bigness, concentration, efficiency and optimal size.[1] They push for concentration. They encourage 'co-operation' instead of competition within industries, but they try to participate in the post-war generation of cartels. Given the French planning machinery, it is in fact far easier to plan for big firms and cartels than for medium-size, competitive firms.[2] Dealing with big firms makes planning easier – not only, as we have seen, at the bargaining tables – but also, as we shall see, in every phase of planning. The planners find themselves in the happy situation in which their strongest convictions coincide with their interest: they believe in big firms co-operating with each other as an enlightened and modernising cartel – under the surveillance of the Planning Commission. As a second best they will accept, temporarily, an *entente* in a low-concentration sector. The methods and structures of French planning necessitate such forms of industrial organisation.

SUMMARY

In the fourth stage of the planning process, the outline plan prepared by the planners and the Treasury is filled in with detailed investment, output and modernisation programmes for each sector. This is done in the modernisation commissions attended by representatives of the major economic groups: management, labour, consumers, Government officials, planners and 'experts.' Representation is extensive; for the fourth plan, the various commissions, sub-commissions and working groups included over three thousand individuals. But participation is restricted. The contents of the sectoral plans are worked out by an informal process of bargaining among the planners, the Treasury officials, and the managers of big business. The other groups represented in the commissions exert no significant influence on decisions.

The principal sources of the planners' power in the bargaining

[1] Joe Bain, 'Economies of Scale, Concentration and the Condition of Entry in Twenty Manufacturing Industries,' *American Economic Review*, Vol. 44, 1954, pp. 15–39.

[2] See Gourney and Viot, (Grenoble Paper), pp. 3–4; Shonfield, *Modern Capitalism*.

sessions are (a) the general attractiveness of most of their programmes to big business, (b) the support of the Treasury, and the reluctance of any prudent businessman to put himself on the wrong side of the Treasury's widespread and discriminating economic powers, and (c) the incentive system.

Business strength in the bargaining sessions stems from the fact that many of the planners' projects coincide with their own expansion and development programmes, so that co-operation entails little loss and often results in a free gift of incentive-subsidies. Business also maintains its own direct lines of influence to the Treasury and the Government. In dealing with the planners it can use this influence as either a carrot or a stick. It can bring pressure on the planners and force them to change an objectionable programme; or it can use its influence to help the planners secure State support for a project business favours, or as a log-rolling lever. Finally, it can simply ignore many of the plan's programmes and targets. This generally happens not to specific reform and restructuring projects, which are the subject of hard bargaining and careful supervision, but to the Plan's output and investment targets which, as we shall see, have a built-in tendency to become irrelevant after a short time. Here, the rationality of the market, rather than that of the Plan reigns supreme, and initiative and responsibility remain with the firm, not the plan or the Treasury.

The sectoral, or industry, plans are broken down into investment and output programmes for individual firms: planned growth and modernisation is divided up within the industry by the industry itself, acting as a cartel or *entente*. The planners, however, participate actively in the workings of the cartel.

By the end of the fourth stage, a planning document consisting of separate plans for each sector, prepared within the framework of an over-all outline plan, has been established. Less officially, each firm has its own share of the state subsidies, and its own share of the industry's planned development.

The planning process then continues to the fifth stage, where an attempt is made to co-ordinate the various sectoral plans.

7 THE FIFTH STAGE: *Coherence*

In the fifth stage of the planning process the separate sectoral plans are checked against one another for consistency and against the primary supply constraints on over-all expansion. The institutional setting consists of five 'horizontal' commissions, similar to the vertical commissions of stage four in composition and mode of operation. The most important horizontal commission is concerned with the overall balance of the plan and with its financing. The others treat manpower, research, productivity and regional development.[1] Co-ordination, or as the planners like to call it, coherence, is the primary concern.

The term coherence designates a basic approach to planning. A coherent plan emphasises interdependencies; it defines balances among sectors; it relates every important industry to every other important industry and to detailed patterns of final demands and primary inputs. Essentially it is a detailed, general equilibrium or resource allocation model, in the form of an operational input-output table of the type described in Chapter 1. Coherent planning means preparing targets for each major industry as a function of the demand for all other industries. In a coherent plan, all economic activities are carefully co-ordinated, all markets cleared, and the entire economy is in balance.

What the French call coherent planning is what most economists have in mind when they say planning. The French use the adjective to distinguish the basic approach to planning they have used since the preparation of the second plan from that which they used for the first plan. Planning, at the time of the first plan, consisted in selecting several problem sectors and preparing detailed programmes for their intensive development.

[1] Hackett and Hackett, *Economic Planning in France*, London, 1963, pp. 144–152 describes the tasks and composition of the five horizontal commissions.

The general resource allocation function of planning that the word coherent emphasizes was not the primary function of the first plan: the first plan was not a complex pattern of carefully balanced interdependencies; it was a short list of top priorities. Unlike its successors it did not consider the task of harmonising all economic activities to be its chief concern; it was more interested in concentrating resources into a small group of strategic activities. The contrast between these two approaches to planning will become sharper in the following parts of this study which examine the successive plans and their effects on the economy.

The horizontal commissions were created for the preparation of the second plan when coherence first became a primary concern of the planners. They have not been very effective; the successive plans have not been particularly coherent. In the planning texts all output targets are carefully co-ordinated. Investment programmes mesh with financial programmes, with demand estimates and with estimates of primary supplies. The successive plans balance on paper but, as we shall argue, those balances are purely paper balances, with little likelihood of realization.

Historically, French economic growth has not been coherent. The past twenty years have been marked by recurrent inflations, foreign exchange crises, devaluations, deliberate deflations, sectoral imbalances and class strife over income distribution. The planned *patterns* of development have not been realized.

Furthermore, the discrepancies between planned and actual development have demonstrated a pattern that is, to an important extent, explainable in retrospect and predictable in prospect. This pattern of discrepancies between planned and actual development is best viewed as systemic. The discrepancies are a natural output of the planning process rather than a series of unique events or a kind of inefficiency analogous to friction. In other words, if a pattern of discrepancies between planned and actual development has in fact been generally predictable, then the published planning texts have been paper plans and the predictable patterns of discrepancies have been the more operational programmes.

It is during the fifth stage of the planning process, when the planners check the separate sectoral plans against one another for consistency and against the primary supply constraints on over-all expansion, that the official general resource allocation plan and the operational plan begin seriously to diverge: the official resource allocation plan remains coherent; the operational plan does not. The assumption that the explicit targets of the general resource allocation plan do not necessarily define the plan's operational role leads to the realisation that the principal functions and effects of the plan may be very different from those suggested by the carefully balanced production data of its targets. Indeed, to equate the balanced production targets with the role of the plan is to assume away all serious inquiry directed at finding out what the plan actually does. Once the initial error is made – as in an effort to gauge the plan's effectiveness by measuring the degree to which its explicit targets are realised – other errors follow. The machinery of the planning process is misunderstood because it is seen as relating to an end that may not be the plan's principal purpose, perhaps not even its second most important function. The argument that will be advanced in this study is that the primary function and effectiveness of the plan are not defined by the coherent pattern of interdependent demand estimates that constitute the plan's explicit targets.

In order to understand the real functions of the plan and its pattern of effectiveness, it is necessary to study its historical development. The following chapters examine the interplay of planning and actual economic activity and trace the development of a role for planning within the political economy of post-war France.

PART III

THE MONNET PLAN: A HISTORY

In the summer of 1945, several months before it had been officially established, the Planning Commission began work; by the autumn of 1946 a four-year modernisation and equipment plan had been drafted.[1] The most striking characteristics of the planning document were (1) a manifest lack of technical sophistication in its preparation and presentation; and (2) the limited breadth of its detailed programmes: the plan concentrated resources on the long-term development of a small group of industrial sectors.

[1] Commissariat Général du Plan, *Rapport Général sur le Premier Plan de Modernisation et d'Equipement*, novembre 1946–janvier 1947, is the basic planning document, henceforth referred to as the First plan or the Monnet plan. The Planning Commission was created by an Executive decree dated 3 January 1946; it was, however, already at work during the summer of 1945. See J. Fourastié, *La Planification Economique en France*, Paris, 1963, p. 19.

8 PRIORITIES

THE TEXTS

The Monnet plan was technically unsophisticated, in comparison with present French practice and with econometric techniques of the late forties. It consisted of a set of detailed investment and modernisation programmes, prepared separately for each of a selected group of industries and enveloped together in a rudimentary analysis of the national economy. It contained no input-output analysis of sectoral interrelations; no explicit analysis of alternative uses of scarce resources; no systematic study of *how* necessary resources would be diverted to the investment programme without further adding to inflationary pressures; no consideration of induced demand for imports resulting from the heavy investment programme, and no studies of the effects of that programme on consumption, income distribution, price levels and general political, social and economic stability.[1]

AVAILABLE DATA

In fairness to the Monnet planners it must be noted that available economic data were totally inadequate to support very elaborate computation. When the Monnet planners set to work, they could find no reliable set of national accounts: there had

[1] See Harold Lubell, *The French Investment Plan: A Defense of the Monnet Plan*, unpub. Ph.D. thesis, Harvard University, 1951, chapter 2; Warren Baum, *The French Economy and the State*, Princeton, 1958, p. 23, discusses some of the shortcomings of the plan, especially its inadequate studies of induced demand and alternative uses of resources, in phrases very similar to Lubell's. See also, S. Wellisz, 'Economic Planning in the Netherlands, France, and Italy', *Journal of Political Economy*, June 1960, especially p. 272, where he is particularly critical of the inadequacy of the plan's macroeconomic analysis and maintains quite simply that 'my own observations corroborated by a perusal of the writings of former officials of the Commissariat (who, having no official capacity, were free to say what they believed), incline me to the belief that the majority of the Commissariat personnel are quite unfamiliar with macroeconomics.' John Sheahan, *Promotion and Control of Industry in Postwar France*, Cambridge, Mass., 1963, pp. 171–172, is clear and more reasonable on this point.

been no agricultural census since 1929; no industrial census since 1931.[1]

A government report of 1953 observed that:

Of all the developed nations, France is without a doubt the least informed of its economy. Most of the instruments of [economic] analysis that modern nations have developed are still lacking in our country.[2]

It is almost impossible to describe the state of French economic statistics between the end of World War I and the mid nineteen-fifties without appearing facetious or sardonic: even Government reports read like parodies.[3]

The index of industrial production which served as the basis of French industrial data up to the Second World War, was established in 1924 by a determined civil servant, M. Jean Dessirier, who ran about in his own car at his own expense, begging for the simplest kind of economic data.[4] Automobile production had to be estimated from the number of licence plates issued; the companies that made the cars refused to tell how many they produced. Michelin, one of the largest industrial enterprises in France, would volunteer no information on tyre production. The chemical industry kept secret the amounts of sulphuric acid and carbonates it produced. Hundreds of other examples could be cited without even entering into the twin-ledger accounts of small family businesses or peasant farmers.[5]

[1] Baum, *French Economy . . .*, pp. 9–10.

[2] Ministère des Finances, SEEF, 'Rapport du Service des Etudes Economiques et Financières sur les Comptes de la Nation des Années 1951 et 1952', *Statistiques et Etudes Financières*, no. 18, 1953, p. 156.

[3] See Conseil Economique. 'Etude sur le Revenu National', *Etudes et Travaux*, no. 19, especially pp. 144–150; the *Journal Officiel, Avis et Rapports du Conseil Economique et Social*, 23 mars 1963, p. 249, offers a more wry humour than the slapstick laugh-getters of French parliamentary debates.

[4] This story is to be found in Conseil Economique, 'Etude sur le Revenu National', p. 144; and in Ehrmann, *Organized Business . . .*, pp. 279–280.

[5] An interesting history of the problems of French economic statistics is provided by M. Alfred Sauvy in Annex VII to Conseil Economique, *op. cit.*, (Etude sur le Revenu National). M. Sauvy outlines the role of powerful trade associations in watering-down a 1938 law to make the provision of basic business statistics mandatory (p. 145). He even manages to explain to the august *Conseil* how businessmen's fears of being exposed in adulterous philanderings impair the collection of economic data (p. 149). He discussed the problems of French economic statistics in a much drier tone in *Collection Droit Social*, no. 7, 1941, llr fascicule, pp. 19–21, when he was a deputy director of the Statistique Générale de la France under Vichy. The article offers some interesting comparisons with his later expressed views on the role of trade associations, etc.

M. Dessirier's index continued to be published until 1938, when his successors, under the direction of Alfred Sauvy, decided that the moment had finally come 'when it was more honest to cease publication'.[1]

Explanation of why French statistics were either non-existent or unreliable entails reference to the French mania for privacy and secrecy, to a long tradition of distrust of government, to a flair for tracing the ultimate destination of all economic information to the police prefect and the tax collector, and to the general conclusion that the *système dé* dies slowly in France.[2]

The atmosphere in which the first plan was prepared had little in common with current images of computerised planning. It was more the handiwork of an artisan's shop than the refined product of a 'think factory'. Two young men, with a mechanical desk adding-machine, sat up all night to put together a final version of the plan's agricultural programme; they worked with pencils, so as to be able to erase and revise any estimate that did not fit. When a vital statistic was missing, they telephoned about for a few estimates and then 'established' the parameter by themselves.[3]

During the period of the Monnet plan, the state statistical agencies were reorganised and strengthened, and a crash programme was begun to develop a reliable set of national accounts. The subsequent development of French economic data has been remarkable, and the plan has played an important role in that development.[4] But the effects of these reforms were not to begin to be felt until 1953.[5] The economic information the Monnet planners needed to prepare a more sophisticated plan was simply not available.

[1] Conseil Economique, *Etudes et Travaux*, No. 19, p. 144.

[2] Ehrmann, *Organized Business*, pp. 279–284, offers a most accessible and representative explanation of why French economic statistics were what they were. See also *J.O. Avis et Rapports du Conseil Economique et Social*, 23 March 1963, pp. 218–256, for a survey of the present state of French economic information and the history of its development.

[3] This anecdote is taken from one of the interviews described in the introductory section. Despite its obvious nostalgia, I believe that it is 'true' in terms of the image it evokes.

[4] See David Granick, *The European Executive*, (Anchor paperback) 1964, p. 145; Pierre Massé, 'French Economic Planning', *French Affairs*, #127, New York, 1961, p. 8; Andrew Shonfield, *Modern Capitalism*, New York, (O.U.P. paperback), 1965, pp. 127–128.

[5] See Bernard Gourney, '. . . les grands fonctionnaires', *Revue Française de Science Politique*, vol. XIV, No. 2, April 1964, p. 236; Massé, *French Affairs*, p. 8 and below, pp. 121–3.

This absence of reliable data sufficiently explains the first plan's lack of technical sophistication: shoddy data precludes elaborate computation. The technical crudeness of the plan did not bother Monnet and his team very much. It will be argued below that even if such data had been available, the Monnet planners had good reasons for avoiding a more elaborate plan than they prepared – reasons their successors underrated.

PRIORITIES AND THE TARGETS OF THE MONNET PLAN

The Monnet plan concerned itself explicitly with just a few 'basic sectors': economic recovery and expansion were to be promoted by concentrating resources on the development and modernisation of a group of industries which were considered essential to future economic development whatever direction that development might take. The plan defined six basic sectors: coal, electricity, steel, cement, agricultural machinery and transportation.[1] It scheduled investment programmes and structural reforms for each of them. The rest of the economy was left largely outside of the plan's active attention – and out of the government-financed reconstruction programme for which the plan was to be the principal framework. In the difficult economic conditions of the early post-war period – especially the penury of private investment finance – exclusion from the plan's investment programmes would make large scale expansion extremely difficult, if not impossible.[2] The plan could concentrate on promoting approved investment projects; the tight capital market would hold back non-approved projects.

The plan set the following increases in 'national production' as its principal objective:

(a) To catch up to the 1938 level by the end of 1946.

(b) To attain the 1929 level, [which was about twenty-five per cent above that of 1938], by the middle of 1948.

(c) And finally, to exceed the 1929 level by about twenty-five per cent in 1950.[3]

[1] *Monnet Plan*, p. 33; shortly after, petroleum, basic chemicals, synthetic fertilisers, synthetic fibres and shipbuilding were added to the list of 'basic sectors'. See *Reponse Française . . . à L'OCEE*, 1948.

[2] See above, pp. 22–3.

[3] First plan, p. 23. These global targets are vague, and there is nothing else in the planning document that clarifies them. Baum remarks that 'it is not even clear from the language of the report whether it applied to industrial production or to the gross national product'. *First Plan*, p. 23.

The plan called for a vigorous investment programme,[1] and concentrated investment on the long-term development of the basic sectors which received well over one half of all planned investment.[2]

The first step in the planned development was reached only slightly behind schedule: industrial production regained the 1938 level in April 1947.[3] The second step – to advance twenty-five per cent beyond that level by the middle of 1948 – proved to be too ambitious.

During reconstruction, that is until Spring 1947, a good portion of investment was used to repair damaged production facilities. To advance production beyond pre-war levels, however, required investment in new plants and equipment and not

[1] Gross investment was targeted at 23–25% of gross national product over the four year period, 1947–1950, (*First Plan*, p. 88). In 1938 only 3% of gross national product was devoted to investment. (H. Lubell, 'The Role of Investment in Two French Inflations', *Oxford Economic Papers, NS*, Vol. vii, no. 1, Feb. 1955, p. 48). The French definition of gross investment differs from that in use in the U.S. It includes repairs and upkeep. Crucially, it includes expenditures on armaments and public works. The last two items are treated as government consumption in the U.S. Department of Commerce accounts. Richard Ruggles, 'The French Investment Program and its Relation to Resource Allocation', in E. M. Earle, ed., *Modern France*, Princeton, 1951, pp. 373, 380–381, provides a rigorous treatment of the statistical adjustments necessary to compare the ratio of gross investments to gross national product as established by French definitions with American definitions of the same categories. He converts actual gross investment in France in 1949 – 20.4% of G.N.P. by French definitions – to 11.8% of G.N.P. by U.S. definitions. Lubell '. . . Two French Inflations', p. 48, makes similar conversions. John Sheahan, *Promotion and Control*, pp. 16–19, discusses further problems connected with his efforts to compare French and American ratios of gross investment to gross national product. He finds that in 1950 the ratio of prices of investment goods to those of consumer goods was about 25% higher in France than in the U.S., so that the simple investment to G.N.P. ratio does not accurately reflect the 'investment effort', nor, as we shall see below, does it reflect the productivity of new investment.

The overall investment target of the Monnet plan was, as we shall see, a vague, exhortatory figure. The plan does not even provide a breakdown of investment so as to make possible the kind of calculation Ruggles suggests (e.g., there is no indication of anticipated military expenditures). The global investment target, like the overall growth target, should be understood as a thoroughly vague, albeit quantified, rallying point. Its function, as we shall see, was more to give the nation something to shoot for than to balance a coherent economic plan. All the numerical targets in the Monnet plan – except those relating to specific industries – ought to be understood in that sense.

[2] See Table III, p. 90 below, for a sector-by-sector breakdown of the bulk of planned investment.

[3] See Baum, *The French Economy*, Table I, p. 20. Agricultural production advanced more slowly, but the 1948 harvest reached the 1938 level.

See below, pp. 98–100.

just in repairs, however big, of war-damaged facilities. Instead of removing specific bottlenecks, which impeded the full utilisation of existing capacity, new capacity had to be created. Consequently, after such a reconstruction period, the rate of increases in output per unit of new investment could be expected to fall.[1] The Monnet plan, drawn up in 1945–6, counted too heavily on the high reconstruction rates of return on investment. It also over-estimated the amounts of investment funds that would be forthcoming. By 1948 it was apparent that the targets of the plan were over-optimistic.

Over one-third of planned investment in the years 1948, 1949, and 1950 were financed out of Marshall plan funds.[2] The *ECA*'s request that the plan's timetable be made to coincide with that of the European Recovery Programme (terminal date 1952)[3] provided a convenient occasion for a general downward revision of the plan's targets. The revised version of the plan called for an investment effort over the extended life of the plan (1947–52) roughly equal to that originally fixed for the four year period 1947–50.[4]

[1] The INSEE attributes the speed of France's reconstruction to the fact that pre-war levels of output could be restored by removing certain key bottlenecks:
'Industrial installations were not, in general, severely damaged by war-time bombardments or destruction. . . In fact it was the near total paralysis of the transport system which extremely reduced economic activity in the summer of 1944.' *INSEE, Mouvement Economique*, 1944–1957, p. 70.
Ruggles, 'French Investment Programme. . .', p. 371, advances a similar argument.

(*In billions* of current francs*)

[2] Year	U.S. Aid to FME	Planned Investment	a. as % of b.
1948	104	317.7	33%
1949	225.7	453.5	50%
1950	155.1	509.6	30%

Source: Commissariat du Plan, *Rapport Annuel*, 1952. (Paris, 1953). Tables 29 and 33, pp. 78, 84.
* 'Billion is used throughout this study as thousand million, like the French '*milliard*'.
FME: Fonds de Modernisation et d'Equipement.
See also, *ibid.*, p. 84, on extent of Marshall Plan aid.

[3] *ECA:* European Co-operation Administration, the administrative agency of the Marshall Plan. On reason for extending the plan, see *Le Monde*, 20 Oct. 1953, p. 10; *Rapport Annuel*, 1952, p. 3.

[4] See Table III, below. To column two of that table, add (sector by sector) actual investment achieved in 1947–48; (for that information, see *Rapport Annuel*, 1951) Compare the horizontal total with column one of Table I for a rough appreciation of the extent of target revision. See also, Clough, S.,

The revised version of the plan emphasized the planners' basic ordering of priorities: investment was even more heavily concentrated in the basic sectors. As Table III shows, investment credits were reduced in some sectors more than others, and in some sectors they were actually increased, both in terms of quantities of funds at constant prices and as a percentage of total investment. Investment in coal production increased from 56.5 billion 1946 francs for the original four year period, 1947–50, to 88 billion 1946 francs for the four-year period 1949–52, an increase of 56% in volume; and it more than doubled as a proportion of total planned investment. Electricity received a constant proportion of investment credits. Energy as a whole increased from just under 1/4th of total investment to just above 1/3rd. Transport too received a slightly larger chunk of the investment budget. Agriculture however was cut – heavily. Originally scheduled to receive 357 billion 1946 francs for the four-year period 1947–50, the revised version of the plan allotted only 183 billions to agriculture for the four-year period 1949–52, a reduction of fifty per cent. Credits for the manufacturing industries were similarly slashed: the revised plan reduced investment credits by fifty-five per cent. And as we shall see below, housing was cut back most of all, although no figures are given in the 1948 report (or in any other planning document) for a housing programme in the years 1949–52.[1]

In brief, the heavy priority that the Monnet planners assigned to investment for the modernisation and development of the small core of basic industrial sectors is evident from the targets of the original plan. In 1948 the planned investment pro-programme had to be reduced and the revision of the plan emphatically reinforced the planners' basic ordering of priorities.

'Economic Planning in France', *Political Science Quarterly*, December 1956, p. 547; Lubell, 'Two French Inflations', p. 55–56, and Baum, *French Economy*, p. 24.

[1] I could find no numerical estimate for a housing programme to replace that of the original 1946 version of the plan in any of the documents supporting the 1948 *Réponse Française*, or in the 1949, 1952, 1953 reports of the plan. Consequently I requested a staff official at the planning commission to try to find such a figure for me. He wrote back, in a letter dated 5 mars 1964, 'Je n'ai pu retrouver trace de l'objectif d'investissements pour la branche 'bâtiment et travaux publics' dans les comptes rendus d'exécution.' The problem of the planned housing programme is discussed below, pp. 104–9.

TABLE III

COMPARISON OF FOUR-YEAR INVESTMENT TARGETS OF NOVEMBER 1946 AND 1948, BY SECTOR.*

Investment Targets (Billions June 1946 francs)

Sectors	Monnet Plan of Nov. 1946 for 1947–50	1948 OEEC revision for 1949–52	% variation OEEC/ Monnet Plan	% Monnet Plan 1946 Total investment	OEEC 1948 % of total investment
Coal	56.5	88	+56%	4.6%	11.3%
Electricity	198	126	−37%	16%	16%
Gas	—	11.8	—	—	1.5%
Fuels	40	42.4	+6%	3.3%	5.4%
Total Energy	294.5	268.2	19%	23.9%	35%
Railways	125	85	−30%	10%	11.3%
Merchant Marine	85	71	—	6.9%	9.1%
Inland Waterways	20	5	—	—	—
Total Basic Transportation	230	164	−29%	18.6%	21%
Agriculture (including agricultural machinery and fertilizers)	357**	183	−50%	29%	23.5%
Steel	33	35.5	+8%	2.7%	4.6%
Cement, construction material	33.5	128.5	−55%	2.7%	16.5%
All other industries	285			23%	
Housing	660	***			
Urban equipment and transport	363				
Total all sectors	2250				

Source: Conseil Economique, *J.O.*, *Avis et Rapports du Conseil Economique*, 27 janvier 1951, Table II, p. 9. Also printed in Conseil Economique, *Etudes et Travaux*, no. 7, Annex, p. 29.

* Figures are for net investment in Metropolitan France. Military 'investment' is not included. For industries not represented by a Modernisation Commission figures are 'provisional estimates' [1st Plan, p. 85]. A list of Modernisation Commission is provided in the Appendix to 1st Plan.

** Of which 192 billion for Agricultural Machinery; cf. First Plan, p. 160.

*** See footnote 1, p. 89.

9 INFLATION AND PRIORITIES

Choosing targets for the first plan was expected to be a simple job. To the Monnet planners what had to be done seemed clear, straight-forward and urgent. A new and modern economy had to be built to replace the archaic methods, obsolete machines and discredited ideas of the inter-war period. To these men, no other long-term goal was thinkable; no other priority for immediate action tolerable.

At the same time, they were confronted by a short-term situation of scarcity and run-away inflation. Between January 1945 and December 1948, the wholesale price index rose by about eight hundred per cent,[1] and the wholesale price index is a conservative indicator of the degree of price inflation; it does not take into account black-market prices, which were important in the 1945–8 period, and often as much as two or three times the official price.

The inflation complicated target choice. It forced the realisation that the plan was essentially a list of priorities, and that considerable disagreement about the ordering of those priorities was possible. It pulverized the broad consensus that was expected to form behind the plan's choice of 'imperative targets', as each group multiplied its pressures on the government for immediate aid and protection.

The inflation emphasised the potential conflict between the demands of the heavy, long-term investment programme of the

[1] See Ministère des Finances, *Inventaire de la Situation Financière*, 1951, p. 144, for 1946–48 prices: INSEE, *Bulletin de la Statistique Générale de la France*, 1945–46, for 1945. Also INSEE, *Mouvement Economique en France de* 1944 *à* 1957 for the entire period beginning in April 1945. In all cases the estimates are only very approximate. Weights were constantly being changed; ministers were manipulating the indices for their own purposes, and as the *ECA* warns users of the *France, Data Book* (1951) p. 34, 'the data used reflect official prices, and do not include black market prices. These are probably too low for that reason.' Thus an eight hundred per cent price increase can be considered to be a most conservative estimate. Dilbert Snider discusses black market prices and the official price index in *American Economic Review*, June 1948, p. 318.

plan and the immediate demands of economic stability, balance and equity. As it continued, the choice of targets became increasingly the sacrifice of stability and equity for future growth.

A succession of insecure governments quickly proved unable to effect the fiscal reforms, monetary policies and direct controls which were a minimal pre-condition for undertaking the planned investment programme without further accelerating the inflation. One government after another from De Gaulle through Blum, via Bidault, filled the press and the parliamentary record with exhortations (varying only in eloquence): fiscal reform, mopping up ill-gotten gains, and price-wage pauses were the by-words. They tinkered with direct controls, price freezes, wage freezes, propaganda campaigns, bond issues, and currency reforms at the same time as the political pressures generated by the inflation squeezed out of them higher prices, higher wages, higher pensions, higher subsidies and higher military expenditures.[1]

The ineffectiveness of the governments fed back into the planners' initial problem of conflicting long-term and short-term objectives, forcing them to realize that the price of the investment programme and increased inflation would be continued.

The inflation had its roots in the economic legacy of the war: a scarcity of buyable goods, a crippled industrial plant, and a vast supply of stored-up liquidity.

In May 1945, industrial capacity was about 40 per cent of the 1938 level (itself a depression year).[2]

During the war the occupying power and the Vichy government had been pumping liquidity into the economy. Between 1938 and 1945 the money supply increased from 192 billion francs to 1,013 billions.[3]

The inflation was nourished by indecision and impotence in government, by a frenzied effort to 'catch up' by labour, by large scale inventory speculation, by heavy demands by and for

[1] See the following works for descriptions of the various unsuccessful attempts to stop inflation: Chapsal, *et. al.*, *op. cit.*, pp. 717–727; Dilbert Snider in *AER*, *passim*; John Sheahan, 'Problems and Possibilities of Industrial Price Controls: Postwar French Experience', *American Economic Review*, June 1961, pp. 345–348; Paul Delouvrier, *Politique Economique de la France*, Cours fait à l'Institut d'Etudes Politiques 1957–1958, pp. 165–169, 219–225; Baum, *French Economy . . .*, pp. 43–65; and Lubell, *Two French Inflations*, Part I.

[2] Ministère des Finances, *Inventaire de la Situation Financière*, Paris 1951, Annex C, p. 117.

[3] *Ibid.*, Annex IV, I. D., pp. 524-525.

the military and by a calculated decision on priorities on the part of the planners.

The governments ran persistent and heavy budget deficits averaging one-third to two-thirds of total budgetary expenditures.[1]

War-time inflation created a fundamental disequilibrium in the distribution of purchasing power: 'Wages had been systematically kept at an abnormally low level by the occupying power and the Vichy government';[2] and the working classes awaited liberation with its implicit and explicit promise of 'catching up'.[3]

They never did catch up, although they tried; wages continued to lag behind skyrocketing prices. From 1946 to 1949 prices rose by just over four hundred per cent, while wages rose by less than three hundred per cent.

*Wholesale Price Index** 1938 = 100		*Hourly Wage Index* Jan. 1946 = 100	
1946		1946	
Jan.	479	Jan.	100
Apr.	559	Apr.	104
July	571	July	111
Sept.	727	Sept.	138
1947		1947	
Jan.	874	Jan.	143
Apr.	—	Apr.	147
Sept.	1096	Sept.	179
Dec.	1217		
1948		1948	
Feb.	1537	Feb.	239
Apr.	1555	Apr.	246
July	1698	July	249
1949		1949	
Jan.	1946	Jan.	287

* *Source:* Ministère des Finances, *Inventaire de la Situation Financière*, (1951), p. 144 for the price index; p. 148 for the wage index. Neither index is very reliable. See INSEE, *Mouvement Economique* 1944–1957, pp. 107–123, for a detailed discussion of price-wage movements.

The continuing disequilibria in purchasing power soon

[1] ECA: *France, Data Book*, 1951, p. 5.

[2] Rist, Charles, 'The French Financial Dilemma', *Foreign Affairs*, April 1947, p. 453. Averill Harriman makes a similar statement in *Le Monde*, 16 March 1952, p. 5.

[3] On the explicit promise, see Baum, *French Economy*, p. 48; Paul Delouvrier, *Politique Economique de la France*, Cours de l'I.E.P., 1957–58, Paris, Les Cours de Droit, 1958, pp. 142–145.

became an almost independent motor of the inflation. R.V. Roosa, a high-ranking official of the US Treasury called attention to this problem:

> One of the several cumulative forces behind the continued inflation grows out of the distortion of income distribution, which, though initially a result of the inflation itself, has acquired an independent causal force in accelerating the inflationary process . . . Wages and salaries have continued to lag behind prices and . . . profits.[1]

Liberation restored great power status to France: General de Gaulle insisted on a heavy military budget, 'to create the active army he should have possessed at the beginning of the war. His aim seemed to re-establish the prestige of France in the eyes not so much of the beaten enemy as in those of her allies',[2] and perhaps in her own eyes. Such prestige was expensive; by 1946 France had 1,800,000 men in the armed services[3] and a runaway inflation. The Economic Council, as well as lesser bodies and numerous individuals, warned that 'the nation cannot support both the financial burden of the re-armament programme and that of the investment programme at the same time: it must choose . . . between re-armament and investment'.[4]

The planners pushed for their investment programme which channeled about twenty-five per cent of national income into investment, for the most part into long-term projects such as steel mills, cement plants, tractor factories, and most prominently, high-dam hydro-electric power stations.

In September 1944, General de Gaulle delivered a speech on the problem of inflation which called for courage, discipline, self-sacrifice, organisation, work, and strength. As the director of the Institut d'Etudes Politiques remarked: 'His resolute language explained very well what it would have been necessary to do, and not less well what was not done.'[5]

The General's rhetoric was a stirring preface to a dazzling display of insecurity and ineptitude: an all-out inflation ensued

[1] R. V. Roosa, 'The Problem of French Recovery', *The Economic Journal*, June 1949, p. 156.

[2] Rist, *French Financial Dilemma*, p. 452.

[3] *Ibid*, p. 452.

[4] Conseil Economique, *Etudes et Travaux*, no. 7, p. 5. See also *Le Monde*, 1 Jan. 1952, p. 5.

[5] Chapsal, *et. al.*, *France Depuis* 1945, p. 518.

as the Governments (including his own) could not initiate effective programmes of fiscal reform and monetary austerity. Again and again the planners watched a new Government conjure up ghastly images of the evils of inflation and then fail to do anything to halt the inflation. Repetitions of this routine convinced the planners that the governments could not halt the inflation and that they would have to fit their investment programmes to a continuing inflationary gyre.

ONE EXEMPLARY FAILURE

In 1944 the provisional Government, anxious to establish its authority, quickly granted the vociferously demanded wage increase which had been promised by the Resistance before Liberation. A price-freeze was instituted, but commodity shortages and excess liquidity brought on increased black market activity which circumvented the officially frozen prices. In November of that year the Government tried to cash in on patriotic fervour and launched a great bond issue – *l'Emprunt de la Libération* – with massive publicity hammering home a flattering theme of sacrifice and patriotism. The money taken in went into a special account at the Treasury, but immediately returned to circulation as partial cover for the running current deficit. A proposed currency reform modelled on the Belgian experience of October 1944 was potentially the most important of these unsuccessful efforts at halting the inflation; it was also the most exemplary. At the beginning of 1945, the Ministry of the National Economy (under the direction of Pierre Mendès France) proposed to call in all bank notes and exchange them against new notes. The issuing of new notes, however, would be phased over an extended period, thus freezing part of the over-liquid supply of purchasing power. Long and heated debate followed, centering around the crucial question of the 'freeze'. Supporting the motion was the Socialist bloc, led and personified by Mendès France (then a near Radical). Against it were the Conservative parties led by René Pleven (the Minister of Finance) which were anxious not to lose the peasant vote in the coming elections, and the Communists who were hoping to gain peasant support. (The Communists were not yet 'in opposition'.) The Conservative-Communist coalition prevailed and in June 1945 bank notes were called in, to be exchanged for newly issued notes without the *blocage* (freeze).[1] The decision on the currency reform was a sacrifice of the best opportunity to mop up the stored-up liquidity – one of the principal motors of the inflation – for the support of the peasant vote. Subsequent efforts by the Governments to mop up the excess liquidity and hold back the inflation were futile, but numerous. They tried rationing, meat requisitioning, price freezes, wage freezes, bond issues, and producer subsidies.

THE PLANNERS' STRATEGY

The planners learned the lesson. Examination of the investment projects undertaken in the framework of the plan leaves one with the strong impression that the planners tended to accept continuing inflation as an unalterable condition – an unfortunate by-product of an unfortunate political situation. They abandoned all serious hopes of influencing the Government's management of short-term economic policy and concentrated their efforts on their programmes of long-range industrial development and modernisation, treating the inflationary effects of their projects as very secondary considerations. Some conversation with the Monnet planners strongly re-enforces that impression.[2]

They were, nonetheless, obliged to prepare and to defend their investment programme (representing about twenty-five

[1] On the currency reform, and the subsequent efforts to halt the inflation see Chapsal, *et. al.*, *France Depuis* 1945, pp. 717–727; Paul Delouvrier, *Politique Economique*, pp. 161–169; Lubell, *Two French Inflations*, Part I; D. Pickles, *French Politics*, London RIIA, 1953, pp. 57–69; Snider, in *AER*, p. 318.

The decision on the currency reform was also an important turning point in the intra-bureaucracy struggle between the Treasury and the Ministry of the National Economy (discussed above, pp. 37–9). It put an end to the Ministry of the National Economy's ambitions to become a super-ministry of the economy and subordinate the Treasury to its own programmes. Shortly thereafter, Mendès France resigned, not to return to a ministerial position for a decade. (His letter of resignation is reproduced in J. Fauvet, *La IVe République*, Paris, Fayard, pp. 363–368). The important functions of the Ministry of the National Economy were taken over by the Treasury, except for the planning function, which was passed on the soon-to-be-created Planning Commission. On the Communists' courting of the peasant vote, see *La Terre*, nos. 1–5, Oct. 1944, and *Humanité*, 30 June 1945. The peasants, it was thought, had vast quantities of currency hidden in their *lessiveuses*.

[2] Paul Delouvrier, one of Monnet's original team, later remarked: 'the plan was prepared with too little attention to the general equilibrium. . . . We were satisfied with rather vague views on its financing.' *Politique Economique de la France*, p. 198.

per cent of national income) in terms of its impact on an inflationary economy. This defence was based on the planners' analysis of the causes of the inflation. It was partially successful: many of the plan's projects, conceived essentially to promote long-term growth, were successfully defended as anti-inflationary measures. Where justification of the investment programmes as a co-ordinated set of anti-inflationary actions was not possible, the planners were forced back to a straight-forward value judgment: priority must be given to long-term industrial development over any consideration of its effects on the inflation.

In this manner, the plan's strategy for dealing with the shorter-term problem of the inflation, was blended into the original long-term programme of a heavy investment effort concentrated in a few key industries that were actual or potential bottlenecks to increased production.

In the planners' analysis, the key to the inflationary situation was on the supply side: the broken-down industrial plant incapable of turning out the necessary quantities of goods. The only way to overcome this basic cause of inflation was to stress the investment programme – at all temporary costs – so as to create in the future an industrial plant able to mass-produce a flow of buyable goods.[1]

They did not dismiss the importance of action on the demand side. The planners repeatedly called for the end of the large and persistent Government budget deficits, for fiscal reforms, and for rigorous enforcement of direct controls.[2] But the lasting solution, they felt, lay in overcoming supply bottlenecks. Furthermore, the planners were convinced that the supply side was where there was the greatest possibility of actually getting something done. They were convinced that without a rigorous anti-inflation programme the inflation would continue – even if the investment plan were cut – and that such a programme would not be implemented.

The planners analysis of the basic causes of the inflation (supply bottlenecks) was a clever and quite legitimate way to offer the nation the long-term investment programme, as both

[1] See *Rapport Annuel*, 1952, pp. 86–90. Harold Lubell, 'The Role of Investment in Two French Inflations', *Oxford Economic Papers*, Vol. 7, no. 1, NS, Feb. 1955, offers the best exposition of the planners' analysis of the causes and cures of the 1945–1948 inflation. See also Paul Delouvrier, *Politique Economique de la France*, p. 89.

[2] See *First Plan*, pp. 89, 107, and Monnet's cover letter for the first plan.

the best long-term policy and the best short-term policy. Events soon appeared to give additional support to this thesis.

THE END OF THE INFLATION

In December 1948, the wholesale price index began to fall. In November 1948 it had reached 1,977 (1938 = 100). By December 1948 it had stopped climbing and fell to 1,974, and by June 1949 it was down to 1,812.[1]

The fall in the price index (and the concurrent stability in the wage index)[2] is often attributed to abrupt changes on the supply side: a sudden increase in buyable goods. This increase in buyable goods was due to the investment undertaken immediately after Liberation and to the 'normal ripening' of the production process, i.e., repairs of war-damaged plants had been completed and goods were coming out of every stage of the production process in steady flows.[3]

Even though an eight hundred per cent price inflation had, by itself, sterilised the liquidity stored up under Vichy, and a devaluation and a reduced ratio of deficit to budgetary expenditures had helped to alleviate some of the inflationary pressures, Uri's analysis seems quite defensible in its essentials: buyable goods did become more plentiful in 1948.[4]

If the end of the first post-war inflation can, in some measure, be attributed to an increase in the supplies of buyable goods, the relationship between the plan and that increase is less certain. (a) The greater part of the increase in output came from sectors rather removed from the plan's targets, and for reasons difficult to attribute to the plan's programmes, and (b) many of the plan's heaviest investment programmes were clearly not aimed at maximizing the outflow of buyable goods in so short a time.

The 'decisive element' came from the agricultural sector when

[1] *Inventaire de la Situation Financière*, p. 144.

[2] *Ibid.*. p. 148.

[3] See INSEE, *Mouvement Economique*, 1944–1957, (Paris, 1958), pp. 121–123; Lubell, *Two French Inflations*, pp. 47–52; Baum, *The French Economy*, pp. 65–66; Pierre Uri is most closely associated with the normal 'ripening of production' argument; see 'L'Evolution de l'Economie Française Jugée par la Théorie Moderne', *Réalitiés* (Economiques), Paris, December 1950.

[4] On the end of the first post-war inflation, see Lubell, 'Two French Inflations', Baum, *The French Economy*, pp. 58–65; Snider, in AER; Chapsal, *France Depuis 1945 . . .*, pp. 720–727; *Mouvement Economique*, 1944–1957, p. 67.

the excellent harvest of 1948 reached the markets.[1] 1948 was a rich harvest – equal to pre-war levels; 1946 was a poor year, and 1947 was disastrous. The 1947 wheat harvest was less than half that of 1946 and about forty per cent of pre-war levels.[2]

Total Agricultural Production[3]
(1938 = 100)

1946	84
1947	75
1948	96
1949	95

The most important factor in this abrupt change in agricultural output was the weather.[4]

It would be an extremely difficult task to defend the choice of investment projects in the Monnet plan as efforts to remove bottlenecks in the short-run supply of buyable goods. For this was certainly not the primary objective of many of the major investment projects in the plan. The most conspicuous instance was the heavy programme for hydro-electric power stations. Investment in hydro-electric stations was five times as great as investment in thermal stations, the principal alternative source of power.[5]

In view of the urgent need for investment and the acute shortage of capital in the reconstruction period, it is extremely doubtful whether any benefit-cost analysis of the two alternatives, using reasonable interest rates, would justify the immediate construction of hydro stations. Such calculations, however, do not seem to have been made; post mortem debates contain no references to any study of alternatives.[6]

Similarly, one can argue that the Plan 'over-developed' the basic sectors – especially railways and the coal industry – at

[1] INSEE, *Mouvement Economique*, 1944–1957, p. 67.
[2] *Mouvement Economique*, p. 67.
[3] *Inventaire de la Situation Financière*, p. 128.
[4] *Ibid.*, p. 67.
[5] *Rapport Annuel*, 1951, p. 92.
[6] Sheahan, *Promotion and Control*, pp. 165–167, is by far the best short treatment of the hydro-electric case. I have drawn heavily on his argument. See also Baum, *French Economy*, pp. 197–200; M. Maillet-Chassanage, *L'Influence de la Nationalisation sur la Gestion des Entreprises Publiques*, Paris, 1956, p. 200; and Gabriel Taix, *Le Plan Monnet, est-il une Réussite?* Paris, 1953, pp. 83–84. (Taix's book is a rather curious right-wing critique of the plan.)

the expense of housing, manufacturing and agriculture.[1] The 'over-allocation' of scarce investment resources to certain industries may be partially explained by the way the plan was assembled, especially by the absence of any systematic studies of alternative uses. But the case of Electricité de France, where productive capacity lagged behind demand for electric power while an enormous volume of planned investment went into 'the ultimate capital-intense method, hydroelectrical power derived from high dam, large reservoir systems',[2] can only be explained (without accusing the planners of gross incompetence and stopping there), by assuming that the planners treated the effects of their investment projects on the inflation as a very secondary consideration. The plan's extensive programme of railway electrification, in a time of capital scarcity and electricity shortages, is another of the plan's investment projects which has clearly not conceived as an anti-inflation measure.[3]

Many observers have called the plan a primary motor of the inflation. R.V. Roosa provides a summary statement of this view:

> . . . the basic reason for the continuance of inflation after 1947 has been the French attempt to impose an ambitious programme of new investment (the Monnet Plan) upon her economy, without accepting forthrightly the sacrifices, in voluntary or compulsory saving, which such a programme implies. . . . Instead of rationing their limited resources through direct controls, or of rationing in effect, through heavy taxation . . . the French chose to do their rationing by means of raising prices. . . . M. Monnet . . . had repeatedly insisted that his plan must be financed from current income stream. Successive governments have agreed in principle without successfully raising revenues or reducing other expenditures. Meanwhile . . . the Monnet plan has gone on steadily demanding more resources than could be made available under existing taxation and savings patterns, without resort to inflationary credit expansion.[4]

The plan was a deliberate choice for financing the investment programme by inflation. But that choice was made only after the planners had become convinced that the governments

[1] See Baum, *The French Economy*, pp. 37, 192; Sheahan, *Promotion and Control*, p. 195.

[2] Sheahan, *Promotion and Control*, p. 195.

[3] See *First Plan*, p. 49.

[4] Roosa, 'French Recovery', pp. 155, 156, 157.

lacked the courage (or the power that gives courage) to stop the inflation and finance the desperately needed investment and modernisation programme by more equitable means. Indeed, the planners could reasonably believe that the inflation would have continued even without the investment programme.

SUPPORT FOR THE PLAN

From the very beginning the Monnet planners made no serious attempts to influence short-term economic policy. They concentrated all their efforts on their long-term investment and modernisation programmes. But the inflationary thrust of those programmes brought them into conflict with the Governments and the powerful permanent staff of the Treasury which were trying to halt the inflation. As we have seen, these attempts to control the inflation were overcome by the political power of various groups: the power of the peasant vote blocked the currency reform; the power of the trade unions and the Left-of-Centre parties kept wages rising; the power of the military lobby won a heavy military budget. The obvious question is: what powers supported the plan? What forces kept the plan's long-term investment programmes from being slashed as the Treasury searched for some area to cut expenditures? At that time the Treasury officials were the plan's enemies – its most powerful enemies; only years later were they to become its allies.[1] The enthusiastic support of the CGT (the largest trade union, Communist affiliated) ended in 1947, when the cold war put the CGT in opposition to the plan.[2] The CFTC, the FO, the Left-of-Centre parties and certain of the new 'technocrats' in the Treasury could all be counted on for some support, but not for sustained, dedicated support: they had their own immediate interests to protect. The plan could count on the dedicated support of the industries that were particularly benefitting from its programmes, the basic sectors. But the fact of the matter is that the Monnet planners' most powerful support in their struggles to maintain their investment programmes came from foreigners, from the administrators of the Marshall Plan.

The problem here is proof. There are no published documents

[1] See above, Part II, Chapter 4.
[2] See below, pp. 123–4.

that support this assertion.[1] There are no facts which can be arranged to demonstrate that within the upper ranks of the French governmental structure there was a widespread conviction that the Monnet office had the support of the Marshall Plan and was the most useful point of contact with the Marshall Plan administration.

The assumption that within the upper ranks of the civil service it was widely believed that the Monnet office had the ear, and the active support, of the Marshall Plan administration helps to explain how the Monnet Plan was able to insulate its investment programmes from the short-term economic situation and from political events. This assumption helps to understand the prominence and influence, quite out of proportion to its own power, that the Monnet Office maintained within the Governmental structure. And it helps to appreciate the problems Monnet's successors encountered when they had to carry on without the support of the Marshall Plan.

It is a useful assumption. But the only available proof comes from the interviews discussed in the introduction, and from the inadequacy of alternative explanations of the sources of Monnet's influence. Several people closely associated with the original Monnet office spoke of the Marshall Plan when questioned about the sources of that office's influence. Similarly, several Treasury officials, who held ranking posts at the time of the Monnet plan, explained what seemed to be the mysterious force of the Monnet office, in terms of the impression that Monnet gave of having the complete support of the Marshall Plan administration – support that extended directly to Washington. Repeatedly the interviews presented the same pattern. The source of Monnet's influence was questioned. The initial reply referred to his extraordinary personal qualities – his ability to stay people's opposition, to change their opinions, to recruit their talents. Eventually, however, when asked if Monnet had any powerful support, they referred to the influence of the Marshall Plan. They explained that many people,

[1] Secondary sources are of no help either. None provides evidence. None provides even the dubious comfort of concurring opinion. None of the secondary sources cited in the bibliography refers to the Marshall plan's support of the Monnet office. None even raises the question of where the Monnet office derived its influence – at least, not to levels beyond repeated references to its dynamism, intellectual acumen and political neutrality – which do not make for a totally satisfying explanation.

especially at the Treasury, viewed the Monnet office as the principal link with the Marshall Plan and with Washington. They pointed out that in their own dealings with the Marshall Plan administration, they often worked through Monnet's office.

10 PRIORITIES THREE: *Housing*

This time it vanished quite slowly, beginning at the end of the tail, and ending with the grin, which remained some time after the rest of it had gone.

(Lewis Carroll, *Alice in Wonderland*)

Another pressing economic problem of the early post-war period that illustrates the planners' ordering of priorities is the housing problem – which competed with the investment programme for scarce resources.

In the late 'forties, the housing shortage in France was critical: the Monnet plan estimated that about two million dwellings had been damaged or destroyed by the war;[1] the average age of the remaining French dwellings in 1945 was estimated at sixty years.[2] The population was growing, and a massive population shift from the countryside into the cities added further urgency to the already critical situation.[3]

The plan, however, did not contain any detailed programme for housing that was comparable to the plan's schedules for industrial reconstruction and development. The *Conseil Economique* maintained that the absence of a clearly-defined, long-range programme for housing was one of the 'serious gaps in the targets of the Plan'.[4] Though lacking in detailed discussion the plan's programme for housing was quite explicit. It stated that 'a hierarchy of objectives must be established for the uses of scarce resources, especially steel and cement', and that housing must necessarily yield precedence to the 'imperative' targets of the plan – the industrial development and modernisation programme.[5] Residential construction was given priority

[1] The Monnet Plan, p. 11.
[2] *Rapport Annuel*, 1952, (Dec. '52), p. 11.
[3] INSEE, *Mouvement Economique*, 1944–1957, p. 34.
[4] *J.O., Avis et Rapports du Conseil Economique*, 27 Jan. 1951, p6. .
[5] *Monnet Plan*, p. 27.

only where it was necessary to house workers employed in the 'basic sectors' – in other words, only when housing could be considered a necessary part of the industrial development programme.[1]

Nonetheless, the 1946 draft of the plan allotted 660 billion francs to the construction and reconstruction of housing and public works, out of a projected investment of 2,250 billions – or 29.3%.[2] The plan called for the reconstruction or repair of two million lodgings by 1950, plus the construction of half a million new urban lodgings by that same date.[3] It was, perhaps, a smaller programme than some wanted,[4] but it was certainly not an indefensible programme in terms of a responsible ordering of reconstruction priorities. Indeed, it was surprisingly generous, in view of the Plan's repeated apologies and justifications for postponing an attack on the housing shortage until industrial recovery had been achieved.[5] (Recovery must be taken to include 'development and modernisation', that is, something more than just the 1938 level of industrial production.)

Most important, however, the housing programme was a paper programme, and the paper houses depreciated even more rapidly than the paper money that was to pay for them. By 1950, instead of half a million new housing units, only 174,000 had been built;[6] instead of two million reconstructed or repaired lodgings, 789,715 were actually repaired or rebuilt.[7] It was not simply a question of underestimating real per-unit costs. The money was never allotted: actual investment in housing between 1947 and 1950 (in constant prices) amounted to 234 billion francs, or one-third of the originally planned 660 billions.[8] The contrast with industrial sectors such as steel or coal is striking. For the same time period, actual investment in steel was one hundred and eleven per cent of the plan's original target; and in coal, one hundred and twenty-nine per cent.[9]

[1] *Ibid.*, p. 28.
[2] *Ibid.*, p. 86, Table XX.
[3] *Ibid.*, p. 61.
[4] *J.O.*, *Conseil Economique*, 27 Jan. 1951, p. 6.
[5] *Monnet Plan*, p. 28.
[6] ECA, *France*, *Data Book*, (1951), Table b–2, p. 19.
[7] *Ibid.*, p. 19.
[8] *J.O.*, *Conseil Economique*, 27 Jan. 1951, p. 12.
[9] *Ibid.*, p. 12–13.

The most satisfying explanation of why the houses were not built is also the simplest: the state and the planners attached a lower priority to housing than to long-term industrial development and modernisation.

Thus, in 1948, when the time came to cut back the plan's targets, the planners were willing to take the biggest cuts out of housing. They fought with the Ministries to maintain investment outlays in basic industrial sectors (including the high dams and railway electrification), – and were largely successful in that fight. But they abandoned the housing programme.[1]

The pattern has not changed very much since the first plan. Each plan contained the kind of housing programme that representative bodies such as the *Conseil Economique* found a bit too frugal, but not intolerable.[2] Then, several years later, the *Conseil Economique* and the news-in-depth journalists (of more or less Centrist political orientation) are surprised that the housing programme was drastically under-achieved. The news analysts offer deep-probing explanations of why the programmes were not realised, often concluding with a tirade against the 'archaic and anarchic' methods of the building trades. Education, meat, and telephones follow similar syndromes. After each plan, the French press is filled with articles analysing why so many of the Paris schools still do not have central heating, and why a course at the Sorbonne bears a strong physical resemblance to a learned lecture in the Metro at rush-hour, and why the French '*Gouamba*' (an African word meaning meat-hunger) is still unsatisfied.[3]

The ambitious (660 billion francs) housing programme of the original 1946 Monnet plan was under-achieved because immediately after it was written into the plan, it was considered unrealisable. Whether the housing programme was originally drawn up in the good but innocent expectation of realisation, or cynically sketched into the plan to trump the opposition is

[1] *J.O., Conseil Economique* 27 Jan. 1951, p. 13.

[2] See *J.O., Avis et Rapports du Conseil Economique*, 3 août 1954, p. 658; 28 fév. 1959; 12 déc. 1962, p. 1113. See Also *Le Monde*, 13 déc. 1952, p. 6; 4 fév. 1953, p. 10; 2 juin 1953, p. 1; 17 juillet 1953, p. 10; 1 juillet 1953, p. 14; 30 oct. 1965, p. 20.

[3] 'Archaic and anarchic' is from Alfred Sauvy, who provides a good example of this kind of reporting in *Le Monde*, 7–8 juin 1964, p. 7. See also *Le Monde*, 27 Sept. 1953, p. 1; *Entreprise*, 18 juillet 1964, pp. 26–28; *Cahiers des Amis de la Liberté*, Nos. 41, 42, 43, 1955; and *Etudes et Conjoncture*, issue of Oct.-Nov. 1957.

largely a speculative pursuit.[1] But when the time came to reconcile the original targets of the plan to economic reality, (1948), the basic priority of the planners – the heavy concentration of resources on the development and modernisation of the basic industrial sectors – was re-emphasised more strongly than ever. Non-imperative targets were sliced down. Agriculture, manufacturing, and housing were the principal non-imperatives. Of the three, housing was cut most vigorously. It was also cut out of the plan: no housing programme appears in the revised four year plan or in the supporting texts.[2] Its omission was, perhaps, prudent. There was not enough room under the inflation ceiling of the French economy for the investment programme, the armament programme and the housing programme.[3] At the same time, the Planning Commission, anxious to establish itself as a permanent institution, stood to gain very little by publishing what would necessarily be an unpopular housing programme (targeting one third of the original 1946 programme). Furthermore 1948 was a time of bitter political fighting, and the Communists were using the housing crisis, and their tactic of 'squatting' in temporarily vacated quarters, as an important vote-getting device.[4] There is, therefore, some basis for suspecting that the omission of a housing programme from the revised plan may not have been entirely a clerical error.

The under-achieved housing programme – the Cheshire cat smile of the Monnet plan – reveals the basic ordering of priorities that lay behind the text. In a time of optimism, (or if you prefer, as a sop to popular opinion), a serious housing programme may be written into the plan. But when inflation forces the Ministry of Finance to prune the plan (as often happens), it is the industrial development programme that the planners defend; housing is the first programme they sacrifice.

The housing programme provides some insight into the relation of the original planned targets to economic and political reality. The targets may well indicate what the planners would like to see, and also what they really expect to see. But if the plan must be modified during the course of its four-year life,

[1] See *J.O., Conseil Economique*, 27 Jan. 1951, p. 12.
[2] See above, pp. 89 footnote.
[3] See *Le Monde*, 1 jan. 1952, p. 5; 3 jan. 1952, p. 1
[4] *Le Monde*, 21 fév. 1952, p. 10.

the original planning document is only an approximate guide to what the planners will fight to save, and even less indicative of what the Ministry of Finance will agree to. Thus, an analysis of the effects of the plan on the economy, which strictly limits itself to determining the percentage realisation of the plan's original targets, is largely a futile and misleading exercise, irrelevant to the question of how French planning affects the economy. For the planners must always be ready to prepare a stripped-down version of the plan – when the Ministry of Finance begins a belt-tightening austerity programme as a short-run response to an inflationary situation. The pruned version of the first plan abandoned non-essentials, that is, everything not directly related to the development and reform of the nation's basic industrial plant. It abandoned the housing programme. It abandoned efforts to influence the short term economic situation and concentrated on promoting the long-term modernisation and development of the basic industrial plant, underneath short term ups and downs.

11 PRIORITIES FOUR:
Other criteria

The importance of an industry's product to industrial rehabilitation and development – and not the industry's structure, geographic location or political power – has been the only criterion for selecting the plan's targets discussed so far. This 'bottleneck approach' to target choice was by far the most important determinant of the targets of the first plan; it was not, however, the only one. Several other considerations influenced the planner's choice of targets, These secondary criteria are useful for explaining some of the more curious aspects of the first plan's targets; they are essential for analysis of the later plans, when the 'self-evident imperatives of reconstruction' had become less imperative and less self-evident.

The ease with which a plan can be drawn up and implemented for a given industry was the second consideration in selecting the targets of the Monnet plan.

The Monnet planners anticipated minimal difficulty in implementing the plan in the nationalised enterprises; the mere promulgation of the plan was assumed to be a binding order for its implementation in the nationalised sectors.[1] They expected to use the purchasing and pricing policies of the public sector as a 'fundamental instrument' for the modernisation of other industries – especially those for which the public sector constituted the principal client.[2]

The planners also anticipated minimal difficulty in *drawing up* a plan for the nationalised sectors. Three of the Monnet plan's six 'basic sectors' – electricity, coal, and railways – were nationalised monopolies. And a nationalised monopoly is the ideal industrial structure for the modernisation commission method. The planners would only have to deal with one 'firm', and they could assume, though perhaps mistakenly, that there

[1] *First Plan*, pp. 102–103.
[2] *Ibid.*, p. 103.

was no basic conflict of interest between that one nationalised firm and the national economic plan. Furthermore, these industries were run by men who personified the goals of the plan: e.g., Pierre Massé at *Electricité de France*,[1] and Louis Armand at the *SNCF*. These were the prototypal 'modern executives', who were in fundamental agreement with the planners on the need for rapid changes in the machinery, structures and methods of French industry. They understood and shared the planners ways of thinking – and their vocabulary. They had at their disposal advanced economic data, econometric techniques and skilled personnel, and knew how to use those tools. Few other firms were so well prepared – in terms of market structure and managerial methods – to participate in planning. The smaller enterprises, and the traditional French family firms, were largely ignorant and suspicious of these methods, and of planning.[2] Thus, the monopoly structures and progressive management of *EDF* and the *SNCF* – in addition to their nationalised statute – contributed to the planner's anticipation of minimal difficulty in drawing up the plan for these sectors.

Drawing up the plan turned out to be even easier than anticipated. *Electricité de France* and the *SNCF* came to the Planning Commission with detailed and comprehensive investment programmes already prepared. To a significant degree, planning in these sectors was conducted on the basis of their own draft programmes, and consisted in little more than enveloping them into the global plan.[3] [The hydro-electric programme, the electrification of the railways, and the 'over-investment' in coal, which were targeted in the first plan, might, to some degree, have been influenced by the fact that these programmes were

[1] The same Pierre Massé who later became the Director of the Planning Commission.

[2] See Gourney and Viot, 'Planificateurs et décisions . . .', pp. 3–4. David S. Landes, 'French Business and the Businessman, A Social and Cultural Analysis', in E. M. Earle, ed., *Modern France*, New York, 1951, pp. 334–353, describes the traditional family firm. On the methods of planning within a firm, and their relation to successful participation in the national plan, see *Entreprise*, 18 juillet 1964, pp. 37–39. See also, above, Part II, Chapter II, and below, Part V, Chapters I & II, for further discussion of the organisational and personal requirements for successful participation in planning.

[3] Lubell observed: 'in these industries [SNCF, EDF] detailed investment projects were already in existence on paper.' Harold Lubell, *The French Investment Plan: A Defence of the Monnet Plan*, Ph.D. thesis, Harvard, 1951, unpub. My own interviews support Lubell's findings.

prepared by the management of those nationalised industries prior to the preparation of the national plan.]

The non-nationalised industries stressed in the first plan shared important structural similarities: steel, cement, basic chemicals, agricultural machinery and synthetic fertilizers are all highly concentrated industries.[1] They are also industries in which management is fairly sophisticated; long-term planning is practiced within the firm. The planners would prepare a modernisation and development programme for such sectors by dealing with only a few people, and could anticipate enough technical sophistication on their part to make the preparation of a plan for that industry possible.

Lastly, successful participation in French style economic planning depends, to a certain extent, on the personal qualities of an industry's representative. He must be an '*interlocuteur valable*' – like Louis Armand or Pierre Massé or Paul Huevlin – who can work with the planners and Treasury officials who understands their aims, methods and vocabulary, and, preferably, who knows them personally. In the intimate and informal dealings of French planning, such 'accomplishments' are crucial, and they work against small and medium size firms just as they work against the trade unions.[2]

Hence,

> The real reason why [the steel industry] can be readily planned and the [textile industry] not, is that the steelmasters are few and powerful; once you have half a dozen of them round a table, you can make an agreement which will determine the shape of the industry, with some precision, for a period of years ahead. Moreover, in such an encounter the government planners are dealing with industrialists who are equipped with the fairly sophisticated apparatus that is required nowadays to take a long-range view of industrial prospects, and even more important, to adapt it intelligently, as circumstances change.[3]

Similar consideration influenced the curious agricultural programme of the Monnet plan – a programme confined to agricultural machinery and synthetic fertilizer plants, which avoided more direct involvement in agriculture.

[1] See Jacques Houssiaux, *Le Pouvoir de Monopole*, Paris, 1955, pp. 226, 228, 209–250; *Entreprise*, 22 Sept. 1962, cover article.

[2] This subject is discussed in some detail above, Part I, Chapter I; Part II, Chapter II; and below Part VI, Chapters I & II.

[3] Andrew Shonfield, *The Listener*, 13 Dec. 1962, p. 992.

The Monnet Plan did not concern itself directly with agriculture because agriculture is a much too dispersed sector in which the number of firms is very large and the entrepreneurs act for highly individual motives. Direct and systematic control is therefore impossible. The plan consequently concentrated on one of the necessary means for the modernisation of agriculture: agricultural machinery.[1]

And the same analysis could be applied to the very important case of the machine-tool industry, the low-concentration sector which constituted perhaps, the most crippling bottleneck to French economic development.[2]

OTHER SECONDARY CRITERIA

A guiding objective for a planning agency that seeks to establish itself as a permanent institution, is to survive; it should avoid programmes which may lead to its own annihilation at the hands of the powerful. The Monnet plan, unlike the *Ministère de l'Economie Nationale*, accepted the supremacy of the Ministry of Finance right from the beginning: to challenge it was to risk destruction. The plan's decision to approach agriculture so indirectly, reflects the same well-developed instinct for survival.

The agricultural problem of marginal producers, byzantine subsidies, medieval land tenure – all kept alive in a hothouse of infinitely complicated protectionism – was an economic rationaliser's dream-playground. But the political forces that would have been stirred up by any systematic effort to rationalise the agricultural muddle, could well have destroyed the Planning Commission; along with a frontal assault on the Ministry of Finance, a serious attempt at rationalising agriculture would have been one of the surer ways to jeopardize the continued existence of the plan. The planners stayed far away from these political pitfalls – confining their agricultural programme to promoting the production of more chemical fertilizer and more tractors..

This tendency to avoid politically dangerous areas has been a marked characteristic of the Planning Commission throughout its twenty year history. It colours the curious relations of the

[1] Chapsal, *et. al.*, *France Depuis* 1945, p. 509.

[2] Sheahan provides an excellent case study of the machine tool industry; see, *Promotion and Control*, pp. 89–101.

plan to the military, to the agricultural sector, to popular causes such as housing and schooling, and to the price-incomes question. Parts IV and VI of this study trace the history of the plan's actions – and inactions – in politically dangerous areas up through its present 'forced involvement' in incomes policy, a question which is logically at the centre of any balanced economic plan, but which the French planners managed to avoid for almost twenty years.

For the first plan the degree of difficulty of planning for a given industry was determined largely by examining the structure of that industry – concentration being the essential structural element – and by weighing the political forces that would be hostile to the rationalisation of that industry. As the scope of planning increased with each successive plan, three other considerations entered into the planners evaluations of the difficulty of planning for an industry. They were: the volatility of an industry's demand curve; the effects of international competition on an industry's behaviour; and the needs of regional development.

These criteria were all of minimal importance to the first plan. They came to occupy an increasingly important place in the planners' strategy as time passed and the economy developed.

SUMMARY

The Monnet planners set out to rehabilitate the French economy from the ravages of war and twenty years of pre-war decadence. They sought to modernise the attitudes and structures of the economy as well as the physical, productive plant.

To an important extent, political conditions determined the objectives and methods of the plan. The fundamental political promises adopted by the plan were that the regime of private property would not be threatened, nor would the power structure within the State bureaucracy: the Ministry of Finance's control of the levers of economic power would not be challenged by the new Planning Commission.

The basic outline of the Monnet planning system follows logically from these two assumptions. The plan would have to be a meeting place or bargaining table, where the major economic groups (most notably big business and the Treasury), would bargain out the conditions and direction of economic development. The planners would function as a team of economic rationalisers and political brokers. Their power to influence economic development would have to come from the compatability of their own objectives with the interests of big business or the Treasury or both. Their role in the bargaining process would have to be essentially that of a mediator or go-between. They could, of course, function as teachers, supplying information and advice to all; but, any direct power they could hope to wield, would have to come from their influence with the two principal power groups.

Monnet's genius – if one chooses to view the Planning Commission as the handiwork of a gifted artisan – lay in recognising these constraints and in fitting the Planning Commission into the role they dictated: the previous planning body, the Ministry of the National Economy, failed to appreciate these limits.

Political conditions also determined the areas where the planners' influence could be significant – and where it could not.

The most pressing problem of the post-war economy – inflation – was too serious a business to be left to economists. The planners learned that they could exert little influence on the exercise of short-term policy, especially on the demand side. Their potential influence was on the long-term development of the supply side. Their investment projects, especially the hydro-electric and railway electrification programmes were not aimed at halting the run-away inflation in the shortest possible time. The Monnet planners abandoned all serious attempts at influencing the short term situation and concentrated all their resources and influence on the long-term development of the industrial infrastructure, the area in which they had their greatest political strength: the Marshall Plan administration vigorously protected the investment programme.

The narrow range of the Monnet plan's activities, and their long-range nature permitted the plan to remain relatively independent of short term economic and political changes. The successful implementation of the plan did not depend upon forces which the planners could not control. A more ambitious plan, one that attempts to co-ordinate the growth of all major economic activities is far more vulnerable. Its successful implementation depends upon controlling all major economic variables; an unplanned change in one variable (e.g., a fall in exports or a rise in wages) would distort the entire pattern of planned development. The Monnet plan made minimal demands – not on the resources of the economy, (for the investment programme was ambitious) – but on the resources of the planners: it could operate successfully even if short term policy was not co-ordinated with the plan's objectives. It was brilliantly designed to function in a situation where the implementation of the plan would not be the primary purpose for which the powers of the Government were to be used. Monnet did not try to extend the plan's influence beyond its powers.

The Monnet plan was crude in an economic sense. It was sophisticated in a political sense. The second, third, and fourth plans were just the opposite.

PART IV

THE SECOND PLAN: A RESPONSE TO CHANGE

The objectives of successive economic development plans should change. The change is not merely a matter of extrapolating the old targets so as to quantify 'more of the same'; it involves revision of the basic schedule of economic priorities from which a plan's objectives are derived. In the context of a slightly altered economic environment, development of a previously low-priority sector may well take precedence over the most heavily stressed sector of the last plan. One plan may focus attention, efforts and resources on the development of basic industry. The next plan might emphasise consumer durables, while the third will stress collective consumption. Evolution in planning means a continual rescheduling of priorities, a shifting of emphasis from sector to sector, rather than a simple straight-line progression of quantatative increases in the sectors stressed by the first plan.

The entire planning process must undergo a similar evolution. A planning process designed to realize one set of priorities within a specific environment must change along with the priorities and the environment. Direct dealings – negotiation, subsidisation, and regulation – may be an effective way to implement production programmes in industries dominated by just a few firms. It is not likely to be as effective in industries composed of thousands of independent firms. Measures that proved effective in implementing planned programmes for industrial expansion are not likely to be suited to the task of implementing an incomes policy. Even the kinds of data and computational techniques needed to prepare a plan change with its objectives. An incomes policy requires much more elaborate information about income distribution than a plan confined to promoting expansion in the basic industries; computational techniques adequate for planning the modernisation of a few basic industries will not be sufficient if the plan is to develop into an over-all pattern of resource allocation.

An ongoing and multipurpose planning process – as distinct from such single shot, single purpose enterprises as wartime or reconstruction plans – is continually evolving new implementation methods, new kinds of data, new computational techniques, new processes of legitimisation, new processes for scheduling priorities, new ranges and forms of participation.

The following pages see the French planning process as a continuous effort to adapt to changing conditions in order to influence future changes. They examine how changing conditions confronted the plan with new problems, and how the plan succeeded or failed in developing ways to deal with these new problems.

12 CHANGED CONDITIONS

By 1952, the terminal date of the Monnet plan, economic conditions had changed so significantly since the plan's inception that a major rethinking of the objectives and methods of French planning was necessary before a second plan could be prepared.

1 CHANGES IN 'WHERE THE ACTION IS'

The 'basic sectors' of the first plan no longer constituted the critical bottleneck to economic expansion. The very successes of the first plan determined the tasks of the second. The entire productive plant of the French economy now needed the rationalising, modernising and developing that the Monnet plan had begun in the basic sectors.[1] In order to maintain its position of leadership, the plan would have to extend the range of its activities. The basic pre-condition for the continuing vitality of the plan – perhaps for its survival – was the adaptation of the Monnet planning system to a wider range of industries, including industries which were less concentrated than electric power or cement, and industries which faced more volatile demand curves than the basic industries of the first plan.

2 CHANGES IN INVESTMENT FINANCING

By 1952 two important trends in the structure of investment financing had become evident. They worked in the same direction: to decrease the importance of public funds for new investment projects.

The first was business increased capacity to self-finance its own expansion.[1] In 1947, self-financing (financing out of retained earnings and depreciation allowances) accounted for only 22.7% of total investment. In 1948, the figure was 23.7%.

[1] See *Second Plan*, p. 24; *Rapport Annuel*, 1952, p. vi; Pierre Massé, *La Planification Française* (La Documentation Française, 1962) p. 5; Fourastié, *La Planification*, pp. 41–42.

In 1949, 30.1%. In 1950 it was up to 34.7%, and by 1952, 47.6% of investment was self-financed.[1]

At the same time the supply of public moneys for the investment programme was menaced with serious cuts. The Marshall Plan was over. US aid continued to pour into France in massive quantities, but it no longer came to promote investment. The military authorities – not the Planning Commission – now handled the inflow of dollars. From 1948 through 1950 Marshall aid to France was used almost exclusively for investment and reconstruction.[2] In 1951, 25% of American aid went to the military; in the first half of 1952, 90% of US aid went to the military.[3] The Pinay Government (established in March 1952) took the burden of anticipated military expenses and the rising price spiral that brought it to power, as a signal to hold-back on public expenditures – including the planners' investment programmes.[4]

The increased ability of business to self-finance investment transformed the planners' principal coercive tool – the granting of cheap investment credits from publicly controlled funds – into an incentive; it had, during most of the Monnet plan, been a control.[5] As explained above, financial incentives could be sufficient to induce a firm to undertake an expansion or modernisation programme. But they were inadequate to prevent a determined firm from going ahead with an investment project

[1] Data is from *Rapport Annuel*, 1951, table 131 and *Rapport Annuel*, 1956, table 13. A more complete discussion of the evolution of investment financing during the early fifties is provided above, pp. 22–3. See also *Le Monde*, 3 October 1952, p. I.

[2] On the uses of Marshall Plan credits see *Le Monde*, 2 January 1952, p. 4 and *Rapport Annuel*, 1952, p. 85.

[3] *Le Monde*, 23 July 1953, p. 10.

[4] The 'expérience Pinay' is discussed below, part IV, pp. 169–70. For what it appeared to be at the time, see *Le Monde*, 14 March 1952; p. 1; 16 March 1952, p. 5; 21 March 1952. *Economic Policy in France*, (Amsterdam 1964) Vol. III, pp. 324–327, offers a rapid review of the Pinay programme and follows the ups and downs of the government investment budget, which Pinay first cut by 88 billion francs in the spring of 1952, and then increased by 100 billion for the following year (p. 325 and 327). *Rapport Annuel*, 1956, table 13, p. 21, maps out the evolution of state credits for investment. For 1952–1953 the amount of state funds for investment (in current francs) decreased relative to the previous year, and the average of the three previous years.

H. Lubell is interesting on the difference between anticipated effects of the military burden and the actual economic effects of rearmament. See, *Oxford Economic Papers, NS*, Feb. 1955, p. 47.

[5] On the distinction between incentive and control, and the importance of the crippled post-war capital market to the Monnet plan, see above, pp. 23–4.

that was contrary to, or beyond the scale of the plan's programmes. For the first plan, the scarcity of investment funds performed this crucial controlling function. If the plan was going to orient development in a different direction from that which the economy would have taken in its absence, some way would have to be found to control the 'excessive' or unplanned expansion of certain sectors.[1]

3 CHANGES IN PERSONNEL

In 1950 Monnet left the plan to assume the direction of the European Coal and Steel Community. He was succeeded by Etienne Hirsch, who had been his deputy commissioner.[2] M. Hirsch enjoyed a reputation for competence.[3] He was also most acceptable to big business. No socialist, M. Hirsch respected profits and respected the independence and rights of private business; he had formerly been a director of the Kuhlmann Chemical group, one of the largest and most powerful big businesses in France.[4] Hirsch was an engineer, not a *débrouillard* like Monnet,[5] but despite his often praised competence, he did not possess the personal prestige and influence of his predecessor.[6]

4 CHANGES IN AVAILABLE ECONOMIC INFORMATION

By 1952–3 French economic statistics had improved enough to permit the planners to prepare a technically sophisticated plan. Coherent quantative target planning – meaning a comprehensive scheme of resource allocation in which all major economic activities are co-ordinated in a general equilibrium model – now became possible. Commissioner Massé describes the

[1] We will have a great deal more to say on this theme in the following chapters.

[2] See B. Cazes, *la Planification en France et le IVe Plan*, Paris, 1962, p. 36.

[3] See, M. MacLennen (PEP), p. 382; Bauchet, *Economic Planning, The French Experience*, London, 1964, p. 4; Hackett, *Economic Planning in France*, London, 1963, pp. 42–43, who all speak highly of M. Hirsch's abilities.

[4] Bauchet, *Economic Planning*, p. 4, provides the bare essentials of M. Hirsch's biography; so does *Who's Who in France*. For a description of the Khulmann group see *Entreprise*, 31 October 1964.

[5] 'Specialiste des idées générales' is the way J-F Gravier describes Monnet in *Preuves*, Dec. 1953, pp. 32 and 26.

[6] *Le Monde*, 15–16 août, 1952, p. 4, comments on the loss of 'prestige and means of action' that Monnet's departure represents for the plan – despite the recognised abilities of his successor.

improvement in national accounting in terms of the new possibilities it opened up:

The progress in national accounting, which permitted an overall view of the economy, came at the right time to provide the necessary tools with which to attack the problems of coherence.[1]

The remarkable contrast between the present state of development and conditions prior to 1952 should not conceal the many shortcoming of the French economic information establishment. Statisticians and economists are still in very short supply. In March 1963, the Economic and Social Council reported:

It is striking to note that the élite of this country, educated by centuries of classical culture, does not consider economics as belonging to general culture. An educated man today cannot remain ignorant of existentialist philosophy . . . or abstract art, but he feels no compunction at knowing nothing about the expression of national income. . . . It must be known that French economic science, which is one of the most brilliant, lacks men . . . that the INSEE gets on with difficulty, that it doesn't possess twenty teams of economists to cover its twenty economic regions, and that there are not more than one hundred business economists capable of meaningful discussion with the services of the national accounts.[2]

Important economic information such as data concerning non-wage incomes is still not available,[3] and regional statistics are poor.[4] Such information is essential for a politically-acceptable incomes policy, and for regional planning: two problems that are rapidly becoming central concerns of the Planning Commission.[5] By 1952–3 the Hirsch planners felt freed from the limitations that the national accounts data had imposed upon the Monnet planners. Their technical sophistication, which had

[1] Massé, *French Affairs*, p. 8. Commissioner Hirsch's request for authorization for the second plan stated that 'for the first time . . . thanks to progress in national accounting, it has become possible . . . to evaluate the volume and rate of investment compatible with a general equilibrium' *J.O. Documents Parlementaires*, 20 Legislature, 1954, annex no. 8555, p. 899. See also Bernard Gourney, 'Les Grands Fonctionnaires,' *Revue Française de Science Politique*, April 1964, p. 236, on the timing of improvements in France's national accounts.

[2] *J.O. Avis et Rapports du Conseil Economique et Social*, 23 March 1963, 'Inventaire des Moyens Actuals d'information Economique,' p. 233.

[3] See M. N. Susini, 'La Comptabilité Nationale et les Plans,' *Le Plan Français*, Ministère de la Co-opération, June 1962; and Pierre Massé, *Rapport Sur la Poiltique des Revenus établi à la Suite de la Conférence des Revenues Oct.* 1963–*Jan.* 1964, Pait II, La Documentation Française, 1964.

[4] *J.O. Council Economique*, 23 March 1963, p. 249.

[5] See Fifth Plan.

been belied by foreign observers,[1] could now be demonstrated. An ambitious plan (in the sense of planning techniques) which balanced all major economic activities – a coherent plan as they called it – could now be prepared.

5 CHANGES IN ATTITUDES

By 1952, business had regained confidence, at least its own confidence. The fear and guilt which had obsessed the business community during the Liberation period had been overcome.[2] The threat of massive nationalisations had passed,[3] and after five years of contact with the Monnet plan, the word 'planning' no longer evoked any nightmares – at least not for the more progressive business leaders. Business' diminished reliance upon state funds for investment increased feelings of independence, and the one year hiatus in planning (in 1953 there was no plan)[4] further added to those feelings of independence *vis à vis* the plan. For business, the early fifties marked a 'return to normalcy.' 'Leaders of private industry were again confident of the possibilities of either using the government for their own purposes, or resisting government intrusion.[5]

In December 1946, when the Monnet Plan was presented, the CGT, the Communist dominated and largest trade union, heralded it as a positive beginning and promised its support; by the time the second plan was in preparation, the CGT was staunchly opposed to the plan calling it reactionary and a tool of the monopolies in their efforts to dominate the workers.[6] The intrusion of the cold war into French political life was, of course, the principal factor behind this complete switch. But it was not the only factor.

[1] See, for example, S. Wellisz statement quoted on p. 83 above.

[2] Henry David Harbold describes the attitudes of the French business community to Liberation and their relation to planning in the introductory chapters of *Le Plan Monnet*, Harvard Ph.D. thesis, unpub. 1954.

[3] See *L'Express*, 6 juin 1953, p. 10.

[4] See below, p. 125.

[5] Quotation is from Sheahan, *Promotion and Control*, p. 176.

[6] *Le Peuple* (a CGT paper) of 14 Dec. 1946 carried a long description of the plan and a box story under the heading: 'l'application du Plan Monnet . . . n'implique pas la régression sociale.' *Le Peuple* of 7 dec. 1946 speaks of the 'adhésion réflichie que la CGT apporte au Plan,' and goes on to say 'nous aurions . . . mauvaise grace à ne pas nous féliciter de l'élaboration de ce plan . . . il ne s'agit donc pas de socialisation ou de collectivisation . . . mais plus modestement, et plus éfficacement aussi, d'un début de mise en order accompagné d'un essai de modernisation de notre économie.' Comparison with later positions by

Like the *Patronat*, the CGT now saw the reality of French planning practice instead of the myths the word planning had previously evoked. By 1952 it was no longer possible to believe that the plan would bring Socialism to France. The planners, it seems, gave up on the trade unions, or at least the CGT. They made no serious efforts to court its favour, certainly nothing comparable to the constant overtures the plan made to the business community. The first report of the Hirsch planners even went out of its way to antagonise the trade unions. It blamed the inflation on 'wage pressures . . . to increase salaries which are already high.'[1] At the time, wage increases were lagging behind price increases.[2] The planners seemed to feel no need of the CGT nor to expect anything constructive from it; the CGT seems to have felt the same way about the plan.

The CGT did not participate in the preparation of the second plan. It claimed that it was 'refused access to the modernisation commissions.'[3] The planners take the view that the CGT refused to participate.[4] The complex problem of trade union participation in the plan is the subject of the concluding section of this study. For the purposes of our present list of changed conditions, it is sufficient to note that the absence and opposition of the largest trade union shattered the carefully cultivated image of the plan as a great cathedral – as the society's central project, prepared through the harmonious

---

the CGT is striking: l'orientation réactionnaire que le Commissariat du Plan entend donner à l'économie . . . Comment ne pas s'opposer à ce Plan réactionnaire?' *Le Peuple* 15 février 1954, p. 2; 'Le Plan est un instrument pour réaliser les objectifs de domination des monopoles contre la classe ouvrière et les masses populaires,' *Supplément du Journal Le Peuple*, no. 643, p. 4, 1962.

[1] *Rapport Annuel*, 1952, pp. vi–vii.

[2] See INSEE, *Mouvement Economique* (1957), pp. 260–261, 283. Statistics on this particular subject are notoriously unreliable. One INSEE index shows a decline in the purchasing power of wage earners between Sept. 1951 and Sept. 1953. INSEE *Mouvement Economique*, (1957), p. 283. pp. 260–261 of that INSEE study discusses some of the problems associated with wage-price indices at that period. Averill Harriman, who cannot possibly be suspected of any affiliation or special sympathies with the CGT remarked, in the spring of 1952: 'In France, the worker does not receive a fair share of the national income.' *Le Monde*, 16 March 1952, p. 5.

[3] *Le Peuple*, 15 février 1954, p. 2.

[4] See, Bernard Gournay et Pierre Viot, 'Les Planificateurs et les Décisions du Plan,' paper presented to the *Colloque sur la Planification* at Grenoble, 2–4 May 1963. Reference is to p. 23 of the mimeographed text distributed by the Planning Commission: paragraph 2D of the 2nd part of the paper.

co-operation between all the groups of the realm. It was not until the advent of the Fifth Republic that serious efforts were again made to cloth the planning process in a veil of communitarian rhetoric.[1]

The planners' attitudes had also changed. The urgency and unity of thought and action which characterised the early days of planning[2] had given way to uncertainty and caution. These new attitudes were largely determined by the planners' new situation, but they in turn became an important determinant of that situation. The planners became increasingly cautious as the strength of their position became increasingly unsure, and the nature of their task increasingly uncertain.

The terminal date of the first plan was 1952, but the second plan was not put into effect until 1954. For the Planning Commission, 1953 was labelled a year of transition.[3]

The last half of 1952 and the first quarter of 1953 were marked by a general business recession. Industrial production stagnated below the levels of the preceding year; so did investment.[4] Most important, a substantial margin of excess productive capacity had developed.[5] The growth projections of the second plan – for which 1952 served as the base year – were considered by most observers to be 'cautious,' or 'modest.'[6]

[1] See below, Part IV, Chapter IV.

[2] Harbold, *le Plan Monnet*, introductory chapter, provides a good description of the atmosphere of the early days of the Planning Commission.

[3] See, *Rapport Annuel*, 1952, p. 321; INSEE, *Mouvement Economique*, p. 127; Baum, *The French Economy and the State*, p. 28.

[4] *Quarterly Index of Industrial Production*

Year	*1st*	*2nd*	*4th*
1951	99	103	104
1952	106	103	103
1953	99	106	111

Source: INSEE, *Mouvement Economique*, p. 151. Total investment (net) in constant (1949) francs for the year 1951 was 1,196 billion; for 1952 it fell to 1,154 billion; and in 1953 stayed at 1,158 billion.

Source: Ministère des Finances, Commission des Investissements, *Rapport Annuel*, (Paris, 1952), p. 88–1. See also INSEE, *Mouvement Economique.*

[5] The planning Commission estimated excess productive capacity – that is, unemployed capital and labour – at about 10% of industrial capacity, see *Rapport Annuel* 1952, (Paris, 1953), p. vii.

[6] INSEE, *Mouvement Economique*, p. 127 calls the objectives of the second plan 'relatively modest.' Baum states: 'a striking feature of the second plan is the modest character of its goals,' *The French Economy . . .*, p. 31; Sheahan cites Baum's judgment and agrees with it, *Promotion and Control*, p. 177. The targets of the second plan – and the reasons why they can be called modest – are discussed below, p. 136ff.

The fact that those projections were made from the trough of 1952 might, in part, explain their cautious nature.[1]

During the prolonged preparation of the second plan, the planners were subject to a growing volume of criticism from the Right, from the Left and also from the Centre. The Right attacked the plan as a menace to free-enterprise.[2] The Left denounced its lack of social policy and its domination by big business.[3] The Centre criticized the plan's tendencies to promote inflation, and the Centre was where the plan's political strength lay.[4] Confronted by allegations that the plan had been 'responsible' for inflation – and by their own uncertainty about the outlook for expansion in the coming year or two – the Hirsch planners adopted a cautious attitude about the anticipated rate of economic expansion and about attempting to influence its direction.

The Government's attitude towards the plan further added to the planners' realisation that they lacked 'bottom'.[5] The Monnet plan ran-out its last months in an economy that was directed by Antoine Pinay's 'personal programme,' which lasted from March through December 1952.[6] The period of renewed

[1] INSEE explains the 'relatively modest' goals of the plan in terms of the planners' uncertainty about the strength of future demand, *Mouvement Economique*, p. 127.

[2] *Le Monde*, 5 janvier 1952, p. 4, cites a good example of such criticism. The hostility of the *Conféderation du Moyennes et Petits Entreprises* towards the plan can be clearly seen in a letter to *Le Monde* 15–16 août 1952, p. 4.

[3] See, for example, *Le Peuple*, 15 février 1954, p. 2.

[4] Paul DeLouvrier (one of Monnet's original team) discusses criticism of the plan's inflationary tendencies in *Politique Economique de la France*, (Cours Fait à l'Institut d'Etudes Politiques 1957–58), p. 198; R. V. Roosa, 'The Problems of French Recovery,' *Economic Journal*, June 1949, pp. 156–157 is a good example of the US Treasury's view; Harold Lubell, 'The Role of Investment in Two French Inflations,' *Oxford Economic Papers, NS*, Feb. 1955, pp. 47–49, defends the plan as does *Le Monde*, 5 Oct. 1952, p. 1. *Rapport Annuel*, 1952, p. 85, touches on this question. Baum states that the second plan's 'modest goals no doubt reflect concern over the frequent allegations that the first plan "failed to" reach its goals and was "responsible" for the postwar inflation and financial instability,' *The French Economy*, p. 31.

[5] 'In the eighteenth century, but particularly under the Regency, a gentleman was expected to have "Bottom." It was a word of composite meaning, which implied stability, and also what the twentieth century calls "guts." It meant being able to keep one's head in emergencies, and, in a financial sense, that one was backed by capital, instead of being an adventurer. Bottom, in fact, was synonymous with courage, coolness, and solidity. The metaphor was derived from ships.' T. H. White, *The Age of Scandal*, (Penguin ed.) p. 68.

[6] Malcolm MacLennan notes the possible importance of various finance ministers wanting to leave their own name on a major economic programme or

expansion which began in the autumn of 1953 was more clearly associated with the 'Personal' Eighteen Month Plan for Economic Expansion of Finance Minister Edgar Faure than with the second plan.[1]

In 1954, during the period of the Faure Plan, the Planning Commission was detached from the Prime Minister's office and placed under the direct, personal authority of the Minister of Finance Faure. It was not, however, 'integrated' into the Ministry of Finance, 'une solution nuancée, qui combine des liens d'allégéance personelle, avec une vocation à l'indépendence intéllectuelle.'[2] Bauchet and the Hacketts pass over this change quickly, indicating only that it was without any real importance.[3] In one sense it was without importance; the methods of planning, as described above, were not changed. The modernisation commission system was kept, as was the autonomy and small size of the Planning Commission. In another sense, the movement of the Planning Commission within the bureaucracy marked an important change in the government's attitude towards the plan.

The Governments were de-emphasizing the plan. Economic policy was prepared and put into effect without reference to the

---

plan; see, 'French Planning: Some Lessons for Britain,' *Planning*, vol. XXIX, no. 475, 9 Sept. 1963, p. 382. The Pinay Programme and the Faure Plan were two of the earliest and most important of these 'personal plans.' See below, pp. 286–290; 301ff, for a detailed discussion of the Pinay Programme, the Giscqud d'Estaing stabilisation plan, the Faure Plan, and relation of short-term economic policy to the plan.

[1] See *Le Monde*, 5 Feb. 1954, p. 14 and 6 Feb. 1954, p. 5, for an outline of the Faure plan which went into effect that month. The association of renewed expansion with the Faure Plan was particularly important in the press which repeatedly discussed the Faure Plan and measured economic activity in reference to it. The eclipse of the second plan in the press is striking. During the period Jan. 1953 through Feb. 1955, *Le Monde* contained almost no mention of the second plan. Government officials, especially M. Faure, also tended to leave the second plan out of major pronouncements on economic policy. See, for example, Faure's speech in *Le Monde* of 18 Jan. 1955; the French Senate's statement on investment credits reported in *Le Monde* of 4 Feb. 1953, p. 10; and *L'Express*, 24 Oct. 1953, p. 5. Faure maintained his position as Minister of Finance until Jan. 1955 through the Laniel and Mendès France Governments. In Feb. 1955, M. Faure formed his own government which stayed in power until the end of that year.

[2] Quotation is from Pierre Massé, *Histoire, Méthode et Doctrine de la Planification Française*, La Documentation Française, 1962, p. 5; Décret no. 54–729, 10 juillet 1954, (*J.O. Lois et Décrets* 17 juillet 1954), relocates the planning commission.

[3] See, Hackett, *Economic Planning in France*, pp. 38 and 59; Bauchet, *Economic Planning: The French Experience*, p. 42.

plan. Government officials and the press spoke of the plan infrequently. There was no Marshall Plan anymore to keep the Planning Commission in the centre of things, and to support it.

The planners had good reason to be unsure of the strength of their own position. The continued relevance – even the continued existence – of the plan was in doubt.

They were also unsure about what to do next. The Reconstruction plan was over. If they were going to succeed in institutionalising the plan – in converting the post-war investment programme into an ongoing planning process – they would have to redesign the Monnet system to fit the new conditions. And in designing the new planning process they would be defining a new role for planning in France.

13 THE NEW PLANNING PROCESS:
A two-component model

The new planning process was not a streamlined design of smoothly fitting parts. Its formal structure told little about its functional structure. Its explicit targets did not define its operational role. The plan was a collection of different activities which were never integrated into a single, coherent process. That, perhaps, is why there has been so much confusion about the way French planning operates: it operates in several ways at once.

The new planning process had two principal components. The first was the complex institution of pragmatic, daily state intervention in the activities of the major industries. The second was the coherent set of detailed output targets, the general resource allocation plan. Each was a complex system, possessing a powerful logic of its own. As a result the plan was forced to assume different, often contradictory, roles.

The first component (direct intervention) operates within what François Bloch-Lainé calls the *économie concertée*: the close partnership between the state and big business aimed at managing rapid, but orderly, increases in output and productivity. It shares all the strengths and limitations of the larger form. It is effective. Participation by the state in the management of the most important industries, has been a major force in promoting economic restructuring, modernisation and expansion. But its effectiveness is limited largely to programmes which can be realised through the direct action of large corporations, for the most part, to programmes consistent with increasing the long-term productivity, size and profits of the major corporations.

The first component operates in what is essentially an *ad hoc* or case by case manner. The determination of where energies and resources ought to be channelled owes more to the pragmatic judgments of the planners and the ranking civil servants than to the formal econometric models of the plan. That judgment, and the eagerness with which it is exercised, is informed by what we called the Myth of Modernisation: a complex collection of motivating images which insists upon the importance of increasing national production, modernising production processes, industrial structures and product lines, and upon the responsibility of the ranking civil servants to guide and insure such developments. The *économie concertée* uses the formal econometric models of the plan more for the legitimation of reform and production programmes than for their determination.

Participation in the *économie concertée* is as narrow as its goals. Because its efforts are directed at strengthening the industrial core of large enterprises, there is no need to obtain the active co-operation of a wide range of groups. The trade unions, consumer groups, small business groups, peasant organisations, and Parliament are outside the system. They are not needed either to choose objectives or to carry out programmes.

As the managers of the state and the giant corporations see it, broad representation would bring in peasant and shopkeeper groups, nostalgic for an irrational past; trade unionists nostalgic for an irresponsible future; and politicians all too eager to serve those groups. It would complicate matters, perhaps even destroy the system. As the range of concerns broadens to include a new sector, the management of its firms – whether they be private or public firms – can be brought in. And places can be kept at the conference table for the 'responsible' trade unionists that the planned industrial evolution is supposed to produce. When they arrive they can make positive contributions to the smooth management of the core of the economy.

The *économie concertée* is not a framework designed to elucidate the choices confronting the nation. It is not an institution designed to facilitate a conscious and democratic determination of the direction of development. The *économie concertée* is an answer to questions about the direction of development.

The *économie concertée* and the component of the planning process it circumscribes operate relatively independently of political and economic pressures elsewhere in the society. The plan's role, within the *économie concertée*, is to assist the stewards of state and corporate power to manage the development of the growth sectors. Planning is, potentially, a superb instrument to aid in the democratic choice of the direction of growth by, among other things, articulating the implications of alternative policies. But the logic of the Plan's involvement in the *économie concertée* is to pull it away from such a role, and away from the traditional political arena. The purpose of the *économie concertée* is to keep the state intimately involved in the management of the dominant industries of the economy while keeping 'politics' out.

Its second component – the projection of quantitative output targets in the form of a general equilibrium system – pushes the Plan in the opposite direction, straight towards the centre of all political activities. The thrust is generated by the basic characteristics of the formal econometric system.

First, (within the coherent resource allocation plan) the rationality of the particular quantitative value assigned to each target rests on the assumption that the entire *pattern* of planned targets will be realised without major distortion. When each value is derived from the same projected pattern of economic activity, when each target fits into that matrix of interdependent balances, when each target is a function of all other targets, each target makes sense only in terms of the planned pattern. If that pattern is not likely to be realised without significant distortion, the target values become irrational – to the very extent that they would be rational under the opposite assumption of realisation without distortion.

Second, the planned pattern must be comprehensive. All economic activities must be accounted for so that the partial equilibria represented by each of the targets add up to the aggregate balances for manpower, foreign exchange, investment and savings that define general equilibrium. This does not, of course, mean that the plan must contain explicit, numerical targets for each and every identifiable economic activity. All it must do is account, implicitly or explicitly, for all activities. Fixing numerical output targets for such products as sweaters, sunglasses or tennis shoes is neither necessary, desirable nor possible. Instead, broad product groupings can be established and targets assigned to cover the aggregate impact of those activities. Just how resources are allocated within the category is not important – as long as the totals hold. Similarly, certain questions which stand at the logical centre of the plan can often be treated implicitly. For example, until very recently the plans made no explicit statements about income distribution. But detailed assumptions about income distribution are necessarily incorporated into the projected pattern of final demands from which the rest of the plan is derived.

Because the plan must incorporate targets for all economic activities it becomes the framework for political decisions. It cannot simply ignore the impact of military expenditures, or farm policies, or foreign aid, or motorcar production. To do so would guarantee that the planned pattern of resource allocation would not be realised without major distortion. That predictable distortion would mean that the output targets are automatically 'inaccurate' from the businessman's perspective and 'irrational' – from the economist's perspective. The range of activities for which four year projections must be incorporated into the plan is enormous. The plan has to embody *all* major decisions regarding resource allocation. Omitted or unrealistic targets for foreign aid, or school construction, or pensions would distort the plan quite as badly as similar lacunae for chemical production, highway construction or petroleum imports. Similarly, decisions on the evolution of prices, wages, saving, taxes and government expenditures must be incorporated into the plan. But these decisions are precisely what 'politics' is all about.

Once the planned pattern – incorporating the major decisions on resource allocation – is established, it must be implemented. And the implementation process pushes the plan into the centre of traditional politics almost as vigorously as the process of choosing targets,

In order for the planned pattern to be realised, all the major collective decisions embodied in its targets must be carried through. The word 'decisions' distinguishes the normative objectives from the purely predictive targets, the independent from the dependent variables. Only if the decisions are carried through as planned will 'market forces' steer the rest of the economy to the planned targets. The most important of these decisions, or volitional programmes, concern the public sector.

The Government must outline its programme – in terms of their effects on the rest of the economy – and then implement them. It must commit itself in rather detailed fashion for a long period. During the planned period it cannot launch major unplanned military projects, or space probes or welfare programmes or tax reforms without destroying the plan's coherence. It must co-ordinate its use of short-term economic policy, including all the traditional monetary and fiscal levers of economic control, with the middle term objectives of the plan. But traditional politics focus on the exercise of these short-term measures. Similarly, incomes and prices must somehow be made to evolve along planned lines and rates. As long as there exists a pressure politics concerned with taxes, government spending, tariffs, interest rates and wage policies, realisation of the coherent resource allocation plan will necessitate co-ordinating or subordinating day to day political activity to the middle term objectives of the plan.

Either the interest groups will believe that they can gain satisfaction through the plan and begin to focus their efforts on the choice and execution of its objectives, or they will refuse to take the plan seriously and continue to concentrate their energies on influencing the exercise of short-term policies and pragmatic programmes. The latter course would result in continuing the usual pragmatic-compromise method of policy formulation and execution. Whatever decisions had been previously written into the plan would not be carried out – at least not without the kind of modification that would distort the plan. This, generally, has been the experience of the successive French plans. The actual pattern of sectoral development has differed significantly from the planned pattern. The third alternative – programmes formulated without political participation and efficiently implemented – is, of course, tyranny. Given the necessarily detailed nature of the plan, totalitarianism is perhaps a better word. In order to be rational and effective the plan has to be comprehensive in its targets and uniform in its implementation. To do that it must accommodate all powerful political and economic demands. In brief, in a democratic society a general resource allocation plan can only be effective if it is the output of a participatory planning process.

It ought to be noted that although realisation of the planned pattern without the kind of distortion that robs the targets of their very rationality is impossible unless all these decisions are incorporated into the plan and then systematically carried out, such a procedure will not guarantee the realisation of the plan. Other uncertainties can intrude. Some – for example, foreign trade in an increasingly open economy – are beyond the control of any power that can reasonably be expected to be exercised with the implementation of the plan as a primary objective.

The preconditions for its realisation – comprehensive targets and implementation of the entire pattern – define the role of general resource allocation planning. The only way the coherent plan can operate as both a rational and effective system is if it is the principal framework for political activity.

It can be an excellent framework. The plan presents a clear picture of the implications of alternative policies for the entire economy. This simple, informational function is, potentially, of revolutionary importance. By presenting clear, informed choices it permits – even forces – the society to choose the direction of its development.

The plan's role as an aid in the conscious choice of the direction of development is, we shall argue, the most important of the many possible roles for planning in a modern, industrial society.

Its two principal components pull the plan in opposite directions. The range of concerns of the first component is narrow; the logic of the second component drives it toward comprehensiveness. The targets of the first are technically crude; those of the second are elegant. The outputs of the first component are relatively independent: their conception and execution is generally confined to the managers of big business and the ranking civil servants. The targets of the second component are dependent upon a wide range of exogeneous forces – and upon each other – both in their conception and execution. For the first, targets are chosen pragmatically; criteria are only partially explicit, and the distant effects of any one project or set of projects are not always clear. For the second, each target is derived from formal econometric models, criteria are explicit and so are its effects on the entire economy. For the first component, objectives and implementation devices have fit together nicely. As a result, it has been effective. For the second, means have not meshed with ends. As a result, it has been at a minimum, decorative, at a maximum, indirectly influential. The first component is based on narrow, the second, on broad participation. The first pulls planning away from involvement in politics; the second pushes planning right into the centre of the traditional political arena. The first component defines a role for planning. It makes the plan an instrument to promote the development of the industrial core of the economy. The second component defines an altogether different role for the plan. It makes it into an instrument to aid the society to choose consciously the direction of its development. The first, under the slogan of 'keeping politics out of planning,' confines the plan to the special politics of economic management by the *grands commis* of big business and the state. The second can help to bring planning into politics.

14 THE TARGETS OF THE SECOND PLAN

The second plan had two distinct kinds of targets. They are best understood as independent outputs of the two components of the new planning process. The first kind of targets, proposals for general structural reforms plus detailed developmental programmes for several industries, were direct outputs of the *économie concertée*. The second kind of targets, in the form of a coherent matrix of quantitative production objectives, were outputs of the second component, the general resource allocation plan.

1 THE FIRST COMPONENT: REFORM AND MODERNIZATION PROGRAMMES

(*A*) *GENERAL STRUCTURAL REFORMS*

The second plan was concerned with increasing 'productivity' as well as production; it aimed at lowering the costs, as well as raising the volume of production.[1] The plan's modernisation and development programmes, which covered a much wider area of the economy than those of the Monnet plan, emphasized capital-deepening investment and structural reforms to increase efficiency.

The plan called for a series of 'basic actions,' or structural reforms to overcome the 'extraordinary rigidity of attitudes and structures' which, the Planning Commission insisted, was the principal reason for France's economic backwardness.[2] Each basic action consisted of a broadly defined objective – such as increasing industrial specialisation through mergers and regroupings – followed by specific measures to be taken by the

[1] La Documentation Française, *Notes et Etudes Documentaires*, no. 846, 30 December 1961, p. 15.

[2] *Rapport Annuel*, 1952, p. viii.

Government and business to achieve that objective.[1] The plan listed five basic actions. They all operated on the supply side.

(1) The development of scientific and technological research and the popularisation of modern methods of production.
(2) Industrial restructuring through mergers, regroupings, and *ententes* to promote large-scale, specialised production.
(3) Re-organisation of agricultural markets, and the modernisation of the distribution system.
(4) The establishment of long-term programmes to lower the costs of investment goods especially for the construction industry.
(5) Reconversion of firms in useless and futureless industries into new lines of production.[2]

These five objectives define the orientation of the plan: reform of the productive plant to make expansion without inflation possible and to prepare for international competition by lowering production and distribution costs.

(*B*) *SPECIFIC REFORMS*

The plan's most important specific recommendations for overcoming 'rigidity' in the economy were: (1) a reform of the tax code, and (2) a policy of official encouragement for mergers and regroupings. Both sets of reforms are excellent examples of outputs of the first component – the *économie concertée*.

In place of the 'turnover tax' levied every time inputs passed through the market, the plan recommended the adoption of a value added tax, levied only once, at the final stage of production. The change would eliminate the premium that the cascading (or pyramiding) effects of the turnover tax placed on internal self-sufficiency and the penalty it placed on capital

[1] The specific recommendations do not follow directly in the text. They are dispersed throughout the plan and in the supporting documents. The actual text of the plan gives the impression of having been severely abridged. Programmes for each sector are, at best, outline sketches of the modernisation commission reports. For many sectors, especially agriculture, the text is so condensed that it gives a misleading impression of the planning commission's views. *The Conseil Economique* makes this point in its review of the plan, *J.O. Avis et Rapports du Conseil Economique*, 3 August 1954, p. 679.

[2] *Second plan*, pp. 29–30.

intensive technology. It would encourage specialised production and capital intensive technology.[1]

The value added tax was adopted by the Laniel Government in April 1954 as the keystone of a general tax reform.[2] The tax bill included a provision authorising the Treasury to lower the rates selectively, or to grant total exemptions, in order to encourage certain lines of economic activity.[3] The most important use of this authority has been made for exports which benefit from complete exemption. Many of the plan's incentives described above are derived from the Treasury's authority to apply the value added tax selectively.[4]

Its enthusiastic recommendation of the tax reform[5] in no way separated the plan from its constituency of modernising civil servants and progressive business leaders. Tax reform had been discussed for a long time, and the substitution of a value added tax for the turnover tax had received strong support from the Treasury, from big business and from the press.[6] The plan

[1] The turnover tax penalised long chains of production where semi-finished goods are made by specialised firms and sold to other firms which specialise in the following stage of production. In this way, the self-sufficient firm was favoured. Similarly, the turnover tax was levied on the purchase of capital goods (only materials physically incorporated into the product were deductible) and then on the product (finished or semi-finished) that was made with these capital goods. In this way capital intensive technology was penalised. The plan estimated that the turnover tax had the effect of an 18% levy on investment. *Rapport de la Commission du Financement*, Nov., 1953, p. 24. See INSEE, pp. 206–207 for a rapid survey of the major provisions and advantages of the tax reform. Secretariat d'Etat aux Affaires Economiques, Comité National de la Productivité, *Productivité et Fiscalité*, avril, 1952, provides a complete discussion of the tax reform; so does C. K. Sullivan, *The Tax on Value Added*, Columbia U. Press, 1965.

[2] See loi de 10 avril 1954, *J.O. Lois et Décrets*, 11 avril 1954, p. 5, title I, pp. 3482–3485.

[3] *Ibid.*, title I, article 8; also *Ibid.*, 3 mai 1955, pp. 4371–4375 for extensions and revisions of value added tax.

[4] See BRAE, *Les Moyens de la Politique Economique*, and G. de La Perrière, 'Les Moyens d'Exécution du Plan.'

[5] *The Rapport Général de la Commission du Financement* (second plan) Nov. 1953 contains the plan's study of the tax code and its recommendation for reform. An annex to that report entitled *Fiscalité* provides a more complete discussion of the advantages of the value added tax and a good indication of the plan's position on tax reform.

[6] *Le Monde*'s support of the tax reform can be seen in the issue of 4 July 1953. The Conseil Economique supported the plan's recommendation (*J.O. Conseil Economique*, 4 August 1954, p. 654) and called attention to its own reports on the same subject which for several years had proposed a value added tax. See *Ibid.*, 27 Jan. 1954, pp. 150–159; 1 Nov. 1952, pp. 397–400; and 26 March 1953, pp. 318–320. The voting pattern is as interesting as the final proposal. The best argued, most enthusiastic and most influential report on the tax reform is

confined its proposals for reforming the tax code to measures aimed at increasing productivity. It did not consider the tax code from the standpoints of regulating demand or social welfare. It said nothing about the effects of the regressive French tax structure on income distribution and proposed no reforms aimed directly at the demand side.

The second specific recommendation concerned the promotion of mergers, regroupings and *ententes* with a view towards the creation of firms large enough to benefit from mass-production technology. The plan called for the sweeping away of all obstacles to mergers and *ententes* which could increase specialisation, standardisation and large-scale production.[1] Several tax reforms were recommended along with a policy of easy credit for the financing of mergers 'for the purposes of specialisation.'[2] An information campaign to 'better inform businessmen of the advantages of specialisation' was also proposed.[3] The plan called attention to existing anti-trust legislation, but pointed out, in very definite terms, that the law makes explicit exception for 'useful *ententes*, especially those which encourage specialisation.'[4]

The plan's programme of increasing industrial specialisation through restructuring was not significantly different from the Treasury's own policies, nor was it in advance of big business' views. The need for replacing the traditional small scale, diversified firm with firms capable of specialised lines of mass production was a constant theme in economic studies, political speeches and the press, especially after the creation of the coal

---

presented in *Productivité et Fiscalité*, which was published in April 1952 and bears the signatures of a distinguished panel of civil servants and experts, including several people closely associated with the Planning Commission. The only serious opposition to the reform came from small businesses and agricultural interests. The very smallest businesses – under F50,000 annual turnover – obtained total exemption from the new tax – as did the farmers. See INSEE, *Mouvement Economique*, p. 206, and *J.O. Lois et Décrets*, 3 May 1955, pp. 4371 and 4373, especially article 4.

[1] *Second Plan*, p. 49.

[2] *Ibid.*, p. 49 of *Rapport de la Commission du Financement* 1953, for details of these recommended reforms.

[3] *Ibid.*, p. 49.

[4] *Ibid.*, p. 49; the *Rapport de la Commission des Industries de Transformation*, 1954, pp. 29, 21, 22, discuss the urgent need for greater concentration and the potential conflict with anti-trust legislation. See above Part II, Chapter III, for a general discussion of planning, *ententes*, mergers and anti-trust legislation.

and steel Community, when a Common Market with Germany began to look like an imminent possibility.[1]

The planners had little liking for competition as a form of industrial organisation. They preferred a modernising cartel in which the State (and the plan) would participate actively. The reasons behind the planners' position were discussed above.[2] It is not necessary to insist upon the importance of the modernising cartel to the operations of the component of the planning process that functions within the *économie concertée*: the modernising cartel with State participation *is* the *économie concertée* at the operational level.

2 THE SECOND COMPONENT: THE GENERAL RESOURCE ALLOCATION TARGETS OF THE SECOND PLAN

The quantitative targets of the second plan developed out of the changing conditions at the time of its preparation. Specifically, the need for the plan to extend its range of activities beyond the basic sectors of the first plan led the planners to a general resource allocation approach. The first plan could concentrate on directing scarce resources into a few high priority areas. The second plan had to concentrate on overall economic balance. In addition, the insecurity confronting the planners – insecurity about political conditions, about economic conditions (the 1952 recession) and insecurity about their own positions – led the planners to prepare particularly cautious targets. More fundamentally, the logic of a general resource

[1] The press, especially *Le Monde*, discussed pending anti-trust legislation in terms of the relative disadvantages of oligopolies and *ententes* versus those of too many too small producers. The articles invariably conclude with a demand for more 'good' mergers and *ententes*. See *Le Monde* of 10, 11 and 13 septembre 1953; articles by P. Drouin; *Le Monde*'s coverage of the Celtex merger which restructured the viscose industry, 30 mars 1952, p. III; *Le Monde* 4 décembre 1953, p. 14 and 30 janvier 1954, p. 14 which stress the need for higher concentration, larger scale, more specialised production as the only way to bring down prices through greater efficiency. Business' views are well summed up in the annual statement of the nationalised bank, B.N.C.I. in *Le Monde* 14 janvier 1955, p. 14 which stresses the need for industrial bigness. The Conseil Economique expressed similar views in *J.O., C.E.*, 3 août 1954, p. 700. The Treasury's total support of such a policy is made clear in *Etudes Statistiques*, janvier-mars 1960, p. 53; and in Jean-Marcel Jeanneny's *Forces et Faiblesses de l'Economie Française*, 1959, pp. 258–262; and *The Guardian* 9 September 1964 p. 14.

[2] See above, pp. 60–78, 109–11.

allocation plan implies a responsibility for the entire economy that reinforces just such caution. The first plan could be successful in its own terms despite an inflation. The second plan could not. The success of a general resource allocation plan would be impaired by a recession, inflation or balance of payments crisis. In short, the responsibility implied by more generalised planning coupled with the uncertainties and insecurities the planners confronted led them to the cautious targets of the second plan.

The second plan projected a 25% increase in national product for the period 1952–7.[1] A 25% increase in national product is appreciable, but 1952–3, the base period for the plan's projections, was a recession year, with stagnant industrial production, a poor agricultural harvest and a large margin of excess capacity.[2]

Investment was planned to increase at the same rate as national product so that by 1957 the percentage of national product devoted to investment would not have increased above the comparatively low levels of 1952–3.[3] The OEEC estimated gross investment (including inventory accumulation) at about 16% of GNP for 1952 and about 15% for 1953.[4] In 1948, however, investment accounted for about 18% of GNP, and in 1949 it was also at the 18% level.[5] The 1952 level of investment represented a drop of 17% from the average ratio of investment to GNP that had been maintained over the previous four years.[6] At the same time as it called for a constant, and relatively low

[1] *Second Plan*, p. 29.

[2] (a) 'In 1952 industrial production remained at the 1951 level, and it fell by about 3½% in 1953.' *Second Plan*, p. 15.

(b) Excess capacity was estimated by the Planning Commission at ten per cent of industrial capacity: See *Rapport Annual*, 1952, p. VII.

(c) Index of agricultural production: 1934–38 = 100

1950–51	1951–52	1952–53	1953–54
108	95	104	111

Source: INSEE *Mouvement Economique*, 1944–1957, Paris, 1958, p. 134.

[3] The plan projects investment increases from 2,660 billion 1953 francs in 1953 to 3,330 billion in 1957 (p. 118), or an overall increase of twenty-five per cent; national product was also projected at a twenty-five per cent rate of increase over the same time, hence the percentage of GNP devoted to investment would remain constant.

[4] 1952 figure is from OEEC; *General Statistics*, Nov. 1954, p. 3; 1953 figure, *Ibid.*, April 1956, p. 107.

[5] 1948 figure from *Ibid.*, Sept. 1955, p. 104; 1949 figure from *Ibid.*, April 1956, p. 103.

[6] INSEE, *Annuaire Statistique*, 1952, pp. 332–335.

proportion of national product for investment,[1] the plan projected increases in the proportion of GNP that would go to savings. It suggested that the potential savings surplus that would be generated be used as an opportunity to lower business taxes.[2] The result of this shift, it ought to be noted, was to further reduce business' dependence on the plan.

At the time the plan was being prepared, many observers – ranging from the Communist-dominated *CGT* to the steel industry – were particularly critical of the plan's excessively timid investment programmes.[3] Later criticism increased.

FOREIGN TRADE

The Foreign Trade balance of the plan was based on a projected 40% increase in the volume of exports and no increase whatever in the volume of imports: Imports were expected to remain at 1230 million (1952 francs) level of 1952 despite a projected increase in national product.[4] The plan's defence of its projection for imports – which was certainly not an extrapolation of previous trends[5] – is particularly sketchy.[6] For the most part it deals only with the effects of anticipated developments in import-substitution industries. Increased agricultural production was expected to reduce imports of agricultural commodities by 40%.[7] New petroleum explorations and production

[1] The planned ratio of investments to GNP was appreciably lower than actual ratios maintained in most OEEC countries; see OEEC, *General Statistics*, April 1956, p. 103.

[2] See, *Second Plan*, pp. 119–120; also *Rapport Général de la Commission du Financement* (*Nov*. 1953), p. 15 where the savings projections are explained in somewhat greater detail, and the tax-reduction scheme is put forward along with a proposal to reduce the share of government investment and expenditure.

[3] For the CGT's criticism, see *La Revue des Comités d'Entreprise*, no. 70, janvier 1954 and no. 80, décembre 1954, p. 8; also *Le Peuple*, 15 février 1954, p. 2. The steel industry differed fundamentally from the Planning Commission on the volume of investment that would be needed. The industry called for a much higher volume than the Planning Commission; see *Rapport Général de la Commission de la Sidérurgie*, June 1954, pp. 26–27, 31 where the difference is clearly brought out. For the *Conseil Economique*'s criticism of the too cautious investment targets of the plan see *J.O. Avis et Rapports du Conseil Economique*, 3 août 1954, pp. 651, 655, 657, 659, 658, 661, (esp. 651).

[4] *Second Plan*, p. 134.

[5] Over the period 1950–51–52 national product rose by about 7½%; the volume of imports increased over this same period by about 15%. *Source:* INSEE, *Mouvement Economique* 1944–40, 1957, (Paris 1958), pp. 240 and 313.

[6] The *Conseil Economique* called the plan's study of foreign trade 'insufficient.' *J.O. Conseil Economique*, 3 August 1954, p. 652.

[7] *Second Plan*, p. 134.

in the *Zone Franc* (mostly in Algeria) were expected to meet increased demand for petroleum products, thus saving foreign exchange.[1] The Economic Council questioned the soundness of the plan's import-substitution projections. It warned that the projected increase of 20% in the consumption of fuel was very conservative, and that no past trends seemed to provide any reason for assuming that fuel consumption would increase at a lesser rate than national product.[2] Furthermore, the Council declared, planned investment in agriculture and fuels would be insufficient to realise even the inadequate expansion of production called for in the plan.[3]

The most important shortcoming in the plan's import projections, however, was not so much the studies of anticipated import-substitution, as the total absence of any analysis of the induced demand for imports resulting from a 25% increase in national product. All that the plan says about imports of finished goods for example is 'that they should *at least* reach their 1951 level.'[4] It says nothing about imports of producers' goods except that they should not advance beyond the level of the past three years.[5] Two of those past three years, however, were low investment years, with a rate of industrial expansion about half that anticipated for the period of the second plan, and a level of investment 25% below that projected by the plan for 1957.

INDUSTRIAL OUTPUT AND INVESTMENT TARGETS

The three most prominent characteristics of the plan's industrial targets – cautious estimates of future expansion, investment to lower production costs and not simply to increase output, and restructuring to increase the size and specialisation of firms – are most clearly seen in the programmes for the steel, manufacturing and energy sectors.

For the steel industry the plan stressed caution. The key section of the plan's report on steel, subtitled *programme*

[1] *Ibid.*, pp. 134–135.
[2] See, *J.O. Avis et Rapports du Conseil Economique*, 3 août 1954, pp. 701–702.
[3] *Ibid.*, p. 702 for fuels; pp. 657–658 for agriculture.
[4] *Second Plan*, p. 135 (italics mine).
[5] *Ibid.*, p. 135.

réduit, was a warning against over expansion.[1] It concluded that:

> total production forecast in the programmes of the individual steel companies would clearly exceed estimates of maximum demand[2] . . . this has led the steel industry modernization commission to consider that increases in capacity proposed by the industry, would, in all probability, result in overcapacity of more than one million tons by 1957. Consequently the commission has judged it necessary to define, for the whole area of the steel industry, a reduced investment programme.[3]

The plan's programme for steel cut the industry's own expansion programmes by 1.1 million tons of capacity, about 80% of planned expansion.[4] The plan stressed the need to lower prices so as to increase sales in both the domestic and international markets. Investment was directed towards this end, and reforms of the fiscal and financial structures, transportation facilities, and the purchasing policies of the public sector were recommended for lowering production costs in the steel industry.[5] Unlike its expansion targets, the plan's heavy emphasis on productivity and lower production costs met with enthusiastic support in the Treasury, business and the press.[6]

MANUFACTURING

The manufacturing sector, which employed 40% of the industrial work force[7] was the proving ground for the Planning Commission attempts to extend the range of its activities. The first plan had dealt with only a small part of this broad sector which encompasses such diverse industries as motor-cars, machine-tools, papers, plastics, chemicals, metal working, electronics, business machines, furniture, textiles, household

[1] Deuxième Plan de Modernisation et d'Equipement, *Rapport Général de la Commission de Modernisation de la Sidérurgie*, juin, 1954, chapter III, part III. The targets of the second plan dealt no longer with just capacity, but with marketable output, and after the 1952 experience with excess capacity, the plan appeared particularly concerned about avoiding this danger. See *Conseil Economique*, 3 Aug., 1954, p. 709; *Second Plan*, p. 52.

[2] *Rapport de la Commission de la Sidérurgie*, 1954, p. 31.

[3] *Ibid.*, pp. 26–27.

[4] *Ibid.*, p. 30–31.

[5] *Second Plan*, p. 60.

[6] See below, pp. 147–8.

[7] *Rapport de la Commission des Industries de Transformation du Commissariat Général du Plan*, 1953, p. 3. The report was also published in *l'Usine Nouvelle*, 19, 26 novembre and 3, 10, 24 décembre 1953.

appliances, artificial fibres, wood and glass – to name but a few.

For the manufacturing sector as a whole, the plan outlined general directions for the reform of industrial structures and the modernisation of production methods. The need for restructuring was stressed: there were too many small firms with diversified lines of production to be efficient. Mergers were needed so that mass production methods could be employed. *Ententes* were to be encouraged to permit small firms to specialise in one line of production by eliminating the need for those firms to defend themselves against competitive movements through diversification.[1] The plan reminded business that anti-trust legislation 'protects useful *ententes*.'[2]

Measures recommended to encourage such restructuring were mostly of a general kind so as to be applicable over the wide range of the manufacturing sector with a minimum of detailed study and supervision. They included: reforms of tax provisions which tended to discourage mergers; special credit facilities to help finance mergers and retooling for specialised production: industry wide purchasing and marketing agencies run by the industry to permit more wholesale purchasing and more efficient distribution; and a programme of information and education in modern management methods.[3]

The expansion targets for those industries resembled those for most other sectors: They were extremely conservative. Even the report of the modernisation commission for the manufacturing industries makes that judgment:

> 'If the first plan sometimes sinned by excessive optimism, it seems that the opposite criticism can be made of the second plan – at least so far as the manufacturing industries are concerned.'[4]

For motorcars an increase in production of only 20% above the 1952 level was projected for 1957;[5] for paper a 35% increase;[6] for chemicals, 30%.[7] The target figures are based, not on the limits to attainable increases in capacity, but on estimates

[1] *Ibid.*, pp. 20–21; *Second Plan*, p. 49.
[2] *Ibid.*, p. 20.
[3] See *Rapport Industries de Transformation*, pp. 21–23, (or the summary of that report in the *Second Plan*, p. 49.)
[4] *Rapport Industries de Transformation*, p. 7.
[5] *Second Plan*, p. 46.
[6] *Ibid.*, p. 46.
[7] *Ibid.*, p. 64.

of market demand. The plan repeatedly referred to the danger of overcapacity.[1]

ENERGY

The same themes dominated the plan's programmes for the energy sector (coal, petroleum, and electric power). Investment was aimed at cutting production costs; expansion targets were conservative.[2] In its review of the second plan, the Economic Council noted that the plan called for a 20% increase in the supply of energy to match a 25% increase in national product. The Council remarked that the assumption that demand for energy would increase at a lesser rate than national product had no basis in experience. The Council insisted that the planned increase in energy production was insufficient to sustain a 25% increase in national product and that energy was likely to become a serious bottleneck to future expansion.[3] It predicted that the low rate of planned expansion in the energy sector would probably create a serious foreign exchange problem as industries would import the fuels needed for expansion.[4] The Council argued that the plan's programmes for energy production were occasionally inconsistent, dangerously conservative and based on inadequate studies of market demand. It recommended that 'investment in the energy sector be significantly increased so as to permit the production of energy necessary for the realisation of the general objectives of the plan.'[5] Despite a legal obligation to consider the recommendations of the Economic Council, the Planning Commission went out of its way to impede the Council's study and completely ignored its recommendations.[6]

[1] See, for example, *Ibid.*, pp. 52–53.

[2] See *Second Plan*, pp. 52–61; *J.O. Conseil Economique*, 3 août 1954, pp. 701–707.

[3] *Ibid.*, pp. 701–702, 665.

[4] *Ibid.*, p. 702.

[5] *Ibid.*, p. 665.

[6] The Economic Council's report on the plan's energy programme complains bitterly of the 'inadmissable' conditions imposed on the Council by the Planning Commission 'contrary to the will of the law which charges the Economic Council with the duty of a continual surveillance of the preparation of the plan,' p. 701. The report goes on to say that the plan's energy programme was dated Nov. 1953, but only on the 15th of June did the Planning Commission turn over the document to the Council demanding that the Council's report be completed by the 1st of July. 'Furthermore,' the Council reflects, the Planning Commission 'did not even supply a sufficient number of copies to permit each member of the

In energy, as in steel, the plan stressed the need to lower production costs.[1] In part as a cost consideration, and in part as a surrender to strong political pressures, the second plan abandoned the first plan's emphasis on hydro-electric power stations in favour of a greater use of thermal (coal) stations.[2] The plan's emphasis on 'productivity' included thermal stations. The Treasury, the press, most politicians, the Economic Council and even the CGT enthusiastically applauded this aspect of the plan's energy programme – despite their own reservations about the levels of planned expansion.[3]

The planners' justification of the cautious investment programme for energy – and they recognised the conservative nature of their programme[4] – provides an insight into the difficulties they encountered in their efforts to build a general resource allocation plan in an environment of uncertainties.

The planners' argument begins by recognising their own uncertainty about future demand for energy because of the recession during which the second plan was prepared. It goes on to say that although there is a clear need for a sharp increase in the volume of available energy, heavier investment in energy

Council's energy study group to work in convenient physical conditions. The Council judged that it had sufficient grounds to register 'the strongest protest' with the Government about the working conditions imposed by the Planning Commission to prevent the Council from fulfilling its constitutional obligation of analysing and discussing the plan's programmes in detail. 'This obligation,' the Council added by way of *obiter dictum*, 'seems to be still further justified because, in fact the composition of the energy commission of the plan does not permit businessmen, workers, and consumers to participate in making the choices which have serious consequences for them. . . . It must be understood that decisions concerning the choice among investment in alternative forms of energy are difficult to realise only among the producers, and that the opinions of the users, whose interests are represented in the Economic Council, is indispensible,' p. 701.

[1] *Second Plan*, p. 52; *Le Monde*, 2 août 1954, p. I.

[2] *Second Plan*, p. 54.

[3] See *Le Monde*, 12 décembre 1953, p. 14; 25 juillet 1952, p. 10; 23 juillet 1952, p. 10; 2 août 1953, p. I. – where *Le Monde* reports on the positive reaction of various groups to the plan's productivity drive and to the emphasis on thermal power stations. It then adds its own approval. The CGT's support was limited to the use of thermal stations which pleased the miners, and was surrounded with complaints that the use of coal was too little, too late and in the context of a thoroughly 'reactionary' plan. The productivity drive was also attacked by the CGT, violently and on the level of polemics, as a further menace to the health of already overworked workers. See: *Le Peuple*, 1 septembre 1954, p. 15, février 1954, and *J.O. Conseil Economique*, 18 août 1954, p. 166 explain the CGT's position.

[4] See *Second Plan*, pp. 52–53.

would necessitate a reduction of investment elsewhere. But the growth of demand for energy depends upon the rapid modernisation of the rest of the economy. Hence, if investment in energy were to increase beyond the planned rate, the modernisation of other sectors would slow down, and so would the rate of increase in the demand for energy. The result would be overcapacity in the energy sector and imbalance in the planned pattern of development.[1] The other risk, the planners acknowledge, is too little investment in energy and a resulting bottleneck.[2] If the rest of the economy were to grow at exactly the planned rate, with that growth distributed according to the planned pattern, the plan's energy programme would provide what the planners (but not the Economic Council) considered to be just the right addition to output to meet all demands.

The rationality of the plan's energy programme – and all the other programmes – depended on the uniform realisation of the planned growth pattern. The planners recognised this fact. But, as we shall see, the likelihood of realising the planned pattern was anything but uniform; it varied from sector to sector. For example, those economic activities which generate demand for energy – general manufacturing, household appliances and motorcars – were least likely to expand to just the planned target. The explicit, numerical targets of the plan were prepared by an elaborate method that was based on the assumption of uniform realisation, but the plan was to be implemented through procedures that guaranteed non-uniform realisation.

[1] *Ibid.*, pp. 52–53.
[2] *Ibid.*, p. 53.

15 THE SECOND PLAN: Results and explanations

The foundation of the plan was the basic sectors. It was a certain foundation. In these sectors the planners could project future demands reliably and, with the active co-operation of the Ministry of Finance, control investment and output effectively.

But the keystone of the plan was the intermediate category of industries – motor cars, chemicals, industrial equipment, textiles, plastics, consumer durables, electronics, etc. Here, uncertainties prevailed.

The planners were uncertain about how closely short-term economic policy would be co-ordinated with the middle-term programmes of the plan and about the willingness and ability of the Government to include all its major economic activities (such as military and public works projects) in the plan and then stick to those programmes. They were uncertain about the evolution of prices and incomes, and about foreign trade and international economic forces in an increasingly open economy. As a result the planners were uncertain about the reliability of their demand projections and implementation devices in the industries of the intermediate category, where all these uncertainties would be most strongly felt. The only certainty the planners possessed was that should inflation pull demand for the products of the intermediate category beyond the plan's projections, the planners could not prevent those industries from expanding beyond target. The result would be not a simple overfulfilment of the plan, but a major distortion of the planned growth pattern. That is precisely what happened.

The basic sectors expanded right to the planned targets:

By 1956 national product had already reached the level that the plan had scheduled for 1957.[1] In September 1956, Premier Guy Mollet, in a rare reference to the plan, proudly announced:

[1] *Rapport Annuel*, 1957, table 4.

TABLE V

INDUSTRY	ACTUAL INCREASE IN OUTPUT AS A PERCENTAGE OF PLANNED INCREASE
(a) Coal	98%
(b) Electricity	105%
(c) Steel	99%
(d) Housing	112%
(e) Railways	100%
(f) Gas	95%
(g) Aluminium	100%

Sources:

(a–c) *Third Plan*, table 1.

(d) *Ibid.*, para. 7. See also *Rapport Annuel* 1958, pp. 345–350.

(e) Refers to volume of freight carried. Source: *Rapport Annuel*, 1958, pp. 280–281; see those same pages for other indices of performance in the railways sector.

(f) *Third Plan*, table 1.

(g) Target is from *Rapport Annuel*, 1957, table 67; actual output is from *Rapport Annuel*, 1958, table 55. Employment in these sectors also closely followed the plan's targets. Actual change in employment in the coal industry was 99% of the targeted increase; 101% in the gas industry; and 95% in electricity. (*Rapport Annuel*, 1958, table 7.)

Industries in the intermediate category, however, expanded well beyond the planned targets.

TABLE VI

INDUSTRIES	ACTUAL INCREASE IN OUTPUT AS A PERCENTAGE OF PLANNED INCREASE
(a) Automobile	380%
(b) Paper	208%
(c) Chemicals	280%
(d) Farm machinery	200%
(e) Diverse manufacturing	200%
(f) Wood	246%
(g) Machine tools	50%
(h) Electrical equipment	233%
(i) Textiles	213%
(j) All manufacturing	196%

Sources:

(a) *Rapport Annuel*, 1958, table 3.

(b) *Ibid.*, table 3.

(c) Target, *Second Plan*, p. 65, *Rapport Annuel*, 1957, para. 199; actual output, *Third Plan*, para. 3.

(d) *Rapport Annuel*, 1958, table 3.

(e) *Ibid.*, para. 210; includes plastics, cosmetics, sporting goods, musical instruments, etc.

(f) *Rapport Annuel*, 1958, table 3.
(g) *Third Plan*, para. 3. On the failure of the machine tool industry, see Sheahan, *Promotion and Control*, Chapter 6.
(h) *Rapport Annuel*, 1958, table 3.
(i) *Ibid.*, table 86.
(j) *Ibid.*, table 67.

'The second plan has been achieved one year ahead of schedule.'[1] The planners made similar announcements, with equal pride.[2] The principal text of the third plan, completed in 1958, began with the observation that 'France finds herself in a severe financial crisis, the expression of a profound economic disequilibrium.'[3] All of the aggregate balances which defined the equilibrium growth pattern of the plan had been destroyed. In their place were imbalances, or, as they were then called, *crises*, which announced the distortion of that pattern, and the presence of an all-out inflation. In 1957 prices rose by about 12% and so did wages.[4] (The plan had projected constant prices.)

The inflation was of the classical variety, motored by an excess of demand over supply.[5] Prices kept rising, wages kept rising, imports kept rising and so did the Government deficit.[6]

The length of the average work week rose to 46 hours,[7] with over three-fourths of those employed in the electrical and mechanical goods industries (the core of the 'intermediate category') working 48 hours and more.[8] Foreign workers were brought in; during 1957 over 112,000 arrived in France, (mostly from North Africa).[9]

[1] Speech of 23 September 1956, cited in *Revue des Comités d'Entreprise*, no. 99, June 1957. On the frequency of M. Mollet's references to the plan see below, pp. 290ff.

[2] For example, 'The objectives . . . [of the second plan] have been reached one year ahead of schedule.' *Rapport Annuel*, 1957, para. 2. '. . . [the second plan] was fulfilled a year ahead of schedule, thus making up for the delay in the first plan.' (Bauchet, *Economic Planning*, p. 186.)

[3] *Third Plan*, para. 2.

[4] (Neither estimate being particularly reliable.) Prices, wholesale price index, INSEE, *Annuaire Statistique*, 1962, p. 342; wages, average industrial wage (hourly), INSEE, *Mouvement Economique de* 1944, à 1957, (1958), p. 283.

[5] See *Rapport Annuel*, 1958, para. 8; *Third Plan*, paras. 11–14; J. Bénard, 'Economic Policy in France,' in *Economic Policy in our Time*, Vol. III, Kirschen and Associates, eds., Amsterdam, North Holland Pub. Co., 1964, pp. 333–335.

[6] See Bénard, 'Economic Policy in France,' pp. 333–337; *Rapport Annuel*, 1958, par. 15.

[7] *Rapport Annuel*, 1958, para. 8.

[8] *Third Plan*, para. 13.

[9] *Rapport Annuel*, 1958, para. 8.

The foreign exchange crisis was the most desperate and the most dramatic. In 1955 exports covered 93% of imports; in 1956, 73%; and in 1957, 71%.[1] The plan had called for a 40% increase in exports; they rose by 70%.[2] But the plan had projected no increase at all in the volume of imports; they rose by more than 50%.[3] By 1957 the current account deficit had reached $1,650,000,000.[4] Devaluation and deliberate deflation followed quickly.[5]

The plan neither caused nor cured the inflation. The Algerian War was at the bottom of France's economic troubles, in part because of the enormous strain it placed on French resources, but also because of the political insecurity and instability it created in Metropolitan France.

It is impossible to isolate the economic effects of the Algerian War, put them aside and then analyse the effects of the plan. But that does not mean that it is impossible to learn anything about the planning process by relating it to actual economic activity. Something more interesting about the relation of the planning process to actual activity can be found in the experience of the second plan than the observation that unique, exogenous forces took over and the planned pattern of resource allocation was severely distorted. John Sheahan attempts to make such a statement.[6]

He argues that even discounting the distortions in the planned growth pattern wrought by the Algerian War, the projections of the second plan were technically inaccurate. The planners, he asserts, missed, and in the worst and most visible way: they underestimated potential growth.[7] For example, they urged the steel industry to reduce intended investment; two years later a drastic steel shortage emerged.[8] Crucially, he finds, 'the second plan grossly underestimated the whole economy's expansionary potential.'[9] This assertion – for it is not a simple statement of

[1] *Ibid.*, table 10.
[2] *Ibid.*, para 11.
[3] *Ibid.*, para. 11. See above, pp. 240–242, for a discussion of the plan's import projections.
[4] *Ibid.*, para. 11.
[5] See Bénard, 'Economic Policy in France,' pp 337–349, for an outline of major economic policies of 1957–59.
[6] In *Promotion and Control*, pp. 181–189.
[7] *Ibid.*, p. 184.
[8] *Ibid.*, pp. 177, 184.
[9] *Ibid.*, p. 184.

fact[1] – is the heart of his argument. Because the plan is likely to underestimate potential expansion it is 'a potentially deadly instrument.'[2] The underestimation was not the result of simple, but, correctable errors, nor of crude, but improvable techniques.

> It is impossible to predict the upper limits of future markets. . . . It is easy enough to retreat to the comfortable notion that better forecasting methods would have given better results, and undeniable that the methods used in France have greatly improved. But the best econometric analysis in the world will never reveal the opportunities that have not yet been created by technical innovation, new commercial opportunities, or new achievements of the human imagination.[3]

The defect inheres in the method. The planned optimum is likely to be less than the actually attainable maximum. Consequently, any attempt to require individual economic units to conform to the targets of a plan that defines a general resource allocation pattern is 'certain to do more harm than good.'[4]

His conclusion is that quantitative target planning, while potentially 'deadly' if implemented, can be useful so long as it remains purely informational.[5] It is an effective form of market research that can improve the information available for making investment decisions.[6] But firms should not be restrained from expanding beyond the targets of the plan.[7]

Many critics of French planning stop their analysis here and close with a hymn to the Market.[8] Sheahan does no such thing. Having disavowed general resource allocation planning because

[1] It is true that by 1957 actual output had surpassed the plan's targets by a substantial margin. But the plan's target was for maximum expansion consistent with stability – defined in terms of several key, aggregate balances. That stability was not achieved. Furthermore, if the fall in the growth rate during 1958 and 1959 can to an important extent be attributed to the disequilibria generated in 1956–57, it is no longer clear that actual expansion exceeded planned expansion.

[2] *Ibid.*, p. 188.

[3] *Ibid.*, pp. 184–185.

[4] *Ibid.*, p. 188.

[5] *Ibid.*, p. 188.

[6] *Ibid.*, p. 188. There is, of course, a problem here. The plan's effectiveness as market research depends upon all parties sharing the assumption that it *accurately* projects future demands, i.e., that the projected pattern will in fact be realised.

[7] *Ibid.*, p. 188.

[8] For example, S. Wellisz, 'Economic Planning in the Netherlands, France and Italy,' and V. C. Lutz, *French Planning*, Washington, D.C., 1965.

it might lessen the rate of expansion, he goes on to applaud the plan's efforts to promote expansion – what we have called the first component of the planning process, the plan's role within the *économie concertée*.[1]

His approval derives from his judgment that the pragmatic interventions of the plan have helped to accelerate growth in many industries. Sheahan recognizes the dangers implicit in the cartel-like operations of the plan but finds that

> The French version of planning has not been deadly for two reasons. On the one hand, its directive personnel have usually been oriented toward investment and expansion, less rather than more inclined than private industry to worry about excessive capacity. On the other hand, the [Planning] Commission has not had the power to block individual firms which did wish to move ahead more rapidly than collective planning seemed to indicate as desirable. Planning helped raise the industries' original targets, and then ceased to constitute a plan in the sense of controlling the result.[2]

Sheahan's analysis is a prisoner of the single and simple set of criteria it incorporates – growth, efficiency, international competitiveness, technological sophistication. The only relevant role it sees for planning is that of promoting activity towards those ends. The existence of other goals is explicitly acknowledged but they are never brought to the centre of the argument. On the basis of these criteria it is hard to criticize the pragmatic promotional activities of the plan and the *économie concertée*, except in the way Sheahan does: in terms of the potential of the cartel system to backfire and impede expansion.

The problem with this perspective is that it prevents an appreciation of what a general resource allocation plan really is. The analysis has no political dimension. But planning is fundamentally a political process. Only when a general resource allocation plan is seen as a major innovation in the way political decisions are taken does it become possible to understand why the second plan was so severely distorted, why some groups support planning while others do not, and why certain kinds of planning fail while others succeed.

[1] *Promotion and Control*, pp. 188–189.
[2] *Ibid.*, p. 189.

PART V

PLANNING MODELS: THEIR POLITICAL MEANING

16 *PLANNING AS A POLITICAL PROCESS*

The rationality of a general, quantitative resource allocation plan derives from its consistency which must extend beyond the mathematical consistency of the targets in the text, to the operational consistency of their realisation. The plan must be implemented uniformly. Distortion represents irrationality and failure. For the second plan, the likelihood of uniform implementation was extremely small, almost non-existent, because the planning process did not meet the political prerequisites for the success of a general resource allocation plan.

The first political condition for the implementation of a general quantitative resource allocation plan is that all major collective decisions affecting the economy be incorporated into the plan and executed as planned. The word 'decisions' it will be recalled, distinguishes normative objectives from purely predictive projections, the independent from the dependent variable. Only if the decisions are carried through as planned can market forces possibly steer the rest of the economy to the planned targets.

The most important of these decisions, or volitional programmes, emanate from the state. All government activities that have important effects on the economy must be included in the plan. Programmes for housing, education, health, communications, social security, roads, science, and technology, public works, art, culture and transportation, must be included in the plan. So too must economically important decisions in such traditionally 'political' areas as foreign policy or military affairs: a change in the size or composition of the military budget (or foreign aid programme) will distort the planned pattern of development quite as much as over-expansion in the motor industry, a change in interest rates, or a spur of the moment moon shot.[1]

[1] A 'contingency planning' approach will, of course, avoid the obvious foolishness of fixing rigid targets for areas of high uncertainty, but, as a moment's reflection will show, no matter how many economic contingencies are taken into account, the plan must still meet these same political conditions.

Crucially, the exercise of short term economic policy must be systematically co-ordinated with the middle term programmes of the plan. Short term policy – especially the full range of monetary and fiscal controls – must be deliberately used to keep the economy moving along the planned path at the planned rate.

The Government must commit itself over a wide range and for a long time. But no Government can be expected to undertake such a commitment except as what one premier is reported to have called, '*un engagement à long-terme qui n'engage pas l'avenir*.'[1] It can promote, promulgate and propagandise, but it cannot seriously anticipate tying itself to the detailed implementation of the resource allocation plan. Such a commitment is simply beyond the Government's range of choice.

A general, quantitative resource allocation plan represents not merely a new programme – however vast, costly and controversial – but a new politics. And no single Government is able, all by itself, to construct a new politics. The Government is part of a political system, and its actions must conform to the logic of that system.

The commitment to planning cannot come from 'The Government' alone but must come from the major political forces. The various political elements – big business, trade unions, small business, peasants, the military, the permanent bureaucracy, etc. – must believe that they can realise their objectives through the plan. They must switch the focus of their efforts from the creation and execution of individual, pragmatically chosen programmes and policies to the choice and execution of the plan's long-term programmes. If they continue to concentrate their energies on initiating pragmatic programmes and on influencing the contents of day-to-day decisions, the Government would have to respond to those pressures.[2] However profound and sincere its attachment to the plan, the Government would have to make its decisions in terms of those forces and not in terms of the programmes contained in the plan. The plan would be distorted. The traditional political process of day-to-day policy formulation and execution based on pragmatic, individual compromises would prevail.

To be effective, the general resource allocation plan must

[1] In Club Jean Moulin, *l'Etat et le Citoyen*, Paris, le Seuil, 1961, p. 357.

[2] The alternative, as noted above, is for the Government to *impose* its plan on the nation. Such a totalitarian model is not relevant to France.

become the principal framework for political decisions and the planning process must become the principal political process. If the plan is to be anything but a decorative *objet d'art* or a self-gratifying list of national New Year's resolutions, it must conform to the logic of the political process. It must be an instrument through which the various groups can seek to realise their objectives and defend their interests. The problem is not whether or not to let politics into planning, but rather how to bring planning into so much of traditional politics. The *économie concertée*, to take one kind of successful planning, is not apolitical or non-political. It is part of the special politics of economic administration by the managers of big business and the state, and conforms to the logic of that special politics. A general quantitative resource allocation plan is a different kind of plan. It presupposes a different kind of politics.

THE POLITICS OF A GENERAL RESOURCE ALLOCATION PLAN

The politics of a general resource allocation plan are comprehensive, simultaneous and explicit. The plan centralises both political space and time. It pulls a vast range of decisions into a single framework and insists that they be decided simultaneously. The politics of frequent, individual and partial decisions becomes a politics of simultaneous, interrelated and long-term decisions. The traditional interplay of issues, interests and marginal adjustments must accommodate to a new politics of social design. For the various political groups this means abandoning the traditional political process of frequent, piecemeal gains and losses for the politics of a single, long-term package deal.

> William James is said to have observed that democracy is a system in which the government does something and waits to see who 'hollers.' Then it does something else in order to relieve the 'hollering' as best it can and waits to see who 'hollers' at the adjustment. [This remark] – epitomizes the experience of self-governing peoples.[1]

One need not define all politics as group pressure politics in order to recognise the existence of a politics of competing

[1] Wilfred E. Binkley and Malcolm C. Moos, *A Grammar of American Politics*, New York (1958), p. 3.

interests, and the importance of frequent and piecemeal decisions to that politics. A process of constant, partial adjustment lies at the centre of traditional, democratic, pluralist politics for good reasons. Whatever its supposed inadequacies in producing coherent, long-term policies, it has proved to be a useful way to sustain a system of opposing interests. The constant process of partial, pragmatic policy formulation holds out to the major groups the promise of chopping away at the substance of defeats and building up structures of small gains. Most important, it provides the best defence against the total defeat of major interests as well as the best safeguard against the realisation of any one vision.[1]

Of the three characteristics of the politics of a general resource allocation plan – comprehensiveness, simultanaeity and explicitness – explicitness is the most important. The plan makes explicit the implications of any contemplated programme, and it presents those implications in the context of a blueprint of the society's future. This is the primary source of the plan's usefulness. But it is also, potentially, a source of important social change and, consequently, a threat to many political groups.

Little direct attention has been paid to the 'explicitness' effect of planning. Most often, analysis fails to sort out explicitness from 'coherence' (meaning internal consistency among quantitative targets, balance between inputs and outputs, supplies and demands). The coherence of the planned pattern for development is seen by most proponents of planning – especially the French planners – as the most fundamental and most important characteristic of planning.[2] Actually, it is neither. Coherence is not a fundamental output of planning. It is an end to which the explicitness of a planned resource allocation can be used. All planning *per se* provides is an explicit pattern of resource allocation. The common presumption is that an explicit pattern of planned allocation will automatically be a coherent, or optimally efficient, pattern. In general, there is strong reason to anticipate such a development – especially in

[1] Except, of course, the vision of compromise and competing interest groups, which it realises.

[2] See above, Part I, Chapter I; and Bauchet, (English edition), pp. 113–115. Here coherence is presented as the crucial characteristic of planning and the desirability of Parliamentary control is denied on the basis of its supposed incompatibility with the plan's coherence.

an economy where market forces play a powerful role. But it ought to be understood that this is merely a likely outcome, and not a general rule or logical imperative. It is quite possible to imagine plans which are not coherent in the general equilibrium sense as the planners use the word. Plans for the agricultural sector in many developed countries can serve as examples; so too, we shall see, can the operational cores of the second and third French national plans.

A failure to distinguish the explicitness which is an inherent characteristic of planned resource allocation from the planned general equilibrium, or coherence it makes possible, generally stems from a conception of the planning process as just another 'economists' tool,' as part of the market system of allocation and not as a new political process.[1] This generally received market research or 'uncertainty reducer-efficiency increaser' model of planning, begins from assumptions about the primacy of efficiency in resource allocation and leads to conclusions about the primacy of coherence in the plan.

But the explicitness of the planning process affects collective decisions at least as strongly as it affects decisions made by individual firms. Few analyses, however, follow through to the implications of this obvious fact. They fail to examine the potential for conflict between a planning process designed to increase the range and effectiveness of collective decisions and one designed to increase the efficiency of resource allocation by increasing the coherence of decisions made by individual firms. Efforts to democratise the planning process reveal the existence of important trade-offs between the democratic control of a plan and its coherence. Serious debate about the desirability and practicability of active parliamentary participation in planning, for example, stems from these conflicting conceptions of the process and role of planning.[2]

Packages of long-term decisions with implications made explicit in terms of a general programme for the society's development characterise the politics of a general resource allocation plan. This constitutes a change in the process of making collective decisions sufficient to warrant consideration

[1] As for example in Massé, *French Affairs*; Sheahan, *Promotion and Control* and Bauchet, *Economic Planning*.

[2] For example, contrast the argument of Part VI of this study with Bauchet's case for 'Executive' rather than Parliamentary democracy, in *Economic Planning*, pp. 113–115 and 123.

as a new politics – a change in the form of taking collective decisions that contains the potential for a change in the substantive outcome of those decisions.

Once the plan is seen as an important innovation in the political process, powerful reasons for the various groups to prefer that it remain essentially inoperative become immediately apparent. For example, from the perspective of the managers of the giant corporations, the most important of the probable outcomes of such a change in political procedures would be an increase in the range and effectiveness of collective decisions. The managers have good reasons for suspecting that such a development is likely to threaten what they consider to be their interests.

As the scope of collective decision expands, the composition and distribution of goods, services, efforts, rewards – even status and values – are likely to change. An explicitly planned income distribution is very likely to differ from the present distribution. Profits might be threatened; so might business' sense of independence and power. The proportion of total output consumed collectively might increase. Social amenities such as urban design, regional balance, safety and health may play a more substantial and more direct role in allocating resources. On a more abstract level, as planning overcomes the limitations of the market as a means for translating social wants into effective demand, important social objectives – such as the desire to preserve or to alter social structures – may become more immediate and more effective forces in allocating resources.

Such outcomes become increasingly probable if one adds the assumption that in order for a comprehensive resource allocation plan to be effective, broad participation in the planning process is necessary. Unlike the *économie concertée*, the general resource allocation plan cannot be prepared and implemented by a small group of business and state officials. The range and explicitness of decisions that must be incorporated into the plan necessitate commitment from a wide range of political forces. Either the resource allocation plan will be the product of a broad range of participants or it will remain ineffective.

Seen from this perspective, the resource allocation plan constitutes a potential threat to the profits, power, prestige and freedom of business. It is against such 'political' outcomes that the managers of big business must balance the potential economic benefits of a general resource allocation plan. From their viewpoint, the losses seem sure and enormous, and the gains uncertain and small.

Big business already enjoys an institution – the *économie concertée* – that provides it with much of what it considers to be the positive potential of planning. The *économie concertée* defines a partnership between the managers of big business and the managers of the state. It provides big business with the active participation and support of the state while keeping broad participation politics away. From the perspective of big business, the *économie concertée* is the most satisfactory reconciliation of its potentially conflicting wants: big business needs the active participation of the state in the management of the economy, but it fears opening economic administration to popular participation.[1]

From this political perspective it is easy to see why the government might not have included all its major decisions in the second plan, and why the government might not have used short-term economic policy to steer the economy along the planned path at the planned rate, and why, in brief, decisions would continue to be made in terms of the traditional political process and the resource allocation component of the plan would be ignored. For that is exactly what happened.

[1] It is, of course, possible to imagine circumstances that will lead business to seek to extend the role of planning beyond the *Economie Concertée*. Parts V and VI of this study examine the kinds of planning big business and the trade unions want.

17 THE SECOND PLAN
and actual economic policy

During the time of the second plan, the exercise of short-term economic policy was not co-ordinated with the plan. Important economic decisions were taken by the Government without reference to the plan. Although its realisation depended upon it becoming the principal framework for political activity and decision-making, the resource allocation planning process had no decision making procedures and no mechanisms for dealing with conflicts. Conflicts, decisions and politics were kept outside the elegant boundaries of the general resource allocation plan, and the general resource allocation plan was kept out of politics and out of contact with actual economic policy.

DECISIONS AND PLANS

In an extraordinarily frank document, *Les Motifs d'Exécution du Plan*, the planners evaluate the relation of the plan to actual decision-making with thoroughness, accuracy and little of the rhetoric that colours most of the Planning Commission's publications. The document states quite coldly that 'the plan remains a marginal organism in the governmental and administrative organisation.'[1] It then goes on to discuss the limits to the plan's influence on the critical economic decisions taken by the government. It observes that the plan played no role in the formulation and execution of France's European policy – including the decision on whether or not to enter into a European Economic Community and the formulation of France's position on what forms and functions the Community ought to

[1] Planning Commission, *Les Motifs d'Exécution du Plan*, (mimeo) 196(3 ?), labelled 'Internal Document, Not for Distribution,' p. 14.

take.[1] Nor did the Planning Commission participate in any way in the decision to undertake the *force de frappe*, France's independent nuclear striking force. Vast and unplanned government expenditures on the *force de frappe* constituted one of the major sources of distortion in the fourth plan.[2] On the level of smaller and more technical single decisions the plan's influence has most often been slight, even negligible. The Mont Blanc tunnel provides a good illustration. The Planning Commission was strongly opposed to the construction of a railway tunnel under Mont Blanc, preferring a more economical route under Mount Cenis. The Planning Commission's recommendations were overruled – although the word overruled suggests a more serious consideration that they received – by a Government and civil service which had to take into account powerful political pressures which the planners preferred not to consider.[3] Similarly, the use of price controls has never been co-ordinated with the programmes of the plan.[4] And the influence of the plan on the extension and functioning of the public sector, on the creation of new, and the diversification of existing, public enterprises, has been in the planners own admission as well as the judgment of outside observers, extremely limited.[5] Furthermore, the distribution of short term credit by the nationalised banks is totally outside the influence of the plan.[6]

[1] *Ibid.*, p. 13: 'on peut néamonins s'étonner que par example, ni sur le plan des principes ni sur celui de la négotiation quotidienne, le Commisariat au [sic] Plan ne soit pratiquement pas associé à la définition et mise en oeuvre de la position de la France à l'égard de la construction économique européene.' Although Mollet and Marjolin, the founders of the plan, played important personal roles in this area, they were no longer associated with the plan.

[2] Military expenditures exceeded the plan's target by 900%: See below, Appendix I, tables 1 and 2. See also, Pierre Bolle, 'Deux Etudes de Cas – Pierrelatte et le Tunnel du Mont Blanc,' in *La Planification Comme Processus de Décision*, Cahiers de la Fondation Nationale des Sciences Politiques, no. 140, 1965; and C. P. Kindleberger, 'French Planning,' paper presented at the National Bureau of Economic Research Conference on Economic Planning, Nov. 27–28, 1964, (mimeo), p. 5.

[3] See Bolle, 'Deux Etudes de Cas,' part II; Kindleberger 'French Planning,' p. 6.

[4] See below, p. 170.

[5] See *Les Motifs d'Exécution du Plan*, pp. 4–5, 19, 46–48, for the most direct and detailed statements. See also, P. Bauchet, *Propriété Publique et Planification*, especially pp. 230–250; Kindleberger, 'French Planning,' p. 6; Sheahan, *Promotion and Control*, pp. 202–209.

[6] 'D'autre part, le crédit à court terme, aussi bien dans ses organismes directeurs (Conseil National du Crédit, Banque de France, Commission de Contrôle des

For our present purposes there is no need to extend the list.[1] The Government did not include all major decisions in the plan and carry out those decisions according to plan. Nor did it use short-term economic policy – especially its monetary and fiscal levers – to steer the economy along the planned growth path. There is no discernable pattern of co-ordination between the exercise of short term economic policy and the middle term programmes of the plan. As we shall see, all available evidence (interviews, published statements, the 'historical record' and analysis of recent proposals for strengthening planning) points to the fact that the co-ordination of short term economic policy with the plans has been extremely limited, if not outright non-existent. It was certainly not the kind of close, systematic harmonisation upon which the successful implementation of the resource allocation plan depended.

INTERVIEWS AND STATEMENTS

Interviews with Treasury officials, businessmen, informed observers of French planning and the planners themselves yielded unanimous judgments: short-term economic policy was not deliberately used as an instrument to implement the plan; the implementation of the plan was only a marginal consideration to the Government and the Treasury when day-to-day economic decisions were made. It was repeatedly emphasised not only that short-term policy was not used deliberately and systematically for the purpose of implementing the detailed programmes of the plan, but that quite often the main trends in economic policy were in contradiction with even the broadest outlines of the plan.[2]

Banques) que dans les banques nationalisées qui en assurent la distribution, échappe totalement au domaine de la planification.' *Les Motifs d'Exécution du Plan*, pp. 11–12.

See also, F. Bloch-Lainé, 'Reform de l'Administration Economique,' *La Revue Economique*, No. 1962, especially p. 875; and P. Bauchet, *l'Expérience Française de Planification*, Paris, 1958, p. 134.

[1] And it is easily extended. For example, the plan's influence has been extremely slight in agricultural policy, much of public works and overseas policies. See, Sheahan, *Promotion and Control*, pp. 80–83.

[2] None of those questioned seriously departed from this general observation although several people – especially the Planning Commission and the Treasury – preferred to discuss the problem of co-ordination in terms of a gradual development: no co-ordination whatever in the first years of planning, then a gradual

Occasionally the planners say the same thing in a published statement:

On day-to-day decisions affecting the immediate state and structures of the economy . . . the role of planning remains quite limited.[1]

The Government has the means [to implement the plan] but for reasons of short-term policy, it does not always use them.[2]

In its own domain, the daily implementation of the plan's medium-term objectives, the Planning Commission is not always fully able to fulfill its function. This is especially true . . . when it comes to including planned investment programmes in the annual budget. . . . Budgetary procedure does not provide the necessary guarantees for the proper implementation of the plan. There is no question that the law gives the Planning Commission the role of policy co-ordination, and . . . its attachment to the Prime Minister's office should give it sufficient weight to exercise effectively this function. . . . The reality is quite different.[3]

Such frankness is, however, exceptional. The problem of co-ordinating short-term policy with the plan is usually discussed in the guarded terms of delicate public pronouncements. For example, Finance Minister Valéry Giscard d'Estaing announced in May 1962 that

For the first time, the Minister of Finance agrees not just to adopt the broad objectives of the plan, but to define his policy in such a way that it becomes an instrument for reaching these objectives.[4]

---

process of improvement. Asked to indicate when this improvement first became significant, almost all said that it was at the beginning of the fourth plan. Furthermore, most found the improvement to have importance only as the beginning of a trend towards increased co-ordination: from the standpoint of the actual implementation of the plan, the situation remains unsatisfactory.

[1] *Les Motifs d'Execution du Plan*, p. 13.

[2] M. Delcourt, *Les Moyens d'Exécution du Plan*, Planning Commission (mimeo), p. 3.

[3] *Les Motifs d'Exécution du Plan*, pp. 14–15.

[4] Quotation is from *J.O.*, *Débats Parlementaires*, 23 Mai 1962, p. 1234. Hackett and Hackett, provide another example of indirect evaluations of the co-ordination of short term economic policy with the plan, when they attempt to show improvement in this area: 'although for a long time there was little co-ordination between the short-term economic situation and the medium-term plan, with the fourth plan the need for such a liason is fully recognised inside the Government departments,' (*Economic Planning in France*, p. 297). They then discuss the fourth plan as though the recent *realisation of the need for co-ordination* was tantamount to desire for change and a guarantee that improvements in the substance of co-ordination as well as the organisational forms and trappings (the central concern of the Hackett study) is, in fact, taking place.

The interesting notion here is not M. Giscard d'Estaing's announced intention to implement the plan – the sincerity and determination of which are debatable – but the initial boast: 'For the first time . . .' which defines, albeit somewhat indirectly, past practice. Often the entire question – essential though it may be to the implementation of the plan – is simply left out of the planners' published discussions of 'problems of implementation,' just as the critical question of incomes is left out of the text of the plans.[1]

THE HISTORICAL PATTERN

The historical record reveals, quite as clearly, the same situation: the exercise of short-term economic policy was not informed by the plan. It was not deliberately used for the implementation of the detailed programmes of the middle term plan. Often, in response to immediate pressures, important changes in short-term policy were made which operated in clear contradiction to even the broadest outlines of the plan.

A blow by blow narration of the long and repetitive history of short-term economic policy decisions and its relation to the plan is precluded by the length and purpose of this study. We can, however, get a useful historical perspective on the co-ordination of short-term policy with the plan by focusing on two critical periods, the years directly preceding the second and third plans – the years in which the plans were being drawn up.[2]

See also Fourastié, J. and Courthéous, J-P., *La Planification Economique en France*, Paris, 1963, pp. 113, 120–125; Bauchet, *Economic Planning* . . . , pp. 92, 97, 107. In June 1962, the Minister of Finance told the National Assembly that the Government 's'engageait *en principe* à financier, par prioritié, les investissements publics du plan . . .' cited in F. Perroux, *Le IVe Plan Français*, Paris, 1962, p. 106 (italics added).

[1] See, for example, Bernard Cazes, 'liasons entre secteur public et secteur privé dans la planification du dévelopment,' *document de travail présenté à la réunion d'experts organisés à Paris par le Département des Affaires Economique et Sociales des Nations Unies sur les Aspects Administratifs de la Planification du Dévelopment*, 8–19 juin 1964 especially Part II, 'Problèmes Posés Lors de l'Exécution du Plan,' where almost all the available *incitations* are catalogued and discussed, where the psychological implementations means are discussed at some length, where even work-load limits (for the planners themselves) are touched upon, but where the whole question of using monetary and fiscal policy as an instrument of implementation is completely unexplored.

[2] A detailed examination of the relation of short-term economic policy to the first plan is provided above, pp. 83–121; the fourth plan, see below, pp. 179–84; 258–65.

CO-ORDINATION IN 1952

1952 was the terminal year of the first plan, and the base year for the second plan's projections. It was also the year of the Pinay experiment. Antoine Pinay ('I am Mr Average Consumer') came to power in March 1952.[1] His aim was to stop inflation, or as he put it in his inaugural address, 'to prevent the fall of the franc, for the fall of the franc would mean despair in the home and disorder in the streets.'[2] Despite his assurance to the French people, 'je ne fais pas l'expérience d'une politique, mais la politique de l'expérience,'[3] he experimented with two methods of halting the inflation.

The first phase of the Pinay experiment began in a classically orthodox manner. State expenditures, including credits for investment, were immediately slashed. But taxes were not increased. Instead, a special bond issue – with the price of the gold Napoleon as an index to encourage purchases and amnesties for past fiscal frauds and undeclared holdings abroad to tap secret hoardings – was floated as a key element in the anti-inflation programme. The bond issue, hailed as a huge success by the Government, brought in an estimated 428 billion francs. Of that sum, however, 233 billions represented older bonds and securities exchanged for the more favourable terms of the new issue. The remaining 195 billion reflected more a shift in the form of savings – away from possibly productive investment – than a shift in resources from consumption to savings.[4] Pinay's

[1] For the Mr Average Consumer speech see *Paris Presse*, 18 April 1952 and, by way of contrast, *l'Humanité* of the same and following days.

[2] M. Pinay's inaugural address of 8 March 1952.

[3] Cited in Paul Delouvrier and Roger Nathan, *Politique Economique de la France*, 1957–1958, Les Cours de Droit, Paris, p. 341.

[4] For an outline of the Pinay programme, including the arithmetic of the bond issue and its economic effects, see J. S. G. Wilson, *French Banking Structure and Credit Policy*, Cambridge (Mass.), 1957, pp. 359–364; Bénard, 'Economic Policy in France', pp. 291, 323–327. M. Pinay is often associated with the psychological or persuasion approach to inflation fighting. He attempted, and not without a certain success, to secure a national agreement to hold price lines. The psychological campaign, the loan, the imports to force down prices, etc., were not without some effect. Most serious economists, however, tend to attribute the stabilisation of prices which coincided with the Pinay experiment only in a small degree to his programmes and in a greater measure to the evolution of a complex series of factors most of which were beyond the influence of the measures Pinay adopted, e.g. changing world commodity prices, the evolution of internal demand, changes in inventories, etc. See, John Sheahan, 'Problems and Possibilities of Industrial Price Control: Postwar French Experience,' *American Economic Review*, June 1961, pp. 345–359 for an excellent analysis of the Pinay experiment.

two principal programmes – slashing state investment credits and shifting the form of savings – both ran counter to the plan which emphasised the importance of maintaining investment.

The orthodox phase of the Pinay experiment was soon transformed into an experiment with direct controls: wages were frozen in the spring of 1952, prices in the summer.[1] These direct price controls were used by the Government and the Treasury with an almost single-minded concentration on holding the general price line. The plan remained irrelevant to the exercise of direct controls.[2]

CO-ORDINATION IN 1956

Following a general election a Left-of-centre Government was formed by Guy Mollet (SFIO) in February 1956. Paul Ramadier (also a Socialist) was named Finance Minister. The new Government, like its predecessors, did not consider, nor pretend to consider, the implementation of the plan to be a

---

See also Harold Lubell, 'The Role of Investment in Two French Inflations,' *Oxford Economic Papers, NS*, vol. 7, no. 1, February 1955, especially pp. 52–56; J. Laux, 'M. Pinay and Inflation,' *Political Science Quarterly*, vol. 74, no. 1, March 1959, and Delouvrier, *Politique Economique de la France*, pp. 341–361.

[1] Bénard, *Economic Policy in France*, pp. 326–327.

[2] The article in the *AER* by John Sheahan, along with Delouvrier, *Politique Economique de la France*, are the two most interesting studies of the French experience with direct price controls. The above argument is based on their findings, and on the results of interviews with those responsible for price controls – especially Louis Franck – (although, of course, the argument above should in no way be interpreted as reflecting their views). Most published studies of price controls do not even consider the plan as an important influence on their use; most of the literature on planning does not speak of price controls as an instrument for the implementation of the plan. See, for example, L. Franck, *Les Prix* (Paris 1958), especially pp. 38, 51–53; André Bisson, *Institutions Financières et Economiques en France*, Paris, 1960, especially pp. 113–123. Even Baum, *The French Economy*, pp. 68–70, remarks that price controls were aimed more at the general price level than at selective control and stimulation. See Cazes, Gourney, Viot, La Perrière and *Les Motifs d'Exécution du Plan* – all planning commission mimeos already cited – concerning the means of implementing the plan where price controls are never listed in the exhaustive catalogues of implementation devices and procedures. Sheahan, studying price controls somewhat more deeply than most, finds that to the extent of their effectiveness, their net effect was to work against investment and expansion – especially in the highly concentrated sectors. If any sectors benefited (relative to other sectors) from price controls, it was the low concentration industries – a pattern of encouraged development quite opposite from that of the plan. Sheahan, one ought to note, does not include the Planning Commission in his discussion of the major determinant of price-control policy, nor does he include the implementation of the growth pattern of the plan as a major concern in price control policy.

major concern in the formulation of economic policy.[1] Under Mollet, major economic decisions were made without reference to the plan. In general, they were clearly contrary to even the basic outlines of the plan.

In the first quarter of 1956, just when inflationary pressures were beginning radically to distort the planned growth pattern, the new Government embarked upon a policy of *expansion à l'outrance*. Pensions, minimum wages and social services were increased; working hours were shortened.[2]

When the plan was worrying aloud about the declining ratio of directly productive investment to national product and about the growing volume of imports, the Government set out to further stimulate expansion through increasing consumer demand and increasing expenditures of public services and housing.[3]

A look at the relation of short-term economic policy to the plan in the years in which the second and third plans were being prepared provides no basis for assuming that short-term policy would be co-ordinated with the plan.[4] Stronger conclusions could be drawn from the same evidence. They are not, however, necessary. For the successful implementation of

[1] See, for example, M. Mollet's speech announcing major changes in economic policy: counter-inflationary measures, new investment policies fiscal reforms, and a host of other measures, some major, many minor, are outlined. A concern for the implementation of the plan is never referred to as informing these decisions; the plan is never even mentioned. Cf., *J.O. Débats, Assemblée Nationale*, 1 August 1956, pp. 3809–3816 and *Le Monde*, 2 August 1956, p. 12. See also Finance Minister Ramadier's presentation of the annual state budget, which is described in a full page in *Le Monde*, 19 April 1956, p. 14, where he makes no reference whatever to the plan. M. Pellenc, Rapporteur for the Finance Commission of the Conseil de la République, discusses the Government's economic policy, again without reference to the plan, in *Le Monde*, 3 August 1956.

[2] For a rapid résumé of these, and similar measures taken by the Mollet Government, see Bénard, 'Economic Policy in France,' pp. 334–337, and Wilson, *French Banking*, p. 373ff. Chapsal, *la France depuis* 1945, pp. 734–740, describes the economic policies of the Socialist Government in detail, but in severely critical tones.

[3] For the planners' views, see *Rapport Annuel*, 1955, pp. 111–112 and *Rapport Annuel*, 1956, pp. 23–24 and vi. For an outline of the Government's measures see, Bénard, *Economic Policy in France*, pp. 334–336; Wilson, *French Banking*, Chapsal, *la France depuis* 1945, pp. 738–739; INSEE, *Mouvement Economique*, 1957, p. 265, and INSEE-SEEF, *Statistiques et Etudes Financières*, no. 95, November 1956, p. 1153.

[4] There are other sections of this study where the co-ordination, or non-co-ordination of short-term economic policy with the plans is examined and similar conclusions reached. See especially, pp. 83–121 (1944–52); 260–7 (1957); 179–84 (1960–63).

the general resource allocation plan depended upon a systematic co-ordination of short-term economic policy with the plan's middle-term programmes.

The simplest, and perhaps best, index of the degree to which short-term economic policy was co-ordinated with the plan are the various proposals which have been made for strengthening planning. Most of these proposals have at their very centre some device for improving that co-ordination. By studying what the proponents of planning hope to achieve in the future, one can fix an upper limit to the degree of co-operation that has so far been achieved.

PROPOSALS FOR IMPROVING CO-ORDINATION

One of the most talked-about innovations for the fifth plan (1966–9) is a system of built-in warning signals. These *clignotants* (blinker-lights) as the alert-indicators have come to be called, are simply a set of index numbers representing the critical economic variables which define the broad outlines of the planned growth path. They include maximum (and minimum) rates of unemployment, price increases, wage increases, imports, etc., compatible with the planned path of development.[1]

The signals 'flash' (to use the planner's language) when the economy begins to stray from the planned growth path. The Government is then supposed to take action to redirect development back to the planned path. Thus, when unemployment or the foreign-trade deficit reaches the warning point of the signal-system, the Government is automatically informed that it must act immediately to steer the economy back to the planned path. In this way the warning signal system is intended to provide a first step towards a systematic and automatic co-ordination of short-term decision-making with the longer-term programmes of the plan.

The key to the system is its immediacy; it is an automatic alert to trigger Goverment action *before* distortions become serious, before remedies have to be drastic. It is hoped that the warning system will also guide, immediately and automatically,

[1] See, *J.O. Lois et Décrets*, 23 December 1964, pp. 11388–11389; *fifth plan*, pp. 23–26; *J.O. Conseil Economique*, 13 November 1964, pp. 873 and 883; *Rapport Sur les Principales Options du Ve plan*, – Projet de loi portant approbation d'un rapport sur les principales options qui commande la préparation du Ve plan, Assemblée Nationale, no. 1154, November 5, 1964, vol. III, p. 50.

the behaviour of non-governmental economic agents and play an important role in developing a more economically aware and sophisticated public opinion.[1]

There is, of course, no binding obligation on the part of the Government or of the Treasury to react to the flashing lights. The decision to do something rests with the Government and the Treasury.[2] The substantive contents of any action which might be triggered by the alarm-indicators are not set out in the plan, not even in the form of 'contingency plans.'[3] All the system does is to indicate that the economy is straying from the planned path. The immediate objective of the new system – for the period of the fifth plan at least – is to take a first step towards linking short-term decisions to the broad outlines of the plan by building some initiative, however small, on day-to-day decisions into the plan.

The indices concern only major aggregates which outline more the rate and smoothness of growth than its detailed sectoral pattern. Lights will flash when foreign exchange gets low or prices high, but not when the rate of growth in the steel, automotive or chemical industries outstrips, in terms of the planned objectives, growth in fertilizers, education or housing.[4]

It is hoped that along with the warning signals, the plan will be able to provide 'advance strategies' to guide current action. The strategies, in a broad and general sense, will outline the kinds of action the plan thinks ought to be taken in response to indications of developing distortions. What influence those recommendations will carry is up to the Government and Treasury.[5]

The linkage is a rudimentary beginning. Its successful development depends upon many factors, and not least on some kind of effective incomes policy. M. Massé is confident about the eventual success of the *clignotant* system, (including the

[1] *J.O., Lois et Décrets*, 23 December 1964, pp. 11389–11401.

[2] *Ibid.*, p. 11401; *J.O., Conseil Economique*, 13 November 1964, pp. 873 and 883.

[3] See, *J.O., Conseil Economique*, 13 November 1964, pp. 873 and 883; *J.O., Lois et Décrets*, 23 December 1964, p. 11389.

[4] The *Conseil Economique* is especially critical of the overly aggregate nature of the indices and doubts the efficacy of the global approach. It recommends a system better able to indicate sectoral imbalances. See, *J.O., Conseil Economique*, 13 November 1964, pp. 883 and 874.

[5] *J.O., Lois et Décrets*, 23 December 1964, pp. 11388–9, 11401; *Fifth plan*, p. 24 and footnote on p. 24.

incomes index) but for the future. For the next few years he sees the alert indicator system working more as an educative device – acting on the Government, the Treasury, powerful economic groups and general public opinion – than as a mechanism which will automatically force the Government's (and the Treasury's) hand when it comes to making real decisions. It is, he stresses, but a first step towards systematic co-ordination.[1]

SUMMARY

The second plan marked the beginning of the two component planning process – the *économie concertée* and the general resource allocation plan. The first component worked. The *économie concertée*, the post-war development in political economy into which Monnet originally inserted the plan, was an important force in the restructuring and invigorating of the industrial core of the French economy. But the general resource allocation plan was not successful. The simplest indicator of its failure is the fact that the pattern of actual economic activity differed significantly from the planned pattern. There are many explanations for this divergence. One is that the planners were new at the game and consequently made errors in projections that could eventually be overcome with experience and methodological refinements. A second is that in a modern complex economy, it is impossible to make accurate projections on the scale demanded by a general resource allocation plan. A third is that unique, unpredictable, exogenous forces intervened and pushed the economy away from the planned growth path. There is something in each of these explanations. But the partial insights each affords come at a heavy price; they lead nowhere. They generate no interesting questions about the planning process and about its role in the political economy of post-war France. They do not even generate explanations to such obvious and important questions as why some groups support the plan while others oppose it. Crucially, they blind

[1] See, La Documentation Française, Recueils et Monographies, no. 47, *Rapport sur La Politique des Revenues Etabli à la Suite de la Conférence des Revenues* (October 1963–January 1964), pp. 3–4, 25, 26, 29; speech by P. Massé at the London School of Economics, October 1964, 'What's New in French Planning,'; *J.O.*, *Lois et Décrets*, 23 December 1964, p. 11423; *Fifth plan*, pp. 18–24; and below, pp. 184–7.

analysis to an appreciation of what a general resource allocation plan really is.

A general resource allocation plan is essentially a political process, an innovation in the way collective decisions are taken. The principal reasons for the failure of the resource allocation component of the second plan were political. The general resource allocation plan simply did not fit into the existing political process.

The general resource allocation plan was produced by a planning process designed to promote modernisation and development within the micropolitical-economy of the *économie concertée*. But a general resource allocation plan is a very different kind of plan from the reform programmes of the *économie concertée*. It implies a different kind of politics. In order to work, the resource allocation plan must be the output of a planning process in which major decisions are taken and important forces accommodated. The comprehensive and explicit nature of these decisions means that the resource allocation plan, if it is to be effective, must be the product of a broadly participatory planning process. It must be the principal framework of political activity. For the second plan, these political prerequisites were ignored. As a result the plan was ignored by the major political groups and by the Government. The new politics implied by general resource allocation planning was never created, and economic policy continued to be guided by the traditional political process.

Only when the resource allocation plan is understood in terms of its political implications and situated within the political economy of the nation is it possible to generate interesting questions and satisfactory explanations about the performance, appeal and role of general resource allocation planning.

But a political analysis can only be the first step towards answering the questions it generates, because even a general resource allocation plan that satisfies these political conditions will not necessarily succeed. Other uncertainties can intrude and distort the planned growth pattern, especially in an open economy.

18 THE COMMON MARKET
and the planning process

The uncertainties in a quantitative, resource allocation plan, increase as an economy 'opens': as imports and exports represent an important and growing proportion of national product; as firms adjust their behaviour to a market which extends beyond the national framework of the plan; and, as production is vertically and horizontally integrated across national frontiers by international, multi-plant firms, international cartels, and international production and distribution arrangements.[1]

The Common Market is making France an open economy;[2] and the exigencies of an open economy will necessitate fundamental changes in the planning process.

OPENNESS AND DEMAND PROJECTIONS

The first imperative for the plan is a reorientation of its efforts away from attempts to prepare a general resource allocation plan by balancing projections of physical outputs. The increasing openness of the economy multiplies the uncertainty

[1] The concept of openness, and its effects on French planning, is developed in Bela Balassa, 'Whither French Planning,' *Quarterly Journal of Economics*, Nov. 1965, and J. Bénard, 'Le Marché Commun Européen et l'Avenir de la Planification Française,' *Revue Economique*, no. 5, 1964. The following pages draw heavily on these two papers which, in turn, draw heavily on Commissioner Massé's analysis of the effects of the Common Market on the plan in 'Projet de Rapport Sur les Principales Options du Ve Plan,' *J.O., Lois et Décrets*, 24 December 1964.

[2] Bénard, 'Le Marché Commun et l'Avenir de la Planification Française,' attempts to measure, in quantitative terms, the rate at which the French economy is becoming an open economy. Balassa makes similar calculations which draw heavily on those of Bénard. These calculations measure, essentially, the place of imports and exports in the economy. Though useful indicators, they are liable to convey a false sense of precision. Imports and exports constitute one of the three principal forces which defined openness in the preceding paragraph. The effects of the other two factors, though difficult to measure, are crucially relevant.

attached to long-term quantitative output projections for specific products. It is very difficult, if not impossible, to make accurate long-term output projections for French motor cars, television receivers, typewriters or electrical equipment when a substantial proportion of demand for those products comes from outside France and, at the same time, a substantial proportion of French demand for those same products is for imported brands.[1] The diminishing reliability of quantitative output projections for specific products is forcing the planners to abandon their attempts to build the plans around detailed projections of physical outputs.[2]

Several studies of French planning discuss this problem and propose solutions. Some call for a Common Market wide plan; others a national plan that de-emphasises physical outputs.[3] The planners, too, recognise the need to reform the planning process in order to meet the imperatives of an open economy. The beginnings of a basic methodological change in the planning process are visible in the fifth plan which insists upon the uncertain nature of its specific output targets and stresses the importance of what it calls 'structural objectives' and 'financial balances'.[4]

By 'structural objectives' the planners seem to mean nothing more than a continuation of the kind of industrial restructuring and reform programmes that were the principal operational output of the first four plans.[5] These were the programmes for state encouraged mergers, modernisations and expansions that

[1] See 'Projet de Rapport' . . . *J.O., Lois et Décrets*, 24 December 1964, pp. 11399–11403, where the problem of output projections is discussed in considerable detail. See also, Balassa and Bénard, who treat the question thoroughly. The Dutch experience in planning in an open economy is instructive: see *Scope and Methods of the Central Planning Bureau*, The Hague, 1956; OECD, *Growth and Economic Policy, Report of Working Party No.* 2 *to the Economic Policy Committee*, 1964, pp. 156–174 and bibliographical references that accompany the report; and BRAE, *Politique Economique et Politique Syndicale, l'Expérience Hollandaise*, Paris, 1961.

[2] See Massé, in *J.O., Lois et Décrets*, 24 December 1964, pp. 11401–11403 and 11414–11416.

[3] Bénard, 'Le Marché Commun et l'Avenir de la Planification Française,' proposes a Common Market plan. Balassa, 'Whither French Planning,' foresees a de-emphasis on physical outputs; so do Andrew Shonfield, *Modern Capitalism*, (O.U.P.) New York, 1965, p. 141, and *The Economist*, 23 May 1964, p. 852.

[4] See *Fifth Plan*, Chapter I; *J.O., Lois et Décrets*, 24 December 1964, pp. 11399–11403; Balassa, 'Whither French Planning,' p. 546; and Shonfield *Modern Capitalism*, p. 141.

[5] See *Fifth Plan*, pp. 67–69.

characterised the workings of the *économie concertée*. Uncertainties surrounding output projections caused by the common market would not seriously affect these programmes.[1]

By 'financial balances' the planners mean an aggregative approach. The national economy can be analysed in terms of a small number of key aggregate balances: prices, employment, foreign exchange, the level of national income; its distribution; its allocation among savings, consumption and investment, etc. By focusing on these aggregate, or financial balances, the plan can overcome the uncertainties of projecting outputs for specific products.[2]

OPENNESS AND INFLATION

The second imperative of an open economy – the necessity of relative price stability – compels the plan to concentrate on financial balances. While the French economy was largely a closed economy,[3] inflation accompanied expansion. During the 1950's, national product (in real terms) increased by over four per cent per year, but do did prices.[4] The plan could concentrate on structural objectives – promoting long-term industrial reform, modernisation and expansion – while ignoring financial imbalances. Long-term modernisation could be attacked independently of short-term stabilisation. The *économie concertée* could be separated from the general resource allocation component of planning, permitting the plan to confine its efforts within the *économie concertée* and remain effective.

In an open economy, such a growth model is unworkable. On a micro level, rising prices means the loss of export markets and domestic sales to French producers; on a macro level, it

[1] It has been argued that the Treaty of Rome deprives the *économie concertée* of the means for carrying out these programmes; see, *J.O., Lois et Décrets*, 12 December 1964, p. 11400. For a discussion of this question see A. C. L. Day, 'The Consequences for Economic Planning of Joining the Common Market,' *The Political Quarterly*, January-March 1963, pp. 47–54.

[2] See *Fifth Plan*, Chapter I; *J.O., Lois et Décrets*, 12 December 1964, pp. 11401–11403, and 11414–11416.

[3] See Balassa, 'Whither French Planning,' Part II, on the extent and timing of the opening of the French economy.

[4] *J.O., Lois et Décrets*, 12 December 1964, p. 11447; and INSEE, *Annuaire Statistique*, 1966, p. 561.

means, in a fixed-exchange rate system, an unacceptable balance of payments deficit.[1] An open economy threatens the effectiveness of the plan's traditional approach of promoting long-term expansion and modernisation while ignoring short-term stabilisation. In an open economy, expansion must be accompanied by price stability.[2] The implementation of the medium-term development plan must be closely linked with the exercise of short-term stabilisation policy.

The principal and permanent short-term objective is to maintain full employment without generating inflation; the principal long-term concerns are expansion and modernisation, for which a growing volume of investment is necessary. In an open economy, if its influence is to extend beyond the *économie concertée*, the plan must combine both long-term and short-term objectives. It must provide a growth strategy that will sustain full-employment, steady expansion, a growing volume of investment, and relative price stability. This is not easy to do. The fourth plan aimed at, but failed to achieve, this crucial quadruple balance.[3]

THE FAILURE OF THE FOURTH PLAN

In 1962 and 1963, the first two years of the fourth plan, gross national product rose by 6.8% and 5.1%.[4] The plan had projected a 5.5% annual rate of increase.[5] Consumer incomes increased by just over 24% during the first two years of the planned period.[6] The four year target was 23%.[7] Crucially, during 1962 and 1963 exports grew at an average rate of 3.5%

[1] See Balassa, 'Whither French Planning,' Parts II, IV and V; *J.O.*, *Lois et Décrets*, 12 December 1964, pp. 11398–11403; A. C. L. Day, 'The Consequences for Economic Planning of Joining the Common Market.'

[2] Or, at least, a rate of price increase that does not exceed that of its principal trading partners: see *Fifth plan*, p. 25. Large foreign exchange reserves can, of course, permit an open economy to run a more rapid rate of price increases than its neighbour and even, thereby, export a bit of inflation – but only for a short while.

[3] For the objectives of the Fourth plan, see *Fourth plan*, pp. 1–46, 'Introduction et Vue d'Ensemble.'

[4] *Rapport Annuel*, 1964–65, pp. 9–10.

[5] *Fourth plan*, p. 7.

[6] *Rapport Annuel*, 1964–65, p. 13.

[7] *Fourth plan*, p. 23.

(the target rate was 4.7%), while imports rose at an annual rate of 14% (the target rate was 5.3%).[1]

While prices, incomes and imports were rising well beyond the planned rates, productive investment fell below the planned targets.[2] The plan projected a 6.4% annual increase in productive investment; the actual increase in productive investment during the four year life of the plan averaged 5.1%.[3] Furthermore, most of that increase took place in 1961–2. In 1963, the volume of actual investment in industry fell below the 1962 level, and in 1964 the downward trend continued with industrial investment falling below the 1963 level.[4]

The planners and several outside observers argue that productive investment, especially private investment, fell because foreign competition restrained price increases in internationally competitive industries so that rising costs could not be passed on in rising prices.[5] As a result, the capacity of firms to finance investment out of retained earnings shrank.[6]

The Government's response to rapidly rising prices, wages and imports was the Stabilisation Plan of September 1963, a deflationary programme associated with the name of Finance Minister Valéry Giscard d'Estaing. Taxes were raised, the volume of commercial and consumer credit cut, resistance to wage increases encouraged and tariffs reduced (beyond the Common Market schedules) on mass-consumption items.[7]

[1] *Rapport Annuel*, 1964–65, pp. 13, 25, 162.

[2] The big increase in investment which permitted the plan to report that its aggregate investment target had been realised was in luxury housing; cf., *Le Monde*, 23 Sept. 1965, and 11–12 July 1965; *Rapport Annuel*, 1964–65.

[3] *Rapport Annuel*, 1964–65, p. 25; G. Mathieu breaks the report's investment data down into more detailed categories and finds that productive investment was closer to 4.5% than to 5.1%. See *Le Monde*, 23 September 1965.

[4] *Rapport Annuel*, 1964–65, pp. 35–36 and 169–170.

[5] See 'Rapport sur les Principales Options du Ve Plan,' *J.O.*, *Lois et Décrets*, 24 December 1964, pp. 11406–11407; Balassa, 'Whither French Planning,' Part II, pp. 548–549. By 1962, the margin for price increases generated by the devaluation of 1958 had been eaten away: from 1958–1962, the general wholesale price index rose from 166.9 to 188.1; the industrial price index (wholesale) rose from 166.9 to 192.1 (INSEE, *Annuaire Statistique*, 1965, p. 445).

[6] See *J.O.*, *Lois et Décrets*, 24 December 1964, pp. 11406–11407; the rate of self-financing fell from 75% in 1960 to 62% in 1963 and, as of January 1965, was still falling; (*ibid.*, p. 11408, footnote #1). It is worth noting that prices for industrial goods rose slower than prices for services, perhaps because the latter were not subject to international competition. See INSEE, *Annuaire Statistique*, 1965, pp. 463 (chart), 446, 450.

[7] For a concise description of the major components of the Stabilisation Plan see OECD, *Economic Surveys, France*, August 1964, and July 1965.

The Stabilisation Plan had some success. As the following table shows, the rate of price increases slowed down, but perhaps not as much, nor as quickly as expected.

TABLE VII

PRICES

	1961	1962	1963				1964				1965	
			1st Qtr.	2nd Qtr.	3rd Qtr.	4th Qtr.	1st Qtr.	2nd Qtr.	3rd Qtr.	4th Qtr.	1st Qtr.	Apr.
Consumer Price Index* (1960=100)	103.3	108.3	111.5	112.7	114.3	115.5	116.3	116.6	117.5	118.2	119.1	
Wholesale Prices** (1949=100)	198.1	188.1	192.4	192.8	195.3	200.3	196.3	198.3	198.0	201.8	200.0	200.8

* 259 *articles (INSEE): OECD, Economic Surveys, July,* 1965, *pp.* 50–51.
*******Ibid., pp.* 50–51. *Note: Sharp fall in wholesale prices from* 1961 *to* 1962 *antedates Stabilisation plan.*

The rate of wage increases also declined soon after the deflationary measures took effect:

TABLE VIII

HOURLY WAGE RATE, ALL PRIVATE ACTIVITIES*
(percentage increase during period)

	1st qrt.	2nd qtr.	3rd qtr.	4th qtr.	1st January to 1st January of following year
1962	2.0	2.5	2.2	2.5	9.4
1963	1.8	2.5	1.8	1.5	7.9
1964	1.9	1.9	1.2	1.5	6.7

**Source: OECD, Economic Surveys, July,* 1965, *p.* 19.

But the balance of trade failed to register any dramatic improvements:

TABLE IX

FOREIGN TRADE – METROPOLITAN FRANCE – $ MILLIONS*

	1961	1962	1963				1964				1965
			1st qtr.	2nd qtr.	3rd qtr.	4th qtr.	1st qtr.	2nd qtr.	3rd qtr.	4th qtr.	1st qtr.
Imports, c.i.f.	433	497	534	590	609	670	699	688	691	732	704
Exports, f.o.b.	445	490	500	553	554	575	610	606	605	649	657
Trade balance	12	−6	−34	−38	−54	−95	−89	−82	−87	−83	−47

* Corrected for seasonal variations: *Source:* OECD, *Economic Surveys*, August, 1965, pp. 54–55. See also, *J.O. Conseil Economique*, 14 Oct. 1965, pp. 656–658 and 685 for an interesting discussion of the trade balance, the Stabilisation Plan and the *Fifth Plan*.

While the benefits of the Stabilisation plan were uncertain, the costs were clear. During 1964, unemployment rose by almost fifty per cent, although the total number of unemployed remained small: in 1963, there were 22,000 registered unemployed; by the first quarter of 1965, the number had climbed to 32,400.[1] The length of the average work week fell from 46.3 hours in the second and third quarters of 1963 to 45.2 hours in the fourth quarter of 1964.[2] The purchasing power of the SMIG (minimum wage) grew by a total of only 1.8% during the thirty-two months from January 1963 to September 1965.[3] The volume of inventories doubled during 1964.[4] Crucially, industrial production stagnated while the growth of productive investment continued to decline. As the following table indicates, the index of industrial production rose rapidly until the first quarter of 1964 when the effects of the deflationary measures began to be felt; for the next eighteen months it stagnated.

In 1962, the volume of productive investment was 8% above the 1961 level; in 1963, it was 6.4% above the 1962 level; in 1964, it was 6% above the 1963 level (most of the increase coming in the first quarter). Official estimates for 1965 projected a decrease in productive investment below the 1964

[1] OECD, *Economic Surveys*. July 1965, pp. 48–49.

[2] *Ibid.*, pp. 48–49.

[3] *J.O. Conseil Economique et Social*, 14 Oct. 1965, p. 662.

[4] *Rapport Annuel*, 1964–65, p. 15.

TABLE X

INDEX OF INDUSTRIAL PRODUCTION: 1960 = 100*

1960	1961	1962	1963	1964				1965		
				1st qtr.	2nd qtr.	3rd qtr.	4th qtr.	1st qtr.	April	May
100	106	112	117	126	128	123	126	125	127	127

* *Source: OECD, Economic Surveys, July* 1965, *pp.* 48–49.

level.[1] Furthermore, whatever growth was achieved during 1964 was largely the result of investment in the public sector which rose by 8.5%. In the private sector, productive investment showed no increase.[2]

The principal objective of the fourth plan – steady expansion within price stability[3] – was not achieved. The general resource allocation component of the fourth plan, like those of the second and third, remained largely irrelevant to actual economic activity. Effective direction of the economy continued to be exercised through traditional, pragmatic policies, as represented by the Stabilisation plan. The results were an unspectacular variant of 'stop-go' 'go-slow': rapid growth, rising prices, deliberate inflation, stagnation. Whatever direct effectiveness the plan asserted remained within the narrow confines of the *économie concertée.*

The fourth plan provided no detailed strategy for achieving the planned growth pattern. It projected a very detailed picture of economic activity for its final or target year, but it did not concern itself sufficiently with detailing the changes in incentives, controls, policies, and institutions that would have been necessary to realise that pattern. It set out 'over precise'[4] long-term physical output targets for specific industries without providing a workable implementation strategy aimed at guiding the day-to-day exercise of short-term policy and con-

[1] See *J.O., Conseil Economique,* 14 Oct. 1965, p. 657, for 1962–64 data; *Rapport Annuel,* 1964–65, p. 23, where a drop in index from 106 in 1964 to 103.3 in 1965 is projected.

[2] *J.O., Conseil Economique,* 14 Oct. 1965, p. 657, footnote, no. 1; the OECD value index shows an absolute decline in the value of investment.

[3] See *Fourth plan,* pp. 3–7, 17–23.

[4] Quotation is from Shonfield, *Modern Capitalism,* p. 141.

trolling the evolution of the key aggregate balances – especially prices and incomes.

Incomes policy was treated indirectly, as an awkward residual, not as a central concern, not as a powerful force for the plan's implementation.[1] Short-term policy was treated as an external force. Its potency was eulogized; its directors propitiated, solicited, instructed. Hopefully it would be used to guide the economy along the planned path (otherwise the plan would surely fail). But the plan provided no detailed guidelines for its exercise. The exercise of short-term policy was never, even on paper, incorporated into the plan; throughout the fourth plan it remained an external variable.

THE STRATEGY OF THE FIFTH PLAN

The fifth plan represents a more sophisticated approach. It marks the explicit recognition of the need to co-ordinate long-term modernisation and expansion programmes with short-term stabilisation policy, and it takes the first steps towards reforming the planning process to meet the new imperative.

Three principal reforms distinguish the fifth plan from its predecessors. First, physical output targets for specific industries are de-emphasised. The fifth plan presents its principal objectives in terms of the financial balances that define aggregate equilibrium: prices, incomes, foreign exchange; national product, investment, savings, government expenditures, consumption, etc.[2] Second, a system of guidelines for the automatic co-ordination of short-term stabilisation policy with its middle-term objectives is built into the plan (the *clignotants* adjustment-indicator system described above). And third, the plan contains an explicit incomes policy.[4]

The aggregate financial balances, the *clignotants* adjustment-indicators and the explicit incomes policy, like the detailed quantitative resource allocation plan they are replacing, con-

[1] See *Fourth plan*, Parts I, II and III, *J.O., Lois et Décrets*, 24 December 1964, pp. 11389, 11391–11392, 11401–11403, and 11423; *Fifth plan*, pp. 18–23; and *La Documentation Française, Recueils et Monographies*, no. 47, 1964, 'Rapport sur la Politique des Revenus Etabli à la Suite de la Conférence des Revenus, (Oct. 1963–Jan. 1964),' pp. 3–8.

[2] See *Fifth Plan*, pp. 18-21 and 151-191; *J. O. Lois et Décrets*, 24 December 1964 pp. 1140-11403.

[4] See *Fifth plan*, pp. 23–24.

stitute only a paper plan. The interesting and difficult reform consists in making them effective.

Relevance – that is, perceptable effectiveness – is the crucial test for the general resource allocation component (the financial balances) of the fifth plan. The second, third and fourth plans failed this test; their effectiveness was largely confined to the *économie concertée*. Their resource allocation components remained largely irrelevant to actual economic activity. The effectiveness of the resource allocation component of the fifth plan will depend upon the co-ordination of stabilisation policy with its longer-term programmes and upon the success of the planned incomes policy. At best it promises to be only a bare beginning towards effectiveness; at worst it threatens collapse.

The planners were forced to bring an explicit incomes policy to the centre of the plan. The opening of the French economy has made relative price stability the necessary condition for expansion and modernisation. The planners can no longer ignore prices; they cannot continue to promote expansion and feed inflation. Of the numerous paths to price stability open to the economy all but one – incomes policy – are closed to the plan. An explicitly planned slack labour market or any 'go-slow' model is a political impossibility for the plan.[1] The same is true for a planned 'stop-go' pattern. The only path to long-term survival and influence for the planners consists of plans that call for full-employment, sustained expansion, growing volumes of investment and price stability, and outline *how* these objectives are to be achieved. The 'financial balances' that the planners must now use to define this growth path bring prices – and incomes – to the centre of the plan. In this way the planners have been forced to tackle the question of an explicit incomes policy – something they have carefully avoided for twenty years.

It is useful to recall that although a successful incomes policy and a systematic co-ordination of short-term stabilisation policy with its medium-term programmes are necessary for the effectiveness of the general resource allocation component of the plan, they are not at all indispensable to the French economy nor, even, to the survival of the plan. The failure of its resource allocation component will still permit the plan to play its traditional role within the *économie concertée* of promoting

[1] Witness the political storm surrounding the choice of an aggregate expansion target for the Fifth plan, described below, pp. 214–19.

expansion, rationalisation and modernisation and of influencing, on a day-to-day basis, important reforms and policy changes. Furthermore, a failure does not preclude another attempt in a sixth or seventh plan. Such a failure is, in the judgment of this writer, the most probable outcome.[1]

THE FIFTH PLAN'S INCOMES POLICY

The particular growth strategy of the fifth plan increases the probability of the failure of its incomes policy and, ultimately, of the distortion of its projected growth pattern, for the distribution of increases in income set out in the plan compromises the incomes policy institution before it is even established.

The fifth plan aims at full-employment, rapid expansion, modernisation and price stability. It projects a 5% annual rate of increase in GNP[2] and an annual rate of price increase not to exceed 1.5%.[3] The key to its strategy for attaining these objectives is more rapid increases in investment than in wages. Productive investment is planned to increase at an annual rate of 5.7%.[4] Corporate savings will grow by 6.4% per year[5] while the proportion of investment financed out of retained earnings is scheduled to rise from 60% to 70%.[6] The plan projects a 5% annual increase in the total wage bill, or a 3.3% annual increase in wages on a per capita basis.[7]

This strategy of rapid rises in investment and even more rapid increases in corporate savings from which to finance the investments will produce a planned increase in profits of 8.6% per year.[8] The contrast with the 3.3% per capita increase in wages is striking. It becomes still sharper when one remembers that the investment strategy places an additional 'tax' on workers' incomes in the form of higher prices to create the profit margins needed to self-finance the investment effort,[9] and that the 8.6% increase in profits does not take into account capital

[1] See below, last chapter, where this argument is developed.
[2] *Fifth plan*, p. 13.
[3] *Ibid.*, p. 19.
[4] *Ibid.*, p. 20.
[5] *Ibid.*, p. 189, Table XXII.
[6] *Ibid.*, p. 187.
[7] *Ibid.*, p. 190, Table XXIII and *ibid.*, p. 191, Table XXIV for per capita.
[8] See, *Fifth plan*, p. 189, Table XXIII.
[9] The Club Jean Moulin characterised the planned increase in self-financing as 'an indirect tax': See, *Le Monde*, 4–5 Oct. 1964, 29–30 Nov. 1964.

appreciations which stand to benefit handsomely from the planned increase in corporate savings.

ECONOMIC OPENNESS AND POLITICAL PARTICIPATION

The opening of the French economy has necessitated basic changes in the planning process. First, the increasing uncertainty surrounding output projections for specific products is forcing the plan to move from a micro to a macro approach. Detailed output targets for such products as chemicals, motor cars and textiles will be de-emphasised. Future plans will concentrate on such aggregates as employment, price levels, foreign exchange, investment, savings and consumption.

Second, the necessity of maintaining price stability compels the plan to make those aggregate balances financial balances and emphasise prices. Until now the planners operated on a growth within inflation model and treated prices rather casually. Henceforth the plan must centre around the question of price stability. The only long-term approach to price planning available to the plan is an incomes policy. An explicitly planned slack labour market or any 'stop-go' or 'go-slow' model is a political impossibility for the plan.

Beginning with the fifth plan, the success of the resource allocation component of the plans depends upon its incomes-prices policy. But an incomes policy, unlike modernisation and expansion programmes for the steel, cement or aluminium industries cannot be effectively implemented by the big business-civil servant partnership of the *économie concertée.* It demands a much broader range of positive participation. Crucially, the incomes policy for the first time makes positive action by the trade unions necessary for an essential part of the plan.

The advent of the Common Market is forcing the plan to confront the problem of participation – especially participation by the trade unions. And the problem of participation raises the broader question of democratising the plan.

PART VI

PLANNING AND DEMOCRACY

19 DEMOCRACY
as direct participation

The unanimity of approval of planning in France can henceforth be nothing but a façade; for what some celebrate as the final point of an evolution, others accept only as a point of departure.[1]

The French Left has traditionally demanded national economic planning as a cure for economic stagnation, political degeneration and social injustice. It has always been the Right – especially the business groups – that has been hostile to planning. Twenty years of experience with the practice of planning in France have significantly altered both these traditional positions.

Many who hesitated – notably in business circles – are now convinced of the necessity of a Plan. Not only because it permits them to obtain, in the name of national interests, public funds at low interest rates and tax exonerations, but also because it 'orients, organises and sets the rhythm of the development of production' [Albin Chalendon], while publicly outlining the economic future of the country.

The Trade Unions, and in a more general sense, the Left – planners by tradition – were convinced of this efficacy from the very beginning. But they expected quite different things from planning; a clear and courageous choice of the economic future of the country, as well as a more equitable distribution of the fruits of economic growth. They insist on their expectation! Thus, while a great majority of the business community now sings the praises of the Plan, some of its original proponents have become severely critical.[2]

The swelling stream of criticism directed at the Plan – apart from the eternally recurrent Free Enterprise sermons – now tends to come from the Left. The Left in France has no single voice, no single programme. Three principal themes, however, dominate the proposals for the fundamental reform of planning

[1] Gilbert Mathieu, *Le Monde*, 2 March 1962, p. 17.
[2] *Ibid.*, p. 17.

put forward by numerous Left groups. These can serve as an initial common denominator and a reference point for finer distinctions. The three themes are:

(1) The Plan ought to be more democratic.
(2) The Plan ought to be more normative.
(3) The Plan ought to be more imperative.[1]

Once the planning process is made more democratic, everything else will follow. A democratic planning procedure will not only permit, but will oblige, the Nation to make a conscious determination of the direction of economic development. Once democratic, the plan will automatically become more normative. By more normative, the Left means that the plan must embody bold choices about the direction of development. The Left argues that the plan has been concerned only with efficiency and expansion. It has not seriously tried to change the direction of development.[2] But a more normative plan – a plan that is not merely a projection of present trends – would be meaningless without implementation devices able to guarantee the realisation of the planned pattern of development. Hence, the Left feels that once democratic, the plan will necessarily become more normative and more imperative.

DEMOCRATISING THE PLAN

The absence – or the insufficiency – of democracy constitutes the principal grievance of the Left.[3]

The Left finds that the Plan, '*cette grande affaire de la France,*' as General de Gaulle called it,[4] is the product of a small and

[1] See *Le Monde* 2, 3 and 6 March 1962; articles and symposia on Democratic Planning in *Cahiers de la République*, issues of Dec. 1961, Jan–Feb. 1962 and June 1962; *Cahiers Reconstruction*, Dec. 1961, June 1962 and May 1963; *Cahiers du Centre d'Etudes Socialistes*, Nos. 18–19, 25–26.

[2] The planners too maintain that the conscious determination of the direction of development is an essential function of planning. (See, for example, P. Massé, *French Affairs*, pp. 19–20.) If allowances can be made for the Planning Commissioner's euphemistic prose style, he can be seen to concur with the Left's judgement that the Plan has failed to re-direct growth. Massé judges the Fourth Plan's 'efforts' at concerning itself with the contents as well as the rate of economic development to be 'timid.' (p. 19).

[3] Gilbert Mathieu, *Le Monde*, 2 March 1962, p. 17.

[4] Address of 8 May 1961.

homogeneous group of businessmen and *hauts fonctionnaires*. Parliament has had no real role in planning; neither has the Left.

The Left insists upon two basic reforms for the democratisation of planning. First, broad and effective direct participation must be introduced at every stage of the planning process. Second, planning must be brought under the control of Parliament.

The Left demands that the modernisation commissions be made more representative so that the Left – especially the trade unions – can begin to play a more active role.[1] The modernisation commissions are supposed to be the most democratic element in the planning process. But, the Left argues, they are dominated by business and government executives; even the numerical composition of the commissions reflects how far the actual planning process is from the communitarian images of the official model.

For the preparation of the third plan, 612 people participated in the modernisation commissions.

They were:

TABLE XI

THE COMPOSITION OF THE NINETEEN MODERNISATION COMMISSIONS FOR THE THIRD PLAN[2]

Businessmen	206
Civil Servants	136
Bankers	13
Trade Union Representatives	57
Technical Experts	134
Miscellaneous	66
Total	612

[1] See, 'Pour une Planification Démocratique' *Cahiers de la République*, June 1962; *Formation*, 14 April 1959; Club Jean Moulin, 'La Planification Démocratique,' *Cahiers de la République* Dec. 1961, Jan. 1962; *Cahiers Reconstruction* Dec. 1961; *J.O., Conseil Economique* 7 Dec. 1963, p. 715; *Perspectives Socialistes*, Jan.-Feb. 1961; *Le Monde* 2, 3, 6 March 1962.

[2] Source for Table 11, Pierre Bauchet, *Economic Planning, the French Experience*, (London, 1964 ed.), p. 36. Miscellaneous includes: representatives of local chambers of commerce, doctors, inn-keeper groups, architects and agricultural groups.

Bauchet counts twenty-five representatives of organised agricultural groups in with the trade unionists – making thereby a total of 82 'syndicalists.' I have placed the farmers' representatives in the 'miscellaneous' category. The history of co-operation between organised farm labour and industrial trade unions in France does not justify putting them in the same category.

Even if one assumes that the 'technical experts' and the 'Miscellaneous' people are neutral, the bankers and businessmen outnumber the trade union representatives by more than 6:1, (355 to 57).

Much was made, in official circles at least, of an alleged increase in democracy in the preparation of the fourth plan.[1] The modernisation commissions were expanded to include over one thousand people; the total number of participants increased to over three thousand. But the official rosters of the various commissions show that the relative strengths of the groups did not change significantly.

FOURTH PLAN[2]

	TABLE XII ALL PARTICIPANTS: MODERNISATION COMMISSIONS, SUB-COMMISSIONS, STUDY GROUPS	TABLE XIII PARTICIPANTS IN MODERNISATION COMMISSIONS
Farmers	107	20
Businessmen	1277	437
Civil Servants	781	202
Trade Unionists (Ag. and Industry)	281	(Industry) 114
		(Agriculture) 20
Misc.	691	233
Total	3137	1006

In Table 12, (all participants in the plan), businessmen outnumber trade unionists (including agricultural labour) by 4½:1. Businessmen and civil servants combined outnumber trade unionists (still including organised agricultural groups) by 7:1. In the modernisation commissions alone, Table 13, the ratios are similar: businessmen outnumber trade unionists by almost 4:1; businessmen and civil servants combined outnumber trade unionists by 5½:1.

[1] See, for example, Massé, *French Affairs*, p. 12; Bauchet, *Economic Planning*, pp. 108–120; Hackett and Hackett, *Economic Planning in France*, London, 1963, pp. 192–204, 249–254.

[2] Table 12 is from Bauchet, *Economic Planning*; (B. Cazes, *La Planification en France et le IVe Plan*, [Paris, 1962] p. 71 provides an identical table.) Table 13 is from *J.O. Avis et Raports du Conseil Economique*, 7 *December* 1963, p. 715. See Table 11, above, for definitions of categories.

These numbers only indicate a problem; they do not explain very much. They do not show *why* labour is so under-represented. Furthermore, in a system where decisions are *not* taken by vote, the implications of a numerical increase in representation are not altogether clear. We will first examine why trade union participation continues to be so very limited, then explore the question of participation in terms of the institutional structures of planning and conclude with an analysis of the political implications of an increase in trade union participation.

REASONS FOR INEFFECTIVE TRADE UNION PARTICIPATION

Despite occasional allegations to the contrary,[1] the trade unions are not excluded from the organs of planning; they are voluntarily under-represented. Many more trade unionists are invited to participate than actually do – at least since the beginning of the fourth plan. There are several reasons commonly offered to explain this voluntary under-representation. The first, heard from various quarters, is that the French trade unions simply do not have enough properly trained men to represent them in the subtle and technical deliberations of the planning process.[2] The small number of technically qualified trade union representatives lack the support of professional staffs to gather and organize the information necessary in order for them to participate effectively. One reason commonly advanced to explain these inadequacies is that the French trade unions are poor.[3]

[1] See, for example, CGT, Le Plan: *Mythes et Réalités*, Supplément du journal *Le Peuple* no. 643, p. 8 and CFTT, *La CFTC et le IVe Plan*, Supplément à *Formation*, no. 49, Nov.–Dec. 1962, p. 12.

[2] Pierre Avril (CFTC), 'Perplexité Devant le IVe Plan,' *Cahiers de la République*, Jan.-Feb. 1962, esp. pp. 45–46: A. Soulat (CFTC) in *Ibid.*, June 1962, pp. 475–477; Roger Jacques, 'Pour une Approche Syndicale au Plan,' *Esprit*, July 1961, esp. p. 27; Gourney and Viot, (Planning Commission) 'Les Planificateurs et les Décisions du Plan,' *La Planification Comme Processus de Décision*, Cahiers de la Fondation Nationale des Sciences Politique, no. 140, pp. 71–72; Philippe Bauchard, *La Mystique du Plan*, (Paris, 1963), pp. 210–215; Club Jean Moulin, 'La Planification Démocratique,' *Cahiers de la République*, Dec. 1961, p. 40; Chapsal *et. al.*, *La France Depuis* 1945, p. 590; Bauchet, *Economic Planning*, p. 54.

[3] See E. Descamps (Secretary General of the CFTC) 'Socialisme et Planification,' *Cahiers de Centre d'Etudes Socialistes*, 1962; A. Soulat, *Cahiers de la République*, pp. 475–478; D. Granick, *The European Executive* (Anchor edition), pp. 194–195; P. Beregovoy, 'Optimisme et Sectarisme,' *Cahiers de la République*, July 1961, pp. 55–57; Chapsal, *La France Depuis* 1945, p. 590; Val Lorwin, *The French Labour Movement* (Cambridge, Mass., 1954), pp. 176–190.

Dues-paying members are few; probably no more than two to two and a half millions, and about half of those belong to the CGT.[1] The trade unions are not just poor, they are weak – at least at the plant level, where union activity is not even 'recognized' in the sense of the US Wagner Act. Management prerogatives are wider in France than in the US or Britain. French management can introduce new production techniques, hire, fire and transfer workers with a freedom that is envied by British and American management. The unions have little influence on the organisation of production in the plant.[2]

INFORMATION AND EFFECTIVE PARTICIPATION

The trade unions' lack of material means is a real problem, but a shallow explanation. The trade unions do possess men who understand economics and statistics; the high calibre of many trade union publications on planning and economics attests to their capabilities. If a shortage of such men was an important problem, that is, if the trade unions were seriously committed to participation in the planning process as it now exists, it could soon be remedied. The trade unions could build technical staffs; they could recruit or borrow economists, statisticians and technical experts.[3] Rather, it is in a different sense that this 'qualified personnel' explanation is most useful, for it leads to some very important questions. Given the nature of the French planning process, in order to be 'qualified' the trade union representatives would have to have access to information and

[1] Hackett and Hackett, *Economic Planning in France*, p. 342, estimates paying membership at two to two and one half million, of which half belong to the CGT; Granick, *The European Executive*, suggests a range between two and four million; Macridis and Ward, *Modern Political Systems*, (N.Y. 1963) estimates three to three and one half million, p. 155; data is notoriously unreliable. Chapsal, *et. al.*, remarks, (p. 570) 'It is truly impossible to obtain precise figures about the trade unions.' The CGT in 1962 said the CFTC had 450,000 members; the CFTC that same year claimed it had 750,000 members. See *Le Monde* 3 June 1961 for these and different numbers. See also, Sellier and Tiano, *Economie du Travail*, (Paris 1962) p. 346ff; Lorwin, *French Labour*, pp. 176–189 which provides a good, but not entirely up-to-date discussion of trade union strengths and weaknesses; and Lasserre, *Syndicalisme*, Part III.

[2] See Granick, *European Executive*, pp. 197–199 for a brief discussion of the wide range of management perogatives in France compared with the U.S. and Britain; see also, Henry Ehrmann, *Organized Business in France* (Princeton, 1957) pp. 420–470; Lorwin, *French Labour*, pp. 212–277 (esp. 274–276); Sellier and Tiano, *Economie du Travail*, chapters 7–8, 11–14.

[3] *Le Syndicalisme Ouvrier en France*, Cours de l'I.E.P., 1964–65, (mimeo), Part IV, para. 9 reports on recent developments in this area.

knowledge possessed only by businessmen. The planning commissions generally work from information supplied by business; often, the projects are initially drafted by the business-representatives.[1] Thus, in the planning situation, business has a quasi-monopoly on certain kinds of 'qualification,' that gives business the initiative. Philippe Bauchard has described the position of the trade unionist in the planning process under these conditions.

The trade unionist arrives at the Plan and finds himself an isolated man. The businessmen know one another, they *tutoient* one another, and they pass around statistics prepared by their own well-equipped, professional staffs. . . . The trade unionist is the only one to feel lost. . . . He will try to pose some questions. He will worry about the sources of the statistics being used and he will seek aid from the representative of the tutelary ministry (usually the Ministry of Industry). . . . The civil servant, however, will rarely be disturbed. He will generally accept the statistics supplied by the business groups without having the inclination – or the technical resources – to check them out.

The trade unionist will be presented with a technical report of some 400 pages and asked for his views. He might ask some additional questions but then the businessmen, civil servants and experts will begin to express their disapproval of this man who only criticizes and questions – and that only in general terms – without offering any detailed, constructive alternatives.[2]

The trade unionists feel like interlopers in some club meeting

[1] See Descamps, *Socialisme et Planification*, p. 9; Granick, *European Executive*, Chapter 11; A. Soulat, *Cahiers de la République*, pp. 63–66, 71–72; Rene Bonéty, 'Le Plan et les Syndicats.' *Cahiers de la Fondation Nationale des Sciences Politiques*, no. 140, pp. 87–88, 210–212; Hackett, *Economic Planning in France*, pp. 334–343; MacLennen, 'French Planning,' *Planning* (PEP), no. 475, 9 Sept. 1963, pp. 341–349; Bauchet, *Economic Planning*, p. 53; P. Bauchard, *La Mystique du Plan* (Paris, 1963) pp. 210–215; Georges Ducaroy, 'Socialisme et Planification, II' *Les Cahiers du Centre d'Etudes Socialistes*, no. 25–26, 1–15 March 1963, pp. 15–19; CGT, *Le Plan, Mythes et Réalités*, pp. 8–9; La Documentation Française, 'Rapport sur la Politiques Des Revenus . . . Conférence des Revenus, Oct. 1963–Jan. 1964,' *Recueils et Monographies* no. 47, pp. 11, 17–19; and above, pp. 115–145, 179, 193–194; Hatzfield and Freyssinet, *L'Emploi en France*, (Paris, 1964) p. 205 observes: 'The fact that statistical information comes almost exclusively from the civil servants or the businessmen makes it impossible for the trade union representatives to exercise an important influence on the debates.'

[2] Quotation is from Bauchard, *La Mystique du Plan*, pp. 211–212; See *Les Motifs d'Exécution du Plan*, p. 15 on the general tendency of the civil servants to accept business-supplied statistics and on the planners' lack of resources to check many of those statistics; see also, Shonfield, *Modern Capitalism*, pp. 137–138.

or family circle. Their presence is cheerfully tolerated. But they do not participate. They cannot participate effectively. The vertical commissions deal with specific projects of a technical nature.[1] But effective participation – not to mention 'constructive alternatives' – is impossible without the kinds of information to which the trade unions are denied access. In the commissions of the plan the trade unions representative is an outsider.[2]

SOCIAL ISOLATION

The trade unionist delegated to the plan is not only an outsider in respect to access to critical information about business decisions and practices, he is also socially isolated from the businessman and civil servants. The business executives and government officials are of similar social backgrounds. They share the same attitudes, the same values, the same modes of expression. They have a common intellectual formation and orientation. They have the same way of defining a 'problem' and they think about those problems in the same manner. Often, they know one another. They attended the same schools. They frequent the same social circles and they marry each other's sisters. The trade unionist, by his intellectual and social formation is an outsider. By a thousand subtle nuances – and an occasional blunt collision – he sets himself apart.[3] Even François Bloch-Lainé, one of the most highly respected civil servants, remarks that too many people, including many ranking civil servants, seem to feel that in the Plan, the executives of big business and the civil servants

> decide everything among themselves, behind a curtain of opaque 'technicity,' in clandestine meetings where agreements are too easily reached among civil servants who have already *pantouflés* (moved into private firms) and civil servants who would like to *pantoufler*.[4]

[1] See above, Part VI, Chapter 3 and François Bloch-Lainé, 'Economie Concertée et Planification Démocratique,' *Cahiers de la République*, July 1962, pp. 573–589 (esp. p. 578), for a description of the technical nature of the work of the vertical commissions.

[2] See *Ibid.*, pp. 576–579; MacLennan, *PEP*, p. 349; Bauchard, *La Mystique du Plan*, pp. 210–215; R. Jacques, 'Pour Une Approche Syndicale au Plan,' *Esprit*, July 1961 (the 'interloper' image is from Jacques, p. 17).

[3] This social dimension of planning is discussed above, pp. 35–71.

[4] Quotation is from 'Economie Concertée et Planification Démocratique,' p. 579. Twenty-five percent of all Inspectors of Finance, for example, switch into executive positions in private firms: see above, p. 66.

Of course, trade unionists might accept all these handicaps and still go along with the planning process. That is to say, the French trade unionists might recognise the right of businessmen and civil servants to collaborate in the planning of the economy and try to get what they could from such a situation. One could easily imagine American trade unions doing this. French trade unions have not, and their reasons for not playing the game will be of great interest in our consideration of democratic planning.

TRADE UNIONS AND PARTICIPATION: AN OUTLINE OF THE TRADITIONAL POSITIONS

Political life provides no *tabulae rasae*. The trade unions have a tradition, and they bring that tradition to the Plan.

French trade unionists by tradition are fundamentalists. They preach and maintain a position of fundamental opposition to the capitalist system, including what they call 'neo-capitalism.' The trade unions see themselves as an arm of the working class engaged in a struggle with the ruling bourgeoisie, and not as a pressure group, accepting the fundamental structures of bourgeois society, and fighting for a larger chunk of the pie. Their function is to contest the basic legitimacy of the capitalist order. Their goal is to replace capitalism – whether it be 'neo' or traditional capitalism – with a fundamentally different socialist society.[1]

Reformism – participation in the organs of the capitalist system in the hope of working gradual change in that system from within – is the great strategic issue that confronts and divides the trade union movement. To some trade unionists it means risking terrible and imminent dangers for a slim and distant chance of working fundamental changes; it is a deadly illusion. To others, it is the only alternative to the sterility of fundamental opposition.

THE DANGERS OF REFORMIST PARTICIPATION

The first danger of reformism is a loss of freedom. The outsider

[1] See G. Declercq, 'Democratie Nouvelle et Syndicalisme Moderne,' *La NEF*, April-June, 1961; CGT, *Le Plan: Mythes et Réalités*, Supplément no. 643 of *Le Peuple*; J. Juillard, 'La CFTC Devant Son Avenir,' *Esprit*, September 1963; André Gorz, *Stratégie Ouvrière et Néocapitalisme*, 32ᵉ Congrès de la CFTC; *Manifeste Aux Travailleurs de France*; Lasserre, *Syndicalisme*, Parts II, III and V; Ehrmann, *Organized Business in France*, pp. 103–123, 420–460; Lorwin, *French Labour*, pp. 29–46.

is free to oppose and condemn fundamentally and totally. He claims no influence on decisions. The reformist has no such freedom. His constructive participation implies his acceptance of the legitimacy of the capitalist system. How can one maintain a position of fundamental opposition to a regime and its policies if one co-operates with that regime and participates in the formulation of its policies? How can one lead a strike against an incomes policy one has helped to formulate? To participate constructively in the plan, or in the management of a plant, means to be associated with and responsible for the contents of that plan or the management of that plant.

The fundamental oppositionists dread association. They fear, first of all, a loss of ideological purity through protracted contact. If they begin to co-operate, they might lose sight of their original goals over the long reformist haul. They might be corrupted; bought off by small gains; caught up in the system they originally wanted to destroy. Reformist participation implies, in the words of a CFDT Secretary, the 'risks of integrating the leadership of the working class into the system.'[1] Crucially, the trade unions fear that reformism will ease class antagonism thereby lessening class consciousness in the working class and working class solidarity. This could be disastrous. It could be the condition for the triumph of neo-capitalism. The trade unions fear that once class hostility and class consciousness in the working class are weakened, the illusion of *individual* upward mobility – so easily fostered in the neo-capitalist system – could erode demands for a transformation of society along Marxist lines and destroy the means for that transformation, class action. The illusion of individual action could dilute class consciousness. Working class consciousness is the very bed-rock of the trade unions' long-term programme for the transformation of society. It is their driving force and the basis of whatever strength they possess at present and of whatever strength they possessed in the past. Any weakening of class consciousness would, the trade unions fear, sap their traditional power to oppose and contest the capitalist order as the militant arm of the working class.[2]

[1] G. Declercq, 'Démocratie Nouvelle et Syndicalisme Moderne,' *La NEF*, April-June 1961, p. 97; see also, CGT, *Le Plan: Mythes et Réalités*, for a vivid exposition of this view by its principal proponents.

[2] For example the CGT's reaction to the Fourth plan: 'The plan is a new attempt to snare the working class into class collaboration. No! No thanks! . . .

In brief, reformist participation is a trap. The bait is the possibility of making the capitalist order more palatable. But when the gate snaps shut the reformist finds that his initial goal of the total transformation of capitalist society into a fundamentally different socialist society has been left outside. The capitalist order prevails. The reformist has sold out the working class, for the illusion of effecting change without struggle, and a few crumbs.

NEO-CAPITALISM AND REFORMISM

But reformist participation has an attraction for the working class leadership.

Reformism does not appeal to the revolutionary trade union tradition. It appeals to a desire to break with that tradition. The French come to reformism on the rebound, after admitting the failure of the traditional trade union attitudes.[1] They do not deny the justice of the traditional negative stance of fundamental contestation; they doubt its effectiveness.

The growth of reformism into an active and potentially dominant influence in the trade unions is largely a post-war development; it is related – in time at least – to the post-war transformation of traditional French capitalism into neo-capitalism.[2]

'Neo-capitalism' is the Left's name for the political economy symbolized by the plan: 'Capitalism' because the motive force of the economy remains private profit; 'neo' because the Left

---

there is no question whatever of the CGT approving – and even less of supporting – such a 'plan'. No trade union worthy of the name could take a different position in face of a manoeuvre so dangerous for the working class. . . . It has not been through class collaboration that the working class had progressed, but through class struggle and working class unity!' CGT, *Le Plan: Mythes et Réalitiés*, pp. 13–14; see also, J. Magniadas in *Economie et Politique*, July 1965, p. 31; A. Heurteault, 'Planifier n'est pas socialiser,' *Partisans*, No. 18, Dec. 1964 – Jan. 1965.

[1] See Lorwin, *French Labour*, pp. 29–46, but esp. pp. 43–46 for a brief history of reformism as a long-term opposition to the principal revolutionary current of the trade union tradition. It is so well rooted in the movement, and has appeared in so many forms over so many years that it can be considered to be a conflicting minority current, a traditional anti-tradition position – rather like Reform Democrats in New York.

[2] See Marcel Gonin, pp. 89–90 in 'La Planification Comme Processus de Décision,' *Cahiers de la Fondation Nationale des Sciences Politiques*, #140 (Paris, 1965) for an example of a reformist view adopted as a response to the neo-capitalist situation.

recognizes the importance of such development as full-employment, steady expansion and giant corporations.[1] Because of these changes capitalism has survived. In the Left's view they are the result of one central innovation in the organization of the economy, the greatly increased role of the State. The State's role, in this analysis, is to provide the conditions for full-employment, stability and expansion and to promote the kind of economic activity which would enable the French economy to compete in world markets. Since the French economy is capitalist, the State increasingly functions as the vanguard of French capitalism, sometimes acting independently, sometimes in alliance with dynamic elements of the private sector to find solutions and economic strategies which private firms alone would have been unable to find. In short, the State assumed major new responsibilities for the conduct of the economy.

The plan fits snugly into this analysis. Here civil servants and businessmen collaborate to map out the future of the economy. Basically, private economic decision-makers retain their autonomy and their profits, but the Government uses certain levers and incentives to persuade such private power holders to make decisions which fit in with a broader view of the development of the economy. How much of an overview the government does and can impose, particularly on dynamic sectors of the economy or firms operating in an international market, is difficult to judge, and analysts on the Left differ about this. (In certain circles the planners are seen as the complete creatures of the giant corporations, and in others a large measure of autonomy in shaping private decisions is credited to the State.)[2]

Up to this point the Left's analysis of neo-capitalism and planning has an empirical accuracy, the main themes of which

[1] See, for example, André Gorz, *Stratégie Ouvrière et Néocapitalisme*, (Paris, 1962); CGT, *Le Plan: Mythes et Réalités*, pp. 1–14; P. Lebrun, in *Cahiers de la République*, June, 1962, pp. 463–464; Declercq, 'Democratie Nouvelle,' pp. 95–105; J. Juillard, 'La CFTC Devant Son Avenir,' *Esprit*, Sept. 1963, pp. 292–295; Serge Mallet, *La Nouvelle Classe Ouvrière*, (Paris, 1963); Ernest Mandel, 'The Economics of Neo-Capitalism,' *The Socialist Register*, (London, 1964); Hatzfield et Freyssinet, *l'Emploi en France*, Chapter 3, and *Manifeste Aux Travailleurs de France*, 32e *Congrès de la CFTC.*

[2] Compare, for example, Declercq, *Démocratie Nouvelle*, or *La CFTC et le IVe Plan*, Supplément #47 to *Formation*, Nov.-Dec. 1962 with *Le Plan: Mythes et Réalités*, or Magniadas, *Economie et Politique.*

many non-leftists accept.[1] Where Left differs from Centre is, of course, on the implications of this analysis. Expansionist businessmen and the planners who promote their success claim that the general welfare is served by such activity, that in the long run the interests of all will be advanced by the development of the new French capitalism.[2] The Left and the trade unions disagree; to them capitalism remains an order of exploitation; the quest for profits, whether made more rational by State intervention or not, is not in the interests of the working class.[3] It follows from this that inadequate technical qualifications, and social exclusion are not sufficient explanations for the lack of trade union participation in planning. To varying degrees, French trade unions do not want to participate, at least not 'constructively,' in planning, for such participation would sanction an economic order which French trade unions and the French Left oppose fundamentally. The Left's answer to the question of democracy in planning is, then, that planning can never be democratic as long as the process of planning involves a monopoly of decision-making by giant corporations and civil servants whose aim is to persuade the businessmen that a broader view means greater, long-term profits. To the Left 'democratic' means a change in the distribution of economic power; it means working class organizations effectively challenging the monopoly of economic decision-making of big business and the State. Planning could only be democratic when workers, through their trade union representatives had sufficient power in the planning process to make working class priorities prevail. In other words, as planning presently exists, trade unionists have no real power over decision-making, thus their presence on planning bodies is decorative at best, comprising at worst.[4]

[1] See, for example, Shonfield, *Modern Capitalism*, for a similar analysis from a definite non-Leftist standpoint.

[2] For examples, see A. Chalendon, 'Une Troisième Voie, l'Economie Concertée,' *Jeune Patron*, Dec. 1960; Louis Armand and Michel Drancourt, *Plaidoyer Pour l'Avenir* Paris, 1961); *Le Monde*, 4 July 1964, p. 15; *Jeune Patron*, no. 162, Feb. 1963, pp. 17–21; *Patrie et Progrès*, issue of Dec. 1961.

[3] See, for example, Heurteault, 'Planifier n'est pas socialiser,' p. 21; Magniadas, *Economie et Politique*, Gorz, *Stratégie Ouvrière et Néocapitalisme*.

[4] See, Gorz, *Stratégie Ouvrière*; Magniadas in *Economie et Politique*; CGT, *Le Plan: Mythes et Réalités*; G. Ducaroy, 'Socialisme et Planification,' *Les Cahiers du Centre d'Etudes Socialistes*, Nos. 25–26, 1–15 March 1963; Declercq, 'Rapport au Congrès de la CFTC,' *Formation*, 14 April 1959; E. Descamps,

Such general remarks can only serve as an introduction to the question of the trade unions, the Left and planning. The Left is far from united, both organisationally and politically, as differences between Communists, Left Socialists (largely in the PSU at the moment) and the Social Democrats of the SFIO demonstrate. The French trade union movement is also divided organisationally, reflecting different political attitudes. The largest confederation, the CGT, is affiliated with the Eastern World Federation of Trade Unions (WFTU) and is closely connected with the French Communist Party.[1] The second largest confederation, the CFDT (Confédération Française Démocratique du Travail), the ex-CFTC, is Socialist, if its constitution and recent policy statements are to be taken seriously, but associated with the Western International Confederation of Free Trade Unions (ICFTU).[2] The third large central, also ICFTU, the CGT-Force Ouvrière, is much smaller than the other two and developed out of a Cold War split off the CGT in 1947.[3]

'Socialisme et Planification,' *Les Cahiers du Centre d'Etudes Socialistes*, Nos. 18–19, 1962, and also articles in *Ibid.*, No. 1, 15 July 1962; Heurteault, 'Planifier n'est pas Socialiser'; Barjonet, 'Un Plan, Pourquoi Faire?'

[1] The existence of a real connection between the Communist Party and the CGT too often discourages further investigation into its internal organisation, and its modes of decision-making. The CGT's General Secretary and 7 of its 14 national secretaries were open Communist Party members as of 1966, but the other 7 national secretaries were not, and of these, three – LeBrun, Duhamel and Schaeffer – were open PSU members (although LeBrun resigned from the CGT in 1966). Much very real debate goes on within the CGT, although major decisions tend to go the way the Communists in the leadership desire. See below, pp. 362 where the LeBrun history, and the internal workings of the CGT are discussed. See also Lasserre, *Syndicalisme*, Part IV Section III and Lorwin, *French Labour* for descriptions of the three confederations.

[2] In 1964, after much give and take and long years of discussion, the CFTC 'deconfessionalised' and became the CFDT, dropping the religious references in its constitution and adopting more explicitly Leftist positions. There was some resistance to this at the conference when it took place, and a minority of 10%, under the leadership of Santy of the miners and Jacques Tessier split off into a separate confederation, keeping the religious reference and the old CFTC name. The new CFDT has shown signs of moving Left, with PSU members rising in the leadership, and gestures towards unity of action with the CGT (here a preliminary accord was actually signed between the two Centrals for certain ends of unity in action in January 1966). See M. Maurice, 'L'Evolution de la CFTC' in *Sociologie du Travail*, Jan.-Mar. 1965; J. C. Poulain, 'La Transformation de la CFTC en CFDT' in *Economie et Politique*, March 1965 and G. Levard 'CFTC – CFDT' in *Formation*, Sept.-Oct. 1965.

[3] The CFT-FO is close to the traditional Socialist party. It has less influence on the working class movement, both on the organizational and ideological levels –

The organisation and political disunity of the Left and labour predisposed them towards a divided reaction to planning. This tendency to division was undoubtedly further encouraged by the way in which planning emerged and developed. Planning grew and matured within the *économie concertée*. Its primary focus was on influencing the policies of economic decision-makers, on making sure that their decisions made sense for the economy as a whole. Effective planning was carried on between civil servants and businessmen, and the initiative in the planning situation lay with these two groups. The trade unions, then, could not act, only react. Moreover, the trade unions were peripheral to this critical business-functionary core of planning. Planning could be, and was, carried on essentially without the trade unions. Thus the unions were placed in a 'take it as it stands or leave it' position *vis à vis* planning. If they 'took it as it stood' they could not expect to exercise any significant power on the core groups of planning since there existed no reason why these groups should be any more than courteous to trade unionists, in the absence of either a greatly altered political situation or of any desperate need to secure trade union co-operation for planning itself.[1] Thus the question of whether to participate in planning or not was for the trade unions, a difficult one, one which involved responding to a *fait accompli*. It seemed that little could be gained, one way or the other. On one hand, it was important to calculate whether participation in planning was necessary to defend the economic interests of the trade union membership. On the other hand, it was necessary to calculate how much union participation, and what kinds of union participation, might commit working people, and thereby legitimise an arrangement which most unionists saw as benefitting only the interests of capital. In any case, the critical point is that elements which the Left and the unions considered enemies had thoroughly shaped a situation to which the unions had to respond. The positions of the unions *vis à vis*

---

than either the CGT or the CFDT. See Lorwin, *French Labour*; Granick, *European Executive*, pp. 187–202; and Lasserre, *Syndicalisme*, Part III, Section 3.

[1] Here, as noted above (Part V, Chapter II) as price planning becomes increasingly necessary, the situation may be changing. The trade union co-operation may become essential to the success of the plan. The implications of this development for the trade unions – and for the democratisation of planning – are examined below, pp. 227–37.

planning was difficult. That several strategies were advanced was, then, no surprise.

TRADE UNION STRATEGIES

One can distinguish three basic trade union strategies for dealing with the plan and with the political-economy the plan has come to symbolize: Unconditional Participation, Fundamental Opposition, and Contestative Participation.

UNCONDITIONAL PARTICIPATION

Defenders of the plan often stress that planning is *l'affaire de tous.* Communitarian rhetoric is often heard from such men who argue that the success of French capitalism is in the interests of the French working man. Albin Chalandon, for example, one of the more intelligent advocates of planning, puts his argument in this form.

> ideologies, yesterday's idols, are dying one after another. From this point on, the facts govern us. . . .
>
> France now finds herself, and will continue to find herself, more and more integrated into a Western economy, facing nations with superior industrial histories. We must be equal to this confrontation if we are to remain in the first rank in the race for prosperity. That is the imperative to which all other considerations must be subordinated.[1]

This, of course, is the language of the technocrat; 'From this point on, the facts govern us.' The implications of this are that radical politics and a radical interpretation of class struggle are luxuries which can no longer be afforded. The success of the French economy is primary and that means success within the capitalist framework. If they accepted this view, trade unions would recognise the permanence of French capitalism and accept the position of a pressure group within a capitalist society. This would mean accepting as permanent the present distribution of economic power. Big business would retain the initiative; the State, through such institutions as the plan,

[1] Albin Chalendon in *Le Monde*, 4 July 1964, p. 15; see also his articles in *Jeune Patron*, December 1960 and in *Nouvelle Frontière* July 1963. See also Bauchet, *Economic Planning*, pp. 233–249; President de Gaulle's address of 8 May 1961; Louis Armand, *Plaidoyer Pour l'Avenir*, Paris, 1961; Jean Fourastié, *La Planification Economique en France*, Paris, 1963.

would try to make their decisions more rational, and more socially beneficial. Constructive trade union participation in the plan under such conditions has been described by another technocrat, one with a trade union background:

> Although it would be difficult for the trade unions to participate effectively in discussion on what and how to produce, they could, nevertheless, provide competent advice on labour problems and on the regionalisation and localisation of economic activities.[1]

Trade union participation in planning under such circumstances would amount to a complete acceptance of the system. Such 'constructive participation' has its defenders in the trade union movement. Its justification is simple and clear. The primary function of trade unions must be to protect the interests of workers *within* the present capitalist society. In the words of Roger Jacques

> Because its essential purpose is to defend the interests of the workers, it (the trade union) is necessarily led to participation and, to a certain degree, to integration.[2]

The traditional negative stance has proven to be futile: capitalism will not collapse of its own, nor will the Left overthrow it. The fundamental opposition of the trade unions has not impeded the growth of the system nor significantly menaced its security. It has only served to prevent the Left from influencing that growth. Fundamental opposition has proven to be less a strategy of contestation than a strategy of abdication. The protection and advancement of immediate working class interests demands trade union participation in the decision centres of the economy. Fundamental opposition has not prevented the capitalists from planning, it has only served to

[1] Jacques Delors (Conseiller pour les affaires sociales au Comm. du Plan), 'Planification et Réalités Syndicales' *Droit Social*, Feb. 1965, p. 157. See also F. Bloch-Lainé, 'Economie Concertée et Démocratie,' *Les Cahiers de la République*, no. 46, July 1962 for a similar description. See also below, pp. 220–8 where trade union participation is discussed in terms of the institutions of the plan.

[2] R. Jacques, 'Pour une Approche Syndicale au Plan,' p. 38. The most perfect model for this position is, of course, the U.S. trade unions. Such a position has its advocates in France, although few trade unionists dare speak in such terms in public debate, given the radical tradition of French trade unions, and the even more radical tradition of their public pronouncements. De facto, unconditional participation exists, although it is far from being the dominant attitude at present. See Laserre, *Syndicalisme*, Part III, Section 2, for a description of one group of unconditional participationists.

prevent the Left and the trade unions from having anything at all to say about planning. Thus, to those who advocate participation, the possibility of making the economic development of France more palatable for the working class, even if critical economic decisions do remain the prerogative of big business, is better than nothing at all. They are willing, though not necessarily eager, to pay the price of accepting the permanence of capitalism, and they are also able to imagine a gradual transformation of the system, resulting perhaps from forces other than class action.

UNCONDITIONAL OPPOSITION

At the opposite end of the spectrum from 'constructive participation' is, of course, 'unconditional opposition.' The leadership of the CGT (excepting a minority who will be considered later) and the Communist Party hold strongly to this position. Planning, in this view, is part of the post-war offensive of 'state monopoly capitalism,' and one of the aims of planning is to promote class collaboration and thereby to disarm the working class.[1] Participation in planning, then, is not just a proposition involving getting scraps off the table for workers which would otherwise be thrown away, the attitude of the 'constructive participators,' but is a very real trap. Since the planning process can go on quite well without trade union participation, since the trade unions have no strategic position of power from which to bargain within the planning process, the unconditional opponent reasons that any concessions by planners and business to the unions concerning planning would have to be paid for by the unions in terms of their freedom to defend the interests of their membership by the usual tactics. Thus by 'participating' in any real way, the unions could gain only minor returns in exchange for vital trade union liberties which, once traded away, would give the workers' class opponents much greater power to manipulate wages and working conditions and to direct the economy along the path of development they choose. Speaking of the reforms trade unions might get out of participation, Jean Magniadas, a CGT leader, commented:

> it is obvious . . . that these reforms constitute the small change

[1] See, for example, CGT: *Le Plan: Mythes et Réalités*, J. Magniadas, in *Economie et Politique*, July 1965; *Le Monde* 4–5 June 1961, p. 11.

that they mean to 'offer' to the trade unions and that they link to an acceptance, or at least to a setting up, of a general framework of class collaboration including the creation of the appropriate institutions in which trade union action would be limited. . . .[1]

In this view, the interests of the working class can best be promoted by action along traditional lines outside planning, by trade union militancy and political organisation. Unconditional opposition has the virtue of assuring that these two means of carrying on the class struggle remain uncompromised, such that the initiative in trade union and political struggles remains in the hands of working class leaders. In the last analysis, the Left view can be summarised in the words of André Heurteault,

> . . . If we are in a capitalist regime, in a regime of exploitation, to participate in the realisation of the capitalist plan means, in good French, to participate in the exploitation of the workers.[2]

Unconditional opposition need not mean that the CGT has nothing to do with the plan. Although this was true for earlier plans, from the fourth plan on, CGT representatives were sent to the various planning commissions, but were sent as *observers*, not *participants*. As André Barjonet, until May '68 Secretary of the Economic Department of the CGT noted in a debate on trade union unity,

> Insofar as the Plan is not a joke, as we have pretended in the past, but a river that capitalism has to ford at the present stage of its development, our being there gives us at least a means of knowing what is happening. . . .[3]

An *observer*, apparently, does not engage in the active operation of planning (in Barjonet's experience with the steel commission of the plan this proved impossible in any case since the steel industry representatives 'make the planning. They are the only ones who know about the secrets of the industry, investments, ploughback and all that, there [on the commission] you can see for yourselves that having the means of production means pulling the levers of real power'),[4] while a

[1] J. Magniadas, in *Economie et Politique*, July 1965, p. 31.

[2] André Heurteault, 'Planifier n'est pas socialiser,' *Partisans* #18, December 1964 – January 1965, p. 21.

[3] André Barjonet, 'The Triple Foil of the Unions,' *International Socialist Journal*, No. 18, Dec. 1966, p. 571.

[4] *Ibid.*, p. 571.

participant at least assumes public responsibility for the content of the plan.

Observer vs. Participant is a subtle distinction. In practice it sometimes appears to wither away as the self-proclaimed observer role degenerates, in the eyes of some, into the *de facto* situation of an ineffective, irresponsible participator. The same is true of the more important distinction: Unconditional Opposition – Unconditional Abdication. It too tends to blurr, and that has been the principal basis for radical criticism of the unconditional opposition position. For the CGT and the Communist Party, the twin bastions of unconditional opposition, are under attack these days from the Left.

Their Left critics argue that the unconditional opposition position fails to provide a workable strategy for challenging the growing dominance of neo-capitalism.

Inaction comes easily. The unconditional opposition viewpoint provides a powerful, sometimes almost automatic, machinery for demonstrating the dangers of any proposed action, while maintaining a purity of revolutionary expression. From that position, any action, short of successful revolution itself, can easily be denounced as either a short-sighted, if not ill-willed, reformist sell-out of the working class, or else as an adolescent flirtation with adventurism.

The result may be such that instead of creating a dynamic revolutionary movement, revolutionary consciousness, sentiment and rhetoric (along with the vitally important communion they generate)[1] get locked into a pattern of inaction that *de facto* supports the *status quo*. Add to this the structures of old (both in their institutional age and in the age of their office holders) and rigid (Stalinist, their critics claim) organisations, the Communist Party and the CGT, and it is not a difficult matter to understand the desire for another Left position, one that can lead to action: not the sell-out, or reformist action of the unconditional participators, but positive, revolutionary action.

[1] It is important not to underestimate the powerful positive role that this communion plays in French working class life. It is one of the most important reasons the French working class has not taken the path of the US working class – a path of individual, privatistic quests. As a result, the French working class has, in a large measure, been spared the isolation, loneliness, alienation and fear that has so badly brutalized so many US workers and led them (in this year of the Wallace campaign) to desperate flirtations with fascism – the apolitical responses of isolated workers, lacking any class consciousness to social threats.

CONTESTATIVE PARTICIPATION

The radical response to the sterility of fundamental opposition can be called contestative participation – a strategy of piecemeal revolutionary actions, or 'non-reformist reforms.'[1]

This group of evolving trade union strategies shares the objective of the traditional Left position – replacing capitalism with a fundamentally different socialist society. It is not reformist. But it is radically revisionist.

Its basic premise is that capitalism has changed, and as a result the traditional Left strategy for challenging the capitalist system is ineffective when it confronts neo-capitalism.[2] The contestative participationists find that under neo-capitalism the revolt against society has 'lost its natural base. . . . Poverty can no longer be the basis of the struggle for socialism.'[3] Workers trapped in poverty and misery 'are for all practical purposes a rear guard,'[4] and while it is still necessary to demand the satisfaction of their immediate needs, 'this struggle no longer brings the entire social order into radical question.'[5]

The contestative participationists accuse the traditional Left of ignoring this essential fact of modern political life: the immiseration model is obsolete. The intolerability of the worker's life as a consumer – his poverty – will no longer function as the motor force of revolution, and struggles based on the immiseration model, struggles for higher wages, will not threaten the capitalist system nor will they generate a consciousness in the working class of the need for a socialist alternative.[6]

The traditional assumptions of absolute and immediate intolerability allow the Left to 'dispense with a strategy of progressive conquest of power and of active intervention into capitalist contradictions. . . . The impasse predicted for capital-

[1] Contestative participation is essentially an Italian strategy developed by the Italian Communist Party and by such Left wing Italian Socialists as Vittorio Foa and Lelio Basso. The clearest statement of the strategy and its application in a French context is to be found in André Gorz, *Stratégie Ouvrière et Néocapitalisme*, Paris, Seuil, 1964, recently and skilfully translated by Martin Nicolaus, under the title *Strategy for Labour*, Boston, Beacon Press, 1967. [See also Gorz's recent collection of essays, *Le Socialisme Difficile*, Paris, Seuil, 1968.] In this brief sketch of the contestative participationist strategy I follow Gorz closely with a maximum of direct quotation.

[2] See, *Strategy for Labour*, pp. 3–10.

[3] *Ibid.*, p. 3.

[4] *Ibid.*, p. 4.

[5] *Ibid.*, p. 4.

[6] *Ibid.*, pp. 20–33.

ism becomes finally the impasse of the revolutionary waiting game.'[1]

The essential problem for the Left is to 'determine in which needs the necessity for socialism is rooted now that the urgency born of poverty is blunted,' to 'shape a strategy that will lead to the consciousness that society must be radically transformed,'[2] and to begin that process of radical social transformation.

The contestative participationists respond to these problems with a strategy of partial, but revolutionary reforms, anti-capitalist wedges into the subtle, but very real contradictions of neo-capitalism. One favourite example of such piecemeal revolutionary reforms is a successful strike in Italy in which workers won the right to produce what they wanted to produce – tractors for nearby farming villages – rather than the luxury motor cars management had decided they would produce.[3] These 'mediating' objectives create consciousness of the critical qualitative intolerabilities of neo-capitalism; they demonstrate the desirability and the possibility of socialist alternatives; and they also secure autonomous bases of working class power – anti-capitalist instances that cannot be reabsorbed by the system.

In the words of Gorz, because 'the intolerability of the capitalist system is no longer absolute but relative, supplementary mediations are necessary to make the intolerability felt. And these mediations must be *positive*: they must reveal the urgency of the qualitative needs which the neo-capitalist ideology ignores or represses. They must make these needs conscious by demonstrating the possibility and the positive conditions of their satisfaction.'[4]

The contestative participationist strategy of challenging the basic structures of neo-capitalism on all levels and in all areas of society instead of the traditional strategy of watchfully waiting for the correct moment for the one-shot revolution, leads to an active Left role in the factory, the university and the plan.

In the plan the contestative participationists hold that the interests of the workers are best served by an active trade union

[1] *Ibid.*, p. 23.
[2] *Ibid.*, p. 4.
[3] *Ibid.*, pp. 59 and 73.
[4] *Ibid.*, p. 4.

role in the planning process. They hold that the purpose of such a presence should be not merely getting 'scraps from the table' but the step-by-step public exposure of the plan and the politi-cal-economy it symbolises as capitalist and profoundly inimical to the real interests of French working people. In other words, what distinguishes contestative participationists from un-conditional participators in the plan is their desire to use the planning process as an educative battleground to elevate the political and class consciousness of the workers. What sets them off from fundamental oppositionists is a belief that a counter-offensive using planning as a base of operation is a sensible tactic in response to the capitalist offensive which is planning.[1]

Here as elsewhere, the Left is far from united; but the many varieties of contestative participation do all have some common characteristics. For example, they all stress the possibilities open to trade unionists to make plans more socially conscious, to stress collective needs and goods publicly in the planning process, to change the content of plans if possible, or at worst to expose the negligence of the planners should substantive change prove impossible. In general, a far broader concept of social utility than profit ought to be governing the planning operation. Specifically, the usual collective goods and goals, full employment, schools, hospitals, roads, social security, recreational facilities are stressed along with more esoteric collective problems such as redistribution of incomes, regional backwardness, reconversion of failing industry and professional retraining for those employed in such industries, and so on.[2]

Putting public pressure on the planners to broaden plans in this way is only one tactic in the larger strategy of contestative participation. Even the most moderate of the social democratic groups claim that their goals in planning are larger than this. J. Piette sees the strategy's primary objective as 'la remise en question du mécanisme de la production.'[3] The plan simply

[1] See *Strategy for Labor passim*; 32 Congrès de la CFTC, *Manifeste Aux Travailleurs de France*; Pierre LeBrun, *Questions Actuelles du Syndicalisme*, Paris, 1965; *Pour Un Front des Travailleurs*, Paris, Juilliard, 1963; *France-Observateur* 12 Nov. 1964; and works cited in following pages.

[2] See *Le Monde*, 24 Nov. 1964, p. 18; *France-Observateur*, 1 Oct. 1964, p. 4; 'La CFTC et le IVe Plan,' Supplement no. 47 to *Formation*, Nov.-Dec. 1962 and below, pp. 355–360.

[3] Jacques Piette, 'Socialisme et Planification,' *La Revue Socialiste*, no. 185, July 1965, p. 155.

as an 'uncertainty reducer,' a reinforcer of the market, is unacceptable says Piette, 'our positive participation . . . imposes a simultaneous structural action aimed at reversing the mode of private appropriation of the means of production.'[1] Likewise, as early as 1961, the CFTC at its congress stated that 'the CFTC opposes modern capitalism – in whatever form of planning – it disguises itself with a socialist economy . . . the economic orientation of the CFTC is socialist, which is presently not the case of the plan.'[2]

The objectives of the contestative participationists in terms of changes in the contents of the plans are clearly articulated in the counter-plan they promulgated at the time of the Parliamentary debate on the fifth plan.

We will first examine this counter-plan carefully not only because it sets out the contestative participationist alternatives for the contents of the plan so clearly but also because it represents the foremost example of the effects of an institutionalised plan on political discourse.[3] We will then examine the two other principal lines of the contestative participationist strategy: first, concrete proposals for the democratisation of the planning process itself, that is for giving the trade unions some real power in the proceedings; and second, the structural changes in the economy and in the relation of the plan to the economy that would have to follow from such reforms in the planning process.

THE COUNTER PLAN

The idea behind the Counter Plan was to seize the political initiative in the debate on the plan from the big business-civil servant axis by presenting a coherent alternative plan for economic development. An authentic alternative plan is an important first step towards the politicisation of planning. The true nature of a plan, that is, an ordering of priorities, can be exposed only when the technocratic mystique of planning is shattered and the Nation presented with a real choice among alternative plans, all technically competent, but each representing a different ranking of priorities. The Counter Plan would

[1] *Ibid.*, p. 156.

[2] *Manifeste Aux Travailleurs de France*, 32e Congrès de la CFTC; Also, *Le Monde*, 4–5 July, 1961, p. 11.

[3] In the sense of the argument of Chapter 16, above.

place the Left in the position of setting the terms, or at least some of the terms, of public debate on the plan and on the larger question of general economic orientation. For the first time, the planners, the civil servants, and the businessmen would have to respond to a Leftist initiative in planning. In other words, if the Counter Plan did not itself provide the decisive political change needed to make planning democratic it would, nonetheless, said the contestative participationists, provide a tactic which, in exposing the true nature of the official plan and in proposing alternatives, might raise the level of economic sophistication and stir the political consciousness of French working men and thus in some way bring closer decisive political change. Additional goals were posited for the Counter Plan. It was also seen as a base on which the unity of the Left might be built, both politically and in trade unions, as the beginning of a common programme useful both in the immediate political future (unity was desirable for the upcoming Presidential and legislative elections) and in pointing the Left towards the consideration of new strategies for combating neo-capitalism.[1]

The Counter Plan was a creation of the French New Left (no relation to the American New Left) and as such fit well as a tactic into the revisionist Marxism of New Left theorists such as André Gorz. To cite Gorz,

> Mobilisation aimed at the conquest of power and the establishment of socialism . . . must proceed by the '*mediation*' of intermediary mobilising objectives: the struggle for partial objectives that speak to profound needs and challenge the capitalist structures. . . .[2]

The Counter Plan appeared in the early autumn of 1964 when the Government was preparing to present the preliminary 'Principal Choices' of the fifth plan to Parliament.[3] Its outlines were unveiled on October 1st in *France-Observateur*, then a quasi-PSU publication, in an article entitled 'What the Fifth Plan Should Be,' under the pseudonym '*Rungis*.' Rungis pointed out what he claimed were the 'three fundamental

[1] See 'Esquisse d'un Autre Plan,' *France-Observateur*, 12 Nov. 1964; also issue of 1 Oct. 1964; 'Le Contre Plan PSU' *Tribune du Parti Socialiste Unifé*, 28 Nov. 1964.

[2] Gorz, *Stratégie Ouvrière et Néocapitalisme*, p. 16 (p. 11 US ed.).

[3] 'Projet de Rapport sur les Principales Options du Ve Plan,' *J. O.*, *Lois et Décrets*, 23 Dec. 1964.

vices' in the government's presentation: the proposed 5% rate of expansion was too little, the plan had many 'clearly reactionary' aspects, and, paradoxically, the plan was too ambitious for the government. To Rungis, a 5% a year growth was not the maximum growth rate possible, but it was the maximum growth rate consistent with the government's liberal predisposition; a higher growth rate would necessitate too many state interventions in the economy, too many illiberal controls for the government's taste. The Counter Plan proposed a slightly higher growth rate of 5.6% per year.[1] As for reactionary priorities in the government's proposals, Rungis listed several. The first was military spending. Rungis pointed out that the *force de frappe* (France's independent nuclear striking force) was costing the French taxpayer more than the Algerian War. The second was the Government's programme of promoting increases in retained profits as the principal path to higher investment. [The Government's plan called for the proportion of investment financed out of retained earnings to rise from 60% to 70% and for corporate savings to rise by 6.4% per year.][2] This, in Rungis' words, 'amounts, practically, to asking the consumers and wage earners to finance the enrichment of the stockholders.' The other 'reactionary' aspects of the Government's draft were the proposed incomes policy; [a 9% annual rate of increase in profits compared to a 3.3% rate in wage increase];[3] the failure to reduce working time; cuts in social security; rises in the prices of basic public services such as buses and the Paris Métro; and the total failure of the plan even to address itself to the question of a more equitable distribution of income. Then, despite the liberal nature of the plan, despite its obvious catering to big business interests (in addition to the retained earnings schemes, another objective of the plan was to promote the concentration of industry) Rungis asked whether the plan was realisable. He pointed out that the plan remained largely indicative insofar as its output targets were concerned, and stressed the massive disregard of the third and fourth plans both by private industry and Government. He doubted whether the Ministry of Finance could be counted on to go along with

[1] For the planning Commission's brief sketch of a 5.5% overall growth rate and their reasons for choosing the 5% variant, see *ibid.*, pp. 11418–11419.

[2] See above, p. 186.

[3] See above, p. 186.

the plan, given the liberal predilections of Premier Pompidou and Finance Minister Giscard d'Estaing. And he asked why the workers should go along with the incomes policy, since they get nothing in return. Rungis' conclusion was that

> practically speaking, although its ambitions are relatively modest, there is a strong probability that the fifth plan will not be realised precisely because the reforms which could permit its realisation will not have been undertaken.[1]

The Counter Plan aimed at all of the weaknesses Rungis pointed out in the Government's draft. A higher rate of growth could be maintained *and* the work week reduced if the state intervened actively to deal with the 'tensions' in the labour market and in financing investment. The state would actively intervene in redistributing incomes between social groups, particularly towards lower strata. Drastic reductions in military spending would make possible increased collective spending for housing, schools, public health, public transportation and regional development. Finally, structural reforms such as nationalisation of building land to end real estate speculation, the nationalisation of big monopolies and the use of selective public enterprise to promote new sectors of the economy were proposed.

Table 14, which follows, compares the principal targets of the Counter Plan with the government's proposal for the fifth plan:

The political career of the Counter Plan was, alas, rather abrupt. The strategy was to introduce it as an amendment to the Government's plan in the Economic and Social Council (the first body to debate the fifth plan) where it would then serve as a rallying point to unify Left opposition to the Government's proposals.[2] Pierre Le Brun, a national secretary of the CGT

[1] 'Contre Plan Rungis', *France-Observateur*, 1 Oct. 1964.

[2] The device of an amendment to the Government's proposal in the Economic and Social Council was adopted primarily because the conditions for the plan's debate in the National Assembly seemed to preclude the discussion of non-government sponsored amendments. Hence, the choice of the Economic and Social Council, which although the first representative assembly to review the draft plan, can only study, discuss and recommend; it has no legislative authority. The crucial rule concerning amendments in the National Assembly is contained in Article 44 of the Constitution of the Fifth Republic. See W. Pickles, *The French Constitution of October* 4, 1958, London, Stevens, 1960, p. 21; also P. Williams and M. Harrison, *De Gaulle's Republic*, London, Longmans, 1960, p. 143. Dorothy Pickles, *The Fifth French Republic*, NY, Praeger Paperbacks, 1960, pp. 122–123.

TABLE XIV

COUNTER PLAN COMPARED TO GOVERNMENT PLAN[1]

	Government plan annual increase (in %)	*Counter plan annual increase (in %)*	*Difference in 1970 (in % of 1965)*
I. National Resources			
GNP	5	5.5	+3
Imports	9.6	10	+2.5
Exports	9.4	9.8	+3
II. Uses of those Resources			
A. Consumption			
Household	4.5	5.2	+4
Government	6.6	0.1	−37.5
of which: Civilian	(6.5)	(6.5)	0
Military	(6.7)	(−7)	−69.5
Financial Institutions	6.3	6.3	0
B. Investment			
Firms	5.7	6.3	+4
Housing	6	8.6	16.5
Government	9.1	11.2	15.5
Financial Institutions	7.8	7.8	0

and a PSU member, one of those who collaborated in producing the Counter Plan (long an advocate of contestative participation) and a vice-president of the Economic and Social Council, was to introduce the amendment.[2] He never did. The CGT refused to support the Counter Plan. The Old Guard Leadership and the old Fundamentalist attitudes prevailed. So did the old results. In the Economic and Social Council the Government's outline plan encountered only disorganised criticism from fragmented groups as the Left proved, once again, unable to unite behind an alternative. When the CFTC proposed an amendment criticising the 'relative austerity' of the Government's plan, the CGT abstained from voting on that amendment. It abstained on five of seven substantive proposals for positive reform put forward by other Left of Centre groups. The two proposals it supported were straightforward demands for higher wages and shorter hours – the traditional grounds of

[1] Source, all figures, *Le Monde*, 24 Nov. 1964, p. 18.

[2] See 'Esquisse d'un Autre Plan,' *France-Observateur*, 12 Nov. 1964, p. 24 for the LeBrun amendment and LeBrun's views. See also his *Questions Actuelles du Syndicalisme*, for a more detailed elaboration of his views.

CGT contestation. Then the CGT voted to reject the Government's plan *in toto.*[1]

Thus the Counter Plan flopped politically. Criticism of the Government's proposal, though virulent, never found a coherent counter proposal and, as a result, never got beyond the confines of traditional, partial, political discourse.[2] But the idea of a Counter Plan remains alive, and it is just conceivable that the CGT may change its position on the whole question. Pierre le Brun will not be around to savour victory if the CGT does finally come around to his views. After a very long career as resident maverick in the CGT, a final explosion occurred in early 1966. Le Brun had, in addition to his views on planning, opposed the Soviet intervention in Hungary in 1956, and had often expressed dangerous sympathies for General de Gaulle. The final crisis occurred after Le Brun had refused publicly to go along with the CGT's support for François Mitterand in the Presidential elections, claiming that the CGT should have remained neutral and that de Gaulle's foreign policy was preferable to Mitterand's pro-Americanism.[3] When, after the election, he repeated his critical views of the CGT in *le Monde* and added, for good measure, a few remarks about the Counter Plan,[4] *l'Humanité* answered the next day with a scathing attack on him as a 'class collaborator.'[5] Le Brun sought a repudiation of this attack from CGT leaders and, when none was forthcoming, he resigned his post as one of the CGT's National Secretaries.

[1] See *J.O.*, *Conseil Economique*, 13 Nov. 1964, where the CFTC amendment is presented (p. 875), and the results of the seven divisions are recorded (pp. 892–893). The CFTC voted with the CGT to reject the entire plan (p. 893).

[2] See above, Chapter 16.

[3] See *Nouvel Observateur*, 20 Oct. 1965, p. 9; see also, *Le Monde* 4–5 June 1961, p. 11 for a description of LeBrun's difficult position within the CGT five years earlier.

[4] See *Le Monde*, 3 Jan. 1966, p. 6.

[5] See *l'Humanité*, 8 Jan. 1966, p. 1.

20 TRADE UNION PARTICIPATION and the institutional structures of the plan

Given the objectives of the Contestative Participationists, what would a serious trade union effort at participation mean in terms of the institutions of the planning process? We can begin with the most concrete question. Where and how (in terms of the institutions of the plan) could the trade unions begin to participate?

1 THE VERTICAL COMMISSIONS

The Vertical Commissions (steel, transportation, energy, etc.) are the scene of the informal and direct participation which weighs so heavily in official descriptions of the planning process.[1] Trade union underrepresentation in these commissions is the focus of many critiques of the plan; increasing trade union participation is a primary concern of reformers.[2] The vertical commissions, however, are a poor starting place for a serious trade union effort at effective participation in planning. An increase in trade union representation in the vertical commissions will be futile unless accompanied by major changes in the planning process, especially participation by the Left in the choice of the plan's objectives, and more coercive implementation devices; with these changes, it promises to be of only secondary substantive importance.

François Bloch-Lainé analyses the implications of an isolated increase in trade union representation in the vertical commissions. He dismisses its substantive impact, that is, the direct effects on the contents of the plans of such a reformist step, but insists upon its desirability in terms of its psychological or political effects.

[1] See, for example, Massé, *French Affairs.*

[2] See *Cahiers de la République*, issues of Dec. 1961, Jan.–Feb. 1962, and June 1962.

The trade unions have asked themselves . . . if the investment programmes contained in the plan would have been different had the discussions [in the vertical commissions] been different. More precisely, would the four year programmes for steel, or for chemicals have been different if the trade union representatives, theoretically present in the vertical commissions, had been better able to discuss what the management of those two sectors got the civil servants to accept.

I don't think so. But I think it would be very useful if such a suspicion were impossible. Truthfully, it isn't the investment and production programmes which could be taken out of the hands of the 'technocrats' and submitted to a more political decision-making process. . . . Nonetheless, it would be useful if none of the vital forces of the nation had the impression of being kept outside the centre of decision where the investment and production programmes are established and implemented.[1]

The intelligent Centre, well represented by Bloch-Lainé, feels that more trade union participation is necessary, if only to allay Leftist suspicions about the goings-on in those commissions and to stifle charges that the Left was 'excluded.' In brief, it is necessary in order to preserve the impression that planning is democratic. But Bloch-Lainé does not feel that the Left's participation in the vertical commissions will significantly change the contents of the plans. The big decisions, the decisions which most interest the trade unions, he argues, are not made in the vertical commissions. This is true. The important decisions, the ranking of objectives, are made when the skeletal plan is first outlined in what we called stage two of the planning process.[2] But he also seems to be saying that the preparation of investment and output programmes in the vertical commissions is a technical matter, or at least a matter for 'technocrats.' This is not altogether the case. Many non-technical decisions are made in the vertical commission stage of the planning process, if not necessarily at the vertical commission tables. These include the complicated business of managing cartels in growth sectors and the somewhat less complicated business of obtaining the maximum in State 'incentives' for investment and expansion programmes that would be under-

[1] F. Bloch-Lainé, 'Economie Concertée et Démocratie,' *Les Cahiers de la République*, no. 46, juillet 1962, pp. 578–579.

[2] See above, Part II, Chapter I.

taken without the plan and without those 'incentives.'[1] A serious trade union presence in the vertical commissions might curtail or at least expose some of these practices. It could also influence decisions on matters of importance to the unions, such as the location of new plants and the choice of technologies.[2] Furthermore, a corps of technically knowledgeable trade unionists could quickly indicate that many of the 'technical' decisions are not entirely 'technical,' and the programmes prepared by the representatives of big business are not the only ways to achieve the objectives of the plan. Nonetheless, it is quite true that the vertical commissions are not where active trade union participation will produce radical changes in the plans. But active trade union participation might produce radical changes in the workings of the vertical commissions.

The vertical commissions, it was argued above, function as rallying places for expansion-oriented cartels. In the commissions, the more progressive managers of big business, in co-operation with ranking civil servants, prepare investment and expansion programmes for each industry. The Treasury, the planners and the progressive firms, encourage and organise the expansion and rationalisation of the industry. In brief, the vertical commissions function as official task forces of the *économie concertée*. All their other functions are of lesser importance, except one: the vertical commissions give planning the appearance of democracy.

A serious trade union presence in the vertical commissions could drastically affect these two principal functions: the smooth operation of the expansion-oriented cartels, and the projection of an appearance of democracy. It would disturb the atmosphere of common interests and common aims that the *économie concertée* tries to create and in which it works best. Unless their ideologies change drastically the trade unionists would not be satisfied with the simple objectives of the sectoral programmes: modernisation, expansion and rationalisation. They are likely to inject, even at the level of investment programmes for a single industry, such 'political' issues as job

[1] See above, Part II, Chapter 4, where the workings of the vertical commissions are analysed; pp. 63–6 discusses the problem of incentives that generate no real changes in corporate behaviour.

[2] For example, the emphasis on hydroelectric stations in the early plans encountered strong resistance from the trade unions who favoured thermal (coal) stations. See above, p. 147.

security, regional location, workers' control and income distribution, which the commissions have managed to ignore. The trade unionists could also prove embarrassing in the many instances where targets adopted by the commissions are unrealistically low and likely to be exceeded, (as often occurs in the consumer durables' sector), or where the resources allocated for the realisation of planned programmes are not commensurate with the objectives of those programmes (as often happens in construction and public works).[1] Exposure of the plan as a capitalist tool, it will be recalled, is one important objective of the contestative participationist strategy.[2]

If there were a substantial increase in trade union representation, how would 'decisions' be reached in the vertical commissions? Voting is no solution. If a voting procedure were to be instituted, the question of a formula for representation would become the central concern of planning, and the entire character of the planning process would be radically altered. The commissions presently work by 'consensus.' The *rapporteur* prepares a report embodying the views of the commission. Dissenting opinions are usually indicated in the reports, but the report is only a recommendation.[3] The question of a voting procedure raises the questions of what the vote means, and how it will affect the workings of the commissions. As long as the reports are not binding on anyone, the voting approach is meaningless at best, self-destructive at worst. The net effect of the change would not be to redistribute power within planning; it would be to destroy the plan.

Substantial trade union participation could, then, radically alter the workings of the vertical commissions, and in the opposite way from that predicted by Bloch-Lainé. Instead of strengthening the impression that the planning process is democratic, it might destroy that impression. Instead of keeping 'political decisions' out of the 'technical' stages of the planning process it might politicise the vertical commissions. If the vertical commissions were to publish reports regularly marked by sharp divisions between management and labour, the sectoral plans could no longer be presented as technical programmes

[1] See above, pp. 104–108 and Appendices, for examples of such disparities.

[2] See above, pp. 211ff.

[3] See above, pp. 60ff for a description of the 'decision-making' process in the vertical commissions; B. Cazes, *La Planification en France et le IVe Plan*, is brief and clear on these points: see esp. pp. 76–77.

based on the objectives of a democratic consensus. They would appear to be the handiwork of big business and a civil service sympathetic to the interests of big business.

An isolated increase in trade union participation in the vertical commissions might be useful in terms of the contestative participationist tactic of exposure. But even here the benefit promises to be small. The contestative participator has few advantages in the vertical commissions over the CGT 'observer' who is quite able to expose. True, the participator could prepare counter-proposals. Their repeated rejection might be a useful device for the public exposure of the plan and for the important task of public economic and political education. But once again, counter-proposals at the industry level are apt to be less dramatic than aggregate counter-plans where differences between the trade union and Government projects are more likely to make a difference to the public at large.

Given its potential for usefulness within the context of the exposure tactic, it is difficult to agree with Bloch-Lainé when he argues that increased trade union participation in the vertical commissions will enhance the plan's image of democracy. There is a good chance that this Centrist strategy will backfire.

Crucially, however, an increase in trade union participation in the vertical commissions will not of itself even begin to lead to the kinds of changes in the planning process that the trade unions insist upon unless it is accompanied by reforms of far greater significance, (again, more imperative controls, more normative targets). Participation in the horizontal commissions, some suggest, might be a better starting place.

2 HORIZONTAL COMMISSIONS

Participation in the Horizontal Commissions would make smaller demands on the technical and economic resources of the trade unions than participation in the vertical commissions.[1] There are only five horizontal commissions (finance, manpower,

[1] Those who argue that trade union participation is severely handicapped by a lack of technical and financial resources stress the important economies of participation in the horizontal commissions; see Pierre Massé's comments in *Cahiers de la République*, June 1962, p. 459, for a brief review of various schemes for increasing trade union representation and participation without taxing trade union resources.

productivity and regional development) while there are over thirty vertical commissions, each with a full complement of sub-commissions and study groups.[1] The short supply of qualified trade union representatives would restrict trade union activities less severely in the horizontal commissions. Furthermore, though technical, the work of the horizontal commissions is not very specialised. It consists, essentially, of balancing projected demand for critical inputs (manpower, finance, foreign exchange, etc.) against projected supplies of those inputs, whereas the work of the vertical commissions demands, in addition to a competence in general economic, financial and statistical analysis, a specialised knowledge of the technology and the financial and market structures of each industry. Crucially, business' monopoly on certain kinds of critical information – data on costs, financing, production and profits at the level of the firm – which so handicapped the trade unions in the vertical commissions, would be less a factor in the horizontal commissions which work with more aggregated data.

The Horizontal Commissions are supposed to check the industrial programmes which originate in the vertical commissions against one another for consistency, and against the economy's supply constraints, then prune them when those constraints are approached. They should provide an ideal starting place for effective trade union participation. A representative committee that shapes the plan's targets and has the power to implement its priorities, is precisely what the trade unions are asking for when they demand that the plan be made more democratic, more normative and more imperative. It is also precisely what the horizontal commissions do not do.

The Horizontal Commissions simply do not have the power to fill their function properly. They can point out inconsistencies and potential bottlenecks, and often their recommendations will be acted upon by the relevant firms. But, as argued above, their essential problem is that they lack the power to restrain potentially profitable expansion beyond levels compatible with the over-all equilibrium of the planned pattern of resource

[1] See: Comm. du Plan, *Programme de Travail des Commissions de Modernisation Pour 1965*, Part IV, (pp. 13–15) for Horizontal Commissions; Annexe no. 5, pp. 61–62, for a complete list of vertical commissions.

allocation. This inability to restrain expansion has led repeatedly to the distortion of the planned growth pattern. The horizontal commissions cannot compensate for their inability to control excessive expansion in such sectors as motor cars and consumer durables by cutting back planned expansion in other sectors such as housing, education or armaments: the plan must, at least, present a politically acceptable social programme, and military matters are untouchable. The horizontal commissions try to make the best of their responsible, but powerless, position. They try to reconcile the necessity of producing a balanced, detailed plan to the reality of their limited powers by making cuts that are not sure to be respected.[1]

The trade unions are quite aware of the powerlessness of the horizontal commissions, and aware of how that powerlessness makes them as ineffective starting places as the vertical commissions. For unless trade union participation is accompanied by a radical increase in the power of the horizontal commissions to restrain expansion, that is, the power to make the plans more imperative in order to make them more normative, trade union participation in the horizontal commission will lead to all of the difficulties associated with an isolated increase in trade union participation in the vertical commissions.

The contestative participationist exposure tactic would probably be more effective in the horizontal commissions than in the vertical commissions. Counter-proposals dealing with aggregate manpower and financial balances would generally have a greater educative and politicising impact than counter-proposals for single industries. A steady stream of reports containing dissenting opinions by the working class groups would weaken the important illusions that planning – even though it is not controlled by Parliament – is a democratic process. But even if the trade union views were to predominate in the commissions, little could be done to prevent distortion of the planned pattern of development without a radical increase in their power to restrain expansion. If the commissions had such power, trade union participation in the commissions *could* be effective. It could help diminish the persistent tendency for the planned pattern of development to be distorted in such a way as to be even more objectionable to

[1] The assertions of this paragraph are drawn from the argument presented above Part II, Chapter 4.

the trade unions than the initial targets of the plan. Once the powers were available to reduce such distortions – by making the private sector conform to the targets of the plan – those initial targets would themselves be effected. A simple increase in the power to restrain expansion in the private sector would permit the plan's targets to be more normative. The planners' inability to restrain expansion in many sectors is partially taken into account by the planners in the initial preparation of the plan. They write targets for many sectors which are more predictive than normative. These targets represent reasonable concessions to their lack of power; when such concessions are not made, distortions of the planned objectives result. Their general direction, however, is opposite to the objectives of the trade unions. They result in higher rates of *planned* expansion, in, for example, consumer durables, and lower rates of planned expansion in the public services or social security. More potent implementation devices would reduce the need for this kind of reasonable concession to market forces.[1]

An increase in the power of the horizontal commissions to make sure the targets of the plan are followed is the precondition for effective trade union participation in the horizontal commissions. Without that power, trade union participation will not result in significant changes in the plans, and may well create many of the same difficulties (for the trade unions themselves as well as for the plan) as an isolated increase in trade union participation in the vertical commissions. But that is the same as saying effective trade union participation in the horizontal commissions is dependent upon the entire list of trade union proposals for the reform of planning: planning ought to be more democratic, more normative and more imperative. For an increase in the power to restrain expansion is precisely what is meant by making the plan more imperative. More imperative controls would permit the plan to be more normative, and control of the choice of targets by a representative assembly would, the Left feels, guarantee that the plans will be more normative.

[1] This tendency for planned expansion rates in many sectors to exceed rates 'desired' by the planners operates in *addition* to the built-in tendency for distortions which work in the same direction.

21 THE PLAN AND PARLIAMENT

Under the Fourth Republic, planning was largely an extra-Parliamentary affair, either never brought before Parliament, in the cases of the first and third plans, or considered by Parliament in conditions which made such consideration pointlesss (after the plan had been in effect for over two years) as with the second plan.[1] This reluctance to risk Parliamentary exposures under the Fourth Republic can be understood partially in terms of the chronic governmental instability of the period; a government's longevity depended greatly on its ability to avoid confronting the National Assembly with issues of consequence.

Moreover, there was little pressure on the Government for greater Parliamentary participation in planning. Parliament itself made no serious efforts to take an active role in the planning process, while the planners, the Treasury and the big business groups made no efforts to interest Parliament in the plan.

In the early days of planning, the planners, and the Treasury officials saw their primary task as leading the French economy towards expansion and international competitiveness, a task which involved developing the industrial core of the economy and educating or coercing (where necessary and possible) those who made economic decisions into new habits. Given the primacy of this process of investment, reorganisation and education within the big business sectors, and given that this process could be effectively carried out within the *économie concertée*, public political debate in Parliament was a luxury rather low on the planners' list of real priorities, and serious Parliamentary participation in planning was potentially disruptive.

Under the Fifth Republic the situation changed somewhat. Early efforts to build a place for planning within the system of

[1] See above, pp. 58–60.

economic and bureaucratic decision-making had been successful. Under planning (whether because of it, is, of course, another question) the economy had grown while the basic distribution of economic power remained unchanged. Thus power holders in the dynamic sectors of the economy and modernising civil servants in the Treasury more and more found planning to their liking, and the priority given planning within the administrative apparatus of state and firm rose. But, for the same reasons, so did demands for its democratisation.

Furthermore, the communitarian aspects of planning – all the corporations of the realm co-operatively planning the future of the nation – combined with its mystique of technology and prosperity had great appeal for the Gaullist government which began a massive campaign to promote planning. For the de Gaulle government one means (among others) of promoting the plan's public relations – and its own notions of constructive and harmonious social and economic relations – was Parliamentary discussion and approval of the plan.

This was especially attractive since political conditions had changed with the advent of de Gaulle's Republic. The political inhibitions which had blocked real Parliamentary discussion under the Fourth Republic had been eliminated since the Parliament returned after 1962 had a Gaullist majority to support a Gaullist Government and approve a Gaullist plan.[1]

Finally, by the early 1960's the plan was beginning to find that the problems it had to confront could no longer be solved within the confines of the *économie concertée* and it began to seek a broader range of participants. Specifically, the Common Market made price stability a necessity. The only path to price stability open to the plan was an incomes policy approach. But the operation of a successful incomes policy demands a much broader range of positive participation than did the modernisation and expansion programmes of the *économie concertée.*

This combination of economic necessity and political considerations led the Government to experiment with a broader role for Parliament in planning.

Thus the fourth plan was discussed by Parliament, albeit

[1] And new Gaullist rules for Parliamentary debate promised to eliminate the possibility of minor embarrassment that could result from debate even though the government did have a majority: see Article 44 of the Constitution of the Fifth Republic and p. 217 above.

most unimpressively, before being put into effect.[1] Then, in 1964, Parliament was asked to pronounce on the critical questions ('Grandes Options') of the fifth plan, then still in preparation. In this case, Commissioner Massé presented the various Parliamentary bodies with a preliminary outline of the new plan which included alternative possibilities for future economic development at crucial points. Whether or not this could be taken very seriously (only one series of alternatives, that favoured by the planners and the government, was worked out in detail[2]) it was an attempt to widen the area of discussion of the plan. A year later, in 1965, the fully prepared fifth plan was discussed and approved by those same Parliamentary bodies.[3]

Critics who maintained that broader Parliamentary discussion of the plan was the answer to the democracy problem were proved wrong by the experience of the Fifth Republic. Discussion occurred. (The fifth plan was even rejected twice by the *Sénat*)[4]. But the government's majority made the discussions purely formal. Perhaps the Parliamentary debates served an educative function in making the issues of planning clearer to the public, but the Government's ability to ram through exactly what it wanted made it quite impossible for anyone to hold the illusion that Parliament had actually *participated* in planning. These issues were, however, secondary. The real problems lay elsewhere.

What, if anything, is achieved when Parliament discusses and approves a plan, even assuming that the currency of Parliament is nowhere near as debased as that of the Parliament of the Fifth Republic? The nation is somehow bound to carry out the plan. In concrete terms this means little. Whether the plan is adhered to or not depends not on its passage through Parliament but on the specific dynamics of economic power. Economic decision-makers, especially the managers of the giant corporations, will go along with the plan insofar as they see it in their

[1] See *J.O. Débats Parlementaires; Assemblée Nationale*, 21, 23, 25, 30 May 1962, 7, 8, 15, 21, 22, 23 June 1962; *Sénat*, 4, 5, 6, 7, 10, 11, 12, and 13 July, 1962.

[2] See 'Projet de Rapport sur les Principales Options du Ve Plan,' *J.O. Lois et Décrets*, 24 December 1964; National Assembly Debates of 24, 25 and 26 November 1964, Senate debates of 7 and 8 December, and *J.O. Avis et Rapports du Conseil Economique et Social*, 13 November 1964.

[3] National Assembly Debates of 3, 4, 5, and 19 November 1965; Senate, debates of 17 and 19 November, 1965.

[4] See Senate debates of 17 and 19 November 1965.

interest to do so. Thus whether the plan has passed Parliament or not will have little effect on the decisions of private firms. Moreover, the plan, whether passed by Parliament or not, need not be treated as a binding obligation by the Government itself. The second plan, passed by Parliament after its second year, was largely ignored by the Governments that came and went during its four years. The third plan, not passed by Parliament, was ignored from the beginning, while the fourth plan was passed by Parliament before being put into effect, only to be scrapped in its last two years in favour of M. Valéry Giscard d'Estaing's Stabilisation Plan.

If the big corporations and the government, the parties that draw up the plan, cannot be expected to be bound by a Parliamentary pronouncement in favour of the plan, what can be expected of groups that have little voice in preparing the plan and stand to gain little from it, such as labour and small business. In short, given the distribution of economic power, discussion and passage of the plan by Parliament can only be symbolic.

Meaningful Parliamentary participation, that is, Parliamentary participation in planning that will result in a change in behaviour on the part of the economic agents, implies a major redistribution of economic power. Either it means that Parliament makes decisions in areas presently considered by the holders of economic power to be their own domain, or it means, in substantive terms, nothing. The Left understands this. That is why it always discusses democratising planning in terms of the consequences of that democratisation: more normative and more imperative plans. And that is why it insists upon the democratisation of planning, because a democratic plan leads to what the Left means when it says democracy: a redistribution of economic power.

The question of the relationship between planning and democracy is one which admits of several possible answers, depending upon whose views of democracy one accepts. Present day holders of economic power – in private corporations, public firms the Treasury and the plan – feel that democratising the plan means persuading key groups in French politics and society that planning as it now stands should be supported. Behind this, of course, is the contention that planning, as it is presently constructed, offers a way to ensure the optimal performance of the French economy and as such is in the interest of all Frenchmen. Implicit is a conservative notion that the problem of democracy is one of convincing people that existing configurations of economic power are legitimate and should be actively supported, i.e., if everyone believed in planned capitalism then planned capitalism would be democratic.

This view is not devoid of sense. If key social groups could be persuaded that planning as it now exists were in their interests, if they were actively to support the present planning process, many of the problems of the economy and of the planners would be more amenable to solution. Moreover, if no one sees fit to challenge the legitimacy of the exercise of existing economic power, then such economic power can be said to have popular support and a democratic base. However, France is not the United States, and such a view of democracy does not go unchallenged. As we have seen, many key social groups, mostly on the Left of the political spectrum take a much more demanding view of democracy and planning, one which holds that unaccountable economic decision making whether by the leaders of big business or by the 'technocrats' of the present partnership of planning is illegitimate and undemocratic.

The key issue of democracy to the Left (and it is worth remembering that the Left here referred to constitutes, in any terms, a significant part of French society) is the extent to which critical centres of economic power are controlled by the people. In these terms, the democratisation of planning involves not the mere popular ratification of the present process of decision making, the view of the Centre (the modernising civil servants and progressive businessmen who dominate the *status quo*), but a real redistribution of economic power involving basic challenges to those who presently make crucial economic decisions.

THE PROSPECTS FOR DEMOCRATIC PLANNING

One may side with either the Left or the Centre on the question of democracy in planning, but it is important to recognise that in the very real conflict between these views of democratic planning lies the future of planning in France. What will happen is difficult to foresee. Two critical variables are involved. The first is the need which planning as presently constituted may feel for broader participation, a need which *a priori* would seem to make the plan more vulnerable to the demands of the Left. The second is the political strength and attitudes of the Left itself which will determine the kinds of demands that will be made. With these two variables in mind alternative possibilities ('ideal types') for the future of planning can be suggested.

The plan sees itself as the institutionalisation of the cutting edge of the economy. It sees itself on the frontier, sighting new problems, new challenges and new opportunities, then rallying and organising the economy's advance into those new areas. In brief, it sees itself as the leader of the economy.

From its beginnings in 1946 until the early 'sixties, the key consideration governing planning was the imperative need to modernise and rationalise France's industrial core. In the first three plans all else – inflation, income distribution, social needs, regional imbalance – was subordinated to these tasks.

The *économie concertée* – a partnership between modernising civil servants and like-minded businessmen – was the response to these challenges. It proved to be an effective instrument for achieving those objectives making active participation by other groups unnecessary. The plan, therefore, did not seriously try to go beyond the comfortable confines of the *économie concertée*. If the plan is to remain in the forefront of things and keep its hard won position of leadership, it will have to change. For the cutting edge has moved. The major problems, challenges and opportunities facing the economy are no longer the need to modernise, rationalise and expand its industrial core, and the major place for leadership by the plan is no longer within the *économie concertée*.

The planners are aware of the need for change. In numerous speeches, papers and reports they single out two areas, previously neglected by the plan, that must now begin to become its central concerns: social investment and price stability.[1] Unlike industrial modernisation and expansion programmes, neither of these objectives can be realised within the big business-civil servant partnership of the *économie concertée*. A broad range of positive participation is necessary for effective programmes in these areas.

Commissioner Massé's speeches are an eloquent testimony to

[1] A third such area, regionalisation, is, as previously mentioned, outside the purview of this study.

the plan's awareness of the need to 'direct demand towards the collective investment services . . . culture, public health, education, housing and urban facilities . . . in preference to the proliferation of consumer goods.'[1] But as the fifth plan demonstrates, these social goals remain distant and indicative. The Common Market, however, has made price stability an immediate imperative. The plan's old growth and inflation strategy is no longer workable. Expansion must now take place within the context of price stability. Of the many paths to price stability all but one – incomes policy – are closed to the plan. An explicitly planned slack labour market or any Go Slow or Stop Go model is a political impossibility for the plan, though not for the Government. Under the new conditions of economic openness in which they must now operate, in order to remain relevant the planners have to build their plans around an incomes policy. The reforms adopted for the fifth plan – the aggregate balances/incomes policy approach – announce the planners' determination to deal with the need for price stability. But, short of an authoritarian regulation of the labour market, an incomes policy cannot simply be decreed.

Until now broad participation – especially on the part of the trade unions – was not necessary for the central purposes of the plan. The Common Market is changing all that. Now an incomes policy is essential to the plan, and active trade union co-operation is essential for an effective incomes policy.

There is little doubt that the planners will try to increase the range of participation in planning, but there is much uncertainty about what that will mean. It is quite easy to envisage irrelevant plans with ineffective incomes policies that are prepared by a broad range of participants. But it is harder to envisage the democratisation of effective planning. The crucial consideration here is the need of the economy – that is, of the present holders of economic power – for an effective plan and an effective incomes policy. If the economy – and not just the planning institution – finds that it wants an incomes policy enough to make real concessions in order to get it, then planning could change radically, and with it, the distribution of economic power.

Assuming that the technocrats and the big business leaders find that they need an incomes policy the critical question

[1] Massé, *French Affairs*, p. 19.

becomes the conditions which the trade unions will be able to stipulate for their participation. Several answers to this question can be foreseen.

(*A*) *A MODEL OF REFORM*

Much depends on the stringency of the demands of France's international economic position. If the situation does *not* necessitate a radical change in stabilisation policy – such as an effective incomes policy – the planners will be granted some margin for manoeuvre. In such a situation the following is likely to occur. Planning itself will be carried on much as it has in the past. The key actors will remain the big corporations and the modernising civil servants. There will be no significant shifts in the locus of economic power: the *économie concertée* will continue to function fairly smoothly. At the same time any and all devices to maintain price stability not involving major concessions of economic power to broader social forces will be employed. The need for an incomes policy will be constantly emphasised and various experiments along these lines will be made. In other words, what will emerge will be a major campaign to convince the French people, including the Left and the trade unions if possible, that participation in an incomes policy and in the aggregate plan that encompasses it, without a change in the structure of economic power, is a good thing. Persuasion will be accompanied by concessions which will not challenge present positions of economic power. (One example of such a concession is the present 'profit sharing' plan advanced by the Pompidou Government. Future 'participation' schemes will surely provide even better examples.) Much leeway of course also exists for the planners to stress collective 'social' goals such as education and housing which the country desperately needs, the Left demands and the more progressive of present day power holders desire, but which do not challenge the fundamental structure of economic power. In short, if France's international position permits, the plan can hold back from any serious confrontation with the trade unions over incomes policy, hoping that a judicious mixture of propaganda, bribery and progress will, in time, bring the labour movement to accept the planning *status quo* and support a real incomes policy with little cost in terms of economic power to those presently in command. Thus, the first hypothetical future for planning would result in the confirmation of the Centrist view of democracy – essentially the popular ratification of the existing configuration of economic power.

(*B*) *A MODEL OF CONFRONTATION*

Other circumstances can be envisaged. Should France's position make an incomes policy with real teeth a necessity,[1] the holders of economic power would have to confront the trade unions and the Left in a real bargaining situation.

Under these conditions the trade unions could demand major concessions in return for their support. What the trade unions would demand depends, of course, on the depth of their commitment to a redistribution of economic power in French society. Assuming that they take their political rhetoric seriously and demand substantive changes in planning and in economic decision-making in the direction of realising the Left's view of democracy, an interesting situation would arise. If a real threat to the holders of economic power existed, big business would probably be sorely tempted to abandon the whole idea of planning and incomes policy and find other means to achieve the necessary ends – perhaps, accepting a reduction in the rate of growth as the price for maintaining power. Also, it is difficult to imagine any such threat developing only as a result of the exigencies of planning price stability. A significant increase in the over all political strength of the Left would be needed to bolster the bargaining position of the unions in a confrontation with the power of the state and business.

Other possibilities of a more extreme nature can be postulated, but they are unlikely in the absence of profound changes in French political and economic life. The Left could, of course, take power. A major change in the configuration of French political forces could bring about the democratisation of planning on the Left's terms. On the other hand, an incomes policy could be imposed on the trade unions by authoritarian means. Much more likely are the alternatives sketched out

[1] The intensity of the economy's need for an incomes policy will be defined by those who presently hold economic and political power; the most relevant measure is their estimation of expansion forsaken for want of an effective incomes policy and their valuation of that expansion in terms of what they would have to sacrifice for an incomes policy.

above, with the first, 'reformist model,' being the most probable.

The future of planning in France centres on the question of democracy, but not on an abstract concept of democracy. Whose view of democracy will prevail will decide not only the nature of planning France, but the nature of French politics and society as well.

Planning began in France with the goals of the technocrats, the civil servants and businessmen who sought to rationalise, modernise and expand the French economy. It must now mature with the goals of the democratic Left: to make planning an instrument to aid the nation, acting through its democratic institutions, to determine the direction of its own development. The first goals have been realised; the second, postponed.

POSTSCRIPT[1]

The 'Events' of May, 1968

In May 1968 a student revolt led to the largest strike in French history. 'The Events of May,' as they have come to be called, have been profusely reported, filmed, tape-recorded and Telstarred. Our purpose here is not to add to that rapidly growing body of descriptive literature. Rather, in this brief note, we shall examine the connections between these events and the shape of the post-war French political economy as symbolised by the plan. Such an analysis makes it possible to make some initial sense, or order, of what happened in May, and to attach significance to the various pieces of the rather confusing pattern of events. It also leads to a clear understanding of the plan's worst failures – failures in its own terms and failures (or inadequacies) of its terms.

1 THE STUDENT REVOLT

Analysis of the forces behind the student revolt should begin from the recent rapid but very uneven growth and transformation of the French economy. Since the war, the French economy has been expanding at an average rate of about 4 to 5 per cent. But most of that expansion has been concentrated in the modernising industrial sectors, which have not only grown but changed their character. The public sector (as distinct from publicly owned industrial enterprises) has not kept pace. The obsolete nature and inadequate extent of public services has been one of the primary failures of the new political economy, or to use symbolic notation, of the plan. Inadequate provision

[1] In addition to the research materials and methods upon which the rest of this book is based, the present essay draws upon information I gathered as an active and enthusiastic participant in the May Events. It took form through a series of long discussions with Mr George W. Ross of Harvard University. Mr Ross, who is the best young political analyst I know, is presently preparing a study of the CGT. Except for misstatements of fact, inadequacies of organisation and conception and inelegancies of expression this essay is as much Mr Ross' as mine.

of public goods and services – even those essential to sustained economic expansion and modernisation – has been the primary failure of the plan in its own terms.

The roots of the student rebellion are to be found in this pattern of sub-system maladaptation. in the failure of the University (and the educational system as a whole) to respond to the demands of the newly formed economy and the new social structures and political forces that economic transformation has generated.

This is not the only cause of the student revolt, or the primary determinant of its strategies and successes, but it is the most advantageous starting place for analysis. Otherwise, Paris in May becomes a re-run (however more glamorous) of Columbia in April, and the complex pattern of forces that shaped the May events and created their confusing character are lost. For the French student revolt was different from the US student revolt, not only in terms of its immediate consequences (beginning with the general strike!) but in terms of its causes.

The University and the economy have grown out of phase. As a result, all kinds of powerful tensions have been created within the University system. The huge influx of students generated by recent economic changes arrives at the University to confront inadequate and outdated facilities manned by inadequate (and, many maintain, outdated) teaching staffs. The new economy generated not just a supply of students but also a demand for technical skills. The University's job, in this crude neo-capitalist model, was to equip the former with the latter. It failed, miserably and visibly.

Aside from the *Grandes Ecoles* (*Polytechnique*, *ENA*, *Ecole Normale Supérieure*), which rigorously educate only an élitist handful, the mass of students at the University were neither being 'educated' in the traditional sense, nor were they being provided with the technical skills upon which economic and social success increasingly depended.

Their extreme dissatisfaction with the substance of their education was combined with acute career anxieties. Thousands of students were herded into programmes in literature, anthropology, sociology and ethnology for degrees that led to no careers. For many, perhaps the majority, the programmes did not even lead to degrees. (This large group of badly steered and poorly-trained literature and social science students was a major motor of the revolt which 'started' in the social science and literature faculty most strikingly characterised by these conditions.)

In brief, the University system failed to respond to the demands of mass education. It tried to contain within its nineteenth (some say eighteenth) century structures, the social forces generated by a rapidly expanding neo-capitalist economy. As a result, whatever integrative bonds existed in the traditional French University structures were destroyed by these new forces. Total lack of communication between students, faculty and administration predominated. The University became a great breeding ground of alienation, aimlessness, resentment and frustration, a powder keg for radicals and a source of concern for reformers. The radicals got to it first, although the reformers had a big headstart.

People with even the most rudimentary knowledge of conditions in the University system did not need the May revolt to convince them that it was desperately in need of reform. The plan had been saying that for years; so had the social technocrats of the Club Jean Moulin and the enlightened businessmen of the Jeunes Patrons. During the past five years there has been no shortage of demands and plans for reform. Most, however, were band-aid jobs, modest construction efforts plus increases in the numbers of underpaid, overworked and, it seems, never-promoted, teaching assistants (who needless to say, played a major role in the revolt). Reforms were decreed from above and implemented (or more often pigeon-holed) through the administrative hierarchy of the Ministry of Education, a highly centralised, inept bureaucracy whose one ability (and in this area it was rivalled only by the New York City Board of Education) was for stripping reforms of their purpose. Crucially, however, it was not administrative unwieldiness that stopped the reform efforts. It was a political choice: neither the determination nor the resources to work fundamental reforms were directed at the educational system.

The failure of the University to adapt to the pressures and demands of the new economy created the conditions that permitted the student radicals to be so successful. In France, unlike the United States, the great mass of largely non-political (and certainly non-radical) students were dissatisfied and frustrated not just with the social relations prevalent in the

University, and not just with the great injustices perpetrated in the nation and the world (especially in Vietnam), but with the immediate damage that the University was doing to them personally. Beyond all else – beyond the international student revolts, beyond the dehumanising social relations, beyond the impact of New Left ideologies – what made the student revolt so powerful was the inability of the University to provide the great mass of students with what they most wanted, with what seemed most legitimate: training for the technical skills that would lead to good careers and upward mobility. Thus, the mass of students who normally (i.e., in the typical US or UK setting) remain indifferent to the radicals' calls to action and thereby determine the radicals' failure by isolating them (and occasionally, actively opposing them) were ready to demand fundamental reforms. All it would take would be the slightest spark to trigger, not just an outburst from a small group of radicals protesting distant injustices, or making demands that the average student would not consider worth getting excited about, but a massive protest movement firmly rooted in the great majority of students demanding what they felt to be vital, legitimate and long overdue reforms.

It could have started anywhere. But for admirers of elegant irony it is best that it started at Nanterre. For Nanterre is the concrete example of the reformers' failure. It is a new campus for social sciences and literature just outside Paris. Some of the planning was clever; its students are drawn from the 16^{e} *arrondissement* of Paris, mostly from rich families. In this way social stigmas associated with a new campus are overcome. But mostly, the planning was a disaster and the realisation even worse. Nanterre was supposed to be a low-budget spectacular; the only thing spectacular about it was the way in which its failure was finally demonstrated. Everything about the place seemed to conspire to mock the planners.

A new subway line will, one day, link Nanterre directly with Paris. At the moment a commuter train services the campus; the station is called *La Folie – Complex Universitaire*. The drive to Nanterre takes you through a tour of all the contradictions of French society. Students take the drive twice daily. The road twists through construction projects and great bulldozed lots and ditches. The background is provided by vast, high-rise, faded concrete housing projects. In the foreground is a *bidonville* (shantytown) – a good sized cluster of rotten little shacks in which the Algerians who are digging the roads and subways live in conditions that are supposed to be found only in underdeveloped countries. Nanterre is classic; at no place since Versailles have the social relations been more perfectly expressed in the architecture.

The 'learning process' takes place in an enormous horizontal structure that consists, essentially, of a vast corridor – at least as long as a football field and about fifty feet wide. The corridor is made, of course, of grey concrete. (The students have taken to painting bright designs along the walls to dent the oppression a bit.) Off the corridors are enormous lecture halls, some equipped with tell-tale TV set-ups. At one end is a pathetic snack bar: stand up tables. What goes on is clear. Vast numbers of students flow from lecture hall to lecture hall through the corridor. (The lay-out is similar to Orly Airport; so is the traffic flow function.)

At Nanterre, communications were non-existent; so were any sense of purpose or achievement.

There was little contact among students. The physical plant, like that of the Sorbonne, did not provide any places for informal contact among the commuter students, and the isolation of the campus precluded the use of local cafés – the basis of social relations at the Sorbonne. Faculty contact was simply out of the question. There were too many students and too few teachers. The teachers would, typically, drive out to the campus, read a lecture, and vanish.

Few of the students seemed to have any idea of what they were supposed to be studying, and fewer still knew why. They hung around taking courses here and there and preparing for exams that had little to do with anything. They knew they were being processed, not educated, and they resented it. The painfully obvious fact that they were being purposelessly processed to fit into disappearing economic and social structures turned their resentment to rage.

The radicals understood that for most of its students Nanterre represented a combination of purposeless processing in an environment of oppressive social relations; it was potentially explosive. The University administration and government officials did not; their lack of understanding defeated them.

The radicals drew examples, impetus and ideology from the

international student movement and from the political ferment generated by the Vietnam War. Tactical audacity coupled with ideological timidity, a refusal to go beyond general leftism in defining a positive programme (which would have been divisive) was the radical formula. Under the correct conditions – a series of incidents to engage the mass, reinforced and accelerated by ill-informed reactions by the University officials – they could precipitate a substantial student protest movement. With luck and skill, it could become massive and radical.

They had more luck than they could imagine – and more skill too. They also benefited enormously from the ignorance of the University officials. The student radicals triggered a series of small incidents. The University authorities, acting on their unlimited faith in the efficacy of minority isolation-manipulation-repression and their total unawareness of the mass support for the protests, found themselves locked into a spiral of student demonstrations, administrative repression; larger demonstrations, more repression (coupled with some minor reforms); etc., etc., . . . Of course repression can stop protest movements – especially ones that have no popular support. In this case, however, it provided the radicals with the necessary unifying and mobilising issues and led to the progressive mobilisation, politicisation and radicalisation of ever-greater numbers of students. Then the movement spread, first to the Sorbonne, then to the other French Universities, then to the *lycées*, to important segments of the adult intelligentsia and finally to nine million workers.

In the student rebellion that triggered the largest strike in French history, a radical minority took the leadership and provided direction for a mass movement of reformist origins; in the general strike, an established leadership of short-run reformist objectives kept its grip on a mass outburst of radicalism.

2 THE GENERAL STRIKE

Sans la CGT nous sommes perdus
Avec elle, nous sommes cloués.
(a striker)

At least one thing about the strike is certain: it did not begin in the executive councils of the CGT. It was a chain reaction of wildcats.

Our purpose in this brief note is not to trace out a blow-by-blow history of the strike. Rather, it is to propose some ideas and some questions that might help to make sense of what happened. And the critical factor in all that happened – and all that did not happen – was the Communist Party and the CGT.[1] Nothing makes sense without an understanding of the actions (and inactions) of the Communists.

COMMUNIST STRATEGY

May caught the Communists by surprise. A major social crisis – let alone a potentially revolutionary general strike – was absolutely the last thing the French Communist Party expected. Indeed, during the past few years, the French Communist Party, following slowly behind its Italian counterpart, had reached the conclusion that the kind of revolutionary crisis that its traditional insurrectional strategy depended upon was unlikely to occur in neo-capitalist France.

The Party's re-evaluation of the realities of advanced capitalism meant abandoning the idea of a one-party dictatorship of the proletariat coming to power through mass, armed insurrection. In its place the Party slowly and painfully elaborated a new strategy for 'a peaceful French road to Socialism.'

Peaceful meant legal and legal meant electoral. The broad tactical implications of this new 'de-Stalinised' strategy are quite clear: Left alliances. A vast United Front of all potentially Left forces would have to be built. The Party would have to win over the non-Communist Left, and to do this it would have to live down a lot of history: Stalinist strategy, tactics and organisation would have to be abandoned: so would the whole Comintern image.

[1] In the following pages I have generally merged the Communist Party and the CGT into one political force. This might bother some readers. I am well aware that there are many non-Communist members in the CGT and that some even hold leadership positions (see below, p. 204). Nonetheless, in the interests of both brevity and a certain kind of realism, it is foolish to ignore the constant similarity of positions taken by the PC and the CGT and the more or less total domination of the CGT by the Communists. It is simply silly to imagine, for example, that Frachon, Séguy and Krasucki (the three most important leaders of the CGT) change significantly as they shuttle back and forth between the *Bureau Confédéral* of the CGT and the Politbureau of the PC. Nor is it an assertion of militant anticommunism to remark that non-Communist leaders in the CGT rarely hold 'key positions'.

The 'peaceful path' strategy also implied a total change in the traditional Communist scenario for how the transformation to Socialism was to be achieved after the accession to power. 'Democratic, bi-polar Socialism' was the logical new answer. Two Socialist parties, the Communist Party and a revitalised ex-non-Communist Left (re-radicalised somehow, through the dynamics of partnership and struggle) would compete and co-operate, democratically, in bringing about Socialism. Only through a democratic process could Socialism be realised in modern France. The capacity of neo-capitalist society to contain and absorb opposition, the repressive apparatus of the modern state, and the menace of foreign intervention would prevent any violent seizure of power or authoritarian imposition of socialism. Furthermore, should the Communists somehow be able to seize power, the opposition of a majority of Frenchmen would make the transformation of the complex and delicate advanced industrial society into a socialist society impossible without an intolerable amount of coercion.

Following out the tactical implications of this strategic analysis on a day-to-day basis, the Communist Party has, during the past few years, been trying to convince all potentially socialist forces to its right that Stalinism was a thing of the past – and the Cold War too – and that the future belonged to the peaceful and democratic construction of French Socialism. All recent (pre-May) tactics of the Party make sense in this light: unity of action programmes with the non-Communist trade unions; support for Mitterand in the Presidential elections; encouragement of electoral alliances with the non-Communist Federation of the Left, etc. The existence of Gaullism created difficulties, but also special short-run advantages for this strategy. The Gaullist régime was arbitrary, antidemocratic and majestically unresponsive to French social needs. Many people were anti-Gaullist, for many reasons. And the only real alternative to Gaullism was a Left alliance. In this analysis French politics quickly reduces to the Gaullists trying to increase their strength by moving from right to left, and the Communists trying to broaden out from left to right. The CP saw the Left as the eventual winner. It also saw how the continued existence of Gaullism would help in the task of building and testing the United Front alliance. Should Gaullism collapse and the non-Communist Left come to power without the aid of the Communists (as had happened in the past) the CP could be locked back into the sterility of its Cold War isolation, and the post-Gaullist era would be, as far as the CP was concerned, a re-run of the anti-Communist socialism of the Fourth Republic. Furthermore, Gaullist foreign policy was of distinct advantage to the CP. Any success in de Gaulle's efforts to reduce Cold War tensions in Europe would greatly help the CP in its efforts to escape from its Cold War isolation. In brief, the Communist Party would think at least twice before rushing to the kill should Gaullism show signs of collapsing.

THE STUDENTS, THE STRIKERS AND THE PARTY

The student movement was growing bigger and more violent. The Gaullists couldn't suppress it and the Communists couldn't control it. Worst of all, it kept getting more political. The radicals (Maoists, Castroists, Anarchists, Renegade Communists, Trotskyites and, most important, general or New Leftists) had seized the leadership of the student revolt and were succeeding in politicising the mass of previously non-political students. At incredible speed, the student revolt stopped talking about new dormitories and smaller classes and began to talk of Revolution and contact with the working class.

The Party was in a bind. The student revolt was proclaiming an independent revolutionary ideology, Marxist in tone, that was in direct contradiction with the Party's strategy. The students were declaring a Revolutionary Situation and trying to form independent alliances with the working class. What could the Party do? Its new strategy was repugnant to the new student revolutionaries. It had little direct influence over the students. Regular Communists among the students were few; their organisations had lost membership and influence during the past years and they were largely irrelevant to the revolt.

The Party's first response was to try to isolate the revolutionary students from the workers and, if possible, from the mass of students. From the beginning through the end of the May Events, Party officials and Party propaganda organs poured out the invective: Cohn-Bendit was 'a German Anarchist', others were 'provocateurs', 'adventurists', and 'infantile Leftists'. All belonged to 'groupuscules', and were misleading the mass of decent students.

Party logic was simple, direct and traditional. The Communist Party represents the revolutionary movement of the people. The student revolutionaries were opposing Party strategy. Therefore, even though they may *subjectively* have thought they were revolutionaries, *objectively* they were counter-revolutionaries, their actions *objectively* serving the ruling class and hurting the people.

The second step was to try to turn a threat into an asset. If the student movement could be separated from its revolutionary leaders and changed from an adventurist revolt into a powerful and attractive movement for educational reform and democracy, it could well turn out to be an unanticipated blessing for the Party. The Party knew that popular opinion resented the social policies of the Gaullist government and that the students – mostly middle class – had aroused considerable sympathy and support in large segments of the population, including many of those same groups whose support, or at least acceptance, the CP was already seeking. Along with the denunciations of the leaders and their 'irresponsible' actions, the Party issued a steady stream of statements supporting the 'real' grievances of the students: more resources for education, reformed curricula and democratised access.

During the night of 10 May, there was a particularly bloody battle between students and police in the barricaded streets around the Rue Gay-Lussac. The Party decided to respond quickly and to reassert its leadership. Seizing the initiative from the students (and from the CFDT), the CGT called a twenty-four-hour general strike for 13 May (also the tenth anniversary of de Gaulle's return to power). At least 100,000 workers were mobilised to march with the students in an *orderly* demonstration of strength to oppose police brutality and to support the students' 'real' demands. The Politbureau issued the *mot d'ordre*: an end to police repression and a democratic reform of the University.

In many ways the demonstration was a huge success. The Party once again showed its strength, stopping production and mobilising, on instant notice, hundreds of thousands of workers. In other ways, it foreshadowed disaster for the Party. For, even at the demonstration, something began to go wrong. Discipline slipped slightly. Initiative kept shifting from the Party leadership to the base. Adventurist student slogans often replaced the more sober Party slogans. Students persistently broke ranks to fraternise with workers, and they were well received.

That same night (13 May) the students occupied the Sorbonne. Twelve hours later, workers at Sud-Aviation (Nantes) struck, occupied the factory and wrote 'Yesterday Slaves – Today Free Men' on the walls. The next day the Renault plant at Cléon was occupied by its wildcatting workers. Within four days some five million workers were on strike; by the end of the following week, eight to ten million, more than twice as many as in the great general strike of the Popular Front period.

The spontaneity, the speed, the scale and the political intensity of the strike surprised everyone: the students who triggered it; the workers who made it; the Government who tried to stop it; and the Communist Party who lost it and tried to recapture it.

The strike rested on a solid base of traditional, quantitative grievances. Rising prices had eaten up increases in workers' incomes. Unemployment – though negligible by contrast with the US – had risen brusquely and the government continued to talk of belt-tightening and austerity. Working hours were among the longest in Europe. Protections against speed-ups and job shifts were weak. Regional disparities were serious and intensifying, and several regions (such as Nantes, where the first strike occurred) were beginning to suffer. Young workers were especially affected by these conditions and by the fact that starting salaries were disproportionately low, and apprenticeship programmes long, exploitative and closed-end. Finally, recent reductions in social security benefits hurt the workers economically and also underscored the government's arrogant insensitivity in dealing with workers.

These 'bread and butter' grievances were sufficiently pressing to generate a major strike, and many people in France expected a wave of strikes before the summer. But analysis of the May Events confined to these traditional, quantitative matters can never succeed in explaining the unusual nature and dynamic of those Events. For what made May different and important is that it was a 'political' strike as well as an economic strike, a strike against traditional structures of authority and for new forms of social relations at every level of organisation, as well as a strike for higher wages and shorter hours.

The CGT desperately tried to recapture control of the strike movement and turn it away from dangerous adventurism. First it called an official general strike from above, after well over a million workers had already gone out on their own. Then it set about 'de-adventurising' the strike. The revolutionary political demands that emerged from the strikers were repressed and ridiculed by the Party, which called them 'meaningless', 'gauchiste', 'adventurist' sell-outs of the workers' 'real interests'.[1]

The CGT tried to minimise the possibility of contact between workers and student revolutionaries. Its National Festival of Young Workers was called off; the CGT did not want to see what might happen if it united several thousand young workers. In factories dominated by the CGT, strikers were sent home – except for a relatively small number of 'safe' party stalwarts who assured the occupation.[2] In brief, the CGT did absolutely everything it could to bring the strike back to traditional, 'reasonable' demands while it rushed, as fast as it could, to negotiate an end to the strike.

While the Communist Party was desperately trying to demonstrate its new-found devotion to Peacefulness and Legality, Order seemed to be falling apart. The Pompidou government appeared to be inadequate to the situation. De Gaulle's first dramatic television broadcast – his reappearance on the scene – proved to be a disaster. Instead of demonstrating authority and restoring order, he revealed incomprehension, weakness, age and a general inability to master the situation: he accelerated the crisis. Forces within the government began to press for de Gaulle's retirement and the Gaullist Parliamentary majority appeared to be disintegrating.

In an effort to calm the crisis the CGT hastily signed the Grenelle Accords limiting the workers' victory to purely 'economic' gains that were hardly commensurate with the scale and intensity of the greatest strike in French history. Even the *échelle mobile* – the cost-of-living escalator that the CGT, in its

[1] The CFDT, the second largest trade union central, took up some of the strikers' anticapitalist and antibureaucratic longings in large part out of conviction (the CFDT had been drifting towards the Contestative Participationist Socialism described above) and in part out of a desire to steal thunder and members from the CGT.

[2] By contrast, in CFDT-dominated plants, the occupation was often held *en masse* and long political discussions were a principal activity.

battles with the 'gauchistes' had claimed to be the key grievance – was abandoned (or, according to the CGT interpretation of the agreements, postponed for re-negotiation one year later).

Then disaster hit. Beginning at the Renault plant, and continuing in factory after factory, the workers rejected the Grenelle agreements and voted to continue the strike.

At this point most observers – and almost all the participants – were sure that the situation was completely out of control and that major political changes would follow.

General de Gaulle disappeared. The immediate rumour (later confirmed) was that he had gone off to secure support, or at least a no-coup pledge, from General Massu, symbol of *Algérie Française* militarism and putschism. The atmosphere of crisis intensified.

Mitterand declared himself available and Mendès France surfaced briefly as the non-Communist Left prepared to accede to power on the imminent collapse of Gaullism. This revival of the Third Force concept was just what the Party feared. It was, for the Communists, probably worse than Gaullism.

The Communist Party and the CGT desperately trying, once again, to gain control of the strike movement and also to anticipate the immediate collapse of Gaullism, issued a call for a Popular Government. By no means was this a call to revolution. Rather it was an attempt to prepare workers for the legal transfer of power to a new government headed by the non-Communist Left and also an attempt to prevent its own exclusion from that government. It backfired.

De Gaulle returned and attacked. This time he spoke on radio, not television. In tones of anger and authority he announced that he would not retire and that he was dissolving the Assembly immediately and scheduling elections for late June. Claiming to understand the basic longings of the revolutionary strikers and the students, he announced that he would soon propose a plan to establish 'Participation' in all areas of French life. Participation would define a third way, between capitalism and communism. Then he resorted to the old bugaboo of warning the nation of the imminent danger of Totalitarian Communist Dictatorship and called for a massive demonstration in support of order and himself.

He got the demonstration, that very afternoon. The strikers militancy in rejecting the Grenelle agreements and the Communist Party's call for a 'popular Government' had precipitated a massive regrouping of the forces of order. De Gaulle capitalised on their great fear. Hundreds of thousands of Gaullists, conservatives, rightists and just scared citizens responded to his call and marched up the Champs-Elysées in an impressive show of strength and support.

He also succeeded in his principal objective of shifting the crisis to an electoral plane. Here, the CP was his most powerful ally. Despite the fact that its determined defense of legality had been dishonestly and cynically ignored by de Gaulle in his efforts to provoke an anti-Communist hysteria, the Communist Party proved to be totally committed to bringing the crisis to a rapid end and espoused the 'electoral solution' with even greater enthusiasm than the Gaullists. The dênouement was rapid.

3 CONCLUDING REMARKS

The Events of May were a confusing mixture – part a traditional protest and part an apparently new kind of rebellion. At this early date, it is impossible to 'weigh' these two components so as to define and evaluate the role and importance of each. But it is possible to relate them to the new political economy and to its chief symbol, the plan. For both components of the May Events were directed against the plan.

The traditional protests stemmed from, and were directed against, the failures of the plan *in its own terms*: an archaic and unproductive University system that frustrated the great mass of students in their efforts to prepare for a proper place in the new society; and long hours, low real wage increases, little job security and unacceptable working conditions that belied the promises of ever increasing affluence that the plan made to the mass of workers.

The radical rebellion was a refusal to accept the tight limits the plan proposed for future social changes. The plan, and the political economy it represented, reached their limits at any idea of radical alterations of authority structures, at any attempt to redistribute power at every level of social organisation in order to create fundamentally different social relations.

Student revolutionaries rebelled against the University's role of training a supply of competent technicians to meet the needs of the expanding and modernising economy and against traditional structures of authority within the University and the society at large. The student revolutionaries were refusing and rebelling against precisely what the plan wanted, but failed, to achieve.

Highly skilled and highly paid technical and creative workers and executives at the ORTF (French Radio-Television) – the group most clearly benefiting from the new political economy, the living models of the plan's success – rebelled and demanded, not higher wages or better production facilities, but liberation from the close government control which had reduced the ORTF to a propaganda organ, and democracy. And they defined democracy in a strikingly different manner from the plan.

In industry after industry workers rebelled, but their radical political grievances remained vague, confused and inarticulate. They were never translated into concrete proposals for change in part because of the unresponsiveness of the principal working class organisations to those demands, and in part because of their inherent vagueness, newness and troublesomeness.

Just as one component of the May Events – the protests – represented demands for the realisation of the plan's objectives, for 'success' in the plan's own terms, so the second component – the rebellions – represented a refusal to accept those terms, a demand for a new kind of plan and a new kind of political economy.

Once it had recovered its security, the Gaullist government responded in a predictable fashion: a serious show of force to discourage another outburst and an attempt to correct some of the 'failures' that were revealed in May. Thus, for the students, a strong show of administrative severity and para-police 'monitors' at Nanterre coupled with the Faure Plan, a programme of University reform, ambitious in its conception, but modest in its funding. The goal is modernisation. And despite present difficulties, it will probably be reached: France will finally get low-budget Berkeleys. Modern Universities with less unwieldy administrative structures – such as Vincennes, the instant university – will appear. And student 'participation' will be instituted. University councils with elected student representatives will be created and given some say in some areas of University policy. But how much say and about what, is at present impossible to know. It is easier to anticipate the long-term response to these forthcoming reforms than to predict their detailed substance. More rebellions will follow. At the beginning they will tend to follow the May model in which a minority of student revolutionaries succeeded in turning the frustrations of the average student, which derived from the plan's failure to realise its own objectives, against those objectives. As the reforms achieve some measure of success, the rebellions will not stop. Instead, they will tend to become purer cases of rebellion against the plan's terms, moving in some ways, closer to the American University revolts.

Patching up the plan's failures in areas other than the University will be a different matter. Rising prices are eating away most of the workers' 'traditional victory' at Grenelle – an effect anticipated by all parties, workers as well as government.

De Gaulle's principal response to the strike was his promise to institute 'Participation'. His perception of the need to go beyond business as usual and venture into the area of fundamental political change placed him, as usual, well above other politicians. But in this case, as in so many others, De Gaulle's distinction remains within the realm of rhetoric. The formula – Participation – awaits definition. Beyond personalities, however strong, there are identifiable political forces that will determine the shape and significance of any Participation scheme any Centre-Right Government might propose. In discussing the possibilities open to 'Participation', it is necessary to separate the *forms* it can take from the *importance* or impact it can achieve. For the most likely outcome is an elaborate *tour de force* of change without change. New and complex words and institutions will be created. But they will have little importance, for the distribution of power will not be affected.

Participation will be closer to the old Vichyite *Association Capital-Travail*, with a touch of 'profit sharing', than to any kind of radical redistribution of economic power that would restructure social relations. The Vichyite formula is consistent with Gaullist corporatist ideas of political organisation. It is also in perfect harmony with the plan's traditional communitarian rhetoric and its operational corporatism.

The word corporatism must be cleansed of its Mussolini overtones. There will be no thugs, no vulgarity and no overt brutality. Essentially corporatist participation will involve the institution of some sort of vertical representation. Social roles – business leaders, consumer groups, trade unions, banks, etc., will be represented. The form fits perfectly with the long cherished conservative image of all the corporations of the realm harmoniously co-operating in the construction of the Great Cathedral of modern society – the Plan. In many ways it will represent simply the formalisation of the pressure group, or lobby politics, that have come to dominate large areas (especially in economic administration) of the political life of Western democracies. Attempts to formalise corporatist politics are not new in France. Corporatist Democracy has held a steady and strong attraction not only for the Pétains and the de Gaulles, the peasants and the cartel-minded business leaders, but even for such socialists and democrats as Mendès France as, for example, in his proposal for a corporatist second house of Parliament, in *La République Moderne*.

The form of the proposed Participation will be corporatist, but the importance of the reform is a separate question. Should Participation come to anything at all – and there is a good chance that it will come to absolutely nothing – it is likely to result in purely window-dressing corporatism. For no matter what form the new councils, committees and assemblies take, the present holders of economic power are not prepared to turn over important areas of decision-making to them. A serious shift of power over economic decisions implies a risk of reducing productivity, and neither the Government nor the business groups see any compelling need to run such a risk. Their determination to protect productivity is incalculably strengthened by the direction any major shift in power must take – away from them. The likelihood of a Gaullist or a Right-Centre Government leading a frontal assault on the prerogatives and power of management within the firm is very, very small; the possibility of success in such a matter is even smaller. Nor are the businessmen ready, as the experience of the plan shows, to abdicate any important areas of decision making to any newly formed, corporatist second house of Parliament. Serious redistribution of power is out. Instead, vertical assemblies and councils will be formed at various levels of organisation – perhaps the firm, probably the region, and possibly the nation. Their purpose will be to give workers the illusion of participating in the common endeavour (which will remain economic expansion) and to convince them of the paramount importance of that task and of the necessity of preserving the present distribution of economic power. Communitarian rhetoric will flow. Everyone will be encouraged to 'belong, co-operate and participate'. But the new structures will have little real power. The councils and assemblies will produce advisory recommendations – rather like the present Economic and Social Council, which is a living example of what 'Participation' is most likely to recreate and perhaps, multiply. But the substance of decision making power will not be affected.

Perhaps, over time, the new corporatist bodies will grow and lead France to a third path that will be neither classic capitalism nor communism. But that third path will not be a new path. It has been visible beneath the rather thin surface of liberal democracy in France for years, and it is still best described by the word corporatism. There is not the slightest doubt that the plan, as it is presently constituted, fits snugly into that system. For the plan, with its group representation commissions, its appearance of broadly distributed power, and its reality of a powerful partnership of big business executives and ranking civil servants is the model for it all. It is the most important piece of 'corporatist democracy' in France.

If participation is to mean anything at all, it must mean a redistribution of economic power, a fundamental reorganisation of authority structures. The Gaullists are neither willing nor able to institute that. As a response to the radical rebellion component of the May events, Participation in its Gaullist conception can only be a red herring.

The essential question raised in May was that of the future of democracy in France. De Gaulle's response was to seize its essence in a dramatic word – Participation – and then to present, in its name, a programme for preserving the existing distribution of power. The Communist Party responded to the rebellion with even greater inflexibility.

May was a disaster for the Party. From beginning to end the Party chased after events. All its actions were reactions. But they were consistent. They all aimed at diffusing, controlling and finally stopping the broad and sudden social movement which threatened the Party's new strategy. The Party demonstrated its power. There is no doubt that it played a crucial role in preventing major political changes in and saving the Gaullist Fifth Republic. In the short run, at least, the Party was badly rewarded for its services.

When, for a moment, it appeared that the Gaullist government would crumble, the non-Communist Left began to take careful distance from the Party and to prepare to form a Third Force type of government. The Gaullists rallied the Right, the scared, the confused and the bothered by cynically promoting an anti-Communist hysteria and thereby obtained their greatest electoral victory ever. And the far Left turned its rebellion against the Party, which even more than the Government, became its symbol of outdated repression.

New Left 'groupuscules', against which most of the Party's moves had been directed, challenged the Party's claim to Revolutionary leadership. They attacked the Party as a *de facto* supporter of the *status quo*. The more extravagant claimed that a Revolutionary Situation had finally developed and that the Party had done its best to crush it. The Party responded to its 'infantile leftist' accusers by claiming that no such Revolutionary Situation had existed and that armed insurrection would lead only to fascist repression.

Within the context of such an idiotic debate the Party was, of course, correct. A massive, Communist-led, insurrection was out of the question. But that was not the only revolutionary possibility. Between leading an armed revolution and the conservative role the Party chose to play there were other serious alternatives. But the Party was blind to them. It was this blindness, rather than the irresponsibility of the 'groupuscules', or the power of the Gaullists, that made May a disaster for the Party. The Party was the victim of its own monolithic bureaucracy and its own sterile strategy.

May revealed that de-Stalinisation within the Party was far from complete. The surprise with which the rebellion caught the Party demonstrated that the leadership was out of touch with the base. During the crisis, when important decisions had to be taken, real debate within the Party, and fruitful discussion and disagreement between the Party and the outside, proved to be practically impossible. In brief, May showed that the Party bureaucracy remined as unresponsive as ever, and that serious contradictions existed between the Party's new de-Stalinised strategy and the continuing Stalinism of its organisation.

More important, May also revealed that the new strategy was incomplete and inadequate, and that a major rethinking of Party strategy was desperately needed. The new strategy is still based on a very old image of how revolutionary change is to be achieved. The essential difference is that the scenario now calls for the Party to take power peacefully and legally instead of by mass insurrection. But revolutionary change still comes from the top down and it still happens all at once, after the Party 'takes power'. Until then there can be little positive revolutionary change. The crucial revolutionary process remains that of substituting a bureaucracy which acts on behalf of the people for a bureaucracy which acts on behalf of the capitalists. Thus the new strategy, like the old, is a policy of *attentisme*, or watchful waiting, for the Party's advent to power.

The new strategy, with its promises of bureaucracy, *attentisme* and centralised change from the top down, was completely contrary to the fundamental objectives of the rebellion. When the crisis broke, the Party found that it could either stick to its strategy and try to stop the rebellion, or it could abandon its strategy. The Party chose to follow its strategy, and it did so, throughout the May Events, with an awesome consistency.

May showed that the Revolutionary Situation, the moment for mass armed insurrection, will not come in an advanced industrial society; the Party had been right to abandon its old strategy. But May also showed that major social crises can occur under modern capitalism and that the Party has no strategy for dealing with them.

The prospects for a major rethinking of Party strategy are not very bright. What is likely to happen is that the Party will note the first conclusion and ignore the second. It will draw the lesson that the new strategy had only suffered a minor setback and ought to be pursued; in other words, that the Party had not only been correct to be consistent, but had been consistently correct.

May, once again, raised the question of the future of democracy in France, and once again, action on the question was postponed.

2 *The Recent Evolution of French Planning*

The last few years of the French Plan's history—the years since this book was written—can be well understood as the slow working out of the political logic of our model. The Plan persistently sought to go beyond its original role of spearheading a movement to modernize the industrial core of the economy. It tried one direction, then another and then still another. Each time, it failed.

The first effort was in the direction of what we have been calling 'general resource allocation planning.' The second was planning for public facilities, a new key sector to replace, or at least supplement, the basic industries and define a new role and a new clientele for the Plan. This effort led to planning for the development and the rationalization of public services: the programming of the construction of schools, roads, and hospitals caused planners to raise questions about education, transportation and health systems.[1] These efforts overlapped in historical time. They took root during the fourth plan (1962–65), reached their maturity during the period of the fifth plan and the preparation of the sixth (1966–70), and rotted on the vine during the life of the sixth plan (1970–75).

The attempt at general resource allocation planning was, by far, the most important: it represented not just a new role for the Plan, but a whole new political economy. The broad outlines of this attempted development, that is, the basic approach and the logic of that approach, were sufficiently visible at the point our historical narrative left off—during the period of the fifth plan—for us to have analyzed the implications of such a development and assessed its feasability. It implied radical changes of a specific nature, in both the methods of the planning process and in its political form and role. At the technical level it means a move from 'back-of-the-envelope' reckoning to elaborate inter-industry analysis in physical terms and from there to very sophisticated, but more aggregated econometric models in value terms (prices, incomes, financing, etc.). At the political level it

[1] A fourth effort was in the direction of regional planning. As the book does not discuss the French experience with regional planning, I have chosen to exclude comment on its very complicated development from this second postscript. It is treated in George W. Ross and Stephen S. Cohen, 'The Politics of French Regional Planning,' in Alonso and Friedmann, eds., *Regional Policy*, MIT Press, 1975.

meant a change from informal and very limited participation (the *économie concertée*) to broad participation politics. As discussion of this change and its implications is a major theme of the text there is no reason to go into it here, except to indicate that it followed, with an impressive precision, the lines traced out for it in our analysis. Behind the rich and often confusing historical experience from May 1968 and de Gaulle's departure through the Pompidou government and the advent of Giscard d'Estaing to major changes in world-trade patterns and the international economic crisis, there were no surprises regarding the fundamental lines of the Plan's thwarted development. Neither our analysis of the Plan's historical development, nor our assessment as to why its attempt at resource allocation planning would fail, needs to be seriously modified in light of recent experience. Instead, the experience helps to confirm the method. It speaks well for the possibility of understanding the logics and limits of different planning processes, and for the general approach to that understanding: political-economy.

While the recent technical evolution of the Plan, especially its physical-financial model (FIFI) has been profusely chronicled,[2] the political evolution has not. And there is no place at all in the literature which shows how they are really two sides of the same coin.

PARTICIPATION

The political counterpart of the general resource allocation approach adopted in the fifth plan was participation: participation by the trade unions in incomes policy; and participation by the government in the automatic adjustment of short-term economic measures to the plan (the 'clignotant' or early warning system), and in the programming of public investments. Both forms of participation failed dramatically. May 1968 was not the harmonious progression of a planned-incomes policy based

[2] See Raymond Courbis, 'The Fifi Model Used in the Preparation of the French Plan,' *Economics of Planning*, 12, no. 1–2, 1972; La Documentation Française, 1971, *Le Modèle Physico-financier dans la préparation du VIe Plan*; Courbis et Aglietta, 'Un Outil pour le Plan: Le Modèle FIFI,' *Economie et Statistique*, mai 1969; P. Pasçallon, *La Planification de l'Economie Française*, Paris, 1975, pp. 49–61; Y. Ullmo, *La Planification en France*, Cours fait à l'Institut d'Etudes Politiques de Paris, fascicule II; C. Seibel, 'l'Utilisation du Modèle FIFI dans la préparation du VIe Plan,' in *Le Modèle FIFI, Tome I*, Collections INSEE C-22, 1973.

on consensus and cooperation. The devaluation, the frenzy of short-term economic measures, and the near-freeze on public investment that followed in the wake of May were not the smooth whirring of the automatic adjustment system and the carefully programmed calender of public investments. May destroyed the fifth plan.

After May, the plan was simply forgotten. It was forgotten by the government who ran the economy without the aid of the plan; forgotten by the general public who stopped talking about a plan, and even forgotten by the planners who, after May, prepared a limp memo significantly entitled 'Report on the Problems of Adapting the Fifth Plan,' and turned to the job of preparing a sixth plan.

When it appeared, the sixth plan (1970–1975) was unmistakably the offspring of the fifth. It had the same basic structure: an effort at general resource allocation planning through a financial balances approach. And it met the same fate as the fifth plan. It was shattered by a spectacular 'external event': the international economic crisis of the early 1970s.

The spectacular, and external, quality of the events that brought down the fifth and sixth plans obscured the fact that their basic thrust—the effort at comprehensive planning—was quite dead well before the external events hit. Participation, on which the financial balances approach depended, had not worked. The trade unions had refused to cooperate in the incomes policy, and the government had refused to regulate its use of short term economic policy by the automatic signal system of the plan.

PARTICIPATION I: INCOMES POLICY

The failure of the incomes policy was, in part, a short-term or circumstantial failure. The substantive contents of the plan's incomes policy was a squeeze on wages in favor of corporate profits. The trade unions refused these terms and withdrew from participation in the machinery of incomes policy which had been launched with such great fanfare. But the failure was more than just a short-run refusal by the unions to accept what they saw as a bad deal. Incomes policy has its own political logic, which is, in many essential ways, quite similar to that of general resource allocation planning.

Balanced growth economists, planners and international organizations such as the OECD are forever proposing incomes policy as the way to combat inflation while avoiding the pitfalls of 'stop-go.' Almost every Western country has, over the past ten or fifteen years tried an incomes policy approach. Each time it has been abandoned after a short while, often to be tried again, at a later date, and then again abandoned. This pattern expresses a logic, not a coincidence. Incomes policy is not just another short-term countercyclical device, a technical alternative to higher interest rates or reduced government spending. It has a simple but powerful political meaning. Incomes policy means centralizing and politicizing the distribution of income. That is one thing the present system avoids like the plague. Under the present system (call it what you will: like the poor little match girl, it doesn't even have a name), decisions on income distribution are not decided at one time, in one place, through a political process. A centralized, politicized package decision on 'who gets what' represents an enormous system change. That is why income policy 'has not worked' in France, or elsewhere. Nobody wants it to: not business, not the middle classes, not the unions and not the government. Barring any compelling need—something that would make incomes policy worth its very high price to the present system, or a major political change—the only way it will be used is the way it has been used. In France, no such political change has occurred, and no such need was felt during the fifth and sixth plans.

PARTICIPATION II: AUTOMATIC COORDINATION

The failure of the government to participate in the effort at comprehensive planning and to let the automatic system guide the exercise of short-term economic policy along the paths laid out in the Plan was also not the result of circumstantial or superficial difficulties. Greedy pressure groups, undereducated politicians, recalcitrant finance ministers and violent short-term economic disturbances all played their parts, as did the awkward mechanics of the system—at first over-, then under-sophisticated.[3] But the main, and insurmountable, reason was

[3] See *Economie et Statistique*, Sept. 1974; *Le Monde* 29 Oct. 1974; *Economie et Statistique* Sept. 1971 'Les indicateurs associés au VIe Plan'; Pasçallon, pp. 107–110.

the fundamental difference between the political forces that converge upon the exercise of short-term policy and those that had stakes in the plan. The same political logic—and forces—that prevented such coordination during the first four plans carried on through the fifth and sixth plans. The difference was that the first plans simply discounted any serious possibility of success in that direction. Just because the fifth and sixth plans adopted a comprehensive planning approach that depended on a tight coordination of short-term policy with the middle-term plan is no reason to assume that the political forces that made such coordination impossible in the past would tactfully vanish. They didn't. The elaborate machinery set out in the fifth plan to guide the government's hand and make it participate in the plan was, of course, not respected. Nor was the more stripped-down version of that same machinery in the sixth plan.

The government restricted credit and cut spending at the moment and to the extent it felt it had to; it did not check with the Plan. The budget, in the last analysis the operational planning document, manifested an active disregard for the Plan.[4] This reflected the fundamental political realities of the budgetary process as well as the personal attitudes of Finance Minister Valéry Giscard d'Estaing.[5] During the dog days of the sixth plan (1970–75), the planning commission issued a report on the implementation of the fifth plan which demonstrated that despite the series of economic dislocations triggered by May 1968, the fifth plan came out pretty much on target. Even if one reworks the calculations, using slightly different methods and referrents than those used by the planners, many industries do come out surprisingly on target—a result that raises many interesting questions as to the nature of such targets. Some, however, do not. Public investment came out at 83 percent of target. When compared with the 140 percent of target result for private investment, the disparity takes on significance.

Structural political obstacles blocked the Plan's big push towards comprehensive, financial balances planning. Politics—at a less structural level—also thwarted the Plan's second big

[4] Cf. Conseil Economique et Social, *J.O., Avis et Rapports* 21 Sept. 1974, p. 1262.

[5] For an excellent example see, X, 'Lettre à Un Ami Anglais, II, Sur Le Plan' in *Review Administrative*, 1971.

effort to create a new role for itself, the planning of public facilities.

PUBLIC FACILITIES PLANNING

The reason for the Plan's efforts in this direction are straightforward. France needed massive investments in hospitals, housing, sewers and water facilities, schools and roads to balance the effects of the industrial growth and transformation. The millions of cars needed highways: in *1968* France counted a total of only 700 miles of highway. The new white-collar industries needed telephones: there was one telephone (of infamous quality) for every seven people compared with one phone for every two people in the United States. The newly urbanized population desperately needed more and better housing: 45 percent of Paris housing units had no toilets, and the new and desolate suburbs needed everything; no hospitals had been built in the Paris suburbs for over thirty years, but about four million people had moved in.[6]

Properly planned, these massive investments could play a developmental and not just a compensatory role. The Plan could help make spending on public facilities into investment in 'smart infrastructure.' Good analysis, planning and programming would produce economy, relevance and synergy. The steady erosion of the Plan's role in industrial development, and with it, the support of its traditional clientele (big business and the economic administration) made this new role, and the new clientele it would generate (urban administration and the construction complex), very attractive to the Plan. The expectation that facilities planning would lead to planning for the activities those facilities served—school buildings to school systems, hospitals to health systems—made that attraction irresistible.

As noted above, the effort misfired. The Ministry of Finance simply ignored the Plan when it determined the amount and the timing of the funds to release for public facilities. And the ministries carried out their own ideas, and not those of the Plan, as

[6] Data from *Statistiques et Indicateurs des Régions Française*, INSEE, col. R. no. 15; hospital data from *Schéma Directeur de la Région Parisienne*, 1975, p. 15.

to the composition, character, location and timing of investment projects.

The reasons for the Plan's failure to play a decisive role in public investment are as straightforward as those that first prompted its decision to try to diversify in that direction. First, the structural conflict between the politics of short-term economic policy and those of the Plan blocked the planning, five years in advance, of the amount and timing of government spending on new construction. The government—and especially the Finance Minister—could not tie its own hands when it came to day-to-day regulation of the economy. Government spending may be vast and varied, but only small bits and pieces of it are discretionary. Salaries cannot be cut, nor can transfers. Civil servants cannot be fired. Ongoing investment projects cannot be suddenly stopped, at least not without major embarrassment, and operating budgets cannot be cut without major political battles. If the government is going to vary its own spending to fine-tune the economy, spending on new construction is one of the very few items in its budget that it can cut. It is the classic discretionary item, one of the few that is not pre-spent.[7] It is also the sector that absorbs the impact of the other principal instrument of short-term policy, interest rate manipulation. The structural difficulties that prevent the tight coordination of short-term economic policy with the middle-term path of the Plan focus precisely on public investment—one of the few levers the government can actually manipulate, and the Ministry of Finance had no intention whatever of abandoning its hold on that lever.

The second reason for the failure concerns the nature of a five-year public investment plan. The Plan must publish a high target for schools, hospitals, housing, telephones, etc.—or else publicly explain why not. But year after year, plan after plan, realization falls short of target. Each time this happens it provides ammunition to the government's critics. Just as the Plan was beginning to move into this area, starting with the fourth plan, and accelerating into the fifth and sixth plans, the government began to consider moving out.

Under President Pompidou, the Plan was becoming more and more identified as a Plan du Government and less and less

[7] The Conseil Economique estimates that over 80% of the budget is pre-spent. *J.O. Avis et Rapports du CES*, 19 Dec. 1967 and 21 Sept. 1974, p. 1262.

a plan of national consensus as expressed by the technocrats. A government existed, along with a governing party. Both would be around to take criticism at the end of the plan. Why, therefore, should the government set itself up for trouble? As far as public facilities went, a 'low profile' strategy was best for the government, if not for the planning commission.

One further set of obstacles blocked the Plan's successful diversification into public facilities. The technical ministries—public works, health, education—did not want the Plan treading on their established turfs. To overcome, or even to dent their resistance, would require a powerful and sustained push from the government. It was not forthcoming. Furthermore, even on a technical basis, the ministries had a good case. Though the Plan played an important role in initiating a process of inter-agency planning for public facilities—especially at the urban and regional levels—the Plan had little to offer in the way of superior techniques or methods. The Plan was treating public facilities in very conventional terms: so many schools for so many children; catchment areas defined by aged rules-of-thumb. Once they got started the ministries found that they could use those tools quite as well as the Plan, if not better. Finally, now that they no longer had de Gaulle, the Gaullists were trying to form a political organization. Public facilities spending is a time-honoured approach to such a construction, but not when it is planned by a politically insulated planning commission.

Though it was very positive in terms of its impact on the quality of public facilities planning throughout France, and in this way represents a neat illustration of how the Plan can be very useful to the system as a whole, the effort at public facilities planning was an important set-back for the planning institution in two ways. First, the Plan had failed to create a new and important role for itself in the area of public facilities planning, a new role it badly needed. And second, it was a detour on the path towards the planning of public services, a bigger and more important role than public facilities planning.

RATIONALIZING AND REORGANIZING PUBLIC SERVICES

May 1968 raised for some of the planners the question of the quality, or substantive content, of French economic development. Shortly after May, a small group of 'social technocrats'—as they came to be called to distinguish them from their more steely eyed colleagues—found a sympathetic ear in Prime Minister Chaban-Delmas, and began to push for an expanded program of social services. Their objective was to balance the one dimensionality of recent French economic growth. Universities, they found, were too few and too feudal; so were hospitals. Social security transfers had to be made available to the victims of economic development—the wiped-out peasants and shopkeepers—before they stopped the growth machine; and the whole massive social security system had to be rationalized. Urban transportation was getting worse and worse; the time of the average commute in Paris had passed that of Los Angeles. And in the vast and deadly suburbs new kinds of social services had to be created to help those commuters adapt to the newness, the brutality, and the imbecility of their surroundings.

More facilities were needed, and more services. Crucially, more than mere 'more' was the goal. Services had to be made relevant and sensitive: relevant to human needs and sensitive to costs. For the sorry state of public services was not just creating social malaise, it was also creating budgetary hypertension. The social security budget—health insurance, family allowances and old-age pensions—had grown by 345 percent between 1959 and 1969, with health expenditures leading the way. In the early 1970s the social security budget passed the government budget and became the biggest thing in France. Extrapolations read as though they were taken from pop-ecology articles: by 1986 social security would absorb all of the GNP.[8] And the education budget was keeping pace! During twelve years of rapid industrial growth (1954–68, the two census years) the health sector added more jobs than all of industry combined, and education added more employees than health.[9] The fearful growth of service expenditures compounding away upon their awesome size lay behind the Plan's hope to make an important role for itself by spearheading the Rationalization

[8] The extrapolation is by President Pompidou himself in his press conference of 22 September 1969. Data from Stephen S. Cohen and Charles Goldfinger, 'From Permacrisis to Real Crisis in French Social Security: An Essay on the Limits to Normal Politics,' in Lindberg, Alford, eds., *Stress and Contradiction in Modern Capitalism*, Lexington, Mass., 1975.

[9] *Annuaire Statistique*, 1963, p. 88; *ibid.*, 1969, p. 79.

and Reorganization of Services—just as it had earlier spearheaded the Rationalization and Reorganization of Industry.

During the fifth plan, before May 1968, attempts at rationalization had been made in two different areas: one produced a mess, and the other, a disaster.

The mess was the result of attempts to rationalize social security transfers. At the first official rumor that this time the annual social security budget crisis was not to be *just* patched over but would be used to begin a restructuring of the system, all the traditional political forces took to the streets. The dreaded family lobby, the fierce peasants, the terrible shopkeepers, the Communists, and the formidable white-collar unions, all opposed tampering with the delicate balance of social security transfers. Rationalization was postponed; the fundamental reforms were quickly withdrawn and replaced with stop-gap.[10] An end-run by the technocrats, backed by a squeamish bluff by the government, would not do. Reorganization of the big services meant massive conflict in the central political arena.

The second attempt, the expansion and rationalization of the French university system, has become world famous. The Plan sought to bring the university into line with the demands of the newly modernized economy. Furthermore, twentieth-century enrollments had already destroyed whatever value remained in the nineteenth-century university. The system was ripe—indeed over-ripe—for reorganization. New facilities were constructed in a hurry, and a beginning was made at defeudalization. Geographic decentralization was to be the first step towards administrative decentralization—the new campuses were located in the suburbs to serve what had become a largely suburban student population and to reap the political tranquility that suburban campuses were supposed to yield. The first concrete achievement of the program was Nanterre, the prototype suburban campus. And the first concrete achievement of Nanterre, or so the students like to boast, was the student revolt which triggered May 1968.

At least one lesson was waiting to be drawn from the two initial attempts at service rationalization. It could not be done quickly; it could not be done easily; it could not be done invisibly. It would be a massive and dangerous political struggle.

[10] Cf. Cohen-Goldfinger, *passim.*

For many years it would occupy the central place in the political-economic agenda of France, quite the way the reorganization of industrial and agricultural production had dominated public policy since the early 1950s. This complex lesson, including the necessity of reorganizing the service sector, as well as the scale and difficulty of that transformation, has yet to be fully appreciated. At the time, however, it was obscured by a more spectacular event, May 1968, which had its own lessons. These, everyone learned; but everyone, it seems, learned something different.

The social technocrats found in May an expression of dissatisfaction with the one-dimensional (or at least lopsided) character of French economic development and, therefore, a confirmation and a powerful impetus for their efforts to offset unbalanced industrialization with more and better services.

De Gaulle seems to have heard a demand for participation. He seized that theme right after May, and through the final moments of his reign he stressed the need for participation and proposed new forms: participation by the workers in the enterprise and participation by the citizen in a more decentralized government.

The Pompidou government never explained what it felt to be the questions raised by May, but it made its answer to those questions very clear: 'l'Impératif Industriel.'[11]

THE INDUSTRIAL IMPERATIVE

The 1969 devaluation was followed by a redoubling of the all-out effort to increase the scale and efficiency of French industrial production in order to meet the struggle of international competition in the Common Market and in the world market. There was nothing particularly new in all this. It was essentially a continuation of the pre-May policies, but with determination and pride.

The economy steamed through the last two years of the fifth plan, 1969 and 1970, in a vigorous, but 'very unplanned way.'[12] GNP grew at 5.7 percent per year, just slightly ahead of the

[11] Title of a 1969 book by L. Stoleru, a close adviser to Valéry Giscard d'Estaing.

[12] *Conseil Economique*, report of 24 Sept. 1974, p. 1260. No dissenting opinions were recorded on that point.

Plan's target. But within that overall, close-to-target figure, private investment, as noted above, ran 140 percent and public facilities 83 percent of target.[13] During the first three years of the sixth plan, 1971, 1972 and 1973, the pace was maintained, and even quickened. Industrial production grew by 7 percent per year—much faster than the 4.5 percent rate in West Germany, while industrial investment piled up a 7.8 percent per year rate of growth. GNP grew at 5.6 percent in 1971, at 6.6 percent in 1972 and at 6.1 percent in 1973 and productivity grew at 5.8 percent per year.[14]

The drive for industrial growth and economic rationalization found expression in all domains, and the government celebrated those expressions. The modernization of Paris was unflinchingly pursued. Its monuments—the Montparnasse skyscraper, the massive office complex at La Défense, the expressway along the right bank of the Seine—were criticized by some as expressions of the last days the bourgeoisie felt confident and had a 'projet,' by others as monuments of the last technocrats who knew what 'modern' meant. But everyone understood them to be monuments or statements, and not merely buildings and roads. President Pompidou himself proudly defended them against their critics as the expression of modern, dynamic France and big business and the technocrats shared his enthusiasm. France doubled and doubled again her supply of supermarkets, and the Plan proudly reported that the French supermarket/population ratio has passed that of England and become comparable with West Germany.[15]

Stoleru concocted his industrial imperative doctrine out of a curious mixture of ingredients, some indigenous and some imported. But the imported elements were so Frenchified as to be almost unrecognizable—rather like le Drugstore. One part was a super version of traditional French mercantilism: it's France vs. the world, this time in an all-out industrial competition. But the other part was a most un-French notion: 'The primary mission of the government,' Stoleru writes, 'is to recreate the market when it can exist.'[16]

[13] *Ibid.*, p. 1260.
[14] *Rapport d'Exécution du VIe Plan, Annèxe au Projet de Loi de Finances pour 1975*, p. 25.
[15] *Ibid.*, p. 36.
[16] *L'Impératif Industriel*, 1969, p. 213.

Fears that 'they' were going to dismantle the state ran through French society, from the extreme right to the extreme left and especially at the extreme center. Finance Minister Valéry Giscard d'Estaing's public flirtations with neo-liberalism did nothing to allay those fears. But fortunately, the way to achieve competitive markets, it turned out, was through the direct action of the administrative state. The bureaucracy would set them up, define their limits, control their conflicts and (working closely with industry) select the winner of the competitive struggle in advance. As a result, the industrial imperative became less a practice of competition within industry than a way for the state to strengthen the private sector by turning over important areas of economic activity to the strongest elements of the private sector.

The state sector had grown steadily since the war in both size and importance. Over 39 percent of national income passed through the state, and as Giscard d'Estaing put it so well, 'beyond 40 percent, it's socialism.'[17] Now, when things were going well, when the private sector was strong and confident, and when a strong and stable government was in power, was the time to pull the state back, before it was too late.

The private sector needed financial strengthening. First, the steadily rising tax burden—what Giscard called 'pression fiscale' to include all transfers from the private to the public purse—was to rise no more! Holding the line on taxes became a major preoccupation of the government, and a major element of the political identity of its finance minister. In part it was achieved through real transfers of funds from the public sector to the private. In part it was achieved through very creative bookkeeping and frequent 'debudgetization' and remained largely symbolic.[18] But symbolic acts are necessary parts of an industrial imperative policy, both to create a climate in which real transfers become possible, and also to compensate with expectation for failures to achieve substantial real results. Second, too high a percentage of savings flowed through the state. As a result, private financial circuits remained underdeveloped. The capacity of firms to self-finance out of retained earnings

[17] From interview in *Expansion*, May 1971.

[18] See Principal Options of the 6th Plan, where reducing fiscal pressure and increasing the share of private financing is presented as an absolutely top priority; also, Cohen-Goldfinger, chapter on 'Undue Charges'.

had to be increased, and so did the strength of the banking system. The government set out to divert some of the savings stream into private financing circuits. In this way, it would strengthen the private sector vis-à-vis the state, and it would also develop the Paris financial industry which had failed miserably to compete with the City of London as a world financial center.[19]

Given that international competition was the principal challenge, and the giant, multinational corporation its principal form, the French response followed logically. The state set out to create its own giant, multinationals. Super mergers were promoted in industry after industry to construct a series of national champions that would carry the French flag into battle against the foreign giants. The industrial policy approach of the early plans had now become the dominant, national policy and the government, the ministries and the business groups had so well learned the basic lessons about industrial restructuring that they no longer needed the Plan. In most of the restructurings to produce national champions, including the major ones such as steel and computers, the Plan played only a minor role.[20]

SERVICE RATIONALIZATION: THE EXPERIENCE

The service reorganization strategy was not completely abandoned. Efforts at rationalization persisted, but on a small scale and within the framework of an effort to hold down short-term cost increases. It was tinkering, not restructuring, and most of it took place within the ministries; the Plan was more a cheerleader than a quarterback.

For the university, where major structural reforms had been implemented before May and where a second round of major reforms had grown directly out of May, policy turned defensive and short run. The aim was to sit on the lid, politically and financially. A succession of Ministers each added a few more

[19] In addition to the Options of the 6th Plan, see Parodi, *L'Economie et la Societé Française*, 1971, pp. 53–60; on the role of Paris see DATAR, *Paris, Ville Internationale*, and the various reports on the projected Cité Financière for central Paris published 1973–74.

[20] See the forthcoming excellent study by John Zysman on the role of the state in the reorganization of the French steel and computer industries, University of California Press.

reforms made necessary by previous reforms and, in turn, necessitating subsequent reforms. While administrative rationalization was slowly pursued through its various phases of program budgeting, task definition and output evaluation, the budget shrank in real terms.[21] The role of the *Grandes Ecoles* grew even greater as the prestige—and the substantive quality—of the university sank.

Structural reforms of the social security system were not attempted. If they implied adding or expanding programs, major changes would be too costly in budgetary terms. If they aimed at serious restructuring they would be too risky in political terms. Instead persistent but minor rationalization efforts were added to a general effort to hold down spending increases. The doctrine of the industrial imperative—sacrifices must be made in order for France to meet the grueling demands of international competition—was invoked at every occasion. The text of the sixth plan provides some of the most eloquent statements of this theme, often at the expense of the Plan's ambitions and best analysis.

The social action report of the sixth plan ran some 200 pages (plus reams of annexed materials) and presented all the good ideas for more and better social services. All of them: aid to new-born babies and their mothers; programs for the lame, the blind, the halt, the bored; day-care centers; at-home services for the old; electronic aids to add comfort to troubled lives; new professions to absorb the new professionals the last Plan's educational reform was beginning to produce. The social technocrats had done their homework, and scores of representatives from dozens of interested groups had participated and contributed their ideas. The report of the Plan's Finance Committee took the Social Action report and reduced it to a manageable seven pages. The Finance Committee even found time in their busy lives, and space in their crowded pages, to acknowledge that the Social Action report was a splendid document, and represented a fine piece of work, and that its many authors ought to be congratulated. Then, after the congratulatory paragraphs and the inspirational opening, the Finance Committee breaks the news—under the heading 'Les Limites de la Solidarité':

[21] See *Le Monde*, 4 Nov. 1974, p. 11, for a politically dramatic presentation of this information.

The drive for international competitiveness brings things into question . . . there is a new imperative. The opening of the economy necessitates that the burdens on the French economy not be heavier than those of its principal trading partners, especially in the Common Market. . . . Doubtless the burden of salaries and social changes is not heavier in France than in other Common Market countries. . . . But it is reaching one of the highest rates. It is true that following a similar line of reasoning, each of the member states could only be apprehensive at the prospect of granting new social benefits. Hence the idea of the Plan's Finance Committee: No real progress can be made in this direction by individual states. It is only by concerted action, going beyond the idea of more harmonisation, which in practice is very limited, that the European Countries can begin to give new dynamism to their social policy. (p. 41)

The plan then goes on to proclaim that the new social policy is 'to enhance the capacity of each individual to increase his personal gain' (p. 42). What is really and truly in the interest of each and all is to increase the productivity. The principal and overwhelmingly most important social policy for both development and redistribution is to better 'develop the earning ability of each person' (p. 42).

TOWARDS LIMBO

The causes of economic growth are hard to establish,[22] and when the economy keeps booming there is a tendency towards generous interpretation. Every plausible claimant is entitled to some identification with the success and to some share of the credit.

On the surface at least, things never looked better for the Plan than they did midway through the sixth plan. The economy was breezing along, faster than ever, and right on target, at 6 percent per year. As long as that performance would continue, nothing too bad could happen to the Plan. After all, who had a better claim to credit for the sustained growth than the Plan? And whose claim costs less to honor? Less in terms of money; less in terms of political threat; and less in terms of fear that the cause of growth was controlled by some external power or that it would go away. The fourth and fifth plans had solidified the

[22] See for example, E. F. Denison, *Accounting for United States Economic Growth*, Brookings, 1974; or E. Malinvaud, et al., *La Croissance Française*, Seuil, 1972.

identification of planning with economic growth. By the middle of the sixth plan, after twenty years of steady growth, the nagging French fear that the boom was all too fragile was—on the surface at least—giving way to a general celebration of growth and prosperity. The notion of prolonged boom was yielding to theories about the structural nature of sustained economic growth: the Plan of course was one of the most modern, most estimable and most French of those structures. The sixth plan fit this role well. It looked competent and successful, modern but experienced, and very much in control. It was the biggest plan in scope (and in bulk).[23] Basically a comprehensive plan, in one way or another the sixth plan covered almost every aspect of French life, from aluminum to culture, from corporate cash flow to open space. Participation in the plan's preparation was as massive as its scope: 2,926 people directly participated in the 'modernization commissions' of the sixth plan as compared with 704 for the third plan.[24] Thousands of civil servants prepared five-year investment programs for every government agency—except defense—for 'inclusion in the Plan.' Parliament discussed and approved the preliminary options of the plan and then, a year later, debated and approved the final version. So did the Conseil Economique et Social.

It was also the most sophisticated plan. Much had been learned since the preparation of the fifth plan about the techniques of econometric modeling, and the sixth plan had the biggest (1600 equations), and the most sophisticated model yet. It was not just technically sophisticated, it was smart. Thanks to experience, emphasis had shifted. During the fifth plan, the planners had acquired a new appreciation for the uncertainties of an open economy. The model for the sixth plan—FIFI—was conceived not as a model of control, as in a traditional comprehensive plan, but as a model to inform strategic choice and speedy response. It emphasized basic structures (or relationships) such as prices to investment financing, rather than particular quantities of particular products.[25] The plan supplemented this basic financial-balances approach with a 'softer' methodology. For many sectors it provided not just simple

[23] The sixth plan published about 70 volumes of reports. They are available at La Documentation Française (31 Quai Voltaire Paris VII).

[24] Pasçallon, p. 63.

[25] Cf. Seibel, or Courbis, or Ullmo, Part II.

numerical targets but rather comprehensive reports that analyzed the state of the sector, its role in the economy, the challenges confronting it, and then proposed strategic actions to improve its performance. It was also the proudest plan. The main volume of the sixth plan, and of course, the presentations of the FIFI model, were published in English translation.

But beneath the surface it was rather hollow. The Plan was just drifting, drifting further and further away from an innovative role at the cutting edge of the economy and towards a legitimating role back among the ranks. Pushed to the center of the political stage by its comprehensive form, the Plan was ignored by the political process when it came down to substance—like the budget—and its comprehensive form was turning into a straitjacket. While participation in the preparation of the plan was quantitively massive, the whole participation process had become something of a ceremonial. The proliferation and enlargement of consultative commissions did not necessarily mean more substantive participation. It was, instead, a sign—and partly a cause—of a weakening of the direct function of participation: propagating new attitudes and ideas, exchanging information, ironing-out conflicts and brokering agreements. The new participants were *notables*. As their numbers rose they began to set the tone, prompting the people who counted to pull out and seek serious discussion elsewhere. Most important, the unions walked out. The CFDT and the CGT refused to participate in the sixth plan, thereby shattering the main purpose of the exercise—the mystique of consensus. It was now, unmistakably, the government's Plan—not the nation's Plan—even if the government chose not to follow it.

Each of the Plan's efforts to create a new and important role for itself had failed. It was not the comprehensive plan for the French economy, and it was less and less the plan for the industrial sector. It was not, nor was it any longer likely to become, the plan (or the planning model) for Europe. It was not the plan for government spending, or even the plan for public facilities. And it was not the plan for reorganizing the public services. While things were still going well on the surface, by the midpoint of the sixth plan, the Plan was lost. Then serious trouble first hit. It hit with a one-two punch: the international economic crisis, mercilessly followed by the election of Valéry Giscard d'Estaing. The crisis killed the sixth plan, then Giscard put the planning institution into limbo, where it now sits, waiting.

LIMBO

There is no need to compare the sixth plan's targets with the actual economic situation at its terminal date, 1975. By the end of the planned period, growth had turned negative, unemployment had passed one million, and prices had climbed by about 60 percent.

Right after the 'oil crisis' hit, President Pompidou asked the Plan to prepare an interim plan. The report, which purportedly outlined a 4 percent per year growth rate for 1974 and 1975, was never made public.[26] Then Pompidou died. The oil crisis grew into the economic crisis and Giscard d'Estaing took the presidency with a 50.7 percent to 49.3 percent victory over the Left Coalition.

From his new perspective, Giscard was able to add new reasons for mistrusting the Plan to his long-held and well-advertised opinion that planning was largely claptrap. The first and foremost was failure; the Plan had not foreseen the crisis, so what good was it? The second was a suspicion that the Plan had become divided into two equally untrustworthy groups: There was a group of social technocrats who, especially after the defeat of Chaban-Delmas, supported the Left Coalition, and there was a group of model builders and macro-economists who remained in the thralldom of their own techniques—they were harmless, but useless.

When the time came to start work on a seventh plan, no directives were forthcoming from the government. When the planning commissioner, Montjoie, resigned, no replacement was named. The president missed no occasion to proclaim his commitment to what he called *piloter à vue* (seat-of-the-pants flying). Again and again he announced his intention to pursue a pragmatic, short-term course as distinct from a planning approach, and he emphasized that the stormy seas of international crisis made such an approach not only desirable, but necessary. With no director, and no instructions to begin a seventh plan, and an icy wind blasting down from the Elysée, some of the Plan's best people began to leave. In October 1974, *Le Monde*

[26] Cf. *Le Monde*, 30 oct. 1974.

reported that 'the plan has been completely paralyzed. Its team is demobilized and beginning to break up: it is unsure about whether or not it will simply be allowed to whither away.' Similar concerns and observations began to appear all over the political system and the press.[27] The future of the Plan had become an open question.

The question of the Plan's continued official existence was resolved, at least for the short term, late in the fall of 1974. There would be a seventh plan. Over the years, the Plan had achieved institutional status and great popularity. Eliminating it implied risk; just letting it 'wither away' did not. Furthermore, it could prove handy some day, even to Giscard.

Prime Minister Chirac instructed the Plan to prepare a seventh plan, but to stick to a small number of qualitative objectives. Uncertainty was too great to permit quantitative long term, or even middle term objectives. Comprehensiveness was out of the question. A new planning commissioner, J. Ripert, was named.

A few things about the seventh plan are clear—but only a few. It will not be a comprehensive plan, nor will it be a highly aggregated macro-economic plan. Participation will be dramatically reduced, and so will its political centrality.

Less sure, but still quite probable, is that the Plan will find itself returning to something somewhat akin to the original Monnet Plan approach, but on a bigger scale. A list of critical sectors and critical actions, along with suggestions for improving performance in these areas will constitute its essential contents. But it is highly unlikely to have the clout the Monnet Plan exercised to back up its schemes for improving performance. The macro, financial balances approach will give way to a macro-economic sketch, a kind of general, but not serious, intellectual framework for the plan's studies and advice. Numbers—let alone well-defined partial equilibria that are to sum up to general equilibrium—will be down-played. They might even disappear. The virtues of no growth and quality of life, along with the imperatives of international competition will constitute its thematic message. And no one knows what rela-

[27] Quotation from *Le Monde*, 30 oct. 1974; see also, *ibid.*, 14 nov. 1974, 10 oct. 1974; 'it looks as though those who believe in the inevitable disappearance of the Plan are not wrong'; 9 jan. 1974; *Figaro*, 2 juin 1974; l'*Express*, 'la paralysie du plan inquiet même les finances,' 31 dec. 1973 et 6 jan. 1974; *Entreprise*, 'Faut-il tuer le Plan?' 15 mars 1974.

tion the plan's contents will bear to economic activity and political decisions.

The longer-term future of the Plan—like so much else in current French political-economic life—is even more uncertain. A new, positive role for planning cannot be defined until the economy itself takes on a new and more clearly defined direction. Despite the current president's personal views, France remains committed to the idea of planning, in part out of a persistent national tendency to express things logically and neatly, even if the expression remains divorced from the reality. That is something planning can always be made to do. More important, France remains committed to planning out of a general and complex judgment that its thirty-year experience with planning has, on the whole, been positive: that the plan does play a useful role in elevating discussion and formulation of political-economic policy; that it helps to bring some coordination and some sense of direction to the multifarious activities of the state itself—for even in France, the state is not one and indivisible; that it has some real, though modest, role in bringing order—and thus greater effectiveness—to private-sector activities; that it has helped to improve the rate of economic growth and to improve the direction of that growth. But the commitment is not without reservation. Planning may have helped growth, but growth has proved to be ironic: possession of its fruits has not fulfilled its promise. Sometimes it has been outright destructive, destructive of the traditional French environment and destructive of important social values and relations. Furthermore the particular form of planning practiced thus far in France has not helped to bring democracy to French political-economic life.

In the Preface to the Paperback Edition I discussed the US debate on planning. Here I have turned to the French experience of planning as a way to inform that debate. But France is now rapidly returning to the point where it must start new and equally fundamental debates on planning of its own. It will continue to have a plan, but it must, once again, decide what kind of planning.

Six years ago this study concluded along the following lines. Planning began in France with the goals of the technocrats and business leaders who sought to rationalize, modernize and expand the French economy. It must now mature with the goals of the democratic forces: to make planning an instrument to aid the nation to determine the direction of its own development. The first goals have been realized; the second, postponed.

At this moment, fall 1975, the current economic crisis—and the special crisis of the Plan—once again raise the question of making the Plan into an instrument to expand the scope of democracy. Once again, action on that question seems to have been postponed.

APPENDIX I: THE FOURTH PLAN

TABLE XV

FOURTH PLAN – TARGETS AND RESULTS

(a) Selected Aggregates

	Target annual rate of increase (%)	*Actual annual rate of increase* (%)	*Actual rate of increase as a percent of target rate*
1. GNP	5.5	5.1	93%
2. Productive investment	6.4	5.1	80%
3. Household investment in private housing	1.2	11.6	550%
4. Exports	4.7	6.2	132%
5. Imports	5.3	10.4	196%
6. Government	5.1	8.0	159%
7. Armaments and aerospace	0.7	6.4	914%

[1] Source: *Rapport Annuel*, 1964–65, p. 25; see also *le Monde's* analysis of that report, 23 Sept. 1965; all data for actual increases in this table (unless otherwise indicated) are taken from *Rapport Annuel*, 1964–65. Data includes estimates for 1965 made in the spring of 1965. Item one in table is for *Production Intérieure Brute*, which includes export production.

[2] Source: *Rapport Annuel*, 1964–65, p. 24; also *le Monde*, 23 Sept. 1965; category includes all firms – both private and public. Private investment during planned period fell considerably below target, while investment by public firms was somewhat above target: see, above, pp. 182–3.

[3] From *le Monde*, 23 Sept. 1965.

[4] From *Rapport Annuel*, 1964–65, p. 25, *le Monde*, 23 Sept. 1965.

[5] From *Rapport Annuel*, 1964–65, p. 25, *le Monde*, 23 Sept. 1965.

[6] From *Rapport Annuel*, 1964–65, p. 25, *le Monde*, 23 Sept. 1965.

[7] Source: *Rapport Annuel*, 1964–1965, Table No. 5, p. 165; figures cover 1959–65, as do all Plan's target-realization data for specific sectors. See table on following page.

TABLE XVI

FOURTH PLAN – TARGETS AND REALISATION SPECIFIC INDUSTRIES[1]

	Annual Growth Rates (%)		
	A	B	C
	Actual 1959–64	*Target* 1959–65	*Percentage realised* (*a*/*b*)
1. Coal	−0.7	−1.8	38.9
2. Non-Ferrous metals	5.5	7.7	71.4
3. Steel	4.9	6.3	77.8
4. Agriculture	3.7	4.5	82.2
5. Wood products	4.2	4.9	85.7
6. Metal working	6.0	5.7	105.3
7. Automobiles/cycles	6.2	5.8	106.9
8. Plastics and diverse manufacturing	10.0	9.2	108.7
9. Paper	7.4	6.8	108.8
10. Telecommunications	8.4	7.2	116.7
11. Chemicals and Rubber	9.2	7.8	117.9
12. Construction and public work	7.9	6.5	121.5[2]
13. Glass	8.4	6.7	125.4
14. Petroleum and natural gas	9.9	6.9	143.5
15. Textiles	6.6	4.6	143.5
16. Construction materials	8.4	5.4	155.5
17. Armaments and aerospace	6.4	0.7	914.3

[1] *Source:* All data from *Rapport Annuel*, 1964–65, *Appendix*, *Table No.* 5, *p.* 165.

[2] Housing: Construction of HLM units (low rent, publically financed housing) was projected at 28% of total new housing; actual result was 22%. [See, *le Monde*, 21 May 1966, p. 20]. Similarly, low and middle income housing receiving state subsidies were targeted at 25% of total new construction; actual results were 18% (*Ibid.*) Thus the actual over-achievement of the Plan's aggregate housing targets (see also item 3 in Table 15, preceding page) represented a radically different mix than that projected in the initial targets. The boom in construction was largely confined to luxury housing.

APPENDIX II: THE THIRD PLAN

The third plan [was] checkmated
from its first year. PIERRE MASSÉ[1]

The third plan, for the years 1958–61, was prepared in the context of a rapidly deteriorating economic and political situation: the foreign exchange crisis of 1957–58 and the political crises which brought down the Fourth Republic and parachuted General de Gaulle into power.

The planners tried to keep pace with the rapidly moving events of 1957–58 by pre-publication revision: the plan had been in effect for over a year before a text was finally made public in February 1959.[2] But as soon as the planning documents were completed they were ignored. They had to be. Actions undertaken outside the plan by the new de Gaulle-Debré-Pinay Government had completely altered the economic environment, rendering the plan's assumptions largely irrelevant to actual conditions. Several months later it was officially discarded and work was hastily begun on a new plan, called the Interim plan.[3]

If the birth date of the third plan is somewhat dubious, its parentage is easily established. It differed from the second plan only in surface detail; separating the second and third plans there was nothing comparable to the distinct change in methods, objectives and tone that distinguished the second plan from the first. Methodologically, the third plan was simply a more sophisticated version of the second plan. The data was better, the matrix was bigger. Compared to its predecessors, it was a technically elegant document. Even a CGT counter-proposal calling for its complete and immediate revision on the grounds that among its other defects, it was completely irrelevant to actual conditions, stopped to 'render homage

[1] *J.O., Lois et Décrets*, 23 December 1964, p. 11400.

[2] The published text, Décret no. 59–443 du 19 mars 1959, hereafter called the third plan, covered the four year period 1958–61. The text was prepared, for the most part, during the year 1957; 1956 is the base year for most of its projections; prices used are those of the end of 1957. It was, however, revised, again and again during the course of its first pre-publication year, 1958. cf. for example para. 74.

[3] *Plan Intérimaire*, Paris, Imprimérie Nationale, J.U. 016661, 1960.

to the technical excellence of the project.'[1] But the increase in sophistication was confined to the purely technical aspects of planning; politically, the third plan was as crude and irrelevant as the second plan.

The third plan presented a detailed, general resource allocation plan – a detailed, 'coherent' (as the planners called it)[2] programme for economic development. But the plan's coherence was purely formal, purely internal. Planned investment in steel balanced with projected demand for steel, with projected supplies of coal and with projected growth of the construction and motor industries. Foreign exchange projections meshed with planned increases in production, investment and consumption. But there was no co-ordination at all between those targets and the means through which they were to be realised. The ensemble of the plan was not even co-ordinated with such evident political realities as the government's economic policies in the all-important year preceding the new plan's first year. Only in such a restricted internal sense could the plan be called coherent. All its balances summed to zero, but so did its chances of realisation.

THE TARGETS OF THE THIRD PLAN

All the targets of the plan related to its central core: a programme to achieve a 'lasting equilibrium' in foreign accounts in 1961.[3] The emphasis on foreign balance was dictated by the foreign exchange crisis developing during the plan's preparation, by the progressive freeing of foreign trade and by the anticipated beginnings of the Common Market.[4] GNP was planned to increase by 27% over the 1956 level by the end of 1961; industrial production by 30–35%; and agricultural production by 20%.[5] Exports were planned to increase by 35% over the 1956 level and imports by 10%.[6]

The projection of a 10% increase in imports during a five year period 1957–61 – or 2% per year – appears somewhat questionable, especially in view of the 27% planned growth of GNP and past experience with the relation of growth of imports to growth of GNP. During the four years of the second plan (where imports were targeted for a zero increase) the actual volume of imports rose by 58%.[7] In other terms, the third plan projected an import GNP coefficient of .37: for every 2.7% increase in GNP a 1% increase in

[1] *J.O., Conseil Economique*, 28 February 1959, p. 270.

[2] See Bauchet, *Economic Planning*, pp. 62–63, 113–120; Massé; *French Affairs*.

[3] *Third plan*, para. 21. Lasting equilibrium implied running a slight surplus on current account to cover dollar debts. See para. 23.

[4] *Ibid.*, paras. 19 and 68b.

[5] *Ibid.*, para. 24.

[6] *Ibid.*, table no. 7.

[7] *Second plan*, p. 252; *third plan*, para. 69.

imports. During the period 1952 through 1957 (which includes a recession as well as an inflation and a long period of steady growth and stable prices) the actual import GNP coefficient was in the order of 1.7: GNP rose by about 30%, imports by about 50%.[1]

The import projection of the third plan, like that of the second plan, depended very heavily upon a complicated series of assumptions about and programmes for increasing the production of import-substitutes, both domestically and in the *zone franc*.

The development of domestic sources of natural gas – especially at Lacq – was expected to play an important part in meeting in-increased energy needs while holding down outlays of foreign exchange'[2] The most important savings of foreign exchange in the energy sector however, were to be realised through the development of petroleum production in the *zone franc*, especially North Africa; total increased consumption of petroleum for the five-year period 1957–61 was expected to be met from this source.[3] The second plan contained an almost identical projection for petroleum: total increases in consumption were to be met from new production in the *zone franc*, particularly in North Africa.[4] At the time of the second plan's preparation the Economic Council expressed serious doubts about the feasibility of this basic objective.[5] By 1957, the terminal year of the second plan, petroleum imports from outside the *zone franc* had increased by 20% – instead of the zero planned increase.[6] The Economic Council did not prepare a detailed study of the foreign trade projections of the third plan; too little time was given as the reason for the restricted scope and detail of the council's report.[7] It did, however, observe that the important petroleum projection was particularly 'fragile', and should be revised annually.[8] The trade union delegates to the Council presented minority reports, which included proposals for the immediate revision of the plan's import projections.[9]

Despite the prominence given it in the plan,[10] the petroleum pro-

[1] GNP, *Third plan*, para. 8; Imports, *Rapport Annuel*, 1958, p. 19.

[2] *Third plan*, paras. 69, 177–178.

[3] *Third plan*, para. 69.

[4] *Second plan*, pp. 134–135, see also above, pp. 142–3.

[5] Cf. *J.O.*, *Conseil Economique*, 3 August 1954, pp. 701–702.

[6] Cf. *Rapport Annuel*, 1958, table no. 46, p. 138 (the figure is for the physical volume of imports thus eliminating the effects of changes in world prices.)

[7] The Economic Council had only five days to study, discuss, hold hearings, vote and prepare a report on the third plan: cf., *J.O.*, *Conseil Economique*, 28 fevrier 1959, p. 254.

[8] *Ibid.*, p. 257.

[9] Cf. *Ibid.*, p. 270. The CGT – and the CFTC prepared separate contre-projects, but their observations and substantive proposals are quite similar.

[10] Perhaps a result in part of the peculiar politics of the Constatine plan, and its appeal to those responsible for the French plan: see above, pp. 40–9.

gramme, if realised, would represent only a small part of the plan's import objective. Foreign exchange outlays on petroleum represented, in 1955, only about 8% of total imports; mechanical goods accounted for approximately 15% of imports; chemicals, 9%; textiles, 16%; metals, 10%.[1] Furthermore, import coefficients for other categories of goods had been higher than that for petroleum. During the period of 1952–57, imports of petroleum increased by about 20% while total imports of energy (coal as well as petroleum) rose by 30%. Imports of raw materials, however, rose by 60% and imports of semi-finished goods by 140%.[2] The development of domestic production of goods for which large quantities of foreign exchange were spent was the plan's principal method for holding down the over-all growth of imports. Investment and output programmes were prepared for the major import-substitution industries. Without entering into a detailed analysis of each industry's programme, it is possible to observe that the plan's programmes for these industries varied considerably from sector to sector, in clarity, detail and apparent soundness.

The chemical industry and the 'para-chemical' industries (rubber, glass, and synthetic fibres) were expected to increase output by 45% so as to cut imports of those products *below* the 1956 level, and to supply synthetic substitutes for raw materials which had in the past been imported. In 1956, imports of these goods had amounted to $331 million; the 1961 target was $290 million.[3] For these industries the plan entered into great detail, analysing investment projects, promoting structural reforms and preparing output programmes. The principal area of imprecision was the financing of the 45% planned increase in production. The plan anticipated decreasing profit margins – in part linked to the removal of protective tariffs – and recognised the problem this situation would create for the traditional method of investment financing, self-finance, but it did not spell out alternative methods of finance.[4] Nonetheless, despite the inadequacy of its discussion of the details of financing expansion in the chemical and para-chemical industries, – no small inadequacy – the plan provided a strong and consistent programme for expansion with clear and convincing indications of how that programme ought to be realised.

FOREIGN TRADE

The plan's projection for the balance of payments of the *Zone Franc* did none of these things. It called for a $50 million balance of pay-

[1] See *Third plan*, tables 9 and 22 a complete breakdown of imports.
[2] *Rapport Annuel*, 1958, p. 19.
[3] *Third plan*, para. 69 and 215.
[4] *Third plan*, paras. 213–216; *J.O., Conseil Economique*, 28/2/59, pp. 257.

ments surplus for the *zone franc* (excluding metropolitan France) by 1961. In the past this bloc had run a mounting deficit: 1954 – 11 million; 1955 – 149 million; 1956 – $107 million; 1957 – $160 million.[1] The plan provides no thorough going explanation of why this trend should be reversed.[2] The Economic Council's statement on the programme for the *zone franc* adds nothing to any analysis of the plan, but it does provide a good indication of the climate of political debate in the winter 1958–59:

'The commission . . . estimates that it is not able to issue a statement on the Algerian plan as defined by the General de Gaulle at Constantine . . . the same holds true for the overseas territories and the countries of the French Union.[3]

Whatever the respective merits and defects of the various import-substitution programmes of the plan they had become, for the most part, irrelevant to actual conditions long before they came off the drawing boards. The plan was a four year plan. It was to cover the years 1958–61, not 1957–61.[4] During 1957 it was still in preparation: prices used in the plan are for the last quarter of 1957; national income and foreign trade figures for 1957 (actual not projected) are contained in the plan.[5]

But in 1957, imports increased by 8%, thus leaving room for a total increase in the volume of imports for the four year period 1958–61 of only 2%. The 2% total is an absolute figure. It refers to the volume of imports; not to any differences between imports and exports.[6]

If the 10% total for the five year period appeared questionable, the 2% total for the four year period appears altogether improbable – especially when the other programmes in the plan which had been carefully synchronised with the original foreign-trade projection were not changed to compensate for the severe tightening of a major constraint. Why should a national plan originally aimed at limiting increases in imports to an average of 2% per annum be appropriate for keeping imports down to ½% per annum? Certainly a comprehensive explanation of this projection should be provided. But the plan offers no such explanation. It simply sets out the original five year, 10% target, admits that eight-tenths of it have already been used up,[7] and stops. It neither anticipates nor suggests

[1] *Third plan*, table 12.
[2] *Third plan*, paras. 305–309.
[3] *J.O., Conseil Economique*, 28 février 1959, p. 263.
[4] Title page of *Third plan*.
[5] On prices, see para. 5 of preface to *Third plan*, and para 5 of text; for national income and foreign trade figures see, for example, tables 8 or 10.
[6] *Third plan*, para. 69 states that the 1961 level of imports would exceed that of 1957 by only 2%. It defines imports as total volume (excluding military).
[7] *Third plan*, para. 69.

revision of the original programmes aimed at limiting imports to a 10% increase; it calls for no new devaluations: the March 1957 exchange rate is used for all foreign exchange projections.[1] In brief, although the plan's principal constraint was approached (or used up) by 80% in the year *preceding* the plan's first year, there resulted no revision of the programmes originally designed to keep the economy within that constraint, nor even any explanation of why such revision was not considered necessary.[2]

NATIONAL INCOME

The plan's projections for national income encountered similar difficulties. Serious questions could be raised about their value as a self-contained five-year programme simply on the basis of a close textual analysis.[3] But more important, they constituted a four year, not a five year programme. The first year of the five year period, 1957, had long since passed by the time the text was completed. Actual developments in 1957 augured ill for the planned pattern of development. GNP was planned to increase by about 27% over the period 1957–61.[4] In 1957, however, GNP grew by just over 6%.[5] Consumption was planned to increase at an average rate of 4.8%;[6] In 1957 consumption increased by over 6%.[7] The events of 1957 left the plan with a series of important inconsistencies and contradictions.

[1] The exchange rate used in the plan is '350 francs per dollar for the first months of 1957 and 420 thereafter' [cf, table 9] thus taking into account the disguised devaluation ('operation 20%') of March 1957. 1957 trade figures do not support any assumption to the effect that the March 1957 devaluation would reduce the 1958 rate of imports below the levels of the last three quarters of 1957. By mid-1957 the devaluation should have shown the measure of its effectiveness. Furthermore the effects of the Suez affair were most important in the first months of 1957: the index of volume of imports for all members of the OEEC (combined) registers a drop in the second, third and fourth quarters of 1957 from the volume reached in the first quarter. (*General Statistics*, May 1959, p. 3) French imports, ran counter to this trend and continued to rise throughout the last three-quarters of 1957 (*ibid.*, p. 103).

[2] *Third plan*, paras. 67–77 which discuss the plan's foreign trade projections. Even Hackett remarks: 'the Third plan remained extremely vague as to the annual rhythm for achieving the four year objectives. Yet it was clear by 1958 that this was the key problem.' *Economic Planning in France*, p. 60.

[3] For example, the *Conseil Economique* found the plan's projection of investment increasing more rapidly than consumption 'too optimistic.' This, the Conseil indicated, had not been the tendency in the past and it seemed to the Conseil unlikely to be realised 'without recourse to enforcement procedures which are, not foreseen in the plan.' *JO, C.E.*, 28/2/59, p. 263.

[4] *Third plan*, para. 25.

[5] *Rapport Annuel*, 1958, table 8.

[6] *Third plan*, para. 25.

[7] OEEC, *General Statistics*, July 1959, p. 92.

Presenting the plan, at the end of 1958, Commissioner Hirsch praised its prudence. He indicated that the overall growth target of the plan could be realised with two stagnant years and that expansion in the remaining years would still not have to exceed the rates of growth maintained during the last years of the second plan. That is, after two sharply contrasted years, 1957 (rapid expansion) and 1958 (recession), the growth targets of the plan could be achieved with yet another year of stagnation without exceeding, in the remaining two years, the 1956–57 rates of expansion.[1] But two recession years do not fit with the plan's other objectives and projections such as regional development (largely through increasing the size and specialisation of productive units – especially by creating new ones), and full employment. The Economic Council admitted that it was an objective. If it was to be a prediction, the Council found that the plan admits that the austerity programme then under way (1958), had been 'compressed or even lost' before completion; if it was to be an objective, the plan would 'serve as a stimulant to recession.'[2] Furthermore, the Council expressed a guarded uncertainty as to whether, in the event of a second year of recession, the plan was well designed to insure that the recession would be used for modernising the nation's economic equipment.[3]

The trade union delegates to the Council were less restrained in their language. In a minority opinion, the CGT listed the plan's major shortcomings. 'The plan was based on . . . non-realised hypotheses.' Events in 1957–58 'seriously weakened the chances of realising the plan's programmes in agriculture, foreign trade, investment, finance and its means of orientation and control.' In brief, the plan, at the time of its unveiling, had already lost contact with reality. The CGT proposed that all investment programmes be kept going and that planning be continued, but that a new plan be immediately prepared.[4] The CFTC said, more or less, the same thing: 'Planning is indispensable.' Economic and political developments – and the government's economic policies – have departed from the pattern of the plan. The plan is therefore largely irrelevant and ought to be promptly revised.[5]

Much the same argument can be made about each of the plan's targets. For once an important weakness develops in one of the principal projections of a coherent plan, the other targets share in that defect because they are, quite literally, derived from that projection.

[1] *J.O., Conseil Economique*, 28/2/59, p. 264.
[2] *J.O., Conseil Economique*, 28/2/59, p. 264.
[3] *Ibid.*, p. 264.
[4] *J.O., Conseil Economique*, 29/7/59 p. 270.
[5] *Ibid.*, p. 270.

The third plan was doomed to irrelevance before it was promulgated. Any attempt to compare actual patterns of economic activity in 1961 (the plan's target date) with the targets of the third plan promises to be especially futile and misleading.[1] The general resource allocation component of the third plan never had a chance to influence development. As Commissioner Massé remarked, many years later, 'the third plan [was] checkmated in its first year.'[2]

[1] Under the direction of Jean Bénard, the CEPREL (Centre d'Etude de la Prospection Economique à Moyen et Long Termes) has analysed – and attempted to measure – the implementation of the third plan. The project is massive in scale – three volumes. It compares targets with actual results, and analyses investment and production programmes. Fortunately, the CEPREL used the third plan as an exercise – more as an experiment in the techniques and methodology of measuring the effectiveness of a plan, than as an attempt to produce any precise definition of the degree to which the plan had succeeded. See, *Bulletin du CEPREL*, nos. 2, 3 and 4, July, December 1964 and Juin 1965; Cazes *La Planification en France et le IVe Plan* analyses the effects of the third plan and compares targets to results; see pp. 48–58.

[2] *J.O., Lois et Décrets*, 23 December 1964, p. 11400.

APPENDIX III

TABLE XVII

AVERAGE ANNUAL RATE OF GROWTH OF THE GNP

	Aggregate		Per Capita	
	1950–58	1958–64	1950–58	1958–64
France	4.4	5.4	3.5	4.0
UK	2.4	3.9	1.9	3.1
USA	2.9	4.4	1.2	2.7
USSR	7.1	5.3	5.2	3.5

Source: Joint Economic Committee, US Congress, New Directions in the Soviet Economy, *Washington,* 1966, *Part IIA, p.* 105.

BIBLIOGRAPHY

ARTICLES

Alpert, Paul. 'Planning: Key to Growth,' *Challenge*, December 1962.

Amendola, G. 'Lutte des Classes et Développement Economique depuis la Libération,' *Les Temps Modernes*, vol. 18, septembre-octobre 1962.

Anciant, Jean. 'Economie Concertée: Mythe ou Réalité,' *La Revue Socialiste*, no. 166, oct. 1963.

Antoine, J. 'Peut-on parler d'une Planification Sociale?' *Revue Action Populaire*, décembre 1964.

Aubert-Krier, Jane. 'Monopolistic and Imperfect Competition in Retail Trade in France,' in E. H. Chamberlain, ed., *Monopoly and Competition and their Regulation*, London, MacMillan, 1954.

Auger, Jean. 'On Trade Union Participation in Planning', *International Socialist Journal*, No. 18, December 1966.

Avril, Pierre. 'Perplexité Devant le IVe Plan,' *Cahiers de la République*, nos. 40–41, janvier-février 1962.

Avril, Pierre. 'Conditions Politiques d'une Planification Démocratique,' *Cahiers Reconstruction*, 17(2), septembre 1962.

Bagoilles, L. 'Le Temps des Banquiers,' *Signes du Temps*, 9 juin 1964.

Bailey, R. 'Towards a Euro-Planbureau?,' *Westminster Bank Review*, February 1963.

Bain, Joe. 'Economics of Scale, Concentration and the Condition of Entry in 20 Manufacturing Industries,' *American Economic Review*, Vol. 44, 1954.

Balassa, B. 'Whither French Planning,' *Quarterly Journal of Economics*, November 1965.

Barjonet, André. 'Un Plan, Pourquoi Faire?, *Economie et Politique*, no. 87, oct. 1961.

Barjonet, André. 'A Propos du "Plan" de M. Edgar Faure,' *Revue des Comités d'Entreprise*, no. 75, juin 1954.

Barjonet, André. 'The Triple Foil of the Unions,' *International Socialist Journal*, No. 18, December 1966.

Basso, Lelio. 'Démocratie et Nouveau Capitalisme,' *Les Temps Modernes*, vol. 18, septembre-octobre 1962.

Batailler, F. 'Une Nouvelle Technique d'Economie Concertée: les Quasi-Contrats pour l'Exécution du Plan,' *Revue Sciences Financières*, avril-juin 1964.

Bauchet, Pierre. 'La Croissance de l'Economie et les Plans Français,' *Droit Social*, 25(12), décembre 1962.

Bauchet, Pierre. 'Une Nouvelle Planification,' *Revue Economique*, mars, 1966.

Bauchet, Pierre. 'Politiques d'Investissement des Entreprises Publiques,' *Revue de l'Action Populaire*, no. 160, juillet-août, 1962.

Bauchet, Pierre. 'La Régulation par le Plan,' *Revue d'Economie Politique*, mai-juin 1964.

Beaud, Michel. 'Analyse Régionale-Structurale et Plantification Régionale,' *Revue Economique*, mars 1966.

Belleville, Pierre. 'La Sidérurgie Lorraine et son Prolétariat,' *Les Temps Modernes*, vol. 17, avril 1962.

Belleville, Pierre. 'Perspectives d'Action Syndicale,' *Les Temps Modernes*, vol. 18, septembre-octobre 1962.

Bellon, H. 'Le Rôle du Bureau du Budget dans un Ministère,' *La Revue Administrative*, septembre-octobre 1952.

Bénard, J. 'Economic Policy in France,' in Kirschen and associates, eds., *Economic Policy in Our Time*, vol. III, Amsterdam, 1964.

Bénard, J. *et. al.* 'L'Exécution du IIIe Plan Français,' *Bulletin du CEPREL*, nos. 2, 3 and 4, juillet, décembre, 1964, juin 1965.

Bénard, J. 'Le Marché Commun Européen et l'Avenir de la Planification Française,' *Revue Economique*, no. 5, septembre 1964.

Bénard, J. 'Planification Indicative et Développement Economique,' *Cahiers de L'ISEA*, Institut de Science Economique Appliquée, no. 67, serie D, mai 1958.

Beregovoy. 'Optimisme et Sectarisme,' *Cahiers de la République*, juillet 1961.

Bernoux, P. et L. Lavorel, 'Les Syndicalistes devant la Négotiation Salariale,' *Economie et Humanisme*, no. 169, juillet-août 1966.

Berton, M. 'Bibliographie sur le IVème Plan,' *Economie et Humanisme*, juillet-avril 1963, no. 148.

Berton, M. L'UNR et l'Economie Concertée, *Economie et Politique*, no. 83, juin 1961.

Bertrand, L. 'Economie Nationale et Financière,' *Revue Banque et Bourse*, avril 1954.

Betout-Mosse, E. 'La Comptabilité Nationale dans la Préparation du IVème Plan,' *Etudes et Conjoncture*, avril-mai 1963.

Betout, E. 'Le Rôle de la Comptabilité Nationale dans l'Etablissement du IVème Plan,' *Etudes de Comptabilité Nationale*, no. 4, 1963.

Biard, R. 'Le IVème Plan: La Sidérurgie est Mal Partie,' *Economie et Politique*, mai 1963.

Bienaymé, A. 'La Réorientation de la Croissance Planifiée Française et les Risques de Freinage par le Commerce Extérieur,' *Cahiers de l'I.S.E.A.*, série P., no. 4, août, 1960.

Bing, Jacques. 'Malaise dans la Fonction Publique,' *Etudes*, avril-juin 1956.

Blass, Walter P. 'Economic Planning, European Style,' *Harvard Business Review*, Sept.-Oct. 1963.

Bloch-Lainé, F. 'Economie Concertée et Planification Démocratique,' *Cahiers de la République*, juillet 1962.

Bloch-Lainé, F. 'Les Moyens et les Fins du Pouvoir Economique,' *Entreprise*, 347, 28 avril 1962.

Bloch-Lainé, F. 'Pouvoirs Publics et Pouvoirs Professionels,' *Jeune Patron*, mars 1961.

Bloch-Lainé, F. 'Réforme de l'Administration Economique,' *Revue Economique*, novembre 1962.

Bloch-Lainé, F. 'Sept Années d'Incitation à l'Expansion Régionale: Bilan et Lecons,' *Annales de la Faculté de Droit et des Sciences Economiques de l'Université de Bordeaux: Revue Juridique et Economique du Sud-Ouêst*, no. 4, 1962.

Bloch-Lainé, F. et C. Gruson. 'Information, Prévision, Planification,' *Le Monde en Devenir*, *Encyclopédie Française*, Tome XX.

Boisde, R. 'Planification et Démocratie,' *Revue des Deux Mondes*, 23, 1 décembre 1963.

Boissonat, J. 'Le Vème Plan et la Crise de la Planification Française,' *Esprit*, février 1965.

Bolle, Pierre. 'Deux Etudes de Cas: Pierrelatte et le Tunnel du Mont-Blanc,' in *La Planification Comme Processus de Décision*, *Cahiers de la Fondation Nationale des Sciences Politiques*, no. 140, 1965.

Bonnaud, Jean-Jacques. 'Participation by Workers' and Employers' Organisations in Planning in France,' *International Labour Review*, Vol. 93, No. 4, April 1966.

Bonnichon, A. 'Planification Démocratique,' *Etudes*, 313(6) Paris, juin, 1962.

Boudeville, J. R. 'Formes et Politiques de Développement Economique: l'Economie Concertée,' *Annales de l'Université de Lyon*, *Troisième Série*, *Droit*, 1962.

Boulbaki. 'Le Grand Capital et l'Etat,' *Les Temps Modernes*, vol. 18, septembre-octobre 1962.

Brindillac, Charles. 'Les Hauts Fonctionnaires,' *Esprit*, juin 1953.

Brochier, Hubert. 'La Politique des Revenues et la Planification Française,' *Revue Economique*, no. 6, novembre 1964.

Brochier, Hubert. 'Les Effets de la Planification Française,' *Cahiers Réconstruction*, mai 1963.

Brochier, Hubert. 'Les Effets de la Planification Française au Niveau des Structures Economiques et Sociales,' in *La Planification*

Comme Processus de Décision, Cahiers de la Fondation Nationale des Sciences Politiques, no. 140, 1965.

Brochier, Hubert. 'Reflexions Sur une Politique des Revenus,' *Revue Economique*, mars 1966.

Bulletin du CEPREL, 'L'Exécution du IIIème Plan,' nos. 2, 3 and 4 juillet, décembre 1964, juin 1965.

Bulletin du C.N.P.F. 'Le Financement du Plan Monnet, Epargne ou Inflation,' déc. 5, 1952.

Burdeau, Georges. 'Plan Comme Mythe,' in *La Planification Comme Processus de Décision, Cahiers de la Fondation Nationale des Sciences Politiques*, no. 140, 1965.

Burgess, Eugene. 'Management in France,' *Management in the Industrial World*, eds. F. Harbison and C. A. Myers, N.Y. 1959.

Business Week. 7 April 1962.

Business Week. 25 May 1963.

Bustarret, H. 'L'Industrie Sidérurgique et le Plan.' *Planification en Afrique, Tome VII, Expérience Française*, République Française, Ministère de la Coopération, n.D. (1964?).

Bye, M. 'Le Conseil Economique et Social', *Revue économique* (Paris), nov., 1962.

Cahiers d'Action Réligieuse et Sociale, 'Le 2ème Plan,' février '63.

Le Cahiers du Centre d'Etudes Socialistes. 'Socialisme et Planification' (special issues) nos. 18-19 and 25-26 of mars 1er-15, 1963.

Le Cahiers de la République. 'Demain: Crise dans l'automobile', (special issue) vol. 32, mai 1961.

Les Cahiers de la République. 'Pour une Planification Démocratique', (special issue), no. 45, juin 1962.

Cahier Reconstruction. 'Le Syndicalisme Devant la Planification Française', (special issues), 61-VI, dec. 1961; 62-II, juin 1962; 63-1, mai 1963.

Calan, P. de. 'Le Rôle des Organisations Professionelles et l'Exécution du Plan,' *Comité Européen pour le Progrès Economique et Social*, juin 1962.

Campbell, Peter. 'The French Civil Service', *New Zealand Journal of Public Administration*, XVIII, September, 1955.

Castle, Barbara. 'Le Plan, Miracle or Myth?' *New Statesman*, 29 September 1961.

Cazes, Bernard. 'Comment se Fabrique le Plan', *Gestion*, déc. '62.

Cazes, Bernard. 'Elaboration du Plan et Démocratie', *Economie et Humanisme*, no. 136, nov.-déc. 1961.

Cazes, Bernard. 'Logique et Finalité du Plan Français', *Planification en Afrique, Tome VII, Expérience Française*, République Française, Ministère de la Coopération.

Cazes, Bernard. 'France, Mère de la Bureaucratie,' *Preuves*, no. 173, juillet 1965.
Cazes, Bernard. 'Les Moyens d'Exécution du Plan,' *Gestion*, mai 1963.
Cazes, Bernard. 'Le Progrès de la Planification en Europe Occidentale.' (*Bulletin de l'Administration Centrale des Finances*, juillet-septembre 1962).
Cazes, Bernard. 'Liasons Entre Secteur Public et Secteur Privé dans la Planification du Développement,' *Document de travail presenté à la Réunion d'experts organisée à Paris par le Départment des Affaires Economiques et Sociales des Nations Unies sur les Aspects Administratifs de la Planification du Développement, juin 1964.*
Cazes, Bernard. 'Les Rapports Entre le Plan et les Entreprises Privées dans la Planification Française,' *Revue Economique et Sociale*, Lausanne, oct. 1963.
Centre d'Etudes Socialistes, Analyses et Documents, no. 15, 1-6-61, 'La Concentration Capitaliste en France,' printed in *Cahiers du Centre d'Etudes Socialistes*, no. 5-6, 20 juin 1961.
C.F.T.C. 'La C.F.T.C. et le 4è Plan,' Supplément à *Formation*, no. 49, nov.-déc. 1962.
C.G.T. 'Le Plan: Mythes et Réalités,' Supplément du Journal, *Le Peuple*, no. 643.
Chalendon, A. 'Eléments d'une Economie Nouvelle,' *Nouvelle Frontière*, Juin-Juillet 1963.
Chalendon, A. 'Une Troisième Voie, l'Economie Concertée,' *Jeune Patron*, décembre 1960.
Chapel, F. 'Le IVème Plan et ses Méthodes d'Elaboration,' *Revue du C.N.O.F.*, mai 1961.
Chardonnet, J. 'La Politique de la Planification en France,' *Revue Politique Economique*, août-sept. 1962.
Chatenet, P. 'The Civil Service in France,' *Political Quarterly*, October-December 1954. Reprinted in A. Robson, ed. *The Civil Service in Britain and France*, New York, 1956.
Chevanier, A. 'Le Ministère des Finances,' *Revue Economique*, Paris, nov. 1962.
Cheverny, Julien. 'Les Nouveaux Technocrates,' *Les Cahiers de la République*, nos. 47–48, août-septembre 1962.
Claude, H. 'Qu'est-ce que l'Economie Concertée? *Economie et Politique*, no. 86, septembre 1961.
Clinchamps, Felix de. 'The Role of Private Enterprise in Preparing the Plan' in CEPES, *French and Other National Economic Plans for Growth*, New York, Committee for Economic Development, June 1963.
Clough, Shepard B. 'Economic Planning in a Capitalist Society:

France from Monnet to Hirsch,' *Political Science Quarterly*, December 1956.

Club Jean Moulin. 'La Planification Démocratique (II),' *Les Cahiers de la République*, nos. 40–41, janvier-février 1962.

Club Jean Moulin. 'Nature et Rôle du Plan Dans une Démocratie,' *Les Cahiers de la République*, vol. 39, décembre 1961.

Coser, Lewis. 'The Myth of the Peasant Revolt,' *Dissent*, May-June 1966.

Coulbois, P. 'Les Moyens de la Politique des Revenus,' *Revue de la Défense Nationale*, juin 1964.

Coulbois, P. 'Les Orientations du Vème Plan,' *Revue de la Défense Nationale*, déc. 1964.

Coulbois, P. 'Introduction à la Politique des Revenus,' *Rivista Internazionale di Scienze Economiche e Commerciale*, août 1964.

Crozier, Michel. 'Pour une Analyse Sociologique de la Planification Française,' *Revue Française de Sociologie*, vol. VI, no. 2, avril-juin 1965.

Cuisenier, Jean. 'Risque, Incertitude et Choix Economique,' *Esprit*, janvier 1965.

Cuisenier, J. 'Sur la Logique de la Planification Française, *Esprit*, juillet-août 1962.

Daude, B. 'Le Déterminisme Planificateur,' *Bulletin SEDEIS*, 888, 1er juin 1964.

Davis, O. and A. Whinston. 'The Economics of Urban Renewal,' *Law and Contemporary Problems*, Vol. 26, 1961.

Day, A. C. L. 'The Consequences for Economic Planning of Joining the Common Market,' *The Political Quarterly*, January-March, 1963.

Debatisse, M. 'Les Organisations Professionelles et le Pouvoir Politique,' *Paysans*, février-mars 1963.

Declercq, Gilbert. 'Démocratie Nouvelle et Syndicalisme Moderne,' *La NEF*, avril-juin 1961; also published in *Cahier Reconstruction*, Supplément no. 52, juin 1961.

Declercq, Gilbert. 'Rapport au Congrès de la CFTC 1959,' reprinted in *Formation*, 14 avril 1959.

Declercq, Gilbert et Marcel Guiheneuf. 'Nantes-Saint Nazaire: Une Lutte pour le Socialisme,' *Les Temps Modernes*, vol. 20, 1964.

Delion, A. G. 'Les Participations Financières Directes de l'Etat,' *Gestion*, décembre 1962.

Delors, J. 'Planification et Réalités Syndicales,' *Droit Social*, février 1965.

Delors, J. 'Les Aspects Sociaux du IVème Plan,' *Planification en Afrique, Tome VII, Expérience Française*, République Française, Ministère de la Coopération.

Demonque, M. 'La Firme et Son Rôle dans le Système Economique Français – la Grande Entreprise Française,' *Economie Appliquée*, vol. XVII, nos. 2–3, 1964.

Descamps, E. 'Socialisme et Planification,' *Les Cahiers du Centre d'Etudes Socialistes*, nos. 18–19, 1962.

Descamps, E. 'Reflexions d'un Syndicaliste sur les Plans Français,' *Cahiers du Centre d'Etudes Socialistes*, no. 1, 15 juillet 1962.

Devaud, Emmanuel, 'Le Plan Français: Mythe et Technique,' *Critique*, mars 1965.

Devaux, L. 'L'Organisation Interne de la Grande Entreprise,' *Economie Appliquée*, vol. XVII, nos. 2–3, 1964.

Diamant, Alfred. 'The Republic Changes but the Administration Remains,' in Siffin, Wm. J. ed., *Toward the Comparative Study of Public Administration*, 1957.

Dorfman, R. 'The Nature and Significance of Input-Output,' *Review of Economics and Statistics*, XXXVI, no. 2, May 1954.

Dow, J. C. R. 'Problems of Economic Planning,' *Westminster Bank Review*, November 1961.

Dreze, Jacques H. 'Some Postwar Contributions of French Economists to Theory and Public Policy, with Special Emphasis on Problems of Resource Allocation,' *American Economic Review*, vol. LIV, no. 4, part 2, Supplement, June 1964.

Ducaroy, G. 'Le Contre Plan,' *Perspectives Socialistes*, déc. 1963.

Ducaroy, G. 'Socialisme et Planification,' *Les Cahiers du Centre d'Etudes Socialistes*, nos. 25–26, 1er-15 mars 1963.

Durand, Claude. 'Positions Syndicales et Attitudes Ouvrières à l'Egard du Progrès Technique,' *Sociologie du Travail*, octobre-décembre 1960.

Eckstein, Harry. 'Planning: A Case Study,' *Political Studies*, vol. IV, Feb. 1956, part II.

Economie et Humanisme. No. spécial sur 'Planification Française et Démocratie,' no. 136, novembre-décembre 1961.

Edelmann, K. M. F. 'French System of Planning,' *Volkswirt*, 1 février 1963.

Ehrmann, Henry W. 'French Bureaucracy and Organized Interests,' *Administrative Science Quarterly*, March 1961.

Ehrmann, Henry W. 'French Labor Goes Left', *Foreign Affairs*, April 1947.

Esprit. 'La Planification Française,' (special issue), juillet-août 1962.

Etudes et Conjonctures. 'Les comptes de la Nation 1962' nos. 8–9, août-septembre 1963.

Etudes et Conjonctures. 'Evolution des Conditions de Logement en France Depuis Cent Ans,' vol. 12, nos. 10–11, oct.-nov. 1957.

Etudes et Conjonctures. 'Bilan de l'Industrie Française du Coton,' vol. 5, no. 2, mars-avril 1950.

Etudes et Conjonctures. 'La Comptabilité Nationale dans la Préparation du IVeme Plan.' avril-mai 1963.

l'Express.

Feyzioglu, T. 'The Reforms of the French Higher Civil Service Since 1945,' *Public Administration*, XXVIII, London, Spring and Summer 1955.

Finer, Herman N. 'The French Higher Civil Service,' *Public Personnel Review*, vol. ix, 1948–M 167–176.

Florenzano, Monique. 'La Construction Automobile,' (dans l'Exécution du IIIe Plan),' *Bulletin du CEPREL* no. 4, juin 1965.

Foa, J. M. Vincent and Vittoria. 'Incomes Policy,' *International Socialist Journal*, June 1964.

Fontaine, François. 'L'homme qui Change le Monde Sous nos Yeux,' *Réalités*, décembre 1962.

Formation. 'L'Exécution du Plan,' jan.-fév. 1964.

Forsyth, E. M. 'Economic Planning in the Common Market,' *Yearbook of World Affairs*, London Institute of World Affairs, 1963.

Fossaert, R. 'Subir ou maitriser?' *Esprit*, juillet-août 1962.

Fourastié, J. 'L'Université et la Prévision de l'Emploi,' (*Avenirs*, no. 106, octobre 1959).

France – Observateur. 'Un Plan de la Gauche,' 8 octobre 1964.

France – Observateur – Le Nouvel Observateur.

Franck, L. R. 'Planisme Français et Démocratie,' *Revue Economique*, (IV, 1953).

Frankel, Charles. 'Bureaucracy and Democracy in the New Europe,' *Daedalus*, Winter 1964.

Frisch, Ragnar. *Generalities on Planning*. Momorandum fra Sosialokonomisk Institutt Universitetet i Oslo, 27 February 1957, reprinted by Editrice l'Industria, Milan.

Froidveaux, P. 'Pour une Planification Socio-Economique,' *Economie et Humanisme*, no. 166, mars-avril 1966.

Garcia, André. 'La Planification Sociale,' *Revue Economique*, mars 1966.

Gardellini, R. and P. Covaillier. 'L'Intervention de l'Etat dans le Domaine Economique: Les Entreprises Publiques,' *Revue Administrative*, mai-oct. 1952.

Gelinier, O. 'Planification Démocratique et Direction Moderne,' *Hommes et Techniques*, janvier 1963.

Germains, E. 'L'Actualité Sociale et le Plan,' *Les Cahiers de la République*, janvier-février 1962, no. 40–41.

Germains, E. 'Une Industrie Non-Concertée,' *Les Cahiers de la République*, vol. 32, mai 1961.

Giscard d'Estaing, Valéry, Address at Harvard University, 8 June 1963, *French Affairs*, No. 155, New York.

Giscard d'Estaing, Valéry, 'Les Domaines du Liberalisme et Ceux de la Planification,' *Civisme*, 26, juillet-août 1964.

Giscard d'Estaing, V. Le Quatrième Plan de Développement Economique et Social,' *Revue des Travaux de l'Académie des Sciences Morales et Politiques*, 2ème sem. 1963.

Goertz-Girey. 'Monopoly and Competition in France,' in E. H. Chamberlin, ed., *Monopoly and Competition*, New York–London, 1954.

Gounod, P. 'La Contribution des Actions de Productivité à l'Exécution des Plan,' *Planification en Afrique*, *Tome VII*, *Expérience Française*, République Française, Ministère de la Cooperation.

Gourney, Bernard. 'Les Administrations Verticales,' *Revue Economique*, nov. 1962.

Gourney, B. 'Les Jeunes Fonctionnaires et la Politique,' *Les Cahiers de la République*, no. 47–48, août-septembre 1962.

Gourney, Bernard. 'Technocrates et Politiques,' *Economie et Humanisme*, no. 136, nov.-déc. 1961.

Gourney, Bernard. 'Une Groupe Dirigeant de la Société Française: Les Grands Fonctionnaires.' *Revue Française de Science Politique*, XLV, no. 2, avril 1964.

Gourney, Bernard and Pierre Viot. 'Les Planificateurs et les Décisions du Plan,' in *La Planification Comme Processus de Décision*, *Cahiers de la Fondation Nationale des Sciences Politiques*, no. 140, 1965.

Gozard, Giles. 'Le Financement du Plan Monnet,' *Productions Françaises*, juin 1947.

Gozard, Giles. 'Le Ministère de l'Economie Nationale,' *Productions Françaises*, juillet 1947 et août-septembre 1947.

Gozard, Giles. 'Le IVème Plan d'Equipement,' *Revue Politique*, vol. 50, no. 17, 30 octobre 1961.

Gravier, J. F. 'Le Cerveau du Plan,' *Preuves*, décembre 1953.

Grimanelli, Pierre. 'Politique Concertée des Revenus,' *Bulletin de l'ACADI* [Association de Cadres Dirigeants de l'Industrie Pour le Progrès Social et Economique], Bull. 182, septembre '63.

Gross, Bertram. 'When is a Plan not a Plan,' *Challenge*, New York University, December 1961.

Gruson, C. 'L'expérience Française de Planification,' *Reflets et Perspectives de la Vie Economique*, 2(2), mars 1963.

Gruson, C. 'Une Planification Sans Rivages,' *Cahiers de la République*, no. 29, 1961.

Gruson, C. 'Prix, Profit et Développement Economique: Problème de l'Optimisme Global,' *Economie Appliquée*, 1960, no. 1.

Hackett, J. W. 'Britain and France: Two Experiments in Planning,' *The Political Quarterly*, vol. 37, no. 4, October-December 1966.

Hackett, J. W. 'Sur les Investissements Dans un Plan Indicatif. . . . L'Example du 3e Plan Français,' *Cahiers de l'ISEA*, no. 57, série D, mai 1958.

Hansen, Niles. 'Indicative Planning in France: Model for the Future?' *Quarterly Journal of Economics and Business*, Vol. 4, No. 4, Winter 1964.

Harth, M. 'Can French Planning be Applied to the USA?' *New Leader*, No. 45, 3 September 1962.

Hertman, E. 'Wirtschaftsplanung in Frankreich,' (Economic Planning in France), *Konjunkturpolitik*, 9(1), 1963.

Heurteault, André. 'Planifier n'est pas Socialiser,' *Partisans*, no. 18, décembre 1964–janvier 1965.

Hirsch, E. 'French Planning and its European Application,' *Journal Common Market Studies*, 1, (2), 1962.

Hirsch, E. 'L'Exécution du Plan,' *Annales de la Societé des Ingénieurs Civils*, 1959.

Hirsch, E. 'Nécessité d'un Certain Pragmatisme,' *Les Cahiers de la République*, no. 45, juin 1962.

Hoffman, Stanley. 'Europe's Identity Crisis,' *Daedalus*, Vol. 93, No. 4, Fall, 1964.

Hoffman, Stanley. 'Paradoxes of the French Political Community,' in S. Hoffman, *et. al.*, *In Search of France*, Cambridge, Mass. 1963.

Hommes et Techniques. 'Considerations sur la Planification Moderne,' janvier 1963.

Hoselitz, Bert F. 'Entrepreneurship and Capital Formation in France and Britain since 1700,' in *Capital Formation and Economic Growth*, a Report of the National Bureau of Economic Research, Princeton, 1955.

Huvelin, Paul. 'Un Plan, Pourquoi Faire?' *La Croix*, 6, janvier 1962.

International Confederation of Free Trade Unions, (ICFTU), 'The French Trade Union Movement Past and Present,' *I.C.F.T.U. Monographs*, No. 1, 1953, Brussels.

Irwin, Patrick H. and F. W. Langham, Jr. 'The Change Seekers,' *Harvard Business Review*, Vol. 44, No. 1, Jan.-Feb. 1966.

Izard, Georges. 'Le Socialisme et la Démocratie,' *La NEF*, avril-juin, 1961.

Jacques, R. 'Connaissance et Choix des Bésoins,' *Esprit*, juillet-août 1952.

Jacques, R. 'La Démocratisation du Plan,' *Revue de l'Action Populaire*, 164, janvier 1963.

Jacques, R. 'Pour une Approche Syndicale au Plan,' *Esprit*, juillet 1961.

Jacques, R. 'Quelques Problèmes Posés par la Planification Démocratique,' *Cahiers de la République*, no. 35, août 1961.

Jacques, R. *et. al.* 'Démocratie et Plan,' *Revue de l'Action Populaire*, 164, janvier 1963.

Jallut, M. 'Démocratie et Planification,' *Ordre Français*, janvier 1963.

Jeune Patron. 'Espoirs et Difficulté de la Planification,' 16 (154), avril 1962.

Jeune Patron. 'Planification Economique, Oui. . . . Si. . . .' 17 (162), février 1963.

Joshua, I., et M. Manuel. 'Le Pétrol et les Carburants,' (dans l'Exécution du IIIème Plan) *Bulletin du CEPREL*, no. 4, juin 1965.

Jeuvenel, B. 'Pourquoi une Politique des Revenus: *Bulletin SEDEIS*, nov. 1964.

Juillard, J. 'La CFTC devant Son Avenir,' *Esprit*, vol. 31, no. 9, septembre 1963.

Kerever, André. 'L'Exécution du Plan Démocratique,' *Revue de l'Action Populaire*, no. 164, janvier 1963.

Kesler, Jean-François. 'Les Anciens Elèves de l'Ecole Nationale d'Administration,' *Revue Française de Science Politique*, vol. XLV, no. 2, avril 1964.

Kindleberger, Charles P. 'French Planning,' Paper presented at Universities National Bureau Conference on Economic Planning, Nov. 27–28 1964, Princeton (unpublished).

Kindleberger, Charles P. 'The Postwar Resurgence of the French Economy,' in Stanley Hoffmann *et. al.*, *In Search of France*, Cambridge, Mass., 1963.

Koechlin, J. 'La Réforme de la Structure Gouvernementale,' *La Revue Administrative*, mars-avril 1948.

Kriz, M. A. 'Credit Controls in France,' *American Economic Review*, March 1951.

Lagache, M. 'Les Problèmes de l'Industrie Chimique Française,' *Revue des Ingénieurs*, no. 125, février 1961.

Lamperière, J. 'Structure et Evolution des Exportations des Pays du Marché Commun et de La Grande-Bretagne depuis 1951,' *Etudes et Conjonctures*, mai 1960.

Landes, David S. 'French Business and the Businessman, A Social and Cultural Analysis, in E. M. Earle, ed., *Modern France*, Princeton, 1951.

Landes, David S. 'New Model Entrepreneurship in France and Problems of Historical Explanation,' *Explorations in Entrepreneurial History*, 2nd Series, Vol. 1, No. 1, Fall 1963.

Landes, David S. 'Observations on France: Economy, Society and Polity,' *World Politics*, Vol. 9, No. 3, April 1957.

de La Perrière, G. 'Les Moyens d'Exécution du Plan,' (*Bulletin de l'Administration Centrale des Finances*, juillet-sept. 1961).

Laure, A. 'Les Programmes de Modernisation et d'Equipment des Agglomérations.' (*Moniteur des Travaux Publics et du Bâtiment*, no. 15, 9 avril 1961).

Lautmann, Jacques. 'Recherche sur les Nouvelles Relations entre le Pouvoirs Publics et le Secteur Privé,' (Mimeo), Privately circulated. 1962.

Laux, James M. 'M. Pinay and Inflation,' *Political Science Quarterly*, Vol. 74, No. 1, March 1959.

Lavau, G. 'Colloque de Grenoble: Compte Rendu,' *France-Forum*, 49, juin 1963.

Lavau, Pierre. 'Non-Wage Incomes Policy in France,' in *Non-Wage Incomes and Prices Policy, Papers for a Trade Union Seminar, Supplement to the Report*, OECD, Paris, 1965.

Laysette, H. 'La Planification Démocratique, Espérance ou Chimère?' *France-Forum* 44, nov. 1962.

LeBrun, Pierre. 'Esquisse d'un Autre Plan,' *France-Observateur*, 12 novembre 1964.

LeBrun, P. 'Signification du Plan,' *Les Cahiers de la République*, no 45, juin 1962.

LeCalonnée, J. F. 'La Planification et le Droit,' *Economie et Humanisme*, 21 (140), juillet-août 1962.

Le Guay, François. 'Planning in France,' *Economic Bulletin – Latin America*, No. 8, March 1963.

Le Guay, F. 'Les Projections à Long Term en France,' *Paper presented at International Conference on Input-Output Techniques.* Geneva, September 1961.

Lemerle, P. 'L'Expérience Française du Plan, Peut-elle Servir aux Pays qui Veulent se Développer?' *Tiers-Monde*, janvier-mars 1965.

Lemerle, P. 'Histoire du Plan Français,' *Planification en Afrique, Tome VII, l'Expérience Française*, Ministère de la Coopération, (N.D., 1964?).

Lemerle, P. 'Planning Development in France,' *United Nations, Planning for Economic Development, Vol. II; Studies of National Planning Experience, Part I, Private Enterprise and Mixed Economies.*

Leroy-Jay, P. 'Le Plan Français: une Tentative Empirique d'Economie Concertée,' *Revue Economique Franco-Suisse*, décembre 1963.

Lescop, Rene. 'Planification et Libre Entreprise,' *L'Usine Nouvelle*, décembre 1962.

Levard, G. 'CFTC-CFDT,' *Formation*, sept.-oct. 1963.

Levi, M. 'La Planificazione Indicativa in Francia,' *Mondo Economico*, 2 February 1963.

Lipsey, R. G. and K. Lancaster. 'The General Theory of Second Best,' *Review of Economic Studies*, XXIV, No. 1, 1965.

Lisle, E. 'Le Plan Français et les Prévisions de Consommation,' *Planification en Afrique, Tome VII, Expérience Française*, République Française, Ministère de la Coopération, (N.D., 1964?).

Lisle, E. 'Les Prévision de Consommation,' *Revue Economique*, no. 1, 1961.

Lisle, M. 'Démocratie contre Inflation,' *Issues du Temps*, mars 1962.

Lombard, F. 'Socialisme et Planification,' *Les Cahiers du Centre d'Etudes Socialistes*, nos. 18–19, 1962.

Looking Ahead. National Planning Association, Washington D.C., January 1963.

Louvel, Albert. 'Grands Corps et Grands Commis,' *Revue des Deux Mondes*, 1 janvier 1959.

Lubell, Harold. 'The Role of Investment in Two French Inflations,' *Oxford Economic Papers, N.S.*, Vol. 7, No. 1, February 1955.

Luc de Nanteuil. 'Economic Planning in France,' *District Bank Review*, December 1963.

MacLennan, Malcolm. 'French Planning: Some Lessons for Britain,' *Planning*, P.E.P. London, Vol. XXIX, No. 475, 9 September 1963.

MacLennan, Malcolm. 'The Common Market and French Planning,' *Journal of Common Market Studies*, October 1963.

Madinier, P. 'Les Problèmes de l'Emploi dans le Plan,' *Planification en Afrique, Tome VII, Expérience Française*, République Française, Ministère de la Coopération (n.d., 1947?).

Magniadas, Jean. 'Trade Union Participation in Planning, *Economie et Politique*, juillet 1965.

Maillet, P. 'Le Secteur Public au Service de la Politique Economique d'Expansion en France,' *Actualité Economique*, avril 1964.

Mallet, Serge. 'Aspects Nouveaux de l'Industrie Française,' *Les Temps Modernes*, no. 156–157, février-mars 1951.

Malterre, A. 'Le Quatrième Plan Français, *Annales d'Economie Politique*, 117(13), 1961–1962.

Malve, Pierre. 'La Planification Française à Travers le IVème Plan,' *Economie*, 16 avril 1962.

Mandel, Ernest. 'The Economics of Neo-Capitalism,' *The Socialist Register*, 1964.

Mandy, P. L. 'La Structure et la Dimension des Entreprises dans les Pays du Marché Commun,' *Revue Economique*, mai 1960.

Marchal, J. 'Investment Decisions in French Public Undertakings,' *Annals of Public and Co-operative Economy*, Vol. XXXV, No. 4, October-December 1964.

Mares, V. E. 'The French New Deal,' *Current History*, Nov. 1963.

Mares, Vaclav E. 'The French Planning Experiment, *Current History*, April 1966.

Marjolin, Robert. 'Do We Need a Plan for Europe?' *Bulletin of the European Economic Community*, Vol. 7, No. 7, July 1962.

Massé, Pierre. 'Discretionary and Formalised Planning,' Communication to Conference on Economic Development, *International Economic Association*, Vienna, Sept. 1962.

Massé, Pierre. 'The French Plan and Economic Theory,' *Econometrica*, April 1965.

Massé, Pierre. 'French Planning,' *French Affairs*, No. 127, French Embassy New York, Dec. 1961.

Massé, P. 'L'Investissement Productif,' *Le Développement Economique*, Congrès de Madrid, janvier-février 1961, O.C.E.D.

Massé, P. 'La Pensée Moderne et l'Action Economique,' *Bulletin de l'Administration Centrale des Finances*, no. 11, 1961.

Massé, P. 'La Philosophie des Plans Français,' *Revue des Deux Mondes*, 10, 15 mai 1962.

Massé, P. 'Planification Nationale et Programmes Professionels,' *Assemblée Annuelle du Syndicat de l'Industrie du Jute*, 22 mars 1961.

Massé, P. 'Planification et Provision,' *La Table Ronde*, 177, oct. 1963.

Massé, P. 'Prévision et Prospective,' *Prospective*, no. 4 (P.U.F.).

Massé, P. 'Du 4e au 5e Plan,' *Commerce Franco-Suisse*, avril 1963.

Massé, P. 'Rapport Sur la Programation Economique en France,' *Revue du Marché Commun*, 53, décembre 1962.

Massé, P. 'Le Secret de la Planification Souple à la Française,' *Hommes et Commerce*, 11, (76) nov.-dec. 1962.

Massé, P. 'Situations et Perspectives de la Planification Française,' *Hommes et Techniques*, 19 (218), janvier 1963.
also in: *Cahiers de la République*, no. 45, juin 1962.

Massé, P. 'Why France Adopted Planning After the War, and the Advantages She Sees in Retaining this System,' *French and Other National Economic Plans for Growth*, European Committee for Economic and Social Progress, June 1963.

Massé, Pierre et Gibrat. 'Applications of Linear Programming to Investment in the Electric Power Industry,' *Management Science*, January 1957.

Maurice, Marc. 'L'Evolution de la CFTC,' *Sociologie du Travail*, janvier-mars 1965.

Mendès France, Pierre. 'Les Conditions Politiques de la Planification,' *Les Cahiers de la République*, no. 45, juin 1962.

Meynaud, J. 'Administration et Politique en France,' *Politico*, XXIV, 1959.

Meynaud, J. 'Le Contrôle des Ententes,' *Revue Economique et Sociale*, Lausanne, janvier 1958.

Meynaud, Jean. 'Les Groupes d'Intéret et l'Administration en France,' *Revue Française de Sciences Politiques*, vol. VII, juillet-septembre 1957.

Nataf, A. et P. Thionet. Modèle à Prix Variable et Plans de Développement,' (*Etudes de Compatibilité Nationale*, Imprimerie Nationale, 1962).

Nicolas, Maurice. 'A Propos du Plan de Stabilisation Economique,' *Bulletin de l'ACADI*, septembre 1963.

Niveau, Maurice. 'Monetary Policy in France,' *The Bankers' Magazine*, London, Sept. 1964.

Niveau, M. 'La Planification Indicative en France et l'Equilibre des Paiements Extérieurs,' *Economie Appliquée*, jan.-juin 1962.

Norr, Martin. 'Depreciation Reform in France,' *The Tax Magazine*, May 1961.

Nowotny, Otto H. 'American vs. European Management Philosophy,' *Harvard Business Review*, March-April 1964.

Parti Socialiste Unifié. 'Le Contre-Plan PSU,' *Tribune du Parti Socialiste Unifié*, 28 novembre, 1964.

Patrie et Progrès. 'La Planification Economique,' décembre 1961.

Perroux, François. 'L'Information Facteur de Progrès Economique dans les Societés du XXème Siècle, *Diogene*, 21, hiver, 1958.

Perroux, F. Le 4ème Plan Français. 'En quoi consiste notre Planification Indicative,' *Economie Appliquée*, janvier-juin 1962.

Peterson, W. 'Planning and Economic Progress in France,' *World Politics*, April 1957.

Petrole Information: L'Industrie Française et le IV ^{me} Plan, no. 311, 5 juillet 1961.

Phelps-Brown, Henry. 'The National Economic Development Council,' *Public Administration*, Journal of Royal Institute of Public Administration, No. 41, Autumn 1963.

Philip, André. 'La Planification dans la Liberté,' *Le Cahiers de la République*, no. 45, juin 1962.

Philip, André. 'France's New Elite,' *New Leader*, 22 June 1959.

Piatier, A. 'Philosophie de la Planification,' *Cahiers de l'ILEC*, 4ème trimestre 1962.

Pietri, Francois. 'L'Inspection des Finances au Pouvoir,' *Revue des Deux Mondes*, 15 juin 1962.

Piette, Jacques. 'Socialisme et Planification, '*La Revue Socialiste*, no. 185, juillet 1965.

Plasseques, A. 'A Propos de la Planification Capitaliste,' *Economie et Politique*, mars-juin 1964.

Political and Economic Planning (PEP). 'Economic Planning in France,' *Planning*, 12 August 1961.

Poulain, J. C. 'L'Evolution de la CFTC en CFDT,' *Economie et Politique*, mars 1965.

Poulantzas, Nicos. 'L'Examen Marxiste de l'Etat et du Droit Actuel et la Question de l'*Alternative*,' *Les Temps Modernes*, no. 20, 1964.

Prud'homme, Rémy. 'La Sidérurgie dans l'Exécution du IIIème Plan,' *Bulletin du CEPREL*, no. 4, juin 1965.

Quermonne, Jean-Louis. 'Les Effets de la Planification au Niveau de l'Appareil Politique et de l'Ordonnancement Juridique,' in *La Planification Comme Process de Décision, Cahiers de la Fondation Nationale des Sciences Politiques*, no. 140, 1965.

Rem, M. 'Problèmes de la Planification Démocratique,' *Citoyens*, 6012, 1963.

Revue de l'Action Populaire. 'Aspects Nouveaux du Plan,' décembre 1964.

Revue de l'Action Populaire. 'Démocratie et Plan,' janvier 1963.

Revue Economique (Paris). 'L'Administration Economique,' (Special Issue), nov. 1962.

Revue Socialiste. 'Planifier dans la Liberté,' mai 1962.

Riboud, J. 'Le Plan Français: Critiques et Suggestions,' *Revue Politique Parlémentaire*, mars-avril 1963.

Ripert, M. 'Le Commissariat Général au Plan,' *C.A.F.*, janvier 1961.

Rioux, L. 'C.G.T.: Un Congrès Figé et une Centrale Vivante,' *France-Observateur*, 23 mai 1963.

Rissoyre, Paul. 'Orientation des Investissements et Politique d'Incitation,' *Economie et Humanisme*, no. 136, nov.-dec. 1961.

Rist, Charles. 'The French Financial Dilemma, *Foreign Affairs*, April 1947.

Rist, Charles. 'Plan Monnet contre Equilibre Budgetaire,' *La Vie Française*, 24 novembre 1949.

Rivero, J. 'Action Economique de l'Etat et Evolution Administrative,' *Revue Economique*, novembre 1962.

Rivero, Jean. 'Le Plan et le Droit,' *Cahiers de la Fondation Nationale des Sciences Politiques*, no. 140, 1965.

Rodgriguez Durantez, L. 'La Planification Francesa,' *Revue Internationale des Sciences Administratives*, 29(3), 1963.

Roosa, R. V. 'The Problem of French Recovery,' *Economic Journal*, June 1949.

Ross, George. 'The French Miners' Strike: Anatomy of a Strike in a Manager State,' *New Politics*, May 1963.

Rouquet la Garrigue, V. 'Les Méthodes de Programmation en France,' *Etudes Economiques* (Mons), novembre 1960.

Roustide, P. 'Les Principes de la Planification Française,' *Revue Défense Nationale*, octobre 1963.

Routier, J. C. et C. Lefèbre. 'Planifier dans la Liberté,' *La Revue Socialiste*, no. 153, mai 1962.

Rueff, Jacques. 'Le Comité Institué par le Décret no. 59 – 1284 du 13 novembre 1959,' *Obstacles à l'Expansion Economique.*

Rueff, Jacques. 'The Rehabilitation of the Franc,' *Lloyd's Bank Review*, April 1959.

Rueff, J. *'Rapport sur la Situation Financière, Présenté à M. le Ministre des Finances et des Affaires Economiques en Execution de la Décision du 30/9/1958,' Imprimerie Nationale, 1958.*

Rueff, J. 'Rapport sur la Situation Finançière,' *Statistiques et Etudes Financières*, no. 121, janvier 1959.

Ruggles, Richard. 'The French Investment Program and its Relation to Resource Allocation,' in E. M. Earle, ed., *Modern France*, Princeton, 1951.

Rungis, M. 'Le Contre Plan Rungis,' *France-Observateur*, 1 octobre 1964.

Rungis, M. 'L'Economie Algérienne et le Plan de Constantine,' *Esprit*, janvier 1961.

Rungis, M. 'Les Transformations Economiques Essentielles,' *Le Cahiers du Centre d'Etudes Socialistes*, no. 5–6, 20 Juin 1961.

Sabatier, J. 'L'Avenir de l'ENA,' *Promotions*, janvier 1952.

Saint-Geoura, J. 'L'Actualité du Plan en France,' *Droit Social*, décembre 1964.

Saint-Marc, P. 'Une Politique Nouvelle du Logement: l'Expérience du Ministère des Repatriés,' *Promotions*, 2e trimestre, 1964.

Sauvy, Alfred. 'La Nostalgie de la Crise et le Plan,' *Service Direction*, décembre 1962.

Sauvy, Alfred. 'L'Organisation de la Production Industrielle,' *Droit Social*, no. 7, 1er Fascicule, 1941.

Sauvy, Alfred. 'Le IVème Plan et Planification Démocratique,' *Service Direction*, no. 80, janvier 1962.

Sauvy, Alfred. 'Les Reformes Statistiques Utiles à l'Evaluation du Revenu National,' *Conseil Economique*, *Etudes et Travaux*, Etude sur le Revenue National, Paris 1951.

Sawyer, John E. 'The Entrepreneur and the Social Order: France and the United States,' in William Miller, ed., *Men in Business*, Cambridge, Harvard University Press, 1952.

Sawyer, John E. 'France's New Horizon,' *Yale Review*, Winter 1959.

Sawyer, John E. 'Strains in the Structure of Modern France,' in E. M. Earle, ed., *Modern France*, Princeton, 1951.

Schneider, H. 'French Planning as a System of Normative Information and Coordination,' *Zeitschrift für die Gesamte Staatswissenschaft*, April 1964.

Schumann, Maurice. 'Vive le Plan!' *L'Aube*, 38 novembre 1945.

Seidman, Burt. 'Behind Europe's Boom – Planning for Prosperity,' in *The Federationist*, [AFL-CIO] Vol. 70, No. 9, September 1963.

Serdais, J. 'Le 2è Plan de Modernisation et d'Equipment,' *Revue des Comités d'Entreprise*, no. 70, janvier 1954.

Serdais, J. 'Que Faut-il Attendre du 2è Plan,' *Revue des Comités d'Entreprise*, no. 80, décembre 1954.

Service Direction, Avril 1962. 'Le Moyennes et Petites Entreprises et le IVème Plan.'

Sheahan, John. 'Problems and Possibilities of Industrial Price Control: Postwar French Experience,' *American Economic Review*, June 1961.

Shonfield, Andrew. 'Who Controls the Planners,' *The Listener*, 13 December 1962.

Snider, Delbert. 'French Monetary and Fiscal Policies since the Liberation,' *American Economic Review*, June 1948.

Soulat, A. 'La Participation aux Commissions du Plan,' *Les Cahiers de la République*, no. 45, juin 1962.

Steel Review. 'Steel's Part in the French 4th Plan,' July 1962.

Sturmthal, Adolf. 'The Structure of Nationalized Enterprises in France,' *Political Science Quarterly*, LXVII, 1952.

Suffert, Georges, 'La Planification n'est pas à l'Age d'Or,' *France-Observateur*, 23 novembre, 1961.

Susini, N. 'La Comptabilité Nationale et l'Elaboration du Plan,' *Bulletin de Liaison et d'Information de l'Administration Centrale de Finances*, no. 18, septembre-novembre 1962.

Susini, N. 'La Comptabilité Nationale et les Plans,' *Planification en Afrique, Tome VII, Expérience Française*, République Française, Ministère de la Cooperation (N.D. 1964?).

Sweetman, L. J. 'Prefects and Planning: France's New Regionalism,' *Public Administration*, Vol. 45, Spring 1965.

Taillefer, J. 'Le Développement Economique et les Insuffisances du Plan Français,' *Revue Banque et Bourse*, mai 1962.

Les Temps Modernes. 'Donnés et Problèmes de la Lutte Ouvrière . . .,' (Special Issue), sept-oct. 1962.

Les Temps Modernes. 'Les Problèmes du Mouvement Ouvrier,' (Numéro Special), août-sept. 1964.

Thiery, André. 'L'Economie Concertée,' *Economie*, 18 juin 1962.

Thomas, G. 'Le Vème Plan: Perspective et Conséquences,' *Economie et Politique*, no. 152, mars 1967.

Touchard, Jean et Jacques Solé. 'Planification et Technocratie,' *Cahiers de la Fondation Nationale des Sciences Politiques, no. 140, La Planification Comme Processus de Décision.*

Tourneur, Henri. 'L'Industrie Automobile et ses Problèmes,' *Economie*, août 1962.

Trentin, B. 'Politique des Revenues et Planification,' *Temps Modernes*, août-sept. 1964.

Trentin, Bruno. 'Politique des Revenues et Planification,' translated from *Critica Marxista* in *Les Temps Modernes*, vol. 20, 1964.

Turin, G. 'Le Plan Acte Politique,' *Economie et Humanisme*, no. 136, nov.-déc. 1961.

Uri, Pierre. 'L'Evolution de l'Economie Française Jugée par la Théorie Moderne,' *Réalités*, décembre 1960.

Uri, Pierre. 'La Querrelle des Nationalisations,' *Les Temps Modernes*, no. 45, juillet 1949.

Vancil, R. F. 'So You're Going to Have a Planning Department!' *Harvard Business Review*, May-June 1967.

Van den Plas, M. 'Quinze Ans de Planification Française,' *Moniteur du Batiment et des Travaux Publics*, 7 octobre 1961.

Vedel, Georges. 'Les Problèmes de la Technocratie dans le Monde Moderne et le Rôle des Experts: Rapport sur la France ' *Paper submitted to the Fifth World Congress, International Political Science Association*, Paris, septembre 1961.

Vedene J. 'Débats Autour de la Planification ' *Economie et Humanisme* 3 juillet 1962.

Ventejol, Gabriel. 'French Unions and Economic Planning,' *Free Labour World*, April 1964.

Ventejol, Gabriel. 'Trade Union Analysis and Appraisal of Programming in France,' *International Trade Union Seminar on Economic and Social Planning, October 1963, Supplement to the Final Report, Paris, OECD, 1964.*

Ventejol, G. 'Trade Union Criteria on None-Wage Incomes and Prices Policy,' in OECD, *Non-Wage Incomes and Prices Policy, Papers for a Trade Union Seminar, Supplement to the Report, OECD*, Paris, 1965.

Vergeot, J. 'Plans Indicatifs et Economie Concertée de l'Expérience Française à la Construction Européenne,' *Revue des Sciences Economiques*, mars 1961.

Villiers, Georges. 'Ce que Doit Être l'Action du Patronat,' *Professions*, no. 16–17, août-octobre 1962.

Viot, P. 'L'Organisation Gouvermentale pour le Développement Economique en France,' *Table-Ronde de Lisbonne de l'Institut International des Sciences Administratives*, septembre 1961.

Wellisz, S. 'Economic Planning in the Netherlands, France and Italy,' *Journal of Political Economy*, June 1960.

Wickham, S. 'Development of S.N.C.F. under the French 4-year Plan,' *Bulletin of Oxford University, Institute of Statistics*, February 1962.

Wickham, S. 'French Planning Retrospect and Prospect,' *Review of Economics and Statistics*, November 1963.

Wolff, S. 'Economic Planning in France,' *Swiss Review of World Affairs*, July 1960.

'X' (Une groupe d'Anciens Elèves de l'Ecole Polytechnique), 'Considérations sur la Planification Démocratique,' *Hommes et Techniques*, no. 218, janvier 1963.

BOOKS

Adam, G. *La C.F.T.C.* (1940–1958), Cahiers de la Fondation Nationale des Sciences Politiques, Paris, 1964.

André, René. *Government Action and French Exports*, Cambridge, Mass.: Massachusetts Institute of Technology, M.S. Thesis, 1964 (unpublished).

Ardant, Gabriel, *Technique de l'Etat*, Paris: PUF, 1953.

Armand, Louis. *Plaidoyer pour l'Avenir*, Paris: Colman–Lévy, 1961.

Bauchard, Philippe. *La Mystique du Plan*, Paris: Arthaud, 1963.

Bauchet, Pierre. *Economic Planning, The French Experience*, A translation of *La Planification Française*, 1962. London: Heinemann, 1964.

Bauchet, Pierre. *L'Expérience Française de Planification*, Paris: Editions du Seuil, 1958.

Bauchet, Pierre. *La Planification Française, Quinze Ans d'Expérience*, (A revised edition of *L'Expérience Française de Planification*), Paris, 1962.

Bauchet, Pierre. *Propriété Publique et Planification*, Paris: Editions Cujas, 1962.

Baum, Warren. *The French Economy and the State*, A Rand Corporation Research Study, Princeton, 1958.

Belleville, Pierre. *Une Nouvelle Classe Ouvrière*, Paris: Julliard, 1963.

Bénard, Jean. *Vues Sur l'Economie et la Population de la France, Jusqu'en* 1970, Paris: I.N.E.D., 1953.

Bettleheim, Charles. *Problèmes Théoriques et Pratiques de la Planification*, Paris, 1951.

Billy, J. *Les Techniciens et le Pouvoir*, Paris: PUF, 1960.

Bisson, André. *Institutions Financières et Economiques en France*. Paris: Berger-Levrault, 1960.

Bloch-Lainé, François. *A la Recherche d'une Economie Concertée*. Paris: Editions de l'Epargne, 1959.

Bloch-Lainé, François. *Pour une Réforme de l'Entreprise*, Paris: Editions du Seuil, 1963.

Bonnefous, Edouard. *La Réforme Administrative*. Paris: P.U.F., 1958.

Burdeau, G. *Institutions Politiques et Administratives*, Paris, 1963.

Bureau de Recherche et d'Action Economique, BRAE,
L'Inflation en France, Paris: oct., 1961.
Les Moyens de la Politique Economique, Paris, 1960.
Politique Economique et Politique Syndicale: l'Expériénce Hollandaise, Paris, 1961.

Campbell, Angus. *Economic Growth in the West*, Twentieth Century Fund, 1964.

Catherine, Robert, *et. al. Mission d'Etude des Structures et des Techniques Commerciales Americaines*, Paris: P.U.F., 1951.

Cazes, Bernard. *La Planification en France et le IVème Plan*, Paris: Editions l'Epargne, 1962.

Chamberlin, Neil W. *Public and Private Planning*, New York: McGraw-Hill, 1965.

Chapsal, Jacques, *et. al. La France Depuis 1945*. Cours fait à l'Institut d'Etudes Politiques, 1961–62, Paris: Les Cours de Droit, 1962.

Chenery, H. B. and Paul Clark. *Interindustry Economics*, New York, 1959.

Chenot, B. *L'Etat et les Entreprises Nationalisées*, Paris: P.U.F., 1956.

Chenot, B. *L'Organisation Economique de l'Etat*, Paris: Dalloz, 1951.

Claude, Henri. *La Concentration Capitaliste*, Paris: Editions Sociales, 1965.

Club Jean Moulin. *L'Etat et le Citoyen*, Paris, Seuil, 1961.

Colombe, Paul. *Le Drame Français – du Libre Echange au Marché Commun*, Paris: Plon, 1959.

Comité Européen Pour le Progrès Economique et Social (CEPES) *French and Other National Economic Plans for Growth*, distributed by C.E.D., 711–5th Avenue, New York, June 1963.

Coulbois, Paul. *La Crise Economique et Monétaire de la France*, Centre d'Etudes Politiques et Civiques, Paris, 1957.

Courthéoux, J.-P. *La Politique des Revenus*, Paris: P.U.F., 1966.

Crozier, Michel. *The Bureaucratic Phenomenon*, Chicago: University of Chicago Press, 1964.

de Gaulle, Charles. *Major Addresses, Statements and Press Conferences of General Charles de Gaulle*, French Embassy, New York: 19 May 1958–31 January 1964.

Delmas, Claude. *Quel Avenir pour la France*, Paris: Aubier, 1956.

de Lattre, A. *Politique Economique de la France*, Paris: Les Cours de Droit, 1960–1961.

Delouvrier, Paul et R. Nathan. *Politique Economique de la France*, 4 volumes, Paris: Les Cours de Droit, 1959.

Despres, John. '*Planning and French Economic Growth*,' Honors Thesis, Harvard College, Cambridge, Mass.: March 1963, unpublished.

Dolléans, Edouard. *Expériences Françaises d'Action Syndicale Ouvrière*. Paris: Les Editions Ouvrière, 1956.

Dolléans, Edouard. *Histoire du Mouvement Ouvrier, vol. III, de* 1921 *à nos Jours*, Paris: Armand Colin, 1953.

Drancourt, Michel. *Bilan Economique de la Vème République*. Paris: Edition de l'Entreprise Moderne, 1961.

Drancourt, Michel. *Les Clefs du Pouvoir*, Paris: Fayard, 1964.

Drouin, Pierre. *L'Europe du Marché Commun*. Paris: Julliard, 1963.

Dumontier, Jacques. *Budget Economique et Capital National*, Paris, 1951.

Dupont, Pierre. *L'Etat Industriel*. Paris: Sirey, 1961.

Durbin, Evan Frank, ed. *Problems of Economic Planning*. London: Routledge, 1949.

Duverger, Maurice. *Evolution des Structures de l'Etat*. *Les Cahiers du Centre d'Etudes Socialistes*, no. 32–33, Paris: 1–15 septembre 1963.

Duverger, Maurice. *Institutions Financières*. Paris: P.U.F., 1956.

Duverger, Maurice. *Les Institutions Françaises*. Paris: P.U.F., 1962.

Ecole Nationale d'Administration. *Recruitment and Training for the Higher Civil Service in France*, Paris, 1956.

Ehrmann, Henry W. *French Labor, From Popular Front to Liberation*. New York: Oxford University Press, 1947.

Ehrmann, Henry W. *Organized Business in France*. Princeton: Princeton University Press, 1957.

Elgosy, Georges. *La France Devant le Marché Commun*. Paris: Flammarion, 1958.

Faucheux, J. *La Décentralisation Industrielle*. Paris: Berger-Levrault, 1959.

Fondation Nationale des Sciences Politiques – Institut d'Etudes Politiques de l'Université de Grenoble, *Administration Traditionelle et Planification Régionale*. Cahiers de la Fondation Nationale des Sciences Politiques, no. 135, Paris: Armand Colin, 1964.

Fondation Nationale des Sciences Politiques. *La Planification Comme Processus de Décisions*. Cahiers de la Fondation Nationale des Sciences Politiques, no. 140, Paris: Armand Colin, 1965.

Fourastié, Jean. *La Planification Economique en France*. Paris: P.U.F., 1963.

Franck, Louis. *Les Prix*. Paris: P.U.F., 1957.

Gand, J. *Les Institutions Administratives Françaises*. Institut des Etudes Politiques, Paris, 1961, mimeographed.

Gascuel, A. *Aspects du 4ème Plan*. Paris: Berger-Levrault, 1962.

Girard, Alain. *La Réussite Sociale en France*. Paris: I.N.E.D., 1961.

Gorz, André. *Stratégie Ouvrière et Néo-Capitalisme*. Paris: Seuil, 1962.

Gourney, B. *L'Administration*. Paris: P.U.F., 1962.

Granick, David. *The European Executive*. [Anchor Paperback Edition, 1964]. New York: Doubleday, 1962.

Hackett, J., and A. M. Hackett. *Economic Planning in France*. London: George Allen and Unwin, 1963.

Hagen, Everett E. and Stephanie F. T. White. *Great Britain, Quiet Revolution in Planning*. Syracuse: Syracuse University Press, 1966.

Hamon, Leo. *Les Nouveaux Comportements de la Classe Ouvrière*. Paris: P.U.F., 1962.

Hamon, P. *Les Maîtres de la France*. Paris, 1941.

Harbold, Henry. *Le Plan Monnet: A Critique of the French Investment Program*. Cambridge, Mass.: Harvard Ph.D. Thesis, 1953, Unpublished.

Harlow, John S. *French Economic Planning*. Iowa City, University of Iowa Press, 1966.

Hatzfield, Henri and J. Freyssinet. *L'Emploi en France*. Paris: Les Editions Ouvrières, 1964.

Hoffman, Stanley *et. al. In Search of France*. Cambridge, Mass.: Harvard University Press, 1963.

Houssiaux, Jacques. *Le Pouvoir de Monopole*. Paris: Sirey, 1958.

Institut pour l'Etude des Méthodes de Direction de l'Entreprise, IMEDE, *Economic Planning in France*. Lausanne, 1962, Mimeographed.

Jeannéney, Jean Marcel. *Forces et Faiblesses de l'Economie Française*, 1945–1959. Paris: Armand Colin, 1960.

Johnstone, Allan W. *United States Direct Investment in France*. Cambridge, Mass.: Massachusetts Institute of Technology (MIT) Press, 1965.

Kindleberger, Charles. *Economic Growth in France and Great Britain, 1851–1960*. Cambridge, Mass.: Harvard University Press, 1964.

King, Jerome B. *Executive Organization and Administrative Practice in the Fourth Republic*. Ph.D. Thesis, Stanford University, Palo Alto, 1958. Unpublished.

Lagache, M. *L'Aide de l'Etat aux Investissements Privés*. Paris: Berger-Levrault, 1959.

Lagache, M. *Les Investissements Privés et le Concours Financier de l'Etat*. Paris: P.U.F., 1958.

LaLumière, Pierre. *L'Inspection des Finances*. Thèse pour le Doctorat en Droit, Paris: Université de Paris, P.U.F., 1959.

Langrod, G. *Some Problems of Administration in France Today*. San Juan: University of Puerto Rico Press, 1961.

Laroque, Pierre *Les Classes Sociales*. Paris: P.U.F., 1959.

Laroque, Pierre. *L'Effort Social Français*. Paris: Armand Colin, 1961.

Lasserre, George. *Le Syndicalisme Ouvrier en France*, Cours de l'I.E.P., 1964–1965, Paris: La Cité de Droit, 1965.

Laux, James M. *French Economic Policy Since the Liberation*. Ph.D. Thesis, Chicago: Northwestern University, 1958, Unpublished.

Lavigne, P. *Les Institutions d'Economie Mixte*. Paris, 1952.

Leavasseur, Bernard. *La Construction de Logement en France et en Allemagne*. Fondation Nationale des Sciences Politiques, Paris, 1958.

LeBrun, Pierre. *Questions Actuelles du Syndicalisme*. Paris: Seuil, 1965.

Lecaillon, Jacques. *Croissance et Politique des Revenues*. Paris, Editions Cujas, 1964.

Lecerf, Jean. *La Percée de l'Economie Française*. Paris, 1963.

Lefranc, G. *Les Expériences Syndicales en France de 1939 à 1950*. Paris: F. Aubier, 1950.

Leites, Nathan. *On the Game of Politics in France*. Stanford: Stanford University, 1959.

Lescuyer, Georges. *Le Contrôle de l'Etat sur les Entreprises Nationalisées*. Paris: Libr. Grale de Droit et de Jurisprudence, 1959.

Lévy, Maurice. *Histoire Economique et Sociale de la France Depuis* 1848. Cours de l'I.E.P., Paris, 1951–1952

Lorwin, Val. R. *The French Labor Movement*. Cambridge, Mass.: Harvard University Press, 1954.

Lubell, Harold. *The French Investment Plan: A Defense of the Monnet Plan*. Ph.D. Thesis Cambridge, Mass.: Harvard University 1951. Unpublished. Mimeographed by OECD, Paris, 1951.

Lutz, V. C. *French Planning*. American Enterprise Institute for Public Policy Research, Washington, D.C., 1965.

Maillet-Chassagne, Monique. *Influence de la Nationalization sur la Gestion des Entreprises Publiques*. Paris, 1956.

Malinvaud, E. *Initiation à la Comptabilité Economique Nationale*. INSEE, second edition.

Mallet, Serge. *La Nouvelle Classe Ouvrière*. Paris: Le Seuil, 1963.

Manoussos, Georges. *Inflation, Croissance et Planification*. Geneva: Droz, 1961.

Marchal, André. *La Pensée Economique en France depuis* 1945. Paris: P.U.F., 1963.

Marchal, J. *La Comptabilité Nationale*. Paris: Editions Cujas, 1962.

Massé, P. *Le Choix des Investissements*. Paris: Dunod, 1959.

Massé, Pierre. *Le Plan ou l'Anti-Hasard*. Paris: P.U.F., 1965.

Merigot, J.-G., et P. Coulbois. *Le Franc*, 1938–1950. Paris: Collection d'Etudes Economiques, 1950.

Mendès France, Pierre. *La République Moderne*. Paris: Gallimard, 1962.
Meynaud, Jean. *Nouvelles Etudes Sur les Groupes de Pression en France*. Paris: A. Colin, 1962.
Meynaud, Jean. *Planification et Politique*. Lausanne, 1963.
Meynaud, Jean. *La Technocratie: Mythe ou Réalité*. Paris: Payot, 1964.
Morisot. *Succeès et Faiblesses de l'Effort Social Français*. Paris: A. Colin, 1961.
Norguet, René. *Le Progrès Social en France*. Paris: Plon, 1961.
Padover, Saul K. *French Institutions: Values and Politics*. Palo Alto: Stanford University Press, April, 1954.
Pallez, Gabriel. *Finances Publiques*. Cours de l'IEP, 1961–1962 Paris: Les Cours de Droit, 1962.
Passe, Georges. *Economies Comparées de la France et de la Grande-Bretagne*. Paris: Fayard, 1957.
Perroux, François. *Le IVème Plan Francais*. Paris: Edition 'Que Sais-Je?', 1962.
Peterson, Wallace C. *The Welfare State in France*. University of Nebraska Press, 1960.
Pickles, Dorothy. *The Fifth French Republic*. New York: Praeger, 1960.
Pickles, William. *The French Constitution, October 4, 1958*. London: Stevens, 1960.
Portugall, Fritz. *Le Plan Monnet*. University of the Saar, Ph.D. Thesis, 1954. Unpublished. (In French).
Reynaud, J. D. *Les Syndicats en France*. Paris: Armand Colin, 1963.
Ridley, F. and J. Blondel. *Public Administration in France*. London: Routledge and Kegan Paul, 1964.
Rovan, Joseph. *Une Idée Neuve: La Démocratie*. Paris: Edition du Seuil, 1961.
Sauvy, Alfred. *Le Plan Sauvy*. Paris: Calmann-Levy, 1960.
Sellier, F. *Stratégie de la Lutte Sociale*. Paris: Editions Ouvrières, 1961.
Sellier, F. et A. Tiano. *Economie du Travail*. Paris: P.U.F.-Themis, 1962.
Sharp, W. R. *The French Civil Service*. New York: Macmillan, 1931.
Sheahan, John. *Promotion and Control of Industry in Postwar France*. Cambridge, Mass.: Harvard University Press, 1963.
Shonfield, Andrew. *Modern Capitalism*. New York: Oxford University Press, 1965.
Skeoch, L. A. and David C. Smith. *Economic Planning: The Relevance of Western European Experience for Canada*. Private Planning Association of Canada, 1963.

Sriber, Jean. *La Réconstruction Economique de la France*. Paris: M. Rivière, 1946.

Strauss, Emil. *The Ruling Servants*. London: Allen and Unwin, 1961.

Sullivan, Clara K. *The Tax on Value Added*. New York: Columbia University Press, 1965.

Syndicat Général de l'Industrie Cotonnière Française, *Programme d'Ensemble de l'Industrie Cotonnière Française*. Paris, 1953.

Taix, Gabriel. *Le Plan Monnet: Est-il une Réussite*? Paris: R. Richon et R. Durand-Auzias, 1953.

Tinberger, Jan. *Centralization and Decentralization in Economic Policy*. Amsterdam, 1954.

Tinberger, Jan. *Economic Policy: Principles and Design*. Amsterdam, 1956.

Tixier, G. *La Formation des Cadres Supérieurs de l'Etat en Grande-Bretagne et en France*. Paris, 1948.

Tron, Ludovic. *Métamorphoses de la France, 1950–1970*. Paris: Julliard, 1961.

Vedel, Georges (ed.). *La Dépolitisation: Mythe ou Réalité*? Paris, Armand Colin, 1962.

Visine, Francois. *L'Economie Française Face Au Marché Commun*. Paris: Richom et Durand-Auzias, 1959.

Waline, M. *et. al. Politique et Technique*. Paris: P.U.F., 1958.

Weber, Max. *From Max Weber*, Mills, C. W., and H. Gerth, Translators and editors, London, 1961.

Weber, Max. *Theory of Social and Economic Organization*. Translation by Henderson and Parsons, New York, 1947.

Williams, Philip M. *Crisis and Compromise: Politics in the Fourth Republic*. 3rd edition of *Politics in Post-War France*. Archon Books, 1964.

Wilson, J. G. S. *French Banking and Credit Structure*. Cambridge, Mass.: Harvard University Press, 1957.

GOVERNMENT PUBLICATIONS

I. *Commissariat Général du Plan.*

A. *First Plan*

1. *Rapport sur le Premier Plan de Modernisation et d'Equipement*. Nov. 1946–jan. 1947 (Text of First Plan).
2. *Reponse Française à un Questionnaire de l'OCEE, Sur le Programme à Long-Terme*, octobre 1948.
3. *Documents Relatifs à la Première Session du Conseil du Plan*, 16–19 mars, 1946, Imprimerie Nationale, 1946.
4. *Données Statistiques Sur la Situation de la France au Début de 1946, Rassemblées en Vue des Négociations de Washington*, 1946.

5. Premier Rapport de la Commission de Modernisation
(a) des Carburants, octobre 1946.
(b) de l'Electricité, novembre 1946.
(c) l'Equipement Rural, septembre 1946.
(d) des Houillères, novembre 1946.
(e) de la Main d'Oeuvre, octobre 1946.
(f) des Matériaux de Construction, octobre 1946.
(g) de la Sidérurgie, novembre 1946.
(h) des Transports Intérieurs, septembre 1946.
(i) de la Production Végétale, décembre 1946.

B. *Second Plan*

1. *Deuxième Plan de Modernisation et d'Equipment*, (1954–1957), Loi no. 56–342 du 27 mars, 1956: Imprimerie des Journaux Officiels, no. 1057, 1956.
2. *Rapport Général de la Commission du Financement*, novembre 1953.
3. *Rapport de la Commission de la Main-d'Oeuvre*, 1954, also published in *Revue Française de Travail*, no. 3, 1954.
4. *Rapport de la Commission des Industries de Transformation*, 1953, also published in *l'Usine Nouvelle*, 19, 26 novembre 3, 10, 24 décembre 1953.
5. *Rapport Général de la Commission de Modernisation de la Sidérurgie*, juin 1954.
Commission du Plan, (with SEEF), *Les Perspectives de l'Economie Française Pour* 1965, 1965.

C. *Third Plan*

Troisième Plan de Modernisation et d'Equipement, (1958–1961), Décret no. 59–443 du 19 mars, 1959, Imprimerie des Journaux Officiels, no. 1129, 1959.
L'Equilibre en 1961, *Synthèse des Travaux du 3ème Plan*, 1957.

1. *Rapport Général de la Commission de Modernisation de la Chimie*, 1957.
2. Commission du Plan, *Rapport Général de la Commission de Modernisation de la Sidérurgie*, 1957.
3. Commission du Plan, *Rapport Général de la Commission des Industries de Transformation*, 1958.
4. Commission des Industries de Transformation, *Automobiles, Motocycles, Cycles et Equipements*, 1957.

D. *Interim Plan*

Plan Intérimaire, 1960–1961, Imprimerie Nationale, J.U. 016661, 1960.

E. *Quatrième Plan de Développement Economique et Social* (1962–1965), Loi no. 62–900, du 4 août, 1962, Journal Officiel du 7 août 1967.

Directives Addressées par le Gouvernement au Commissaire Général du Plan en Vue de l'Elaboration du 4ème Plan, June 8, 1960.

(with SEEF), 'Les Perspectives de l'Economie Française pour 1965,' février 1960.

(with SEEF and CREDOC), 'Projection de la Consommation pour 1965,' novembre 19, 1959.

(with SEEF), 'Les Perspectives à Long Terme de l'Economie Française,' 1959.

1. Horizontal Commissions, Reports:
   Economie Générale et Financement, Imprimerie Nationale, 1961.
   Main d'Oeuvre, Imprimerie Nationale, 1961.
   Productivité, Imprimerie Nationale, 1961.
   Recherche Scientifique et Technique, Documentation Française, 1962.
2. Vertical Commissions:
   Carburants, Commerce, D.O.M., Energie, Equipement Culturel, Equipement Sanitaire et Social, Equipement Scolaire, Equipement Urbain, Industries Agricoles et Alimentaires, Industries de Transformation, Postes et Télécommunications, Radio et Télévision, Sidérurgie, Tourisme, Transports. Available at:
   (1) La Documentation Française or
   (2) L'Imprimerie Nationale.
      (a) Artisanat, Chimie, Eléctronique, Pêches Maritimes, Recherche Scientifique et Technique.
      Available at *la Documentation Française.*
      (b) Bâtiment et Travaux Publics – Habitation, published in *Le Moniteur des Travaux Publics et du Bâtiment,* Supplément no. 48, 2 décembre 1961.
3. *Indications sur les Méthodes d'Elaboration du IVeme Plan,* 14 juin, 1960.
4. *Note aux Rapporteurs des Commissions de Modernisation,* Juin 1960.
   Note sur l'Organisation des Travaux de la Synthèse Provisoire du 4ème Plan, 5 janvier 1961.

F. *Fifth Plan*

Programme de Travail des Commissions de Modernisation pour 1965, *La Documentation Française*, 1965.

Directives Addressées par le Premier Ministre Au Commissaire Général du Plan d'Equipement et de la Productivité, Vème Plan, La Documentation Française, janvier 1965.

Cinquième Plan de Développement Economique et Social (1966–

1970), Loi no. 65–1001, du 30 novembre, 1965, Journal Officiel du 1 décembre, 1965, Imprimerie des Journaux Officiels, no. 1278 and 1278 bis.

Rapport Général de la Commission de l'Economie Générale et du Financement, 2 volumes, M. 494 and M. 495, La Documentation Française, 1966.

Rapport Général de la Commission de la Main-d'Oeuvre, mars 1966, La Documentation Française, 1966.

G. *Related Material*

1. *Cinq Ans d'Exécution du Plan de Modernisation et d'Equipement de l'Union Française*, (*Réalisations 1947–1951 et Programme 1952*), 1952.
2. *Rapport sur L'Exécution du Plan*, 1952 through 1964–65.
3. Commissariat Général du Plan, *Les Motifs d'Exécution du Plan*, mimeo, no date, (1963?).
4. *Les Moyens d'Exécution du Plan*, prepared by Gilles de la Perrière, G., mimeo, Fall 1961.
5. *Les Moyens d'Exécution du Plan* mimeo prepared by M. Delcourt, no date, (1962?).
6. *Note aux Rapporteurs des Commissions de Modernisation*, juin 1960.
7. *La Planification Française*, prepared by P. Lemerle, mimeo, décembre 1962.
8. *Réponse à Un Questionnaire des Nations-Unies Sur la Planification et le Développement de l'Industrie*, avril 1963.

II. *Conseil Economique et Social*

A. *First Plan*

1. *Rapport sur le Projet de Loi Relatif au Développement des Dépenses d'Investissement pour l'Exercise* 1951. *Journal Officiel, Avis et Rapports du Conseil Economique*, No. 1, 27 January 1951. Also, *Journal Officiel, Avis et Rapports du Conseil Economique*, 24 décembre, 1948, 8 juin 1949, 27 janvier 1950.
2. 'Contrôle des Ententes Professionnelles', *Etudes et Travaux du Conseil Economique*, no. 13, 1950.

B. *Second Plan*

1. *Rapport sur le 2ème Plan de Modernisation et d'Equipement, Journal Officiel, Avis et Rapports du Conseil Economique*, no. 22, 3 August 1954.
2. *Rapport sur le Projet de Loi Relatif au Développement des Dépenses d'Investissement pour l'Exercice 1953. Journal Officiel, Avis et Rapports du Conseil Economique*, no. 21, décembre 16, 1952. Also, *Journal Officiel, Avis et Rapports du Conseil Economique*, 21 mai, 1952, 25 décembre 1954.

3. *Etude Generale sur le Problème du Logement, Journal Officiel, Avis et Rapports du Conseil Economique*, 21 août 1953.

C. *Third Plan*

1. *Rapports sur le Troisième Plan de Modernisation et d'Equipement. Journal Officiel, Avis et Rapports du Conseil Economique*, no. 4, 28 février 1959.
2. 'Etude sur les Participations Financières de l'Etat,' *Journal Officiel, Avis et Rapports du Conseil Economique*, 19 mars 1959.

D. *Interim Plan*

1. *Rapport sur la Réalisation de la Première Année du Plan Interimaire. Journal Officiel, Avis et Rapports du Conseil Economique et Social*, 14 février 1961.

E. *Fourth Plan*

1. *IVème Plan National de Développement, Journal Officiel, Avis et Rapports du Conseil Economique et Social*, décembre 12, 1961.
2. *Etude presentée par la Section des Investissements et du Plan sur le Rapport de M. J. Delors, Evolution de la Consommation des Particuliers au Cours des Prochaines Années*, 23 février 1960.
3. *Etude Presentée par la Section des Investissements et du Plan sur le Rapport de M. L. Charvet, Perspectives de l'Economie Française pour* 1965, 3 mai 1960.
4. *Problème de la Neutralité Fiscale et des Incitations Fiscales Destinées à Faciliter la Réalisation des Objectifs Prioritaires Définis au* 4ème *Plan. Journal Officiel, Avis et Rapports du Conseil Economique et Social*, 9 August 1962.
5. *Inventaire des Moyens Actuels d'Information Economique, Journal Officiel, Avis et Rapports du Conseil Economique et Social*, 23 March 1963.
6. *Problèmes Posés par l'Exécution du IVème Plan*, prepared by M. Halff, *Journal Officiel, Avis et Rapports du Conseil Economique et Social*, 11 January 1963.

F. *Fifth Plan*

1. *Les Principales Options du Vème Plan, Journal Officiel, Avis et Rapports du Conseil Economique et Social*, 13 novembre 1964.
2. *Méthodes d'Elaboration du Vème Plan*, prepared by M. Halff, *Journal Officiel, Avis et Rapports du Conseil Economique et Social*, 7 dec. 1963.
3. *Projet de Rapport Général sur le Vème Plan, Journal Officiel, Avis et Rapports du Conseil Economique et Social*, 14 octobre 1965.

III. *de Gaulle, Charles,* Président de la Vème Republique
Major Addresses, Statements, and Press Conferences of: 19 May 1958 - 31 January 1964, French Embassy. Press and Information Division, New York.

IV. *Documentation Francaise*
1. *L'Organisation Gouvernementale, Administrative, et Judicaire de la France,* 1952.
2. *Ententes et Monopoles dans le Monde, France,* Notes et Etudes Documentaires, no. 1736, Paris 1953.
3. *L'Evolution du Commerce Extérieur de la France Métropolitaine de 1950 à 1953, Notes et Etudes Documentaires,* no. 1807, nov. 25, 1953.
4. La Documentation Française, *Les Institutions Politiques de la France,* three volumes, 1959.
5. *La Planification Française,* (*Notes et Etudes Documentaires,* no. 2.846), 30 décembre, 1961.
6. *Histoire, Méthode et Doctrine de la Planification Française,* prepared by Pierre Massé, 1962.
7. *Rapport sur la Politique des Revenus Etabli à la Suite de la Conférence des Revenus,* (octobre 1963 - janvier 1964) Recueils et Monographies, 1964.

V. *Institut National de la Statistique et des Etudes Economiques (INSEE).*
1. *Annuaire Statistique de la France,* Annual.
2. *Annuaire Statistique de la France, Résumé Retrospectif,* 1966.
3. *Bulletin de la Statistique Générale de la France,* 1945–1946.
4. *Etudes de Comptabilité Nationale,* no. 10, 1967.
5. *Etudes et Conjoncture,* Published Monthly.
6. 'L'Industrie Française de 1951 à 1956.' *Etudes Statistiques,* jan.-mars, 1960.
7. *Etudes Statistique, Supplément Trimestriel,* absorbé par *Etudes et Conjoncture* en 1964.
8. *Mouvement Economique en France de 1944* à *1957.*
9. *Rapport sur l'Exécution du Plan de Modernisation et d Equipement,* 1957.
10. *Statistique et Etudes Financières,* Published Monthly.
Tableaux de l'Economie Française, Paris, 1958.

VI. *Ministère de la Coopération*
La Planification en Afrique, Tome VII, L'Expérience Française, (N.D.) [1964?].
Ministère de la Coopération: Le Plan Français, (Recueil de Conférences Prononcées au Centre de Perfectionnement pour

le Développement et la Coopération Economique et Technique, nov. 1961 – juin 1962), 1962.

VII. *Ministère des Finances et des Affaires Economiques*

Inventairede la Situation Financière, 1951.

Secrétariat d'Etat aux Affaires Economiques, Comité National de la Productivité, *Productivité et Fiscalité*, avril 1952.

Ministère des Finances – SEEF, 'Rapport du Service des Etudes Economiques et Financières sur les Comptes de la Nation des Anneés 1951 et 1952,' *Statistiques et Etudes Financières*, no. 18, 1953.

'Les Avantages Fiscaux à l'Exportation en France et à l'Etranger, *Statistique et Etudes Financières*, no. 51, mars 1953.

Rapport Général de la Commission Créée par Arête du 6 janvier, 1954 pour l'Etude des Disparités entre les Prix Français et Etrangers, 1954.

Rapport sur la Situation Financière, Presenté à M. le Ministre des Finances et des Affaires Economiques en Execution de la Décision du 20/9/58 (Rueff Report). Imprimerie Nationale, 1958.

Rapport sur les Obstacles à l'Expansion Economique, (Rueff-Armand Report), Imprimerie Nationale, 1960.

Les Comptes de la Nation, 1955, 1960, 1966.

SEEF – *Rapport sur les Comptes de la Nation de l'Année 1960* 1961.

SEEF – *Les Techniques d'Elaboration des Plans*, prepared by L. Blanc, mimeo, 1962.

Les Mondes de Crédit Utilisables pour le Financement des Investissements dans l'Entreprise Industrielle et Commercielle. 4e Edition, jan. 1963.

FDES (Fonds de Developpement Economique et Social) *Rapport Annuel* (1955–1965).

VIII. *Parlement*

A. *Assemblée Nationale*

1. *Second Plan*

(a) *Rapport de N. Gazier au Nom de la Commission des Affaires Economiques* (no. 9133).

Rapport de M. Jacobson au Nom de la Commission du Plan . . . et Avis de l'Assemblée de l'Union Française du 23 novembre, 1954 (no. 9570).

Also Rapports nos. 9710, 10094, 10482, 10614, 10630, 10633, 10701.

(b) *Debates on 2nd Plan*

10, 11, 12, 18 et 25 mai, 1955 – adoption 25 mai, 1955.

2. *Fourth Plan*

(a) *Rapport de M. Marc Jacquet au Nom de la Commission des Finances*, no. 1712, 2e Session Ordinaire de 1961–1962; 2nd Report, no. 1857.
Avis de la Commission des Affaires Culturelles, Tome I, La Répartition du Revenue National, prepared by M. Freville, no. 1714 (1961–62).
Avis de la Commission de la Production, no. 1707 (1961–62).
(b) *Debates on Fourth Plan*, 22, 23, 24, 29 mai 1962; 6, 7, 14, 19, 20, 21 juin. Recorded in *Journal Officiel, Débats Parlementaires, Assemblée Nationale*, 23, 24, 25, 30 mai 1962 et les 7, 8, 15, 21, 22 juin, 1962. Adoption, 21 juin et 23 juillet 1962.

3. *Fifth Plan*
(a) *Rapport de M. Louis Vallon, au Nom de la Commission des Finances* (no. 1638).
Avis de la Commission de la Production (no. 1637),
Avis de la Commission des Affaires Culturelles (no. 1644),
Rapport de M. Louis Vallon, au Nom de la Commission Mixte Paritaire (no. 1786),
Rapport de M. Louis Vallon, au Nom de la Commission des Finances (no. 1687 et no. 1689).
(b) *Debates on Fifth Plan*
24, 25 and 26 novembre 1964 (on Preliminary Principal Choices of Fifth Plan) – 3, 4 et 5 novembre 1965 (Adoption, après Declaration d'Urgence, 5 novembre 1965) – *Projet de Loi Rejeté par le Sénat*, no. 1675, Discussion et Adoption Définitive 19 novembre 1965.

B. *Sénat*
1. *Fourth Plan*
(a) *Reports on Fourth Plan*
nos. 238, 239, 243, 247, *Journal Officiel*, 2e Session Ordinaire 1961–1962.
(b) *Debates on Fourth Plan*
Journal Officiel, Débats Parlementaires, Sénat, 4, 5, 6, 7, 10, 11, 12, 13 juillet 1962.

2. *Fifth Plan*
(a) *Reports on Fifth Plan*
Rapport de M. Longchambon, au Nom de la Commission des Affaires Economiques, no. 40 (1965–1966).
Avis de la Commission de Finances, no. 41 (1965–1966).
Also nos. 56, 58, 73, et 76 (1965–1966).
(b) *Debates on Fifth Plan*
7 et 8 décembre, 1964 (Preliminary Discussion of Principal Choices of Plan).

17 novembre 1965 – First Debate and Rejection of Fifth Plan.

19 novembre 1965 – Final Discussion and Second Rejection of Fifth Plan.

IX. *Communauté Economique Européenne*

Statistiques de Base de Douze Pays Européens, Luxembourg-Bruxelles, February 1958.

X. *U.S. Economic Cooperation Administration, Special Mission to France*,

France: Data Book, March 1951.

XI. *OEEC – OECD*

General Statistics

Industrial Censuses in Western Europe, Paris 1951.

National Accounts Research Unit, *National Accounts Studies, France*, 1951.

Economic Conditions in France, 1953.

An International Comparison of National Products and the Purchasing Power of Currencies,

Report Prepared by M. Gilbert and I. Kravis, 1954.

Management Training in Western Europe,

Prepared by P. Hunt, 1955.

Supply of Capital Funds for Industrial Development in Europe, European Productivity Agency, Project 292, 1957.

Trade Union Training in Europe, 1958.

The Problem of Rising Prices, Papers by M. Fellner, M. Gilbert, *et. al.*, May 1961.

Rapport International sur les Facteurs Intervenant en Matière de Politique des Investissements, novembre 1962,

Prepared by Bruce R. Williams.

International Trade Union Seminar on Economic and Social Programming 1963–2, Supplement to the Final Report, Oct. 1963.

Growth and Economic Policy, An Unpublished Report of Working Party, no. 2 to the Economic Policy Committee, mimeo, Paris, 1964.

Policies For Prices, Profits and Other Non-Wage Incomes, 1964.

International Seminars, 1965–2, *Non-Wage Incomes and Prices Policy, Supplement to the Report, 1965.*

SUPPLEMENTARY SELECTED BIBLIOGRAPHY

The texts of the fifth and sixth plans, including some seventy volumes of reports for the sixth plan, are available at La Documentation Française, 31 Quai Voltaire, Paris 7[e].

Albertini, J.-M. *Faites vous même le VIe Plan.* Editions Ouvieres, 1971.

Balassa, Bella. 'Planning and Programming in the European Common Market,' *European Economic Review*, no. 3, 1973.

Bonnaud, J. J. 'Planning and Industry in France,' in Hayward and Watson, eds., *Planning, Politics and Public Policy, The British, French and Italian Experiences.* Cambridge University Press, 1975.

Borel, G. 'Les relations entre le budget et le Plan en France,' *Bulletin de l'Institut International d'Administration Publique*, juillet-sept., 1971.

Buhler, A., et Sabatier. '*Le VIe Plan, Pourquoi*?' Fayard, 1971.

Carre, Dubois, et Malinvaud. *La Croissance Française* Seuil, 1972.

Cohen, Stephen S., and Charles Goldfinger. 'From Permacrisis to Real Crisis in French Social Security: An Essay on the Limits to Normal Politics,' in Lindberg, Alford, eds., *Stress and Contradiction in Modern Capitalism: Public Policy and the Theory of the State.* Lexington, Mass., 1975.

Conseil Economique et Social. *Journal Officiel, Avis et Rapports du.*, 21 sept. 1974; 23 mars 1972.

Courbis, Raymond. 'The Fifi Model Used in the Preparation of the French Plan,' *Economics of Planning*, vol. 12, no. 1–2, 1972.

Courbis, Raymond, et Aglietta. 'Un Outil Pour le Plan: Le Modèle FIFI,' *Economie et Statistique*, mai 1969.

Courbis, Raymond, et Seibel. *Le Modèle FIFI-Tome I, Presentation Générale et Utilisation*, Collections de l'INSEE, C–22, 1973.

Denison, Edward. *Accounting for United States Economic Growth.* Brookings, 1974.

Dumontier, J. 'Le système d'indicateurs du VIe Plan,' in Rapport au Conseil Economique et Social, *Journal Officiel Avis et Rapports du Conseil Economique et Social*, 23 mars 1973.

Duprat, J.-P. 'La debudgétisation,' *Revue de Science Financiere*, no. 1, 1972.

Economie et Statistique. 'Les Indicateurs Associés au VIe Plan,' no. 26, sept. 1971.

Expansion, mai 1971.

l'Express. 'La Paralysie du Plan Inquiète Même les Finances,' 31 dec. 1973, 6 jan. 1974.

'Fonctions Collectives et Planification,' *Notes et Etudes Documentaires*, La Documentation Française, nos. 3991–3992, 28 mai 1973.

Geistdoerfer-Florenzano. 'Le Modèle Physico-financier. Essai du Critique Syndicale,' *Droit Social*, avril-mai 1972.

Gruson, Claude. *Renaissance du Plan*. Seuil, 1971.

Herzog, Philippe. 'Histoire du Plan Française,' *Economie et Politique*, juin 1970.

Imbert, M. 'L'Environment dans la Préparation du VIe Plan,' *Revue Environment*, no. 1, fev. 1971.

Jobert, Bruno. 'Le Ministère de l'Industrie et la Cohérence de la Politique Industrielle,' *Revue Française de Science Politique*, avril 1974.

Lefournier, Philippe. 'La Bataille du VIe Plan,' *l'Expansion*, avril 1970.

Lepage, H. 'Faut-il Tuer le Plan?,' *Entreprise*, 15 mars 1974.

Mantoux, J. 'Il Faut Ressusciter le Plan,' *Les Informations*, 15 avril 1974.

Modern Capitalism: Public Policy and the Theory of the State. Lexington, Mass., 1975.

Oppenheim, J. P. *La CFDT et la Planification*. Tema, 1973.

Parodi. *l'Economie et la Société Française*. Paris, 1972.

Pascallon, Pierre. *La Planification de l'Economie Française Masson*, 1975.

La Planification Dans La Société Française. Colloque à Uriage, October 1973, published by Université des Science Sociales de Grenoble.

Ross, George W., and Stephen S. Cohen. 'The Politics of French Regional Planning,' in Alonso and Friedmann, eds., *Regional Analysis*, MIT Press, 1975.

Scott, Bruce, and J. McArthur. *Industrial Planning in France*. Harvard Graduate School of Business Administration, 1969.

Sheahan, John. 'Planning in France,' *Challenge*, March-April, 1975.

Stoleur, Lionel. *l'Impératif Industriel*. Seuil, 1969.

Ullmo, Yves. *La Planification en France*. Cours fait à l'Institut d'Etudes Politiques de Paris, 1972.

INDEX

advocacy planning, 214–19
agriculture, 11, 54, 55, 59, 60, 61, 84, 85, 86, 89, 98, 99, 100, 107, 111, 112, 113, 132, 137, 141, 142, 143, 161, 194
Algeria, 47, 48, 143, 152, 242
Algerian War, the, 152, 216, 250
aluminium, 54, 187
America, United States of, *ix*, 47, 48, 72, 75, 94, 101, 102, 120, 196, 199, 219, 232, 239, 240, 241, 248, 253
anti-Republicanism, 41
anti-trust legislation, 139, 145
approved projects, 22, 23, 65, 77, 86
Armand, Louis, 6, 110, 111
austerity programmes, 55, 95, 100, 101, 106, 107, 108, 120, 180
authoritarianism, 18, 63, 234, 236, 245
aviation, 6

balance of payments, 141, 142, 172, 179, 181
banking, 165, 166
bargaining process, the, 30, 62, 63, 65, 69, 70, 76, 77 114, 117
Barjonet, André, 209
Bauchard, Philippe, 197
Bauchet, Pierre, 35, 127
Belgian currency reform, 95
Belle Epoque, the, 48
Bidault, Georges, 92
big business, 30, 38, 44, 51, 52, chap. 6, 113, 114, 121, 130, 131, 134, 135, 138, 139, 158, 159, 163, 174, 187, 206, 214, 216, 222, 224, 228, 232, 234, 236, 255
black market, the, 91, 95
Bloch-Lainé, François, 51, 64, 65, 198, 220, 221, 223, 224
Blum, Léon, 92
bond issues, 92, 95, 96, 169
bottlenecks, supply, 9, 16, 88, 97, 99, 109, 112, 119, 146, 148, 225
bourgeoisie, 41, 48, 199
Brun, Pierre Le, 204, 217, 218, 219
budget, 39, 58, 93, 95, 97, 98, 167
bureaucracy, *ix*, 4, 8, 10, 15, 21, chap. 3. 36, 42, 45, 46, 113, 127, 158, 229, 240, 256, 257
business activity, 21, 120, 123, 139, 142, 145, 225; *see* big business
business attitudes, modernization of, 36, 37, 39, 40, 43, 45, 51, 53, 56, 113, 123
business community, the, 3, 4, 36, 37, 50, 62, 63, 123, 124, 144
business cycle, the 9
business men, 3, 4, 6, 9, 33, 37, 62, 72, 166, 191, 193, 194, 197, 198, 199, 202, 203, 205, 215, 233, 237, 254
business, independence of private, 123
business small, 61, 84, 110, 111, 130, 158

capital, 7, 11, 21, 22, 24, 65, 99, 100, 136, 137, 186, 187, 205
capitalism, *ix*, 50, 199, 200, 201, 202, 203, 206, 207, 208, 209, 211, 212, 213, 214, 223, 232, 250, 255, 257
capitalism, neo-, 5, 199, 200, 201–6, 207, 210, 211, 212, 215, 239, 240, 244, 245
cartels, 71, 72, 73, 74, 76, 77, 140, 154, 176, 221, 222, 254
cement, 86, 94, 104, 111, 119, 187
centralization, *ix* 18, 159
Centre parties, 101, 106, 126, 170, 203, 218, 221, 224, 232, 236, 253
Centre-Right, the, 253, 254, 257
CFDT, the, 200, 204, 247
CFTC, the. 101, 204, 214, 218
CGT, the, 61, 101, 123, 124, 142, 147, 200, 208, 209, 210. 217, 218, 219, 243, 244, 247, 249, 250
CGT—force Ouvrière, 204
Chalendon, Albin, 191, 206
Chemicals, 6, 54, 75, 84, 111, 144, 145, 149, 173, 187, 221
class struggle, 79, 200, 212, 213, 215
Cléon, 248

clignotants, 172, 173, 174, 184
closed economy, 178
Club Jean Moulin, 158, 186,
coal, 11, 86, 89, 99, 105, 109, 110, 139, 146, 147
coercive methods, *ix*, 3, 8, 15, 17, 20, 21–7, 29, 120, 220, 228, 245
coherence, 122, 123, 134, 136, chap. 7, 160, 161, 214
Cohn-Bendit, D., 246
Cold War, the, 123, 204, 245, 246
collaboration, 196–9, 200, 202, 206, 207, 208, 209, 219
collusion, 71, 72
Common Market, the, *ix*, 55, 140, 153, 164, 176–92, 229, 234
competitive structure, 68, 72, 73, 74, 75, 76
communication, lack of student, 240, 242
Communists, Communist Party, 95, 101, 107, 123, 142, 204, 208, 210, 244, 245, 246, 247, 248, 250, 251, 255, 256, 257
Communism, anti-, 250, 251, 256
Comptoir Longwy (1902), 73
'Concerted Economy', 67
Concerted Cartelization, 68
conflict situations, in relation to planning, 15, 16, 17, 18, 20, 51, 65, 67, 91, 161
Conseil Economique, the, 104, 106
Conservatives, 37, 38, 41, 95, 126
Constantine Plan, the, 47, 48
constitutional changes, 49
construction industry 18, 24, 106, 137, 223
consumers, 60, 61, 76, 130, 254
consumer durables, 17, 19, 97, 98, 99, 117, 144, 148, 149, 223, 226, 227, 234
consumption, 15, 17, 83, 117, 169, 178, 180, 184, 187
contestative participationists, 206, 211, 212, 213, 214, 215, 218, 220, 223, 224, 226
contingency planning, 157–60, 173
control, 21, 22, 23, 24, 27, 117, 120, 121, 149, 154, 158, 183
co-operation, between state and management, 51–2, 67, 71–2, 75–7, 124–5, 229
co-ordination of short term economic policy and planning, 25, 55, 56, 77, 114, 115, 121, 133, 149, 164, 166, 167, 169–74, 184, 185
corporations, 44, 65, 129, 131, 162, 202, 203, 229, 230, 231, 235, 254
corporatism, 253, 254, 255
costs, 136, 137, 143, 146, 147, 180
Counter Plan, the, 214–19
credits, 58, 59, 63, 120, 139, 165, 169, 170, 180
currency reforms, 92, 95, 96, 101

decadence, 113
decentralisation, *ix*, 4, 8, 10, 20
decision making, 10, 15, 16, 20, 35, chap. 6, 131, 132, 154, 159, 161, 162, 164, 174, 175, 203, 205, 207, 228, 254
deficit, Government, 151, 152, 172, 179, 181; *see* budget
deflation, 79, 152, 180, 181, 182
demand, 9, 10, 11, 15, 25, 78, 79, 97, 113, 114, 119, 134, 139, 146, 147, 148, 149, 151, 158, 160, 171, 176, 177, 178, 224
democracy, *ix*, 41, 42, 43, 59, 69, 130, 131, 133, 159, 160, 161, 163, 187, 188, 189, 193–219, 220–27, 228–37, 245, 247, 252, 254, 255, 257
depression, 92
Dessirier, Jean, 84, 85
devaluation, 55, 79, 98, 152
developed countries, 161
development, 5, 15, 16, 18, 21, 24, 25, 34, 69, 89, 96, 104, 105, 106, 107, 108, 109, 110, 111, 112, 114, 115, 117, 119, 133, 134, 136, 174, 175, 228
dirigisme, 47
direct controls, 92, 97, 100, 112, *see* control
distortion of plan, 115, 131, 132, 148, 149, 151, 152, 157, 158, 165, 171, 172, 174, 175, 186, 226, 227
distribution, 4, 137
disunity of Left. *see* Left

Eastern Europe, *ix*
Eastern World Federation of Trade Unions, 204
Ecole Libre des Sciences Politiques, 41, 42, 43, 44
Ecole National d'Administration, 40, 43, 44, 45, 46, 47, 48, 56
econometrics, 34, 83, 110, 130, 131, 134, 153
economists, 36, 114, 122, 161, 196
economic backwardness, 136, 152

economic balance, 53, 78, 80, 92, 93, 131, 140, 151, 161, 177, 178, 181, 184, 185, 187, 225, 226, 234
economic system, changes in, 5, 36, 38, 174, 203, 208, 214
économie concertée, the, 51, 52, 129, 130, 131, 136, 137, 140, 154, 159, 161, 163, 174, 175, 178, 183, 185, 187, 205, 222, 228, 229, 233, 235
Economic Council, the, 94, 122, 143, 146, 147, 148, 217, 218, 255,
education, 40, 41, 42, 43, 44, 47, 106, 113, 114, 138, 154, 173, 213, 224, 226, 234, 235
educational system, failure, 239, 240, 241, 251
educative methods. 3–20, 62, 114, 174, 213, 226, 228, 230
efficiency, 8, 16, 39, 47, 52, 67, 75, 76, 136, 154, 189
Electricité de France, 6, 26, 27, 100, 110
electricity, 26, 27, 63, 86, 89, 100, 109, 119, 146
electrification of railways, 106, 110, 114
employment, 18, 39, 179, 202, 213, 248; *see* labour
ENA graduates, the, 46–50
energy, 89, 143, 146–8, 220
enlightened self interest, 3
ententes, 49, 68, 72, 73, 74, 75, 76, 77, 137, 139, 145
entrepreneurs, 112
Estaing Stabilisation plan, Giscard d', 56, 180, 181, 182, 183, 231
Estaing, Valery Giscard d', 167, 168, 180, 217
European Coal and Steel Community, 121
European Economic Community, 164
European Co-operation Administration, 88
European policy, 164
European Recovery Programme, 88
Events of May, the, 238–57
Executive decree, 59
expansion, 4, 6, 16, 19, 24, 25, 36, 39, 45, 48, 49, 52, 64, 67, 118, 120, 121, 126, 129, 137, 143, 144, 145, 146, 147, 152, 153, 154, 171, 177, 178, 179, 183, 184, 185, 186, 187, 192, 202, 203, 216, 221, 222, 225, 226, 227, 228, 229, 233, 234, 237, 238, 239, 240, 255
experts, 33, 45, 60, 61, 76, 194, 196, 197
exports, 11, 24, 55, 62, 64, 65, 115, 138, 142, 152, 175, 178, 179

Faure, Edgar, 127
Faure Plan, the, 56, 129, 252
Fifth Republic, the, 125, 228, 230
finance, 6, 22, 23, 37, 60, 78, 79, 119, 225
financial crisis, 151, 152
fiscal policy, 25, 92, 95, 97, 133, 144, 158, 166
'Flexible Planning', 67
'Flexible Cartelisation', 68
foreign aid, 55, 132, 157
foreign exchange, 9, 11, 21, 53, 55, 79, 131, 143, 146, 152, 184, 187, 225
Foreign Office, 54, 101
foreign policy, 49, 219, 246
Fourth Republic, the, 56, 73, 228, 229, 246
France, great power status of, 94
France-Observateur, 215
free enterprise, *ix*, 73, 162, 191
fundamentalism, 199, 200
fundamental oppositionists, 200, 201, 206, 207, 208–10, 211, 218

Gaulle, General Charles de, 92, 94, 192, 219, 229, 245, 246, 247, 249, 250, 251, 252, 253, 254, 255, 256
general strike, 239, 243, 244, 247, 248, 249, 250
Germany, 72, 92, 93, 140
Gorz, André, 202, 211, 212, 215
Government, the, 3, 4, 10, 16, 19, 23, 25, 33, 35, 38, 39, 42, 50, 51, 52, 60, 62, 63, 65, 66, 69, 77, 91, 92, 96, 97, 101, 102, 115, 123, 126, 128, 131, 132, 135, 140, 149, 154, 158, 159, 163, 164, 165, 166, 167, 170, 172, 173, 174, 175, 177, 180, 193, 202, 206, 207, 215, 216, 217, 219, 221, 230, 231, 234, 242, 248; economic policies, 3, 10, 11, 21, 25, 29, 53, 164–75; expenditure, 18, 100, 120, 132, 133, 149, 169, 184; inefficiency, 92, 94, 96, 100, 101; loans, 21, 22, 24; support policies, 11, 21, 22, 64, 65, 86, 138, 177. 203; weakness, 228
Great Britain, *ix*, 196, 241
grand corps, the, 37, 38, 42, 43, 44
Grandes Ecoles, 239
Granick, David, 66
Grenelle Accords, the, 248, 250, 253

gross national product, *ix*, 39, 86, 141, 142, 143, 146, 149, 171, 176, 178, 179, 184, 186
growth, *ix*, 6, 8, 9, 10, 15, 16, 17, 18, 21, 33, 34, 38, 39, 50, 54, 56, 57, 60, 68, 76, 77, 79, 86, 88, 92, 114, 125, 126, 130, 131, 134, 136, 148, 149, 151, 152, 154, 158, 166, 171, 172, 173, 174, 175, 183, 185, 186, 187, 207, 215, 216, 217, 221, 226, 227, 229, 234, 236, 238, Table V

Hackett, 127, 167
harvests, 99
hauts fonctionnaires, the, 42, 43, 45, 47, 48, 50, 51, 52, 53, 189
Heurteault, André, 209
hire-purchase, 18, 19
Hirsch, Etienne, 36, 53, 121, 122, 124, 126
horizontal commissions, 224–7, chap. 7
hotels, 70
housing, 89, 100, 104–8, 113, 157, 171, 173, 217, 226, 234, 235, 259; 146 scheme, 105, 106, 107, 108; shortage, 104, 107
Humanité, l', 219
Hungary, 219
Huevelin, Paul, 6, 111
hydro-electric schemes, 94, 99, 100, 106, 110, 114, 147

ideology, 46, 47, 48, 51, 52, 130, 200
imperative plan, 25, 192, 193, 224, 225, 226, 227, 231
imports, 18, 55, 62, 83, 142, 143, 146, 151, 152, 171, 172, 176, 180
incentives, 21, 22, 23, 24, 25, 27, 62, 64, 65, 67, 69, 77, 120, 138, 183, 202, 221, 222
incomes, 11, 16, 53, 92, 93, 94, 95, 98, 101, 113, 115, 124, 133, 149, 151, 167, 171, 172, 179, 180, 181, 182, 184
income distribution, 49, 79, 83, 94, 132, 139, 213, 216, 217, 223, 233
income, non-earned, 122
income policy and control, 50, 55, 92, 96, 113, 118, 122, 133, 170, 173, 174, 180, 181, 184, 185, 186, 187, 200, 216, 217, 229, 234, 235, 236
income, national, 94, 96
independence of business, 4
index of industrial production, 84, 85
indicative planning, 3, 7–20, 62; limits, 14–20; techniques, 10–14
industry, 10, 11, 12, 15, 16, 33, 129
industrial capacity (1945), 92, 97
industrialists, 111; *see* businessmen
industrial organisation, 3, 72, 73, 74, 76; *see* restructuring
industrial sectors, 68, 76, 77, 78, 81; *see* sectors
inequality, in relations of State and citizens, 51
inflation, 9, 19, 53, 54, 55, 79, 83, chap. 9, 107, 108, 114, 124, 126, 137, 141, 149, 151, 152, 169, 171, 178, 183, 187, 233, 234
information, 9, 10, 14, 15, 16, 19, 28, 38, 83, 84, 85, 110, 114, 117, 118, 122, 198, 225; *see* statistics
input, 3, 11, 14, 78, 83, 137, 160, 225, Table I
insecurity, 140, 149, 152
INSEE, the, 122
Institut d'Etudes Politiques, 43, 94
integration, lack of, 129
intellectuals, 122
interest, business, 62, 63, 114
interest, general, 50, 51, 52, 203
interest, group, 50, 51, 54, 61, 77, 101, 110, 159, 160, 191
Interest, the National, 67
interest rates, 7, 18, 19, 133, 157, 191
international competition, 3, 5, 24, 33, 39, 113, 134, 139, 142–3, 144, 149, 180, 181, 202, 228
international firms, 176
interventionism, 39
investment, 5, 6, 8, 9, 10, 11, 15, 16, 17, 21, 22, 23, 24, 25, 27, 33, 38, 53, 55, 58, 60, 62, 63, 64, 68, 70, 71, 72, 76, 77, 79, 83, 86, 87, 88, 89, 91, 94, 95, 96, 98, 99, 100, 101, 102, 104, 105, 106, 107, 108, 110, 111, 114, 115, 119, 120, 121, 123, 125, 128, 131, 136, 137, 140, 142, 143, 144, 146, 148, 149, 152, 154, 167, 169, 170, 171, 178, 179, 180, 182, 183, 184, 185, 186, 187, 216, 217, 221, 222, 223, 233, 234
Italy, 212, 244

Jacques, Roger, 207
James, William, 159

Key 'man' negotiation, 69, 70, 71, 111, 162

Keynes, J. M., 9, 42
Kindleberger, C. P., 6, 165
Kléber-Colombes, 6
Korean War, the, 63
Kuhlmann Chemicals, 121

labour, 11, 50, 65, 76, 78, 92, 131, 144, 151, 178, 185, 186, 187, 195, 217, 223, 224, 225, 226, 231, 234, 245, 250, 256
laissez-faire, 18
Laniel Government, the, 73, 138
Le Brun, Pierre, 204, 217, 218, 219
Left, the, *ix*, 37, 101, 126. 170, 187, 191, 192, 193, 201, 202, 203, 204, 207, 208, 209, 210, 211, 212, 215, 217, 218, 220, 221, 231, 232, 233, 235, 236, 237; disunity of, 203, 204, 208, 210, 213, 215, 217, 233, 244
liberal economy, 10, 47
Liberation, the, 40, 93, 94, 95, 98, 123
liquidity, 92, 95, 96, 98
Loire et Centre, 6

Magniadas, Jean, 208
management, 3, 39, 40, 43, 45, 50, 60, 65, 67, 69, 76, 111, 130, 131, 134, 135, 159, 162, 163, 196, 221, 224, 230
mandarins, 46
manufacturing industries, 70, 74, 89, 100, 107, 143, 144, 145, 148, 177
markets, the, 3, 8, 13, 18, 19, 20, 25, 77, 78, 110, 132, 137, 144, 145, 146, 152, 154, 161, 178, 227
market ideology, 51
market research, 7, 8, 10, 153, 161
Marshall Plan, the, 88, 101, 102, 103, 114, 120, 128
Marxism, 200, 215, 246
mass production, 97, 139, 145
Massé, Pierre, 6, 17, 60, 110, 111, 121, 122, 173, 174, 230, 233
Massu, General, 250
meat, 106
mediaevalism, 112
Mendès France, Pierre, 38, 95, 250, 254
mergers, 49, 74, 75, 137, 139, 143, 145, 177
Métro, the, 106, 216
Michelin, 64, 84
middle classes, the, 43
military establishment, the, 54, 55, 93, 120, 158
military expenditure, 53, 54, 55, 92, 94, 101, 107, 113, 132, 133, 149, 157, 165, 216, 217. 226
Ministries, the, 10, 27, 28, 29, 35, 38, 62, 63, 106, 197
Ministries, co-operation with Planning Commission, 35–6, 56, 69
Ministry of Education, 240
Ministry of Finance, 27, 28, 30, chap. 4, 53, 54, 55, 58, 60, 62, 70, 71, 76, 77, 101, 102, 103, 107, 108, 111, 112, 113, 114, 127, 138, 139, 144, 147, 149, 216, 217, 222, 228, 229, 231; Old Ministry, 37. 46; Minister, personality of, 56; *see also* Treasury
Ministry of Industry, 54
Ministry of the National Economy, 28, 29, 37, 38, 39, 95, 112, 114
Ministry of Public Works, 54
Mitterand, François, 219, 245, 250
modernization, 5, 6, 21, 24, 36, 37, 45, 46, 48, 49, 51, 52, 54, 60, 63, 68, 70, 71, 72, 74, 75, 76, 77, 81, 83, 89, 91, 96, 101, 104, 105, 106, 108, 111, 112, 113, 119, 120, 129, 130, 136, 137, 145, 148, 175, 177, 178, 179, 184, 185, 186, 187, 222, 229, 232, 233, 237, 238, 239, 252
modernization commissions, 33, chap. 6, 60, 61, 109, 124, 127, 144, 145, 193, 194, 197
modernization, commitment to, 48, 49, 51
Mollet, Guy, 149, 151, 170, 171
Monde, Le, 73, 219
monetary policy, 25, 38, 92, 95, 101, 133, 144, 158, 166
Monnet, Jean, 4, 5, 6, 29, 36, 86, 101, 102, 103, 114, 115, 121, 174
Monnet Plan, the, 4, 21, 22, 24, 25, 36, 37, 38, 52, 58, 78, 79, chap. 8 *passim*, chap. 9 *passim*, chap. 10 *passim*, chap. 11 *passim*, 119, 120, 121, 122, 123, 125, 126, 128, 136, 140, 141, 144, 145, 147, 169, 228; deficiencies, 81, 83, 85, 86, 88; revised, 88, 89, 117, 119, 133
monopoly, 73, 75, 109, 110, 123, 208, 217
Mont Blanc tunnel, the, 165
Mont Cenis, 165
Motifs d'Execution du Plan, Les, 164
motor cars, 15, 84, 132, 144, 148, 149, 157, 177, 187, 226
Mussolini, 253
myths, growth of, 48, 49

Nanterre, 241, 242, 252
national accounts, 83, 84, 85, 122
National Assembly, 228
nationalization, 4, 43. 49, 123, 217
nationalized industries, 7, 25, 35, 44, 54, 109, 110, 111, 130, 131, 132, 165, 183, 231, 238
New Left, the, 215, 241, 246, 256
New York, City College of, 45
normative plan, 192, 224, 225, 226, 227, 231
North Africa, 151
nuclear striking force, 165, 216; *see* military expenditure

OECC, the, 141
oligopoly, 51, 54
open economy, 134, 149, 175, 176–9, 185, 187, 234
opposition to planning, 4, 37, 88, 126
ORTF, the, 252
output, 3, 6, 8, 11, 16, 33, 60, 62, 63, 70, 71, 72, 73, 76, 77, 78, 79, 83, 88, 129, 131, 132, 136, 143, 149, 160, 177, 183, 184, 187, 221, Table I
over-expansion, 110, 144, 146, 148, 149, 157
overseas projects, 55
Oxford, 45

'pantouflage', 66, 198
Parkinson's Law, 28
Paris, *ix*, 38, 41, 43, 239
Parliament, 16, 33, 34, 35, 50, 52, 58, 59, 61, 71, 74, 130, 161, 193, 214, 226, 228–37, 249, 254
participation, 3, 35, 52, 58, 59, 70, 76, 111, 118, 124, 130, 133, 134, 140, 161, 163, 175, 193–219, 220–7, 228–37, 250, 252, 253, 254, 255
'peaceful path' to socialism, 244, 245
peasants, 95, 96, 101, 130, 158, 254
Pécheney, 64, 75
pensions, 171
personnel, change of, 7, 36, 39, 110
Pétain, 254
petroleum, 63, 142, 143, 146
Piette. J., 213, 134
Pinay, Antoine, 56, 63, 136; government, 120; plan, 126, 169, 170
plan, planning: First, *see* Monnet plan; defence of, 96, 97; Second, 56, 59, 61, 78, 108, 109, 113, 115, 117–54, 157, 161, 163, 164–75, 183, 185, 228, 231; Third, 17, 59, 61, 74, 109, 113, 115, 161, 167, 171, 183, 185, 193, 216, 228, 231; Fourth, 56, 59, 61, 109, 113, 115, 165, 179–84, 185, 194, 195, 209, 216, 229, 230, 231; Fifth, 59, 108, 113, 172, 173, 177, 184–7, 214, 215, 216, 217, 218, 219, 230, 233; Sixth, 186; Seventh, 186
plan, aim of, 16, 17, 112, 222
plan, interim (1959–60), the, 59
plan, implementation of, 30, 55, 66, 63, 115, 118, 132, 133, 134, 149, 154, 167, 168, 170, 184, 192, 220
plan, weakness of, 25, 113, 114, 120, 127, 128, 164, 166, 167, 230, 231
planning, new process of, 128, 129–35, 136
planning, stage one, chap. 4 *passim;* stage two, chap. 4 *passim*, 71; stage three, chap. 5 *passim;* stage four, chap. 6 *passim*, 78; stage five, 77, chap. 7 *passim*
planning, politics in, 131, 132, 133, 134. 135, 154, 157, 158, 159, 159–63, 164–75, 214, 223, 226
Planning Commission, the, *ix*, 16, 23, 27, chap. 3 *passim*, chap. 4 *passim*, 53–5, 58, 59, 60, 61, 62, 69, 70, 71, 75, 76, 81, 107, 110, 112, 113, 114, 120, 122, 125, 127, 128, 136, 144, 146, 154, 164, 165, 167, 197, 209; small size, chap. 3 *passim*, 34
Plevin, René, 38, 95
policy, middle term objectives of, 25, 55, 133, 149, 158, 166, 167, 172, 184; short term objectives of, 25, 55, 92, 96, 98, 101, 102, 108, 114, 115, 133, 149, 158, 163, 164, 165, 167, 171, 172, 173, 183, 184
Pompidou, 217, 235, 249
Popular Front, the, 37, 248
population, growing, 104
poverty, 211, 212
power, power structure, 3, 4, 15, 18, 29, 30, 54, chap. 3 *passim*, chap. 4 *passim*, chap. 6 *passim*, 113, 114
pragmatism, 46, 47, 48, 51, 129, 133, 134, 154, 158, 160, 183
press, the, 5, 106, 128, 138, 139, 144, 147
pressure groups, 30, 53, 54, 62, 77, 91, 101, 130, 133, 147, 159, 160, 165, 167, 175, 191, 199, 206, 213, 254
price controls, 25, 47, 92, 95, 96, 170
price index, 93, 98
price stability, 16, 178, 183, 185, 186, 187, 229, 233, 234, 235, 236

prices, 8, 25, 27, 53, 55, 73, 83, 91, 92, 93, 94. 100, 109, 113, 120, 124, 133, 144, 149, 151, 165, 170, 172, 173, 178, 180, 181, 183, 184, 185, 186, 187, 248, 249, 253
priorities, 27, 30, 53, 79, 86, 89, chap. 8 *passim*, chap 9 *passim*, chap. 10 *passim*, 117, 118, 140, 214, 225
private enterprise, *ix*, 4, 7, 10, 21, 22, 23, 26, 27, 29, 44, 68, 111, 121, 123, 183, 202, 216, 227, 231
private property, 113
production, 4, 5, 13, 98, 125, 141
productivity, 24, 49, 50, 52, 67, 78, 87, 97, 125, 136, 139, 142, 144, 145, 147, 171, 182, 221, 254
profits, 4, 8, 21, 50, 67, 75, 94, 121, 162, 186, 201, 203, 213, 225, 235, 253
progressive businessmen, 3, 4, 6, 64, 110, 123, 138, 222, 232, 235, 240
projects. long term, 81, 87, 94, 98, 158, 159, 172, 177, 185, 187
protection, 39
Provisional Government, the, 38, 95
PSU, the, 204, 215, 218
public funds, 22, 23, 86, 119, 120, 123, 191
public opinion, 173, 174
public sector, 25, 26, 27; *see* nationalized industries
public services, 171; *see* welfare
public works, 55, 149, 157, 223

Radicals, 95
radicals, student, 240, 241, 242, 246, 251
radical politics, 206, 210, 211, 212
radical pragmatism, 46
railways, 11, 99, 100. 109
Ramadier, Paul, 170
rationing, 95, 100
rationalization, 21, 39, 45, 47, 49, 74, 75, 112, 113, 114, 119, 186, 203, 222, 233, 237
realization of plan, 133, 164
recession (1952), 125, 126, 140, 141
reconstruction, 86, 87, 92, 97, 99, 104, 109, 113, 117, 120, 128
Reconstruction Plan, *see* Monnet Plan
reform, educational, 240, 241, 247
reform, industrial, 38, 39, 41, 42, 44, 177, 178, 199, 200, 201, 201–6, 211, 212, 217, 220
reform, planning process, 177, 184, 186, 187, 192; *see* planning
regional development, 65, 78, 113, 122, 213, 217, 233
Renault, 248, 250
representation, chap. 6 *passim*, 130, 193–5; *see* participation
Resistance, the, 95
resources, 9, 16. 17, 18, 19, 47, 53, 79, 81, 107, 115, 117, 131, 152, 169; scarcity, 21, 83, 91, 92, 95, 100, 104, 121, 140, 152
resource allocation, 18, 21, 78, 79, 80, 118, 121, 129, 131, 132, 133, 134, 136, 140, 141, 147, 148, 152, 153, 154, 157, 158, 159–63, 164, 166, 172, 174, 175, 176, 178, 183, 184, 185, 223, 225, 226
restructuring of industry, 49, 62, 70, 74, 75, 77, 86, 129, 130, 136, 137, 139, 143, 145. 174, 177
revolutionary movement, 210, 211, 212, 244, 246, 247, 249, 251, 256, 257
rigidity, economic, 137
roads, 18, 59, 157, 213
Roos, Joseph, 6
Roosa, R. V., 94, 100
Round Table, the, 5, 33
Rousseau, 50

Sauvy, Alfred, 83
savings, 24, 100, 131, 142, 169, 170, 178, 184, 187, 216
scientific research, 24, 137, 157
secrecy, 69, 85, 111
sectors, basic, 86, 87, 89, 97, 104, 106, 107, 109, 118, 119, 131, 140, 149, 225, 228; concentrated, 68, 69, 70, 75, 111, 117, 137; key, 5; low concentration, 68, 72, 73, 74, 76, 112
sectoral imbalances, 79
security, 8, 223
SEEF, the, 28, 33, 34
self financing, 22, 23, 24, 119, 120, 180, 186, 216
SFIO, 170, 204
Sheahan, John, 72, 152, 153, 154
Sherman Act, the, 73
shipbuilding, 63
SNCF, the, 6, 110
social background, of planning administration and managers, 65–7
social change, 160
social democrats, 213, 254
socialism, socialists, 4, 95, 121, 124, 170, 199, 201, 204, 211, 212, 214, 244, 245, 246, 254

sophistication, economic, 19, 20, 111, 115, 121, 122, 154, 215
Sorbonne, the, 106 242, 243, 248
Soviet Union, the, *ix*, 219
Space research, 133, 157
specialization, 24, 74, 75, 136, 137, 138, 139, 143, 145
Stability, 83, 92, 179, 184, 185, 202, 235
stagnation, 4, 37, 125, 141, 182, 183, 188
Stalinism, 210, 244, 245, 256
state intervention, 51, 129, 216, 217
statistics, 10, 13, 14, 28, 33, 34, 38 84, 85, 110, 117, 118, 121, 122, 134, 196, 197, 225
steel, 11, 54, 63, 70, 73, 86, 94, 104, 105, 111, 140, 142, 143, 144, 147, 152, 173, 187, 209, 220, 221
strike, 200, 212; coal miners' (1963), 47
structural objectives, 177
structure of industry, 109, 110, 113
student revolt (1968), 238–43, 246, 247, 249, 252, 253, 257
Subsidies, 49, 64, 65, 67, 69, 96, 112, 117
Super-Caravelle the, 47
supply, 137, 151, 160, 225
survival of plan, 35, 36, 53, 112, 185

targets of plan, 17, 55, 58, 63, 64, 67, 68, 69, 79, 80, 86, 88, 91, 107, 108, 109, 117, 121, 129, 131, 132, 134, 136–48, 149, 153, 154, 157, 183, 184, 187, 222, 223, 227
tariffs, 133, 180; abolition, 47
tax, 18, 21, 24, 85, 100, 133, 137, 138, 139, 142, 169, 180, 186, 188
technocrats, 36, 45, 46, 66, 101, 206, 207, 214, 221, 232, 234, 237, 240
technology, 3, 7 24, 46, 48, 49, 75, 111, 137, 138, 153, 154, 157, 198, 222, 225, 229, 239, 251
telephones, 106
textiles, 70, 111, 144, 149, 187
totalitarianism, 133
tourism, 70
tractors, 11, 94
trade, 73; *see* international competition
trade associations, 49, 62, 70, 72
trade unions, 10, 33, 50, 51, 54, 60, 61, 66, 101, 111, 123, 124, 130, 158, 191, 193, 194, 195, 196, 197, 198, 199, 200, 203, 204, 205, 206–15, 220–7, 245, 254; participation, lack of, 195; unity of, 209; social isolation of, 198, 199, 203; weakness of, 195, 196, 200, 203, 208, 214
transport, 86, 89, 144, 157, 217, 220
Treasury, the, 10, 36, 53, 95, 166, 167, 170, 173, 174, 180; *see* Ministry of Finance

unemployment, 172, 178, 182, 185, 187; *see* employment
University, 238–43, 247, 252, 253
University of Paris, 43
Uri, 98

vertical commissions, chap. 6, 78, 198, 200–24, 226
Vichy government, the, 92, 93, 98, 253
Vietnam, 241, 243
Vitry, Raoul de, 6

Wagner Act (USA), the, 196
Washington, 102, 103
Welfare, 133, 139, 157, 171, 213, 216, 217, 226, 227, 233, 234, 235, 238, 239, 245, 247, 248
WFTU, the, 204
Western International Confederation of Free Trade Unions (ICFTU), 204
working class, the, 42, 43, 93, 123, 151, 194, 195, 199, 200, 201, 203, 205, 206, 207, 208, 210, 212, 213, 215, 217, 223, 226, 242, 246, 251, 252, 254
working conditions, 15, 16, 33, 151, 171, 182, 208, 216, 217, 218, 248, 251
World War, First, 84
World War, Second, 7, 84, 92, 93, 113, 117

Zone Franc, 143